DARWIN ON MAN

Charles Darwin in 1840. *Courtesy of Nora Barlow.*

DARWIN ON MAN

A
Psychological Study of
Scientific Creativity

SECOND EDITION

HOWARD E. GRUBER

FOREWORD TO THE FIRST EDITION
BY JEAN PIAGET

THE UNIVERSITY OF CHICAGO PRESS

To Rhiannon

The first edition of *Darwin on Man* also included a selection of Charles Darwin's early writings, now available in a separate volume.

The University of Chicago Press, Chicago 60637

©1974 by Howard E. Gruber and Paul H. Barrett
©1981 by Howard E. Gruber
All rights reserved. Published 1974
Second edition 1981
Printed in the United States of America

87 86 85 84 83 82 81   5 4 3 2 1

Library of Congress Cataloging in Publication Data
Gruber, Howard E.
   Darwin on man.

   First ed., published in 1974, entered under title: Darwin on man.
   Includes bibliographical references and index.
   1. Darwin, Charles Robert, 1809–1882.
2. Evolution. 3. Psychology, Comparative. 4. Creative ability in science. 5. Naturalist—England—Biography.
I. Darwin on man. II. Title.
QH31.D2D37 1981   575'.0092'4   80-28453

ISBN 0-226-31007-8 (paper)
     0-226-31008-6 (cloth)

Contents

Foreword
to the First Edition

This fine work on the thought of Charles Darwin is an instructive and stimulating example of what the approach of genetic epistemology can produce when applied to the development of the theories of a great scientist. It is not simply a chapter in the history of science, although Professor Gruber has indeed given a faithful and detailed historical reconstruction, based in part on Darwin's published works, but especially on his personal notebooks not intended for publication. These notebooks have been transcribed here by Professor Barrett.* Nor is this work only a study of the psychology of thinking, although starting from these new and highly significant facts, Gruber takes up a problem which the study of the formation of intellectual structures in children has often required us to pose: the rate at which such structures are formed, and the possibility of retarding or accelerating it. Over and above these two dimensions, the present work carries an evident epistemological significance, making us understand how much a new scientific theory differs from a simple "reading" or description of the observed or observable facts.

---

*These notebooks have now been reissued separately in *Metaphysics, Materialism, & the Evolution of Mind: Early Writings of Charles Darwin* (Chicago: University of Chicago Press, 1980). *Publisher's note*

From this epistemological point of view we see here how the construction of a new theory is far from being reducible to the accumulation of data, but necessitates an extremely complex structuring of interpretive ideas which are linked to the facts and which enrich them by framing them in a context. But as the ideas are interdependent with each other and also with previous ideas which have guided even the discovery of the observables, every alteration at one point gives rise to a modification of the system as a whole. This process maintains both the coherence of the system and at the same time the adequacy of its fit to the data of experience and observation. It is this double dialectic, external (subject × object) and internal (relations among ideas or hypotheses), which the present work describes for us minutely, and the analysis is the more instructive because Darwin's theory is relatively simple.

The two results which seem the most interesting to me are first, the time that Darwin needed to become aware of ideas which were already implicit in his thought, and second, the mysterious passage from the implicit to the explicit in the creation of new ideas. Concerning the second point, we know well, from the study of the development of intelligence in children, the manner in which most structures first elaborate themselves unconsciously on the plane of action. This occurs well before thought succeeds in translating such structures into "ideas"—in the form of conscious conceptualizations. This process is accomplished by means of representative and reflective processes. But one might have believed that this passage concerned only the relationships between thought and action, and that, on the level of thought itself, the passage from "implicit" schemas (that is, schemas already playing a role in certain acquired structures, but unconsciously) to their reflective explication, would be much more rapid. The present work shows us, which is most instructive, that even in a creator of the greatness of Darwin the passage is far from being immediate. This delay establishes the point that making things explicit leads to the construction of a structure which is partially new, even though contained virtually in those structures which preceded it.

Hence the great problem of explaining the rate of development of thought. Gruber has the great merit of showing us that we face this question in the creative work of a genius as well as at the beginnings of mental development, which is itself a creative process. We are dealing here with an extremely complex phenomenon. If it is true, as it seems, that an assimilative process can be neither accelerated nor much retarded without harming it, this would tend to show, first, that all assimilation is constructive, and second and above all, that all cognitive construction depends on a series of dynamic interactions in which the factors at play do not consist only of positive "forces" but also of resistances to be overcome. The existence of an optimal speed (which by the way we do not know) would meet with the epistemological considerations pointed out above. The need to maintain a general equilibrium of the system or theory as a whole requires a difficult balance between differentiations and integrations, from which requirement derives the necessity of a certain rhythm.

In a word, this remarkable work is of high interest and we must hail it and be thankful for its original approach to this domain, in general so poorly explored, of scientific creativity.

—Jean Piaget

Preface

The First Edition

Anything new and striving to be born must struggle for life as an interloper among established contenders, often powerful and sometimes hostile. So it is with new ideas. In this book we hope to uncover the traces of one man's thinking, mainly during a two-year period in which he laid the basis for a great new synthesis of ideas. Darwin's outward life, at least after the adventurous voyage of the *Beagle,* seems so secluded, so quiet, and at the same time, such a successful march of accomplishment that it is easy for one to be misled. The examination of the inward working of Darwin's mind becomes a study of a man struggling. The arena in which the fiercer struggle took place was not the public world, but the private world of thought. This was the arena in which Darwin displayed his staying power and his courage. As we consider the growth of Darwin's thought, the inner intellectual difficulties he faced help us to understand his outer hesitations and compromises. The complexities of this relation between private honesty and public courage raise questions that remain urgent in our time: Is there not some set of social arrangements that would welcome the fresh productions of every generation of minds? Is there not some social order that would place less reliance on individual force of character, and the chancy privilege of speaking from protected sanctuaries, in winning a hearing for the really new vision?

Darwin's notebooks on man, mind, and materialism—the M and N notebooks which he himself had seemingly dismissed as "full of Metaphysics on Morals and Speculations on Expression"—held the key to understanding the essential role of his ideas about man

---

This work was first published in a volume combining both my interpretive essay and Paul Barrett's transcription of Darwin's M and N notebooks, as well as a selection of other documents. These are now reissued as separate volumes. These excerpts from the preface to that first edition include some references to my collaborator, Paul Barrett, without whom my work would have been well-nigh impossible.

and mind in his thinking about evolution.

In these M and N notebooks and associated documents, discussed in full for the first time in the present volume, can be seen Darwin's struggle toward the materialist philosophy of biology which he thought he needed in order to support his theory of evolution. Moreover, continued reflection on the relation between two parallel sets of notes—the transmutation notebooks and the notebooks on man and mind—suggests what has become one of the major themes of this book: Darwin's motives for his long delay in publication. His fear of persecution and ridicule was based not only on the unpopularity of evolutionary theory, but on the fiercer retribution meted out against proponents of materialism. It was then widely believed in Christian circles that philosophical materialism led straight to atheism.

Darwin's notebooks of 1837–39 offer an unsurpassed opportunity for the detailed tracing of a scientific thought process. In the period immediately preceding these notebooks, he had arrived at the firm intention of once more attempting what others had failed to do, to construct a persuasive, coherent, factually supported theory of evolution. As the notebooks open, we find his thinking governed by this purpose. We can read an almost day-by-day record of a young man's struggle to construct the theory that became one of the great advances in human thought, transforming, not only the world of science, but humanity's conception of itself.

Darwin's difficult handwriting, his excision of many pages, his kaleidoscopic sequences and often telegraphic style all conspire to make the reader's task a difficult one. There are difficulties of a more general nature. The lack of a well-developed theory of the psychology of creative thinking defeats any effort to map fragmentary data into a clearly worked-out scheme; the data must be used to develop the theory. This is a painful process, since at first, there is no alternative but to proceed one case at a time. Darwin was only one man, which fact forbids any confident psychological generalizations from the study of his thought processes. For a psychologist interested in constructing a theory of creative thinking, the years of labor needed to study one case well might understandably be viewed as a poor risk.

If the experimental psychologist chooses to study some one topic related to creative thinking, such as visual imagery, free association, or problem solving, no one suggests that his work is faulty because he did not study the other topics. The power of experimental sciences depends on our ability to play a narrow but intense beam on a restricted conceptual target. As compared with such laboratory studies of psychological processes, the case-study method has one very important characteristic: it draws attention to the whole person.

This is a mixed blessing. On the one hand, it leads to fruitful consideration of factors and relationships that might otherwise be neglected. On the other hand, a case study must inevitably suffer from many sins of ommission. No one can really study the whole person even as he stands at one moment in time, much less in his total development. Even a case study must have a few foci. We have chosen the inner development of Darwin's thinking about evolution during a two-year period, and the interplay between his evolutionary ideas and his ideas about man, mind, and materialism.

The Second Edition

There is a curious duality in Darwin. He loved the order human beings sometimes see in nature and impose upon it. And he had a passion for the unruly, explosive growth of living things into almost every nook and cranny of the world of possible beings. These two feelings are expressed in the closing "tangled bank" passage of the *Origin of Species*. They found a much earlier expression in the diary he kept on board the *Beagle:* "When quietly walking along the shady pathways & admiring each successive view, one wishes to find language to express one's ideas . . . a true picture of the mind . . . the land is one great wild, untidy luxuriant hothouse, which nature made for her menagerie, but man has taken possession of it, & has studded it with gay houses & formal gardens." (*Beagle Diary,* p. 417)

It is evident that Darwin, although he was writing mainly about nature, saw the parallel with the human mind. The mind is indeed a "tangled bank" full of variety, with innumerable interconnections continuously evolving, and yet displaying some order, permitting at least some description of its workings as an organized system obeying laws that we can ascertain.

The density and complexity of this tangle makes of any one person's mind a world that could be explored endlessly by an innumerable series of collaborating investigators. Each would be a "naturalist" on a new voyage of discovery akin to Darwin's five-year circumnavigation of the earth in the *Beagle*. Of course, there would be some repetitiveness and some contradiction. But repetition serves constructive functions, and contradiction helps us to feel out where to look next, whether at the fragments of nature we are studying or at our own system of ideas. On the whole, our knowledge of a mind so explored would continue to enlarge.

If the subject under scrutiny happened to be a person who,

like Charles Darwin, had transformed our vision of the world, the task would gain both in interest and in difficulty. We want to understand how he did what he did. This requires us to see the world as he saw it when he began, and at other points along his way. But his work has already transformed our view of everything.

These complexities and subtleties, and the importance of his work, help to explain why Charles Darwin remains the subject of such a parade of voyages of discovery. *Darwin on Man* is a progress report by one of the voyagers. This new edition gives me a chance to write a very brief addition to that report.

Not least among Darwin's accomplishments is the superb record he left of his work and thought. To understand Darwin, it is vital to pay some attention to the form of this record. Psychoanalysts have suggested that Darwin's keeping of notes reflects a strong obsessive-compulsive strain in his character. In the present volume, I have proposed an alternative view that note-keeping was an expression of the empirical philosophy of John Locke, handed down to Darwin through family tradition and through his teachers at Edinburgh and Cambridge Universities. It might be argued that these two ideas are not contradictory, that the anal-retentive character born in the Protestant Reformation fostered personal obsessiveness, capitalism, and scientific work. The question becomes one of feeling tone. If Darwin was a happy man, if he enjoyed his work, and if keeping copious and careful notes helped him to do it, how does it help to use the vocabulary of psychopathology to describe his doings?

The details of notekeeping—what sorts of books to use, how to carry them safely, how to label and catalog specimens, and so forth—concerned Darwin (and many of his colleagues) before, during, and after the voyage. It is hard to imagine his work without some very well-developed system. If we want to understand his thinking, we need to look at its supporting structure. Did the maintenance of that structure exact a high psychic price from Darwin? I think not. I think he found every aspect of his lifetime voyage of discovery hard work, and the whole, immensely enjoyable. One of the few times he complained was in connection with a task requiring protracted fussing over details—his eight-year study of barnacles. So he did not enjoy every moment of his work. But was his complaint due to the character of the work or rather to the fact that the unexpected duration of the task made it an obstacle to doing the far grander one that lay just beyond, tackling once more the "species question"?

For the period of the *Beagle* voyage (1831–36), Nora Barlow, Darwin's granddaughter, has produced three major documents. In

Charles Darwin and the Voyage of the Beagle, she published a valuable
series of Darwin's letters, mainly to his family, together with a
generous selection of transcriptions from a group of little pocket
notebooks he carried with him on his numerous and often protracted expeditions ashore. *Charles Darwin's Diary of the Voyage of
H.M.S. Beagle* gives a complete and faithful transcription of the entire diary. Although it contains much of scientific value, it is most
useful in giving Darwin's poetic reactions to the world of natural
history, his reactions to human conduct in the many different
ethnic settings he visited, and some idea of his early views on a
wide variety of nonscientific subjects. Over one-half of *Darwin and
Henslow: The Growth of an Idea* is given over to letters between the
two men during the voyage itself or the period immediately after.
To make sense of his enormous collections, Darwin had enlisted
numerous experts in specialized branches of natural history, reserving the geological work for himself. Professor Henslow was a
botanist, and he was also Darwin's great friend and teacher. The
publication of this correspondence helps to correct the view of
Darwin as a lone wolf. He was an eager and skilled collaborator,
and that is a side of his life which has not yet been fully told.

The main scientific notebooks of the voyage, which are large in
format and take up thousands of pages, remain unpublished and
have been curiously little examined. In 1957 I spent a long summer
looking at little else. I began with a badly chosen goal, to search for
any early expressions of belief in or concern for organic evolution.
Although there was little or nothing of that sort, the effort of the
search led me to an idea that has guided me ever since. The key to
understanding a creative person is to understand his point of view.
To understand the growth of a creative process is to understand
the growth of the point of view that governs it. Having been
trained as an experimental psychologist, I began exploring the
creative process under the conventional assumption that creative
scientific thought was in essence a somewhat complicated kind of
problem solving. But what dictates which problems the person will
sense and which of those he will pursue? This crucial change in my
own perspective, and in the questions it generated, accelerated
sharply during that summer with the *Beagle* notebooks.

But a single summer makes only the barest inroads into those
densely packed notebooks, and much is still to be done on a
number of fronts. Darwin was twenty-two when he set out and
twenty-seven when he returned, ages corresponding to the usual
years of graduate education in the training of a scientist today—
unless he or she interpolates a voyage between degrees. How Darwin conducted his own education, how his ideas grew, what he dis-

covered, and how he did it—in short, his intellectual and personal growth during this whole five-year period—remain largely unexamined subjects.

Incredibly, a thorough, coherent modern examination of Darwin's scientific accomplishments during the voyage does not exist. The chapters in Gavin de Beer's biography are quite good, but they are brief and sketchy and do not touch upon many important topics. Also, de Beer wrote from a rather static point of view. He does not give a picture of the *development* of Darwin's ideas, of his vacillations and struggles and changes during the voyage.

The appendix that I have added to this edition deals with the two versions of the journal of the voyage that Darwin published, the first in 1839 and the second in 1845. What is still needed is a thorough examination of the scientific notebooks he kept during the voyage, far more thorough than what has been done so far. Fortunately, significant new additions to our knowledge of Darwin's early notebooks are being made. Two of the most important appeared after I had drafted this preface, too late for the serious discussion that they deserve. Sandra Herbert's reconstruction and interpretation of Darwin's "Red" notebook[1] (which I refer to only briefly as "R.N.") will help us to fill in our picture of the year from the spring of 1836 to the spring of 1837, that is, the year just preceding the series of transmutation notebooks (B,C,D, and E) on which I concentrated much of my attention. David Kohn's long paper goes over much the same ground that I do in dealing with the B,C,D, and E notebooks.[2] Although he does not make much use of the notebooks on man, mind, and materialism (M and N), which figure largly in *Darwin on Man*, he does connect his interpretation with the reconstructed Red notebook.

I have not attempted the necessary new synthesis of these and other important works. That may well be a task requiring the collaboration of a number of scholars. In my view, the interpretation I have made in *Darwin on Man* remains substantially correct, as far as it goes. The new synthesis will, I believe, show that Darwin's thinking and its development was even richer and more complex than the picture I have drawn.

In 1835, before Darwin came home from the *Beagle* voyage, his father had written to Henslow thanking the professor for all the help he had given his son, most recently the publication of a pamphlet of

---

[1] Sandra Herbert, *The Red Notebook of Charles Darwin* (Ithaca: Cornell University Press, 1980).

[2] David Kohn, "Theories to Work by: Rejected Theories, Reproduction and Darwin's Path to Natural Selection," *Studies in the History of Biology*, No. 4, 1980.

scientific extracts from Charles's letters during the voyage. Dr. Robert Waring Darwin—who has too one-sidedly been painted as a tyrannical bore—wrote, "I thought the voyage hazardous for his happiness but it seems to prove otherwise and it is highly gratifying to me to think he gains credit by his observation and exertion. There is a natural good humoured energy in his letters just like himself."

I began my work believing most of the psychoanalytically derived speculations about Darwin's character and about the psychogenic roots of his undiagnosed illness. But I think that our picture of Darwin is changing. Previously, he was often painted as an obsessive, neurotic, solitary man, forever fighting off the oppression of the great carnivorous dinosaur, Tyrannosaurus Rex, his father. But Darwin was to move the world. For this he needed a stable personal platform on which to stand. He comes through to me now as a steady, serene, and cheerful person.

It was in an optimistic spirit that Darwin began his transmutation notebooks in 1837, which were supplemented by his notebooks on man, mind, and materialism begun in the summer of 1838. These are the main subject of the present volume. During the same post-*Beagle* period, Darwin kept another notebook which has now been reconstructed and analyzed in an excellent monograph by Martin Rudwick. Rudwick shows how in 1838 Darwin's expedition to, and subsequent essay about, a peculiar geological formation in Scotland was neither a tangent to his other efforts nor simply (as has long been thought) a technical mistake. It was, rather, an expression of the same philosophical position that took other forms in the other disciplines Darwin pursued. There was, then, a theoretical connection among Darwin's diverse enterprises.

We can see now that the summer of 1838 was a gathering time for Darwin. It was a moment of regrouping his efforts in evolutionary theory, in philosophy and psychology, and in geology. On the last day of summer, Darwin had his dream of execution, and one week later he achieved his great insight into evolution through natural selection. That summer, his courtship of Emma Wedgwood (proposal accepted on November 11, 1838—the 'day of days' he called it) was at its height.

In a decade or two it will be time for a definitive biography of Darwin, a sort of "modern synthesis" of history of science, evolutionary theory, and the psychology of creativity. We do not yet have all the necessary materials available, and those that are have barely begun to be analyzed. Even the story of the *Origin of Species* remains to be coherently told. His theoretical sketches of 1842 and 1844, although published seventy years ago, have not been much examined. In the years 1854–58 Darwin worked on his "big book," much of which has now been magnficently reconstructed by Robert Stauffer and published as *Charles Darwin's Natural Selection.* Our knowledge of this mammoth undertaking refutes the careless statement that Darwin was waiting and vacillating about publishing his ideas until Alfred Russel Wallace's famous letter arrived in 1858. Darwin was moving steadily forward and would soon have completed the "big book." To be sure, what actually happened was far superior. Wallace's letter did trigger the writing of the epoch making work *On the Origin of Species.* All the circumstances under which it was written converged to make of it far more than the bare statement and documentation of a scientific theory. It is also a masterpiece of scientific literature. It went through six editions during Darwin's lifetime, and the changes he made reflect some of his unresolved doubts and some of the progress he made in resolving them. Morse Peckham has published a variorum text which is an indispensable resource for anyone interested in examining the lifetime process of constructing and reconstructing a great work. But again, these resources have been little exploited.

By now the reader may be puzzled. I promised a progress report, and I have spent most of my ink describing tasks as yet undone. Still, there is some progress, albeit slow, as befits our evolutionary subject matter. As new material becomes available and as we learn how to study it, we get a deeper grasp of and respect for the intricacy of one mind, and that is a sort of progress.

As Mark Twain wrote in his autobiography,

> What a wee little part of a persons's life are his acts and his words! His real life is led in his head, and is known to none but himself. All day long, and every day, the mill of his brain is grinding, and his *thoughts,* not those other things are his history. . . . The mass of him is hidden—it and its volcanic fires that toss and boil, and never rest, night nor day. These are his life, and they are not written, and cannot be written. Every day would make a whole book of eighty thousand words—three hundred and sixty-five books a year.

Darwin produced three master works: his *Journal of Researches,* the *Origin of Species,* and the *Descent of Man.* In spite of the mountains of specialized Darwin literature, we have seen that most of the task of examining and understanding how he produced the first two of these still lies ahead. The same is more emphatically the case for the *Descent* and its companion volume, *The Expression of Emotions in Man and Animals.* The main thrust of *Darwin on Man* is his construction in 1837–38 of the general theory of evolution through natural selection. I pay some special attention to the role of his ideas about human evolution in the development of this general theory. But I do not attempt to reconstruct in any detail the

long path to the *Descent* and the *Expression of Emotions.* Nor has anyone else.

I should qualify this observation by stressing the growing
number of important contributions to many special topics relevant
to the construction of these great works. My point is only that we
lack comprehensive and coherent developmental treatments of any
of them.

For example, the *Beagle* period has been quite well studied in a
fragmentary way. Sandra Herbert has written a particularly good
brief account of Darwin's views on man during the *Beagle* voyage,
and of the collaborative processing of his zoological collections in
the years immediately following the voyage. With Valmai Gruber, I
wrote an account of the development of Darwin's views during the
voyage, stressing his geological thinking. D. R. Stoddart has transcribed and commented upon Darwin's earliest essay on the formation of coral reefs, written during the voyage. Sydney Smith has
analyzed the connection between Darwin's later evolutionary views,
his monumental monographs on barnacles, and one unusual speci-
men he found during the voyage. Nora Barlow, Sandra Herbert,
and others—including myself—have written about the development
of Darwin's point of view during the voyage. However, some topics
have been slighted almost completely, for example, botany, politics,
scientific method. There is much material, but there is little synthesis.

While the appendix that I have prepared for this edition deals
with the *Journal* of the voyage, it focuses on the years after Darwin
came home. We know that these were years in which he did intense
theoretical work. In most Darwin studies, including my own, emphasis has been laid on the fact that he delayed publishing his *conclusion,* the theory of evolution through natural selection. My re-
reading of the two versions of the *Journal* shows that Darwin did,
however, express surprisingly fully many aspects of the point of
view and way of thought that led to that conclusion. Moreover,
since about eight years elapsed between the actual writing of the
two versions, changes made in the later one reflect the very considerable development of his thinking during that period.

To be sure, for reasons discussed below, Darwin hesitated to
publish the entirety of his thought, or even to reveal it to most of
his colleagues and friends. Moreover, his long delays permitted
only a veiled expression of certain key constituents of his point of
view in the *Journal.* After all, the idea of evolution is neither simply
one idea among many nor simply a conclusion. It became the organizing center of all his thinking. Withholding it withheld much.
The fact that Darwin consciously decided to do so makes it all the

more interesting that he actually revealed so much of his point of view, both in 1839 and in 1845. As he wrote his great travel book, his theoretical perspective seems to have bubbled out of him at almost every turn.

Obviously, a great mind like Darwin's does not simply produce a major work every decade or two and lie fallow during the intervals. In addition to his many books, Darwin wrote 152 articles in his lifetime, some of them short notes, others very substantial contributions. Yet until recently, there was not even a complete bibliography in existence. Now Paul Barrett has ferreted out all these papers and brought them together in a wonderful collection. Going through them and integrating the picture they give with our other views of Darwin will add greatly to the completeness of our understanding. They show an assiduous experimenter at work, the careful theoretician forming some of the essential building blocks of his thought. They reveal some of the ways he tipped his hand during the long years of silence, and they help bring to light seemingly unproductive periods in his life. But there are gaps in the public record. Darwin's *Autobiography* and biographies of him have little to say about the years 1846–54. This was the mysterious time that Darwin devoted to his classic monographs on fossil and living barnacles. Even Michael Ghiselin, who has written an illuminating account of Darwin's work on barnacles, refers only to the two monographs on living species.

What I am driving at throughout is a double need. We need to fill many gaps in our knowledge of detail, and we need new approaches to synthesis. The details wanting are by no means fussy bits. They are, rather, organized chunks or even macro-chunks— for example, a longitudinal and critical reconstruction of Darwin's half-century of work on earthworms, or an exhaustive cross-sectional study of one year in his life, say 1844. Studies on this scale will come along rapidly enough now. We also need theoretical approaches that will help us to bring all this wealth together into a more coherent whole, a theory of creative scientific thought that might handle it. For the moment, I ask the reader a question: There have been many very general claims about the philosophy and psychology of scientific discovery. The case of Charles Darwin presents a marvellous opportunity to develop and test ideas, but everyone will grant that to do this we must know the case. And it even such a case as Darwin's—richly documented and of the greatest import—is known only sketchily, how can we hope for a well-grounded general understanding of scientific discovery?

We are just beginning to grasp the immensity of this task of describing one creative life in the detail necessary for understanding the growth of thought. Although we need to fill in our still sketchy knowledge of Darwin's work, we do not want to drown in an ocean of documentation. Clearly, to make sense of it all, at least some provisional theory of the creative process is desirable.

But here we run up against a great difficulty. What we mean by creativity is the achievement of something unique, or at least very rare. There is no reason at all to think that any two creative people are alike in those key respects that lead us to label them as creative: what is most evident about each one is the uniqueness of his or her achievement. We will need a new scientific strategy to cope with this issue, a way of constructing for each creative person (indeed, for each living person) a "theory of the individual." There are, in all probability, infinitely many ways of being organized for highly effective work. What we need is a general approach that grasps this individuality without disregarding the social nature of every human being. Such a theory would not be composed of sentences of the form "all creative people are XYZ," but of the form "this unique configuration interacts with that unique configuration thus and so."

In the past five years, I have been developing, with some students and colleagues, what we call, quite provisionally, "an evolving systems approach to creative work." In essence, we propose that creative work requires three great subsystems: an organization of knowledge, an organization of purpose, and an organization of affect. It cannot be too strongly emphasized that this general list is not a description of some fictional abstraction, the creative person, but a sketch of some of the things to look for in constructing a "theory" of a given individual.

In the newly burgeoning cognitive sciences, the changing organization of knowledge is the object of central concern, as it is in *Darwin on Man.* In *Darwin on Man,* a major theme is criticism of the idea that creative work is characterized mainly by one or a few great moments of insight. Rather, I advance the view that insights occur frequently and express the steady functioning of a productive system rather than its overturning. More generally, rather than one key idea, we need a certain *organized pluralism* to describe the functioning of a creative person: many knowledge structures, many enterprises, many episodes, many insights. Since writing the book, I have had second thoughts about one matter. It seems to me now that I was then too much under the sway of one of Darwin's great images, the irregularly branching tree of nature. But just as there is not a single insight, there is not a single great metaphor. It takes an "ensemble of metaphors" to express and generate a new point of view. In Darwin's case, the following come easily to mind: the free market of Adam Smith, war, artificial selection. It is unfortunate that two others, the irregularly branching tree and the tangled bank, are less often spoken of. They better capture Darwin's enthusiasm for the explosive, complexifying tendencies of evolving systems. To grasp Darwin's thought as a whole, one must see the selective and regulating functions as operating upon this rich and generative matrix of possibilities.

In examining the organization of purpose in a creative life, we need to deal with both continuities and discontinuities. In this volume I introduce the concept of a "network of enterprise" as a way of dealing with the continually changing concerns and interests of a purposeful life. Broadly speaking, this is an idea in the tradition of "thematization" and is one way of giving some unity to a complex and changing picture.

But a creative life is not only thematic; it is also episodic—organized in temporally compact periods within which a given orchestration of effort is played out, and certain projects executed. The central focus of *Darwin on Man* is one such episode, the theoretical work of the years 1837–38. In order to do justice to the complexities of such a life as Darwin's, the constant organization and reorganization of ongoing enterprises into productive episodes must be better understood.

I wish there were more to say about the organization of affect in a creative life. But psychologists have not yet addressed the topic in a useful way. Attention is given one-sidedly to negative emotions, such as fear, rage, anxiety, and guilt. As scientists we know little—although as human beings we may know much—of the positive emotions necessary to sustain a long and arduous creative effort: the passion for truth, the enthusiasm of pursuit, the glory of discovery. There are also the quieter emotions, such as the daily pleasure of competent work, the tranquility of steadily regarding a cherished object, the enjoyment of an easy and generous exchange with a like-minded colleague. A good theory of scientific creativity would have to say something about the relation between cognition and affect, but in order to do so, it would need to take up these positive emotions as a matter of central concern. In *Darwin on Man* and other writings, for want of better, I have only drawn attention to instances of this kind—a far cry from making a scientific theory.

A case in point: arguing for a new and more complex view of the relationships between cognition and emotion is the recurrent and inconclusive discussion of Darwin's motives for years of delay in publishing the theory of evolution. To my surprise, I have been criticized for overplaying Darwin's fear of persecution as a reason for his delay. Those who object stress an alternative reason, the intellectual difficulties Darwin faced, even after 1838, and the continuous struggle he waged to clarify his ideas and improve his theory. Far be it from me to disagree. I appreciate any support of the idea that creative work is a continuous and life-long process.

By the same token, however, during the whole course of the creative life, the individual must shape and reshape his working relations with society as embodied in his family, his teachers, his colleagues, and several wider publics. The ensemble of these relations form the social and emotional context within which intellectual work goes forward. Although the individual can shape his own situation, he is not completely free. His efforts are part of a historical process and take place within it.

In 1859, not only the *Origin of Species* appeared, but John Stuart Mill's great essay *On Liberty*. Mill points out the use in England even then of laws and customs depriving atheists and other heretics of their rights—leading, on the part of some, to an understandable reticence. "Those in whose eyes this reticence on the part of heretics is no evil should consider . . . that in consequence of it there is never any fair and thorough discussion of heretical opinions."[3] Mill was discussing neither hypothetical nor long-past problems, but real contemporary cases. The England in which Darwin grew up and worked was by no means an inviolate temple of freedom of thought.

Evidence for the intellectual difficulties Darwin faced is not evidence against the existence of social and emotional difficulties. Even a simpler person than he could experience simultaneously a passion for discovery, an urge to tell the truth, protective feelings toward a beloved but unfinished idea, and a fear of ridicule and persecution.

In another passage, Mill speaks, in a probabilistic vein remarkably like Darwin's theory of evolution through natural selection, of the origin of new ideas: "when an opinion is true, it may be extinguished once, twice, or many times, but in the course of ages there will generally be found persons to rediscover it, until some one of its reappearances falls on a time when from favourable circumstances it escapes persecution until it has made such head as to withstand all subsequent attempts to suppress it."[4]

But it must be added that a complex scientific theory like Darwin's does not lie about waiting only to be discovered or rediscovered. It must be patiently conceived, crafted, and elaborated. This takes years of brave and patient struggle under conditions of adversity. Darwin had that kind of courage.

---

[3] John Stuart Mill, *On Liberty* (1859; reprint ed., Harmondsworth and New York: Penguin, 1974), p.95. See also June Goodfield's *Seven Sad Stories* (forthcoming), in which she gives striking new material about the case of William Lawrence, which I discuss below.

[4] *Ibid.*, p.90.

ABBREVIATIONS

Frequently used sources will be referred to by the abbreviations listed below. All the manuscripts listed are kept in the Cambridge University Library. In the case of the books, the edition cited below is the one referred to in the text unless otherwise specified.

MANUSCRIPTS

B — Darwin's first notebook on Transmutation of Species (July 1837—February 1838)

C — Darwin's second notebook on Transmutation of Species (February–July 1838)

D — Darwin's third notebook on Transmutation of Species (July 15th 1838—October 2nd 1838)

E — Darwin's fourth notebook on Transmutation of Species (October 1838—July 10th 1839)

M — Darwin's first notebook on Man, Mind, and Materialism (July 15th 1838—October 1st 1838, approximately)

N — Darwin's second notebook on Man, Mind, and Materialism (October 2nd 1838—August 1st 1839, approximately)

"Old and Useless Notes" or [OUN] — "Old and Useless Notes about the moral sense & some metaphysical points" (written mainly from 1837–1840)

Journal — A running record of major events in Darwin's life from 1809–1881. He probably began it in August 1838, the earlier entries being retrospective.

BOOKS

Autobiography — *The Autobiography of Charles Darwin, 1809–1882. With original omissions restored,* edited with appendix and notes by his grand-daughter Nora Barlow (London: Collins, 1958)

LL — *The Life and Letters of Charles Darwin,* edited by his son, Francis Darwin, 3 vols. (London: Murray, 1887)

ML — *More Letters of Charles Darwin,* edited by Francis Darwin, 2 vols. (London: Murray, 1903)

Beagle Diary   *Charles Darwin's Diary of the Voyage of H.M.S. "Beagle,"* edited from the *MS* by Nora Barlow (Cambridge: University Press, 1934)

Voyage, 1839   *Journal of Researches into the Geology and Natural History of the Various Countries Visited by H.M.S. Beagle under the Command of Captain FitzRoy, R.N. from 1832 to 1836,* by Charles Darwin (London: Colburn, 1839)

Voyage, 1845   *Journal of Researches into the Natural History and Geology of the Countries Visited during the Voyage of H.M.S. Beagle Round the World,* second edition by Charles Darwin (London: Murray, 1845)

Origin   *On the Origin of Species by means of Natural Selection, or the Preservation of Favoured Races in the Struggle for Life,* by Charles Darwin (London: Murray, 1859)

Animals and Plants   *The Variation of Animals and Plants under Domestication,* by Charles Darwin, 2 vols. (London: Murray, 1868)

Descent   *The Descent of Man, and Selection in Relation to Sex,* by Charles Darwin, second edition (London: Murray, 1882)

Expression   *The Expression of the Emotions in Man and Animals,* by Charles Darwin, reissue of second edition edited by Francis Darwin in 1890 (London: Murray, 1921)

Zoonomia   *Zoonomia; or the Laws of Organic Life,* by Erasmus Darwin, 2 vols. (London: Johnson. Vol. I, 1794; Vol. II, 1796) . All references are to Vol. I.

SYMBOLS

/ a few words inserted by Darwin /
<crossed out by Darwin>
[added in transcription by Barrett]
[Darwin's own brackets][CD]
((marginal or interlinear passage))
| = end of MS page
e = part of MS excised

CHRONOLOGY

Note: Direct quotations are taken from Darwin's *Journal.*

1809 February 12	Born at Shrewsbury.
1818	Entered Shrewsbury School.
1825–27	Attended Edinburgh University.
1827 March 27	Contributed two scientific papers to Plinian Society. W. A. Browne's paper, on mind as material, read and stricken from record at same meeting.
1827–31	Attended Cambridge University.
1829 Summer	Entomological tour of North Wales with Professor F. W. Hope.
1831 Spring	Began planning scientific voyage to Canary Islands.
1831 August	Geological tour of North Wales with Professor Adam Sedgwick.
1831 August 29	Received offer of post of naturalist on H.M.S. *Beagle.*
1831 December 27	H.M.S. *Beagle* sailed from Devonport, England.
1832 September 23	First important fossil find: various extinct mammals.
1832 December 16	First sight of Indians of Tierra del Fuego.
1835 September	Studied geology, fauna, and flora of Galapagos Islands.
1835 December	First draft of paper on theory of formation of coral reefs.
1836 October 2	H.M.S. *Beagle* docked at Falmouth, England.
1837 May 31	Read paper on coral reefs to London Geological Society.
1837 July	"Opened first notebook on 'Transmutation of Species.'" Formulated monad theory of evolution.
1837 October	Began work leading to *Zoology of the Voyage of H.M.S. Beagle, edited and superintended by Charles Darwin,* published 1840–1843, 5 volumes.

1837 November 1	Read paper on earthworms to London Geological Society.
1838 July 15	Began notebooks on man, mind, and materialism.
1838 September 21	Dream of execution.
1838 September 28	Read Malthus, grasped theory of evolution through natural selection.
1838 November–December	Restated theory as three succinct principles.
1839 January 29	Married Emma Wedgwood.
1839 January–May	Began circulating *Questions About the Breeding of Animals.*
1839 December 27	First child born, William Darwin. Began observations on infant development.
1842, 1844	Wrote preliminary essays, similar in outline to *Origin of Species.*
1844	Robert Chambers' *Vestiges of the Natural History of Creation* published anonymously.
1846 October 1	Finished third and last volume of *The Geology of the Voyage of the Beagle.*
1846 October 1	Began eight-year study of barnacles, resulting in four volumes.
1854 September 9	Finished barnacles.
1854 September 9	"Began sorting notes for Species theory."
1856 May 14	Began writing *Natural Selection,* voluminous work on evolution, never finished.
1858 June 18	Received letter from Alfred Russel Wallace, formulating theory of evolution through natural selection.
1858 July 1	Papers by Darwin and Wallace, announcing theory of evolution through natural selection, read at Linnaean Society, London.
1858 July 20	Began writing *Origin of Species.*
1859 March 19	Finished writing last chapter of *Origin.*
1859 October 1	Finished correcting proofs.
1859 November 24	*Origin of Species* published.
1860 January 9	"Began looking over MS. for work on Variation."
1860–67	Worked on unsolved problems of variation and heredity, published in 1868 as *The Variation of Animals and Plants under Domestication,* various related botanical

	works on plant reproduction, hybridization, and variation.
1863	Began experimental work on climbing and insectivorous plants, continued until his death.
1867 February	Began circulating questions about expression of emotions. Began work on "Man Essay."
1871 January 15	Finished correcting proofs of *The Descent of Man,* published February 24.
1871 January 17	"Began Expression & finished final rough copy on April 27."
1872 August 22	Finished last proofs of *The Expression of the Emotions in Man and Animals,* published November 26, 1872.
1877	Wrote and published "A Biographical Sketch of an Infant," based on observations made thirty-seven years earlier.
1881	"All early part of year Worm book published Oct. 10th." This was *The Formation of Vegetable Mould Through the Action of Worms, with Observations on Their Habits,* an enterprise begun forty-four years earlier.
1882	Died.

DARWIN ON MAN

If all men were dead, then monkeys make men.—Men make angels.
—Charles Darwin, B. notebook, p. 169, about November, 1837.

Introduction

Sept 21st Was witty in a dream in a confused manner. Thought
that a person was hung & came to life, & then made many jokes
about not having run away & having faced death like a hero, &
then I had some confused idea of showing scar behind (instead of
front) (having changed hanging into his head cut off) as kind of wit
showing he had honourable wounds. all this was kind of wit.—I
changed I believe from hanging to head cut off (there was the feeling of banter and joking) because the whole train of Dr. Monro
experiment about hanging came before me showing impossibility of
person recovering from hanging on account of blood, but all these
ideas came one after other, without ever comparing them. I neither
doubted them or *believed* them.—Believing consists in the comparison of ideas connected with judgment.
  What is the Philosophy of Shame & Blushing? [M 143–144]

So runs one of Darwin's entries in a notebook he kept in 1838. A
person is being executed, perhaps for his ideas. He entertains the
thought of running away, but stands fast. The dreamer wants to live
or return to life, so he changes the method of his execution from
hanging to decapitation, which in the dream seems less final. The
dream contains a recollected scrap of Darwin's medical education to
the effect that hanging is irreversible. In recording the dream Darwin
adds a remark about the nature of belief, and in a comment added
later raises a question about shame.
  In this passage we catch a glimpse of a man thinking. We see the

interplay of social and intellectual forces in Darwin's fear of dire punishment for thinking. We see the rapid, easy movement between different kinds of thought: a fragment of a physiology lecture heard long ago, a psychological remark on the distinction between dreams and rational beliefs, and the dream itself. We see, in the change from hanging to decapitation, and the meaning Darwin ascribes to it, the dreamer's wish for immortality; perhaps Darwin would have been satisfied to know that the ideas for which the dreamer was executed would endure a century and more.

The aim of this study of creativity is to describe the growth of thought in a real, thinking, feeling, dreaming person. As in the dream, thinking is not a straightforward advance. From the thinker's own point of view, there are doubts, retreats, detours, and impasses; there are also impulsive moments of decision, leaps into the dark from points of no return. From the standpoint of one hundred years of historical hindsight there are reasonable mistakes, non-essentials, and foolish blunders.

The reader may be disappointed if he approaches the subject expecting a tale leading up to one climactic moment of great insight, like the dubious stories of Archimedes' bath and Newton's apple. Although the progress of Darwin's thought is punctuated by many vital moments of insight, each one filling him with the joy of discovery, it is hard to find any single insight which in the living moment really seemed more vital than the others to the thinker himself.

The search for a moment of truth is probably misguided. Perhaps the concept of a single, crucial, sudden insight is suitable for describing someone solving a single well-defined problem. But we are dealing here with a different sort of thinking: a person striving to construct a new synthesis, a new way of looking at many problems, *a new point of view*.

On the time scale of the life history, the classic topics of the psychology of thinking—problem solving, concept formation, and imagery—are not only processes to be explained: beyond that, they take their places in a longer process of growth, the formation of a point of view. As Thomas Kuhn has urged, the established point of view, the scientists' "paradigm," provides the shared framework within which problems will be recognized as significant and solutions accepted as valid.[1] But in the psychology of thinking, little has been done to study the growth of a new point of view, although the work of Jean Piaget and his collaborators on the development of thinking in

[1] Thomas Kuhn, *The Structure of Scientific Revolutions* (London: University of Chicago Press, 1962).

children has done much to show how we might proceed in a study of adult thinking.

As for problem solving, it takes place in a diverse train of activities: reading and observation, imagination and memory, argument and discussion. For all we really know of it, focused problem solving may be a comparatively rare event. The very act of taking up a problem crystallizes a long history of development.

Given a problem-solving process, we may find reflection, sudden insights, and gradual improvement through trial and error. Even the groping trials are not blind or random: they emerge from the problem solver's perception of the structure of the problem, as he has come to recognize and understand it from his own particular vantage point. Thus, the sudden insight in which a problem is solved, when it is solved suddenly, may represent only a minor nodal point, like the crest of a wave, in a long and very slow process—the development of a point of view.

All this is not to say that problem solving is an unimportant part of the creative process. Indeed, Darwin's notebooks show how he attacked and solved a number of problems. But the total creative process of constructing a novel point of view is so complex that it is impossible to identify the solution of some one problem as a step more crucial than any other. The quest for one such step violates the character of thinking as an organic whole, as would a debate on the relative importance of the heart, the brain, and the liver. Without any one of a number of vital organs, the individual dies; without any one of a number of vital components, an argument fails.

In a case study of creativity one might well expect to find an analysis of the subject's personality and its roots. Although that is not the aim of this study, a description of a man's thinking involves so much of the man that it must reflect something of his personality. For example, in examining Darwin's method of work we find that he is not afraid to examine his own mental processes, including their non-rational components, and something of his own psychosexual life. In the interest of exploring the mind-body problem, Darwin took his evidence where he could find it, and what better place to look than at his own inner world?

Similarly, we learn something about Darwin as a person by studying the pattern of hesitation and delay which grew out of the purely intellectual difficulties of constructing a theory of evolution when these were multiplied by theological problems and by his fear of persecution and ridicule. A discussion of creativity and personality really ought to deal with the kinds of courage necessary for creative work. While there is no such separate discussion in the present study, the very human, cautious, vacillating yet persistent courage of Charles Darwin will become quite apparent.[2]

The fact that the formation of a new synthesis must be seen as a creative *process* rather than as a sudden creative *act*[3] has a deep significance for the relation between the thinker and the intellectual and social milieu in which he works. An isolated and sudden act might conceivably be thought of as occurring out of all time and place. But a long growth process must be seen as rooted in its total human context. There is plenty of time for the individual thinker to see the implications of his developing work for those around him, to test out colleagues and potential allies, to suffer in private the fear of ridicule and then to recover himself and persevere, to shape his argument so that he presents the smallest possible target to his critics and produces the largest possible impact on the general movement of public thought.

Rather than establish the context in which Darwin worked by retelling the general history of the period, in a study of an individual's thought it seems more directly relevant to consider the personal side of that context. Impersonal historical and social forces have no meaning for the individual until they are brought to bear directly on his life. In the present work I approach this matter by examining the points of view to which Darwin was exposed in his university education and in his family circle.

Darwin's notes are rich in useful facts garnered from his omnivorous reading, bibliographic references, and private dialogues with contemporaries whom he met either in person or through their writings. If there were some single specific idea which was central to Darwin's thought, we might hope to discover in his notebooks a clue as to when and from whom he had borrowed this golden key. But, as I have already proposed, preoccupation with the search for the initial appearance of single ideas may obscure more fundamental aspects of intellectual growth. It matters little whether the crucial idea is sought in a study of external influences upon the creative person, or whether the "golden moment" is sought in that person's inner thinking. While of course I am on the lookout for origins, sources, and early appearances, my main concern is the changing structure of an argument. Each idea is to be seen as taking its significance from the structure of ideas, or argument, of which it is a part. The ways in which such structures change will be my central concern.

---

2 Courage is rarely discussed in the literature of academic psychology. "Risk-taking," i.e. gambling, a much studied subject, is hardly the same thing. See my chapter, "Courage and Cognitive Growth in Children and Scientists," in *Piaget in the Classroom*, edited by Milton Schwebel and Jane Raph (New York: Basic Books, 1973).

3 Compare Arthur Koestler's treatment of this subject in *The Act of Creation* (London: Hutchinson, 1964).

For example, the idea of natural selection would, on the surface of things, seem to be Darwin's special characteristic. Yet it is well known that this idea was almost a commonplace before Darwin began his work. Darwin's special discovery was to see how the idea of natural selection could be transformed from a conservative to an evolutionary force. My task is not the unpromising one of trying to detect the first appearance of the idea of natural selection in Darwin's thought; like all ideas, it was almost certainly foreshadowed·and prefigured many times (a few of which I shall discuss) before it took on its mature and stable significance for him. Rather, the task is to see how the idea changes its character as it appears and reappears at different moments in the growth of Darwin's thought.

Bearing all these qualifications in mind, the term *insight* retains some value. Thought is a process in time and it does have its special moments. I shall speak often of Darwin's "Malthusian insight," the moment when, on September 28, 1838, he read the *Essay on Population*[4] and recognized the force of the idea of evolution through natural selection. In one sense, *insight* is a convenient shorthand for the very complexities under discussion. In another sense, it does justice to the emotion of thought, to the surge of joy and dread, excitement and fulfillment whenever the thinking person closes the loop and discovers what he has done.

Since Freud's work on unconscious errors and Köhler's discussion of "good errors"[5] it has been common for psychologists to use the analysis of errors as a tool in the study of thinking. In Piaget's work the concept of "error" is supplanted by the concept of the genesis of adult ways of thinking out of infantile and childish mental processes.[6] Given this background, we might expect that tracing a thought process

---

[4] In Darwin's surviving library there are two copies of the *Essay*, both of the same edition: The Rev. T. R. Malthus, *An Essay on the Principles of Population; or, a view of its past and present effects on Human Happiness with an inquiry into our prospects respecting the future removal or mitigation of the evils which it occasions* (London: Murray, 2 vols., 6th ed., 1826) . One copy, Charles' brother's, has the inscription "Erasmus Darwin 1830," and is presumably the one Charles read in 1838. It has few marks in it, probably none by Charles. The other copy has the inscription "C. Darwin April 1841." It has many of his characteristic markings and notes in the back of Volume 1. The pages of Volume 2 of this copy are uncut. The edition I quote from in the present book is the Everyman Library reprint of the 7th edition (New York: Dutton, n.d.) .

[5] Sigmund Freud, *The Psychopathology of Everyday Life*, authorized English edition with an introduction by A. A. Brill (London: T. Fisher Unwin, 1914), first published 1901. Wolfgang Köhler, *The Mentality of Apes* (London: Routledge and Kegan Paul, 1927). Köhler used the term "good error" to describe moves in solving practical problems which, while unworkable, led the chimpanzee toward solution.

[6] This approach characterizes all of Piaget's extensive works. See for example Bärbel Inhelder and Jean Piaget, *The Growth of Logical Thinking from Childhood to Adolescence* (London: Routledge and Kegan Paul, 1958) or the recent summary by the same authors, *The Psychology of the Child* (London: Routledge and Kegan Paul, 1969).

of great historical interest would invite careful attention to its erroneous—i.e., early—forms. Darwin made this possible for us because his
notebooks contain several very interesting "errors." But a common
tendency in discussing Darwin's thinking has been to ignore this subject and to present Darwin's thought as a successful march from one
good idea to another, all of which were eventually assembled in the
Origin of Species.[7]

It is true enough that if one examines Darwin's notes with sufficient historical hindsight one can find many examples of the early
appearance of "correct" ideas—i.e., ideas which survive in approximately their early form and appear later in the *Origin of Species* or
Darwin's other works. Noticing this aspect of the growth of thought is
certainly significant.

But it is at least equally important to study the transitional ideas,
those which disappear later on, such as Darwin's early attempts to
construct a coherent theory. As we shall see in examining his first
theory of evolution, Darwin was capable of ideas which by modern
standards seem quite bizarre. We should not let historical hindsight or
Great Man worship blind us to these early efforts.[8] By examining
them fully we may better understand the difficulties Darwin faced and
overcame. Without seeing these difficulties clearly, it becomes all too
easy to see Darwin's long hesitation before publishing his ideas as
reflecting nothing but blemishes of character, neurosis or cowardice.

There were at least two varieties of intellectual or scientific doubt
with which Darwin was understandably afflicted. First, since he himself had great difficulty in making whatever progress he did make, it
was clear to him that his most promising ideas could not be self-
evident even to one prepared to accept a theory of evolution. By the
same token, his theory might not persuade his contemporaries, even
those most prepared to be friendly to it, not to speak of avowed
enemies of all evolutionary thought. Secondly, Darwin hardly ever
forgot that his theory had important gaps in it. He was on very sound

---

7 See, for example, Sir Gavin de Beer's succinct and expert biography, *Charles Darwin:
Evolution by Natural Selection* (London; Nelson, 1963); Lady Barlow's introduction to
Darwin and Henslow: The Growth of an Idea, Letters 1831–1860, edited by Nora Barlow
(London: John Murray, 1967); and Michael Ghiselin's recent book, *The Triumph of the
Darwinian Method* (Berkeley: University of California Press, 1966). All of these works
entirely neglect Darwin's first theory of evolution, which is dicussed below in Chapter 7.
8 Ignoring Darwin's erroneous early thought forms may be an inverted form of
the "genetic fallacy," a term used by philosophers to describe the disparagement of
historical and evolutionary outcomes because of their "lowly origins." Admiration
for Darwin's work may have led some scholars to ignore or underemphasize his apparent errors in order to avoid criticizing him. For an interesting discussion of this
general question, see T. Z. Lavine, "Reflections on the Genetic Fallacy," *Social
Research*, 1962, Vol. 29, pp. 321–336.

ground in remaining less than smug. In short, a study of how Darwin moved from one stage of thought to another casts some light on his motives for hesitating to publish his ideas.

A creative thought process is so complex that no single approach can do it justice. In order to look closely at Darwin's thinking as a whole during the richly documented two-year period 1837–39, this study is divided into three parts.

Part One deals with the intellectual setting in which Darwin worked. It is not intended as a historical account so much as a personal mise-en-scène. I discuss the interplay between public and private aspects of Darwin's thinking, and the way in which this interplay shaped Darwin's general strategy of scientific work. This leads me to examine the effects of religious dogmatism on his scientific progress, with special reference to Darwin's personal knowledge of such persecution, when it might have most affected the development of his own sense of scientific identity. These repressive forces must be understood as a counterpoise to other tendencies, such as those expressed in the world outlook Darwin shared with his illustrious grandfather, Erasmus Darwin, and which was prevalent in the extended family circle in which Charles Darwin moved. In addition to his family there were teachers who were important in Darwin's early development. Not only did they help him acquire specialized knowledge in various branches of science, they also conveyed to him their attitudes toward controversies bearing on the conflict between science and religion.

Part Two is a detailed study of the development of the theory of evolution through natural selection, based mainly on Darwin's transmutation notebooks of 1837–38. Three different approaches are interwoven:

1. A specific psychological process is singled out for attention, and illustrated with examples chosen from case material.

2. The whole "argument"—that is, the way in which an ensemble of ideas are related to each other—is reconstructed and examined, first for one moment in the creative person's development, then for another.

3. Single ideas are selected and pursued, one at a time, through their various appearances and transformations in the changing pattern of ideas.

The study moves back and forth over the case material, examining it from different perspectives. Darwin kept many streams of thought going over long periods of time. But he did not label them for us or separate them into neat, coherent essays. In his notebooks, ideas tumble over each other in a seemingly chaotic fashion. The underlying order is something to be constructed, not observed.

Preoccupation with processes of growth and change ought not to prevent us from recognizing the invariants, the structures that remain relatively intact throughout a long developmental process. If we could not identify such invariants, if there were nothing but chaotic flux, it would become almost meaningless to speak of change. If we take the next step and admit genuine change depends on such ordered integrity, we may almost say, "Plus ça *reste* la même chose, plus ça change."

Although I cannot, of course, give an exact measure of the rate of intellectual change, I try to show how it happens that stable changes in ideas evolve at such a moderate rate. The movement of ideas is far slower than the swift but transitory currents of the continuous stream of thought which serves as the "carrier wave" of creative work.

Part III considers Darwin's thinking about man, mind, and materialism. The major theme is that Darwin's thinking about man was not an afterthought or a separate line of inquiry, nor was it the cause or the effect of his evolutionary thinking. Rather, the subject of man and his place in nature was so woven into Darwin's thoughts that it forms an indispensable part of the network of his beliefs. From an early age Darwin thought about all sorts of men, ranging from himself and other Englishmen to primitive men, such as the Tierra del Fuegians of whom he wrote to his teacher Henslow that they "seemed the troubled spirits of another world."[9]

But his thinking about man changed profoundly as his theory of evolution developed. Darwin saw that the species man provided an unparalleled opportunity to study adaptive variation in an organism displaying extraordinary ability to change itself through its own activity. Man, thought Darwin, might well be the organism most useful for studying the inheritance of acquired characteristics. From a relatively simple concern with man's place in nature we are thus led to the question of man's place in Darwin's theory of evolution. To understand Darwin's relation to the Lamarckian idea of the inheritance of acquired characteristics, it is fundamental to see how he grappled with the problem of the causes of variation, and to see how hard it was for him to separate this question, even tentatively, from the problem of evolution itself. His notebooks show how this struggle led Darwin to search for *some* mechanism of selection even before he grasped the idea of natural selection.

To a striking extent, Darwin's thinking about nature seems marked by images drawn from human experience and conduct. The concept of struggle for existence is linked, through Malthus, to human conflicts which periodically decimate our numbers. The concept of

---

[9] Darwin's letter of April 11, 1833, to the Rev. Prof. John Henslow. Published in *Darwin and Henslow: The Growth of an Idea, Letters 1831–1860*, edited by Nora Barlow (London: John Murray, 1967).

Fuegian

natural selection is linked to artificial selection as practiced by the plant and animal breeders whose work Darwin studied closely. The image of the irregularly branching tree of nature, which captures so much of Darwin's thought, is linked to the family trees of human genealogies.

It is tempting to accept the suggestion that human life is the fundamental source of our creative imagery, even when we think about non-human things. From this it might follow that the general forms of scientific thought are directly constrained by existing social relations which govern the limits of our images of man. But I believe this formulation may be both anthropomorphic and un-Darwinian. The great achievement for which Darwin's work is sometimes called the second Copernican revolution was to remove man from the center of the stage in our conception of nature. Just as Copernicus showed how our abode the earth is not the center of the solar system, so Darwin showed how the biological order does not revolve around man. This step in thought has, or ought to have, profound consequences for our conception of scientific imagery.

There are many sources of our images: man in his social relations; man alone—thinking, feeling, sensing; human art and technology, and all their products; and wild nature. These are not strictly separate forms of experience. Rather, each informs the other, and there is a constant and productive interplay among them. Darwin drew on Malthus for a sharper look at the subject of population, but Malthus himself began with examples drawn from Benjamin Franklin, in which botanical and human superfecundity are fused in one image.[10] Darwin drew on artificial selection to clarify the idea of natural selection, but probably not until he had already grasped or almost grasped the essential features of natural selection. It is difficult to decide which idea illuminated the other—a point that plant and animal breeders appreciate.[11] Throughout his thinking Darwin used human invention as a way of understanding biological adaptation. His contemporaries used the marvels of organic nature to demonstrate the supreme intelligence and necessary existence of the Creator who must have devised such intricate and perfect creatures. In contrast, Darwin used the imperfections and irregularities to be found everywhere in living organisms to argue that the design of nature was achieved not by an omniscient inventor but by a groping evolutionary process.

It may well be that man himself is the most fruitful, or at least the first, source of our creative images. But the study of Darwin's thought

---

10 Malthus, *op. cit.*, pp. 5–6.
11 See John Hammond, "Darwin and Animal Breeding," in S. A. Barnett, editor, *A Century of Darwin* (London: Heinemann, 1958) .

reveals the value of abundant and varied images, the time it takes to transform one image into another to meet the requirements of creative thinking, and the effort it takes to escape from primitive modes of thought in which we place excessive reliance on limited sources of imagery. It is in the constant and pluralistic struggle to expand the horizons of thought beyond images derived from our own human past that we see more deeply into nature and into ourselves.

The intricacy of the relations among these different well-springs of thought can be seen in the history of self-regulating machines, or feedback devices. Before the 18th century European inventors interested in automatic machines designed devices that followed rigid clockwork patterns. In the 18th century there was a marked increase in the development of self-regulating machines (float regulators, temperature regulators, centifugal governors, etc.), designed to make corrections for external disturbances so that the machine can maintain some desired state. It was during the same period that the concept of society as a self-regulating system became prominent in the work of Adam Smith and others, as against the more static idea of rigid centralized control which dominated earlier social theories.[12] Both the technological innovations and the new kind of social theory were essential features of the industrial revolution. They cannot be said to have caused it, or to have caused each other: together with a host of real social and economic changes, they *were* the revolution. But it took almost another century before the same conception of a self-regulating system was powerfully reflected in biological theory.

Darwin's thinking, both in biology and in geology, was permeated with the idea of such self-regulating systems. But as far as I can tell, he never did use the analogy of natural selection and man-made feedback devices. Alfred Russel Wallace, however, co-discoverer of the theory of evolution through natural selection, wrote, "The action of this principle is exactly like that of the centrifugal governor of the steam engine, which checks and corrects any irregularities almost before they become evident . . ."[13]

Of the Darwin manuscripts I discuss in detail, unquestionably the most important are his M and N notebooks, dealing with the continuity between man and other animals, the evolution of intelligence, expression of emotions, sanity and insanity, and a host of other psychological subjects. His concern for the material side of the evolution of intellectual functioning inevitably led him to reflect on philosophical and religious questions, such as the relation between

---

12 See Otto Mayr, *The Origins of Feedback Control* (Cambridge: M.I.T. Press, 1970).

13 Alfred Russel Wallace, "On the Tendency of Varieties to Depart Indefinitely from the Original Type," *Journal of the Linnaean Society*, Vol. 3, 1859, p. 62.

mind and body, free will, the natural origins of supernatural beliefs, and the effects of atheism on morality.

Darwin's concern for these subjects was expressed in other important manuscript materials written at about the same time, especially Darwin's notes on an "Essay on Theology and Natural Selection," and a miscellaneous bundle he later labeled "Old and USELESS Notes about the moral sense & some metaphysical points . . ." The material gives clear evidence for Darwin's realization during this period that his ideas were indeed materialistic, tending toward atheism, and therefore dangerous. Darwin's fears of a hostile reception did not stem simply from the widespread antagonism to evolutionary views of all sorts. He knew that his particular theory inescapably located the idea of evolution within the framework of materialist philosophy.

Examination of these notebooks on man, mind, and materialism brings out the discrepancy between Darwin's actual psychological view and his views as presented in the *Origin,* in his chapter on "Instinct." Because his psychological writings are more scattered than the rest of his works, the extent to which Darwin was a psychologist has not been generally recognized. From the entire pattern of his work it becomes clear that behavioristic psychology cannot accurately lay claim to Darwin as their intellectual forebear. I believe that Darwin has been misappropriated by modern behaviorism and that he was actually a pioneer for a much less mechanistic approach to human psychology.

Darwin's view of nature was subtle and complex. He saw it as both deterministic and probabilistic, and he dealt with living beings as both stably organized and adaptively changing. This is a useful perspective for reflecting on the creative process and on its relation to human aims and desires.

Can man be deliberately creative, or is it all an illusion? Are the seeming products of the free mind only chance recombinations of old ideas? Or are they reflections of an inevitable historical process in which individuals are carriers and not steersmen?

The question is important not only for understanding creativity but also for arriving at an image of man's future. Can we plan for a world in which there is some likelihood of the survival of life on earth? Is there anything we can do and ought to do to make our future enjoyable and dignified, worthy of *Homo sapiens* at his wisest?

When we speak of man as a species we run the risk of minimizing the importance of his existence as an individual organism, each of us with his own experience and his own purposes. To be sure, these arise out of life in society under concrete historical conditions. Nevertheless, each of us becomes an individual, bearing his unique share of responsibility for the future of our species. Without the twin ideas of individuality and purpose, both creativity and morality would be meaningless concepts.

Ought implies *can*. There would be no point in saying that we ought to do something if it were impossible. But how do we know what can be done except by using our full powers of invention to explore the possibilities? Morality requires both creativity and choice.

Darwin saw the relation between intelligence and morality. Ruminating about the evolution of conscience, he wrote: "In a dog we see a struggle between its appetite, or love of exercise & its love of its puppies: the latter generally soon conquers, & the dog probably thinks no more of it.—Not so man, from his memory & mental capacity of calling up past sensations he will be forced to reflect on his choice. . . . Hence conscience is improved by attending & reasoning on its action & on the results following our conduct."[14]

The heart of moral conduct is caring for others. Only a being that could elevate the process of caring to a level not known in previous species could become intelligent in the way we know as human. Only an extraordinarily intelligent being could care for others at this level. The evolution of morality and the evolution of intelligence have always been inseparable, as well as their future survival in the body and brain of humanity.

---

14 "Old and Useless Notes," # 43-44, written May 5, 1839.

PART I

The Intellectual Setting

CHAPTER 1

Public versus Private Knowledge

> To avoid stating how far, I believe, in Materialism,
> say only that emotions, instincts, degrees of talent,
> which are hereditary are so because brain of child
> resembles parent stock.
>
> Charles Darwin, M notebook,
> p. 57, about August 1838

Events in the history of science develop at three main levels of expression. They have a public shape, embodied in scientific meetings, in articles published in scientific journals, and in books. They have private shape, in the thoughts of the individual, a shape which may disappear in the course of the transformation from private to public. And they have confidential, or semi-private shape, in the form of letters, discussions among intimates, and other such restricted exchanges. These three levels of expression interact and influence each other in important ways, but these ways are neither simple or direct.

The early development of Darwin's views was expressed in his private notebooks of 1837–38. His public views on the evolution of psychological processes only appeared much later in two major works: *The Descent of Man* (1871) and *The Expression of the Emotions in Man and Animals* (1872). *On the Origin of Species* (1859) contained one chapter on instinct, confined mainly to a detailed examination of egg-laying in cuckoos, slave making in ants, and hive-construction in bees. His intent then was restricted to showing that natural selection could account for the evolution of the "diversities of instinct and of the other mental qualities of animals within the same class." In the conclusion of the *Origin,* however, he predicted somewhat vaguely that "Psychology will be based on a new foundation, that of the necessary acquirement of each mental power and capacity by gradation. Light will be thrown on the origin of man and his history." (*Origin*, 488)

Darwin's restraint in 1859 and his delay until 1871 have given rise to the impression that he was reluctant to make up his own mind as to whether or not his theory of evolution applied to mind and to man. But careful study of his private notebooks makes it clear that Darwin, *from his very first musings on evolution onward,* viewed man as part of the web of evolutionary change.

During the voyage of the *Beagle,* 1831–36, Darwin kept thousands of pages of scientific notes, and wrote many letters expressing the development of his ideas. In these writings there was almost no hint of evolutionary thought; during these years he was preoccupied with geological questions. He began with a notion of a stable, harmonious natural order, in which all organic beings were adapted to each other and to their physical environment in a fashion ordained by the Creator. As he came to accept modern geological views of a constantly changing order in the physical world, a contradiction within his point of view developed as follows: each species was adapted to its milieu; the milieu was undergoing constant change; and yet the species were changeless. Darwin probably began to feel this contradiction during the final months of the voyage, as he was going over his notes and organizing his materials. It was not until July 1837, ten months after returning to England, that he began his first notebook on "Transmutation of Species." It was over a year after that, in September 1838, that the role of natural selection in evolution began to be clear to him.[1]

But Darwin did not await this clarification before applying his still chaotic and murky ideas to man. In 1837 Darwin believed that the chief agent of evolutionary change was the direct influence of the changing physical world. Accordingly, in the very first passage of his transmutation notebooks Darwin writes, "even mind and instinct becomes influenced" by changes in the physical environment. (*B* 3) A few pages further on, his feeling that man is part of the evolving natural order is reflected in an interesting argument by analogy *from* man *to* the rest of that order: "Each species changes. Does it progress. Man gains ideas. The simplest cannot help becoming more complicated; and if we look to first origin, there must be progress." (*B* 18)

[1] H. E. Gruber and Valmai Gruber. "The Eye of Reason: Darwin's Development During the *Beagle* Voyage," *Isis,* 1962, Vol. 53, pp. 186–200.

H. E. Gruber, "Pensée Créatrice et Vitesse du Changement Adaptif: Le Développement de la Pensée de Darwin," in F. Bresson and M. de Montmollin (ed.), *Psychologie et Epistémologie Génétiques: Thèmes Piagetiens* (Paris: Dunod, 1966).

A few months later Darwin makes a different comment on the inevitability of progress, showing that he has come to see some danger in this anthropocentrism: "It is absurd to talk of one animal being higher than another. *We* consider those, where the cerebral structure, intellectual faculties, most developed, as highest.—A bee doubtless would where the instincts were."[2]

By July of 1838 Darwin's interest in psychological matters had risen to the point where he began a separate set of notes, the M and N notebooks, which dealt almost exclusively with the evolution of man, mind, emotions, and behavior. The M and N notebooks include many of Darwin's personal recollections, some of his dreams, and other material of intrinsic interest—all used by him in his reflections on the relation between psychology and evolution.

From the standpoint of the student of creative thinking it is extremely interesting to note that Darwin began these reflections on psychological issues long *before* writing the *Origin of Species,* and, indeed, before the moment in September 1838 when his reading of Malthus led him to his incisive insight into the importance of natural selection. In short, Darwin began to explore the implications of the theory of evolution before he could explain evolution to his own satisfaction. This exploration took the form of a rapid, almost explosive branching out into many problem areas. Even without the central idea of natural selection clearly formulated, he was able to assemble many facts and work out some important partial solutions to these problems. The task that remained, which took many more years, was to formulate a few cardinal points in a well-coordinated theoretical structure, and then to integrate in this new structure the many ideas he had previously sketched. It was only in this slow process of assimilation that these ideas could take their final shape.

From private thoughts to public expression the path is not straight. Effort spent on keeping notes played a large part in Darwin's work. Far from being a personal idiosyncrasy, his almost endless making of notebooks had roots in industrial practice, in his family tradition, and in British empirical philosophy. In good part, the notebooks Darwin used were well-made manufactured articles. In their bindings, their clasps, and their paper, as well in their variety of sizes suited for different purposes, they indicate a history of the social development of a technique. The celebrated British printer John Bell was the manufacturer of Erasmus Darwin's commonplace book in which Charles' grandfather recorded his ideas, diagrammed his inventions, in short, stored a fascinating miscellany.

---

2 *B* 74, about September 1837. Darwin wrote "cerebral structure" above "intellectual faculties" and bracketed the two phrases, indicating how inseparable he thought they were.

M Notebook, p. 57. *Courtesy of Cambridge University Library.*

The first eight pages of Erasmus' commonplace book were printed by Bell; they explain its functions and instruct the user in the technique and philosophy of indexing. Mr. Bell makes it clear that the purpose of indexing is not simply to help find entries in the commonplace book; rather, the very process of forming the index will help the user to organize his ideas and experiences, and facilitate reflective thought. Bell drew heavily on the empirical philosopher John Locke, who believed that knowledge arises out of personal experience through an active process of reflection.[3]

Charles Darwin's notebooks were not exactly commonplace books following Locke's ideas about indexing a miscellany. Each notebook was an attempt to group material on certain broad topics, such as geology, evolution, or man. Any indexing was done after the fact, often long after. These early notebooks were mid-way between a commonplace book and a filing system. As his enterprises grew in size and complexity, Darwin found that notebooks were a clumsy device, and he moved further in the direction of a flexible filing system. This led him to tear out some pages of his notebooks for filing in appropriate categories. Keeping notes, then, was not simply a matter of recording observations. It was the expression of a broad philosophical point of view, and an opportunity for deepening thought and strengthening command of one's personal knowledge.

---

[3] *Bell's Common-Place Book. Form'd Generally upon the Principles Recommended and Practiced by Mr. Locke* (London: John Bell, 1770). Erasmus Darwin's copy is now kept at Down House, Charles Darwin's home.

The relation between the transmutation notebooks and those on man and mind is significant for what it tells us about Darwin's whole scientific strategy. He did not work on "Baconian principles," if that means collecting facts and then drawing conclusions; nor did he work in a "deductive spirit,"[4] as he said of his work on the formation of coral reefs. To be more specific: *he did not* first (a) collect evidence for infra-human evolution, then (b) construct the theory of evolution through natural selection, then (c) see the special difficulties in applying the theory to the human case, then (d) solve these special problems, and finally (e) draw the conclusion that the theory of evolution does indeed apply to man. Nor did he carry out these steps in some other sequence that might be deemed scientifically or logically prudent.

Make what we will of it, those of us devoted to methodological soundness, when he first opened his transmutation notebooks (a) he believed in the occurrence of evolution, (b) he took it for granted that man was included, and, finally, (c) he had what seemed to him a plausible theory but gave it up within a few weeks, without giving up his belief in evolution.

This disparity between the actual and the prudent course of scientific thought gains interest from a parallel discrepancy between the actual and the publicly recorded course of events. In the years 1839–46, after he had developed the theory of evolution through natural selection, Darwin brought out ten books. There were two editions of his *Journal of Researches,* recounting the voyage of the *Beagle.* There were five volumes of the *Zoology of the Voyage of H.M.S. Beagle,* which he supervised and edited, working in collaboration with various specialists. There were three volumes of the geology of the *Beagle* voyage, including his book on the formation of coral reefs. During the same years he published about a dozen scientific papers on the same range of subjects. None of these works contained any unconcealed account of his theory of evolution. With one major exception, the second edition of the *Journal of Researches,* which he worked on for four months in 1845, there were no published traces of his evolutionary thought.

The revision of the *Journal of Researches* reflects the deep strain Darwin had imposed upon himself by deferring publication of his theory. Throughout this edition he deposited paragraphs that could only have been written by Darwin the evolutionist. Taken out of their hiding places and strung together, they form an essay which gives

---

[4] In describing his work on the formation of coral reefs, he wrote: "No other work of mine was begun in so deductive a spirit as this; for the whole theory was thought out on the west coast of S. America before I had seen a true coral reef." (*Autobiography,* 98)

almost the whole of his thought. He used two methods of concealment: fragmentation and dispersal of the relevant passages, a paragraph here and there throughout the book; and omission of one vital ingredient, the principle of natural selection acting to produce new species.[5]

Meanwhile, Darwin wrote two sketches of his theory of evolution, one in 1842 and the other in 1844.[6] The second one, which he "slowly enlarged and improved" during the first six months of 1844, bears a striking resemblance to the *Origin of Species,* in its organization, its scope, often in its wording, and in the essential of its argument. Darwin thought well enough of it to have a secretary copy the 230 pages of his manuscript. But he did not publish it. Instead, we see in Darwin's life an emerging strategy involving two grand detours: the first, a long delay before publishing his general theory of evolution, and the second, another long delay before revealing his ideas on the evolution of man.

After completing the Essay of 1844, he did not go directly to the necessary task, as he perceived matters, of its further "improvement and enlargement." Instead, he wrote a detailed letter to his wife, Emma, instructing her on the choice of an appropriate editor who might prepare the essay for publication in the event of his death. Then he turned to other work.[7]

By 1846 Darwin had exhausted the vein of his geological material. His sketch of 1844, which he believed to be "a considerable step in science" (letter to Emma), was two years behind him. He had suffered from the decision to conceal his views for a while; one might expect that now at last he would turn to the task of perfecting his essay on species.

Instead, the detour continued. Darwin took up what was for him

---

[5] At least one observant contemporary, John Lindley, editor of *The Gardeners' Chronicle,* noticed one of the key revisions Darwin had made. Professor Lindley reprinted in the *Chronicle* a long passage from the *Journal of Researches,* on fossil evidences of the extinction of mammals in South America. In the revised version Darwin had added a very clear statement of the Malthusian principle of the relation between food supply and population growth. Darwin only used it to show how the principle might be used to account for the increasing rarity and eventual extinction of some species. Compare Darwin's *Voyage,* 1839, pp. 210–212, with the 1845 edition, pp. 173–176. See *The Gardeners' Chronicle,* 1845, August 9, p. 546; August 16, p. 563; October 4, p. 675. On August 25, 1845, Darwin wrote to Lyell, "I was much pleased by Lindley picking out my extinction paragraphs and giving them uncurtailed." (*LL* 1, 342)

[6] Charles Darwin, *The Foundations of the Origin of Species; Two Essays Written in 1842 and 1844,* edited by his son Francis Darwin (Cambridge: University Press, 1909).

[7] *LL* 2, 16–18. Letter to Emma Darwin, July 5, 1844. Although he suggested five different men for the job, his preference was to have his scientific remains arranged for display by Charles Lyell the geologist, with the assistance of Joseph Hooker the botanist. For this work he proposed that Emma pay £400, £500 if need be.

an almost wholly new subject, the study of barnacles. He seems to have expected this to take him a year or two; in fact, it took him eight long, long years. At first he spoke of his "beloved" barnacles. Later he came to hate them, and yearned to be finished with the demanding task in which he had permitted himself to become engrossed, or entrapped. When he finally quit the barnacles, it was not because he had done everything he thought necessary, but because he had had enough. His series of four fat monographs on living and fossil barnacles confirmed his reputation as a solid citizen of the scientific community, a biological systematist, and a great specialist in one domain. In a preface to one of the barnacle books, written as he was winding up the last of that work, he admitted that he had intended to do another volume, on

Emma Darwin in 1839. *Courtesy of American Museum of Natural History*

anatomical questions, but "I am unwilling to spend more time on the subject."[8]

Darwin's work on barnacles was very good. A zoologist one hundred years later remarked that in the field of taxonomy we "may still be guided by Darwin's precept and example. His example, in the shape of the *Monograph of the Cirripedia,* has still to be followed as far as most of the animal kingdom is concerned. Few groups of animals have yet received such comprehensive and world-wide treatment. . . ."[9]

The suggestion that Darwin delayed publication of his evolutionary views to avoid offending Emma merits discussion. Was he treating her merely as a member of the "frail sex" unable to face the unpleasant truth of man's origin? Or was he treating her as a reasonable member of the general public whom he wished to persuade rather than antagonize?

Because they were together so much from his marriage in 1839 to his death in 1882 there was little correspondence between them. But we know enough to piece together a reasonably coherent picture. Dr. Robert Darwin, Charles' father, had strongly advised him to be circumspect in religious matters: "Nothing is more remarkable than the spread of scepticism or rationalism during the latter half of my life. Before I was engaged to be married, my father advised me to conceal carefully my doubts, for he said that he had known extreme misery thus caused with married persons. . . . My father added that he had known during his whole long life only three women who were sceptics. . . ." (*Autobiography,* 95)

As late as 1865 Joseph Hooker took a similar view. Darwin's lifelong friend Hooker was the first to whom he confided his evolutionary views[10] and one of the first to support them publicly in 1859. An outspoken man with a trenchant style and an entrenched position in British science, Hooker nevertheless wrote: "It is all very well for Wallace to wonder at scientific men being afraid of saying what they think. . . . Had he as many kind and good relations as I have, who would be grieved and pained to hear me say what I think, and had he children who would be placed in predicaments most detrimental to children's minds by such avowals on my part, he would not wonder so much."[11]

---

8 *A Monograph of the Sub-class Cirripedia with Figures of All the Species: the Balanidae (or Sessile Cirripedes); the Verrucidae, etc.* (London: The Ray Society, 2 vols. 1851, 1854). *A Monograph of the Fossil Lepadidae (Balanidae and Verrucidae) etc.* (London: The Paleontographical Society, 2 vols., 1851, 1854).

9 R. A. Crowson, "Darwin and Classification," in *A Century of Darwin,* edited by S. A. Barnett (London: Heinemann, 1958).

10 Darwin to Hooker, January 11, 1844: ". . . I am almost convinced . . . that species are not (it is like confessing a murder) immutable." (*LL* II, 23)

11 *Life and Letters of Sir Joseph Dalton Hooker,* edited by Leonard Huxley, 2 vols. (London: John Murray), Vol. 2, p. 54, Hooker to Darwin, October 6, 1865.

We have no positive evidence that Charles and Emma ever discussed his evolutionary theories in the early years. But they probably would have discussed his letter of editorial instructions, and, for that matter, the Essay of 1844 itself.

By 1856, from one of Darwin's many letters to Hooker, it is obvious that Emma was by then aware of both men's views.[12] In 1859 she helped him with the proofs of the *Origin*. Although we have no definite information on the early years, he most probably did discuss the subject openly with her. I say this mainly because in his private life he was a very open, transparent man; in his relations with his children and others with whom he corresponded one sees that he was incessantly enlisting their help, taking them some way into his confidence, and maintaining at least a seemingly very free relationship. One has the feeling about the Darwins that within the family everything was discussed.

What is more to the point, we have unmistakable evidence that he did discuss his religious doubts fully and frankly with Emma, thus ignoring his father's advice almost immediately after it was given. Our main source is one quite sophisticated letter from Emma to Charles, written about 1839–40, discussing his religious doubts, asserting her own faith, and assuring him of her love. Her aim in writing seems to have been to express herself clearly rather than to persuade him. She alludes to his brother, Erasmus, as having "gone before" Charles—i.e., lost faith first and perhaps having unduly influenced him; she suggests that the scientific habit of doubting undemonstrated facts and theories ought not to be extended to matters of faith; and she speaks of the value of prayer. It is all written in the tone of someone accustomed to rational argument and careful expression, as indeed she was. (*Autobiography*, 235)

Not only Charles' but Emma's faith faded. Their daughter Henrietta wrote of her: ". . . she kept a sorrowful wish to believe more, and I know that it was an abiding sadness to her that her faith was less vivid than it had been in her youth."[13]

In September of 1854, ten years after the letter to Emma instructing her on the publication of his species theory, he took up the task

---

[12] *Ibid.*, Vol. 1, p. 494.
[13] *Emma Darwin: A Century of Family Letters, 1792–1896*, edited by her daughter Henrietta Litchfield, 2 vols. (London: John Murray, 1915), Vol. 2, p. 175. In 1880 Darwin wrote to Karl Marx (see below, page 72), "Although I am a keen advocate of freedom of opinion in all questions, it seems to me (rightly or wrongly) that direct arguments against Christianity and Theism hardly have any effect on the public; and that freedom of thought will best be promoted by that gradual enlightening of human understanding which follows the progress of science. I have therefore always avoided writing about religion and have confined myself to science. Possibly I have been too strongly influenced by the thought of the concern it might cause some members of my family, if in any way I lent my support to direct attacks on religion." (Quoted in *Darwin Revalued* by Sir Arthur Keith, London: Watts, 1955).

once more. In anticipation, he wrote to his good friend Hooker that he had been finishing up the barnacles, correcting proofs, returning borrowed specimens ". . . and sending ten thousand Barnacles out of the house all over the world. But I shall now in a day or two begin to look over my old notes on species." (*LL* I, 395)

So ended the first grand detour. Even now, he did not really go straight for the jugular. As he began to move steadily and directly toward his lifetime goal, he maintained his deliberate, prudent style of work. He spent some twenty months reading and sorting out his notes. Then, as he wrote in his *Journal* entry for May 14, 1856, "Began by Lyell's advice writing Species Sketch." In spite of his wording, this was hardly intended as a suggestive sketch but rather as a definitive treatment, marshaling all evidence, answering all objections. Encyclopedic in tone, "Natural Selection," as he intended to call it, would have been a bulky, difficult book which might conceivably have attracted the attention of only a few scientists.[14]

But "Natural Selection" was never finished. Working steadily, he finished about ten chapters, or a chapter every two or three months. He was about two-thirds of the way through the task as he had outlined it. Then, on June 18, 1858, something happened which changed his plans and led him to write the *Origin of Species*. Expressing his ideas in a more compact form, the *Origin* was a masterpiece of scientific writing which excited the interest of all literate people everywhere in the world.

What happened on June 18, of course, was the arrival of Alfred Russel Wallace's letter to Darwin announcing privately that he, Wallace, had a theory: the theory of evolution through natural selection. Wallace enclosed a short paper excellently summarizing his—and Darwin's—views, arrived at more or less independently by the two men.

About a year earlier, Darwin had explained his theory of evolution to Lyell. Immediately on receiving Wallace's letter, Darwin wrote to Lyell: "Your words have come true with a vengeance—that I should be forestalled. You said this, when I explained to you here very briefly my views of 'Natural Selection' depending on the struggle for existence. I never saw a more striking coincidence; if Wallace had my MS. sketch written out in 1842, he could not have made a better short abstract! Even his terms now stand as heads of my chapters." (*LL* 2, 116)

Now at last Darwin was galvanized into quick, decisive movement toward the great achievement of his life. There was an initial fuss over the division of priority of discovery between Darwin and Wallace.

---

14 "Natural Selection" is being reconstructed from surviving manuscripts by Professor Robert C. Stauffer and will soon be published by Cambridge University Press.

This matter was handled equitably and firmly by a sort of informal jury, which effected the transmission to the scientific community of a brief summary of the views of both men; these papers were read to the Linnaean Society in London, on July 1, 1858. Neither Wallace nor Darwin was present. Wallace was still off in the Malay Archipelago. Darwin hated public appearances, and in any event only a few days earlier an infant son had died of scarlet fever. His whole family was threatened, and it took them all a few weeks to recover from their grief and panic.

On July 5 Darwin managed to write a very purposeful letter to Hooker, outlining his plan to write the book which became the *Origin of Species*. On July 9 he left for a rest on the Isle of Wight, where he began the actual writing of the book. On March 19, 1859, he had finished the last chapter, and, as he wrote in his *Journal*, "Oct. 1 Finished proofs. 13 months & 10 days on Abstract of Origin of Species. 1250 copies printed."

The appearance of the *Origin* marked the end of Darwin's first grand detour, but it was only a phase in his other roundabout maneuver, the 23-year delay before publicly admitting his well-formed ideas on man's place in nature. In the transmutation notebooks and in the notebooks on man, mind, and materialism, all written in the years 1837–39, he never wavered in his belief that man had evolved from lower organisms according to the same natural laws governing all evolution. Darwin wrote openly in this vein in his preliminary sketches of 1842 and 1844, and also in "Natural Selection."

But in the *Origin* he wrote generally, and did not address himself in great detail to the special problems of accounting for the evolution of any one particular species, least of all man. Of man he wrote only vaguely—of discoveries yet to be made, ideas yet to be thought, not hinting how much of this work he had already done. Eventually, in 1871, he published the *Descent of Man,* the full revelation.

In the *Origin,* the only chapter dealing with psychological issues bore the title "Instinct." The chapter he drafted in 1857 for "Natural Selection" was called somewhat more ambitiously "Mental Powers and Instincts of Animals." In the Essay of 1844, the long descriptive title of the corresponding chapter began with the words, "On the Variation of Instincts and Other Mental Attributes under Domestication and in State of Nature." In all these versions the basic argument remained the same: instincts, like "corporeal structures," exhibit variation and are therefore subject to evolution through natural selection. In all these versions the evolution of instinct is the major subject. None of them has the psychological scope of the M and N notebooks written in 1837–39, or of the *Descent of Man,* published in 1871. But the versions preceding the *Origin* differ from it in three ways. First, his use of evidence drawn from the behavior of human beings makes it reason-

ably obvious that he means to include man and human mental processes in the evolutionary network; second, he makes much greater use
of the idea of the inheritance of acquired mental characteristics; and
third, he is quite explicit about his materialist approach to the relation between mind and body.

In the *Origin* he was always careful to limit himself to drawing
the analogy between the variation and selection of instinct on the one
hand, and variation and selection of bodily structures on the other. He
wrote, "The canon of 'Natura non facit saltum [Nature doesn't make
jumps]' applies with almost equal force to instincts as to bodily
organs." (*Origin*, 210) This stops short of asserting a causal relation
between mental processes and material structures, as he did in 1844:

> These facts must lead to the conviction, justly wonderful as it
> is, that almost infinitely numerous shades of disposition, of tastes,
> of peculiar movements, and even of individual actions, can be modi-
> fied or acquired by one individual and transmitted to its offspring.
> One is forced to admit that mental phenomena (no doubt through
> their intimate connection with the brain) can be inherited, like in-
> finitely numerous and fine differences of corporeal structure.[15]

While the main contents of the chapters written for "Natural
Selection" and the *Origin* are the same, in the latter he deleted a few
key remarks giving the direction of his thinking, and all illustrative
material referring to man. In the *Origin* he permitted himself to say
only that instinct does not operate alone, but "A little dose, as Pierre
Huber expresses it, of judgment or reason, often comes into play, even
in animals very low in the scale of nature." (*Origin*, 208) There is no
passage in the *Origin* where he expands on the point as he did in
"Natural Selection," written only two years earlier:

> . . . instincts are occasionally subjected in some very slight degree
> to the influence of reason, experience, instruction, and imitation;
> and though I believe that such modifications may be of some impor-
> tance from at last becoming habitual, and from habitual actions be-
> coming hereditary, for which reason I have discussed at some length
> the intelligence of animals—yet I must fully admit that all such
> modifications are of subordinated importance in an extreme degree,
> to that blind impulse strictly called an instinct.[16]

---

15 Charles Darwin, *The Foundations of the Origin of Species, op. cit.*, p. 115.
16 "Natural Selection," Chapter 10, pp. 20–21, Darwin MSS, Cambridge University
Library. In 1856 he went through the M and N notebooks, writing on the cover of
M: "Selected Dec. 16, 1856." "Mental Powers and Instincts" was finished by March
9, 1858 (*Journal*). It was eventually published by Darwin's protégé in matters of
animal psychology; see George J. Romanes, *Mental Evolution in Animals. With a
posthumous essay on instinct by Charles Darwin* (London: Kegan Paul Trench and
Company, 1883).

From all these documents we can conclude that Darwin first worked out a thoroughgoing materialist approach to the evolution of mind and brain, man included; then in his various preliminary drafts he decided to put the major emphasis on lower forms of psychological functioning, while at the same time making the human import of his whole theory clear but not conspicuous. In writing the *Origin,* however, he withdrew to a more cautious position, making only the briefest allusions to higher mental processes.

The *Descent of Man* appeared in 1871, twelve years after the *Origin of Species.* Knowing Darwin's persistent, methodical way of bringing his ideas to fruition, it might seem as though he was following a preconceived plan to keep *Homo sapiens* out of the *Origin* in order to do him justice in the *Descent.* But there is some reason to believe that Darwin did not really want to write about the descent of man. He followed the *Origin* with three botanical works. In 1864 Wallace published a paper discussing the limits of the principle of natural selection as applied to man. He argued that the principle had applied to man's precursors, but that man, after attaining a high degree of intellect, no longer remained subject to the rule of natural selection. He concluded that man's highly developed moral and intellectual faculties had not resulted from the operation of natural law.[17] He had already taken the spiritualist path that led him to conclude his book *Darwinism* with a passage asserting that "man's body may have been developed from that of a lower animal form under the law of natural selection; but . . . we possess intellectual and moral faculties which . . . must have had another origin . . . in the unseen universe of Spirit."[18]

In spite of his misgivings and disappointment about the differences between them, Darwin admired some features of Wallace's 1864 paper, and wrote to him, "I have collected a few notes on man, but I do not suppose that I shall ever use them. Do you intend to follow out your views, and if so, would you like at some future time to have my few references and notes?" (*LL* 3, 91)

In 1868 Darwin brought out his compendious two-volume treatise *The Variation of Animals and Plants Under Domestication.* The first volume gives a survey of all the factual material he had collected on variation in domestic animals and cultivated plants, covering a very wide array of species. The second volume was largely an attempt to fill

---

17 Alfred Russel Wallace, "The Development of Human Races Under the Law of Natural Selection," first published in the *Anthropological Review,* May 1864; reprinted in his book *Natural Selection and Tropical Nature* (London: Macmillan, 1895).
18 Alfred Russel Wallace, *Darwinism: An Exposition of the Theory of Natural Selection with Some of Its Applications* (London: Macmillan, 1889) , p. 478.

in two major gaps in the argument of the *Origin,* the need for explanations of the causes of variation and of the mechanism of heredity. The ideas he advanced in this volume were not very successful, although they played a useful role in preparing the way for modern genetics.

But *Animals and Plants* is noteworthy for other reasons. Just as the second edition of the *Journal of Researches* contained a liberal scattering of the fragments of Darwin's evolutionary views, *Animals and Plants* has many references to human variation and heredity and seems to take it for granted that the evolution of *Homo sapiens,* both in mind and body, is part of the natural order. Although in this work Darwin tacitly assumed the evolution of man, he did not examine this proposition systematically, nor did he shout it from the housetops. From what he did write in the introduction, we can gather that his intentions lay in other directions. He announced that the book was the first of three related works. The second would deal with variation in nature, and the third in much greater detail than before with the principle of natural selection. In other words, in the 1860s, as he was writing *Animals and Plants,* his main intention was not to go forward to the subject of human evolution, but to strengthen his general theory as presented in the *Origin.* The second and third parts of this grand work never were completed. In spite of himself, Darwin was more and more drawn into the subject of man.

Perhaps, during the 1860s, he clung to the hope that someone else would satisfactorily dispose of *Homo sapiens.* If so, that hope must have faded rapidly. As he watched the work of men like Huxley, Lyell, Spencer, and Wallace, he must have come to realize that, for varying and complex reasons, there was no one else in the English-speaking world who was willing and able to write a book like the one he saw the need for, the *Descent of Man.* The nearest approach to such a book was Ernst Haeckel's *Die Natürliche Schöpfungsgeschichte* [*The Natural History of Creation*], which appeared in 1868. In his introduction to *Descent,* Darwin suggested that he might not have written his own book if he had seen Haeckel's first. But on November 19, 1868, Darwin wrote to Haeckel, telling him how much he was enjoying the latter's book. (*LL* 3, 106) By this date Darwin was well into the writing of *Descent,* but he could not in any case have abandoned the project in deference to Haeckel because there were many important differences in approach between the two men. I believe Darwin, by this time, felt an inner need to make his own statement about man.

By this time the reader may be troubled by the question: was Darwin a pusillanimous coward, trimming his argument to suit the temper of the times, or was he a master strategist, patiently assembling his forces but withholding his fire until the moment most propitious for a victorious assault?

The answer to such questions is never simple. The book I have been referring to as the *Descent of Man* is really three books. The full title is *The Descent of Man, and Selection in Relation to Sex*. Thus, Descent deals with two quite different issues: first, the continuity of man with other animals in the network of evolution, with regard to both bodily and mental attributes; and second, the whole subject of sexual selection. To these should be added a closely related work, *The Expression of the Emotions in Man and Animals,* which appeared in 1872, one year after *Descent. Expression* was really an extension of *Descent,* originally intended as part of it but developed as a separate book when it grew too large.

Darwin could certainly not have produced these works in 1859, when he published the *Origin,* simply by taking a few more months for the writing. They are based on a great deal of additional hard work, much of it highly original, done in the years 1867–71. The most he could have done in 1859 would have been to admit publicly what he believed privately about the evolutionary origins of man, and to give a brief account of his reasons for having maintained those beliefs for some twenty years.

In the introduction to *Descent* he gives his reasons for withholding his views on man from the *Origin:* "During many years I collected notes on the origin or descent of man, without any intention of publishing on the subject, but rather with the determination not to publish, as I thought that I should thus only add to the prejudices against my views." (*Descent,* 1) This position merits consideration. Is it incumbent upon a scientist to state his case before he feels he can state it effectively?

The conflict Darwin felt about publishing on the subject of man is reflected in the different shading with which he described his own motives in a letter to Alphonse de Candolle, the Swiss biologist, written July 6, 1868:

> . . . I was so much fatigued by my last book that I determined to amuse myself by publishing a short essay on the "Descent of Man." I was partly led to do this by having been taunted that I concealed my views, but chiefly from the interest which I had long taken in the subject. Now this essay has branched out into some collateral subjects, and I suppose will take me more than a year to complete.
> [*LL* 3, 100]

How one evaluates Darwin's behavior depends on two aspects of the general situation. Regarding the outward intellectual climate, what reception could he expect for his ideas? How well developed did they have to be before it was worth the trouble of making them public? Regarding the internal strength of his thinking, did he see himself as having solved the major problems entailed in the development of his theory, or did he see his work as sketchy, incomplete, vulnerable to legitimate criticism?

There is, naturally, a strong interaction between these two factors. If he saw himself as having a finished theory invulnerable to legitimate criticism, withholding publication would be merely defensive, just delaying the moment of coming before the bar of public opinion. If, however, he saw his work as incomplete in fundamental respects, the delay would make sense as a constructive move. Publicly, he could present the part of his work that was well developed, and hope to carry at least some of his readers with him. Privately, restraint would give him the time and the protection from criticism necessary to go on working serenely, deepening his argument and finding effective ways of presenting it.

Darwin decided he needed the time, and, in my opinion, he used it remarkably well. Even more remarkably, in the twelve years 1859–71 no one else managed to plunge into the gap he had left and write the *Descent of Man* before he did.

CHAPTER 2

The Threat of Persecution

Mention persecution of early Astronomers.

Charles Darwin, C notebook,
p. 123, about April 1838

In considering the history of ideas, we tend to focus our attention on the successful version of an idea, the victor in a final bout after many preliminaries with unhappier results. We see the victorious idea successfully weathering storms of opposition, its author greater than his opponents, as he often is. Then, in the writing of history, those lesser lights may be forgotten, and what we remember is a tale of victors.

In the history of ideas, the *persecutors* are often among the vanquished; thus the importance of persecution may be much diminished in historical perspective.

Taken by itself, this would be a relatively small distortion and readily corrected by going back to public sources. But the error is magnified and correction made far more difficult by another and more private factor.

We tend to think of the persecution of men for their ideas as occurring publicly and after the fact. How, indeed, could it be otherwise? An idea cannot be suppressed or ridiculed or used as a basis for action against its author until the idea has been conceived and publicly presented. If the idea threatens some existing establishment, suppression must await its development and expression; and punishment must be public if it is to inhibit the spread of the offending thought. So it would seem.

But it is possible to argue that the prevalence of persecution inhibits the very creation of new ideas, as well as their diffusion. If an idea develops gradually, through the efforts of many workers, its earliest expressions will be the most vulnerable, both to honest criticism and to the defensive reactions of whatever establishment the new idea appears to threaten. This establishment will mount its counter-attack against the fledgling thought, and the struggle will be known to the public at large, including those thinkers likely to carry the new strain of thought forward.

As we will see in examining Darwin's notebooks, personal awareness of the risk involved in expressing new ideas does not simply serve as a counter in the struggle among fully formed contenders in the arena of thought. Vague and confused thoughts, dimly felt questions, and strange images shift and swirl into new patterns. The fear of persecution is only one factor in a complex process of construction. The creator is not always a well-armed knight defending the damsel of truth. Sometimes he is more like a ragged wanderer moving in a certain direction but not at all sure what the next turn in the road will reveal; sometimes an artist trying first this pattern and then that; sometimes a simple builder working to a plan, laying stone upon stone; and sometimes, indeed, he is that knight.

The creative process is a complex human activity, carried forth over months and years, taking different shapes as the work proceeds. In historical perspective, as we move further away from it in time, its human dimensions diminish, and only the product remains—in this case, a series of abstract ideas in the history of science. The interplay of ideas has its own fascination, which makes it yet a little easier to forget or minimize some of the unpleasant human truths associated with man's pursuit of knowledge.

For example, almost everyone today knows the story that Galileo, sometime in the seventeenth century, dropped two weights from the Leaning Tower of Pisa, and that this had something to do with the development of Newtonian physics; and it is well known that he built a telescope which made it possible to see the moons of Jupiter; and that he believed in the Copernican theory that the earth revolved around the sun. We may even remember, a bit hazily, that he had some trouble with the Church over these ideas. But have you tried to put yourself in his place, a man trying to keep his mind clear, to bring new thoughts from cloudy intuitions to crystal purity, working always under the threat of the Inquisition?

Imagine what it was like to do your thinking in a world where you might eventually be forced to swear, as Galileo was forced: "I, Galileo, being in my seventieth year, being a prisoner and on my knees, and before your Eminences, having before my eyes the Holy

Gospel, which I touch with my hands, abjure, curse, and detest the error and the heresy of the movement of the earth."[1]

Now when we turn to Darwin's life and the role of *potential* persecution in his thinking, we must first ask: was he aware of the history of oppression, and how did it affect him?

Certainly he knew the story of Galileo's troubles with the Inquisition. It was discussed in 1837 by the Rev. William Whewell, who wrote: "The story of the condemnation of Galileo by the Inquisition, for asserting the motion of the earth, and of his formal renunciation of this doctrine in the presence of his judges, has been so often told, that I need not here repeat the details."[2] Whewell also discusses Copernicus' hesitation in revealing his thoughts, so that his great work, *Concerning the Revolutions of the Heavenly Spheres,* was published only after thirty years' delay, in the year of his death, 1543, and at that with a preface added by a friend pretending that Copernicus had not actually believed the heliocentric heresy. Whewell also reminded his readers of the fate of Giordano Bruno, one of the earlier supporters of the Copernican doctrine: Bruno was burned at the stake in the year 1600.

Lest the reader conclude that Darwin at Cambridge was an immature student who fell into the hands of a doctrinaire professor, it should be said that Whewell was far from being an implacable critic of Church authority. In his account he writes disparagingly of both Bruno and Galileo for bringing punishment upon themselves by their arrogance. And he ends his discussion with a remarkable display of forbearance, not for the victims but for the Inquisition: "they did not act till it seemed that their position compelled them to do so, and then proceeded with all the gentleness and moderation which were compatible with judicial forms."[3]

Another great recantation in the history of science came nearer the Darwinian knuckle. In the eighteenth century, evidence for an evolutionary history of the earth and its inhabitants was rapidly

---

1 Andrew D. White, *A History of the Warfare of Science with Theology in Christendom* (London: Macmillan, 1896), 2 vols. A full and moving account of Galileo's trials, and a slightly different version of the oath, are given in Giorgio di Santillana, *The Crime of Galileo* (Chicago: University of Chicago Press, 1955).
2 Rev. William Whewell, *History of the Inductive Sciences,* 3 vols. (London, 1837), Vol. 1, p. 399. Darwin mentions Whewell's book in his notebooks, but he may well have heard these stories from Whewell's lips some ten years before, when Darwin was a student in Cambridge and Whewell one of the professors he knew quite well.
3 Whewell, *op. cit.,* p. 404. According to Whewell, Bruno was burned not for his astronomical views, but for a satirical attack on the papal government which proscribed those views. Whewell cites Montucla, an Italian author of the day, who felt that "by his rashness in visiting Italy after putting forth such a work . . . [Bruno] compelled the government to act against him." Whewell, *op. cit.,* p. 385.

accumulating, which would lead eventually to a forced choice between scientific geology and the myth of creation as told in Genesis. A leading French proponent of the new geology was Georges Buffon, who in 1749 published his *Natural History,* in which he argued for the continuous transformation of the earth's surface, in a manner seen as contradictory to Scripture by the Faculty of Theology at the Sorbonne. To save his career he was required to publish the following words: "I declare that I had no intention to contradict the text of Scripture; that I believe all therein related about the creation, both as to order of time and matter of fact; and I abandon everything in my book respecting the formation of the earth, and, generally, all which may be contrary to the narration of Moses."

Darwin could not have missed this story. It was well known in his day, and the full text of the recantation, as quoted above, appears in Volume 1 of Lyell's *Principles of Geology,* Darwin's most important scientific guide during his five long years circumnavigating the earth.[4]

Both Whewell and Lyell discussed the conflict between religious dogma and scientific thought. As we have seen, Whewell took a moderate, "philosophical" view of the matter. Lyell, far more the working scientist, felt the intellectual thumbscrew more directly. He went further into the unpleasant details and drew different morals. He described sympathetically Voltaire's satirical attacks on eighteenth-century geological writings in which "much ingenuity had been employed to make every fact coincide exactly with the Mosaic account of the creation and deluge. It was, therefore, with no friendly feelings that he contemplated the cultivators of geology in general, regarding the science as one which had been successfully enlisted by theologians as an ally in their cause."[5] After a slashing attack on the theological geologists of the eighteenth century, Lyell reminds the reader of Galileo's recantation and similar surrenders: "If they were guilty of dissimulation, we may feel regret, but must not blame their want of moral courage, reserving rather our condemnation for the intolerance of the times, and that inquisitorial power which forced Galileo to abjure, and the two Jesuits to disclaim the theory of Newton."[6]

It may well be that Darwin's most vital knowledge of the suppression of scientific materialism came from more personal experience, and much earlier than the books by Lyell and Whewell.

---

4 Charles Lyell, *Principles of Geology: Being an Inquiry how far the Former Changes of the Earth's Surface Are Referable to Causes now in Operation,* 4 vols. Vol. 1, p. 69. 4th edition, London: John Murray, 1835. Darwin had the newly published first edition with him during the voyage. The two editions are alike in matters relevant to the present work.
5 *Ibid.,* p. 95.
6 *Ibid.,* p. 99.

While a student at the University of Edinburgh, in 1825–27, he was a member of the Plinian Society, a group of students who held weekly meetings to discuss scientific subjects. Since young Darwin's love of science far exceeded his interest in medicine, which he soon abandoned, his contacts with like-minded students during these formative years ought to be taken very seriously, as involving an area of life most important to him.

In the library of Edinburgh University there is a curious document, the Minute Book of the Plinian Society for the years 1826–41. It was the custom of the society for the secretary to write an account of each meeting with which was given a clear and fairly detailed summary of any scientific report. The Minute Book reports Darwin's election to the society. He was proposed by several members, among them one W. A. Browne, on November 28, 1826. On December 5, Darwin was among those hearing Browne read a paper criticizing Sir Charles Bell's *Anatomy of Expression,* a book which later figured in Darwin's work on the expression of emotions. On December 26, the officers of the society proposed that the French and German scientists Cuvier and Blumenbach be elected honorary members. Upon the objection of a Rev. Ritchie, the motion was voted down. On February 27, 1827, Darwin heard Mr. Grey read a paper on instinct, "in which he attempted to prove that the lower animals possess every faculty and propensity of the human mind."

The incident of greatest interest for our present discussion occurred at the meeting of March 27, 1827. Mr. Browne read a paper on the nature of organisms and mind in which he took an outright materialist position: "mind as far as one individual's sense and consciousness are concerned, is material." A discussion followed which must have been very lively, for it was decided to strike Mr. Browne's paper and the discussion of it from the record. The secretary of the society was thorough. He went back to the minutes of a previous meeting, at which Mr. Browne announced his *intention* of reading this paper, and struck that announcement from the record too. But he chose an odd method of doing so, ruling a single stroke of the pen through every line of his carefully written résumé. As a result, we have an almost perfectly legible record of one of Darwin's early exposures to a materialist philosophy of mind and a strong antagonistic reaction to it.[7]

This meeting was significant for Darwin in another way. Before

<hr>

[7] The full text of the minutes showing the suppression of Browne's paper is given in the Appendix. Sir Gavin de Beer, in his biography of Darwin, gives an account of the minutes of the scientific content of some meetings of the society attended by Darwin, including this meeting, but does not seem to have caught the significance of this incident, for he fails to mention it at all. Gavin de Beer, *Charles Darwin: Evolution by Natural Selection* (London: Nelson, 1963).

C Notebook, p. 123. *Courtesy of Cambridge University Library.*

Browne's paper, Darwin informed the society of two small discoveries
he had made, both dealing with marine organisms he had studied in
the waters of the Firth of Forth near Edinburgh. Darwin remembers
these discoveries in his *Autobiography*. But he does not mention the
suppression of Mr. Browne's materialism. The *Autobiography* is written in the mellow spirit of a man who has thought some dangerous
thoughts, worked them out carefully, and convinced the scientific
world of their correctness; a man who has earned a high place in the
eyes of his contemporaries and a resting place in Westminster Abbey.

   But in 1837–38, when he was a young man first entertaining those
thoughts, he was well aware of their explosive meaning for man's
conception of his place in nature, and aware of the risk to himself if
and when he presented these ideas in public. It was this that he had in
mind in the spring of 1838 when he wrote in one of his transmutation
notebooks the instruction to himself:

> Mention persecution of early Astronomers,—then add chief good of
> individual scientific men is to push their science a few years in ad-
> vance only of their age . . . must remember that if they *believe* &
> not openly avow their belief they do as much to retard as those
> whose opinion they believe have endeavoured to advance cause of
> truth.[8]

   As we have just seen, when he jotted down his reminder to himself to "mention persecution" there was an objective historical basis

---

[8] *C* 123. Although the end of the sentence is slightly garbled, he obviously means
that those who do not openly avow their beliefs harm the "cause of truth."

for his fear. His ideas did challenge views cherished by powerful social forces in his day. Darwin's recognition of the social relevance of evolutionary thought and his awareness of the threat of persecution are reflected in his notebooks at several points.

In the first transmutation notebook, the fear of persecution does not emerge. But as he continues to work, he broadens his attack, relating his work to many disciplines and occasionally remarking on the social relevance of his ideas. Thus, by about September 1837 he makes his first explicit criticism of anthropocentrism.[9]

By about January 1838 he is very explicit about man's place in nature as a thinking animal: "The difference [between] intellect of man and animals not so great as between living thing without thought (plants) and living thing with thought (animal)." (*B* 214)

In a summary passage written about the same time, he sees the relation between anthropocentrism, ethnocentrism, and racial oppression: "Animals whom we have made our slaves we do not like to consider our equals.—Do not slave-holders wish to make the black man other kind?" (*B* 231) Reminiscent of "Ozymandias," Shelley's poem on the temporal limitations of political power, is Darwin's remark, written about March 1838, "Man—wonderful man . . . he is not a deity, his end under present form will come . . . he is no exception." (*C* 77)

By May of 1838 the theme of materialism, at that time more outrageous than evolution, is stated in a knowingly provocative form: "Thought (or desires more properly) being hereditary it is difficult to imagine it anything but structure of brain. . . ." He is writing on the inheritance of mental faculties as evidence that they must result from the structure of the brain, which he assumes is all that can be inherited.[10]

The passage continues, "Love of the deity effect of organization, oh you materialist! . . . Why is thought being a secretion of brain, more wonderful than gravity a property of matter? It is our arrogance, our admiration of ourselves." (*C* 166)

By July 1838 he knows that he must avow his most heretical beliefs: ". . . I will never allow that because there is a chasm between man . . . and animals that man has different origin." (*C* 223) These words might well stand as the opening of the M and N notebooks on man, mind, and materialism.

In the M and N notebooks the subjects of fear and anger come up repeatedly. In one passage he discusses unattached fear and the need to find an object for it. (*M* 54) Modern psychologists would agree that

---

9 Quoted above, p. 21.
10 This may seem to assume what he is trying to prove. I am here not evaluating Darwin's logic but tracing the growth of his ideas.

such unattached fears probably have as their cause some repressed impulse. Almost immediately after, Darwin suggests the possible source of his own fears: "To avoid stating how far, I believe, in materialism, say only that emotions, instincts, degrees of talent, which are hereditary are so because brain of child resembles parent stock. . . ." (*M* 57)

A cartoon ridiculing Darwin that appeared immediately after his publication of the *Descent of Man* in 1871. *Courtesy of Cornell University Library.*

Darwin had a real need to ingratiate himself with others, to avoid sharp personal controversy, to feel that he had made the effort to avoid conflict. In an insightful moment he writes of this tendency in himself (see *M* 60). Soon after, he remarks on the psychic cost of inner conflicts when hostility is not ventilated; he writes of "perceiving myself skipping when wanting not to feel angry—Such efforts prevent anger, but observing eyes thus unconsciously discover struggle of feeling. It is as much effort to walk then lightly as to endeavour to stop heart beating. . . ." (*M* 70)

Throughout these discussions of fear and anger and their management, although Darwin does not say what he is afraid of, he is certainly drawing on personal experience of these emotions. It is not speculating too much to suggest that he felt some trepidation at the thought of exposing himself publicly as an atheist. Although it is probably more correct to describe Darwin at this point as a Christian en route to agnosticism, such subtleties would not have done him any good, in the courts either of public opinion or of law.[11]

Then, on September 21, 1838, Darwin records his dream of hanging and decapitation, which I have already discussed briefly in the introduction to this book. Given all that we know, it seems reasonable to interpret this dream of execution of a witty man as Darwin dreaming of himself being punished for his ideas. The impulse to run away, clearly stated, can be understood as Darwin's hesitation to expose his ideas publicly. The desire for eventual recognition and enduring fame is reflected in the dreamer's notion that he can recover from the execution.[12]

Certainly, one ought to be cautious in venturing into any dream interpretation, especially when the subject is long dead and unavailable for questioning. Since Darwin was thinking more and more of marriage to Emma Wedgwood, to whom he proposed on November 11, less than two months after the execution dream, it might be equally reasonable to interpret it as a castration dream, or as a dream with a double meaning. In any case, the two themes of impending marriage and threatened punishment for unacceptable ideas were definitely connected in Darwin's mind.[13] Marriage is a kind of violation of one's privacy, raising the question of sharing one's secret and innermost thoughts. As I have already mentioned, Darwin later wrote to his

---

11 See below, Chapter 10, for further discussion of this subject. To cite only one example, Shelley was expelled from Oxford University in 1811 for writing a pamphlet, *The Necessity of Atheism*. It was published anonymously, and Shelley would not admit to the college tribunal that he was the author, so he was expelled for refusing to testify against himself.

12 The allusion to Dr. Monro's experiments may refer to a suggestion that stopping the circulation of the blood by hanging is a more definite and rapid form of death than decapitation. Dr. Monro believed that nervous energy was distributed throughout the body and was consequently not immediately vulnerable to destruction by decapitation. It will be remembered that the question of death by decapitation was prominent at one time because of the use of the guillotine. The Dr. Monro whom Darwin knew as a lecturer on anatomy at Edinburgh University was the third in a line of Alexander Monros who held the same post. See "Charles Darwin as a Student in Edinburgh, 1825–1827" by J. H. Ashworth, *Proceedings of the Royal Society of Edinburgh*, Vol. 55, 1934–35, pp. 97–113. See also "Descriptions of a Human Male Monster" and "Experiments Relating to Animal Electricity," pp. 215–230 and 231–239, *Transactions of the Royal Society of Edinburgh*, Vol. 3, 1794. Dr. Monro's papers, read in 1792, give some ideas of his views on the circulation of the blood and the distribution of nervous energy in the human body.

13 See above, p. 27.

friend Hooker that telling the secret of his evolutionary ideas was like "confessing a murder."

Six years after this dream Darwin reenacted the pattern of crime and punishment, death and resurrection, in a more realistic way by preparing the sketch of his theory of evolution, with instructions to Emma on editing and publishing it in the event of his sudden death.

Whatever caveats we may express in this murky part of the history of ideas, one thing is clear: we need some explanation for Darwin's long delay in publishing his views, and we need some understanding of the way in which this delay affected his inner life. I do not mean to suggest that Darwin's fears were obsessive or crippling. On the contrary, he managed to go on working steadily and productively, as well as brilliantly, and to have a happy family life. Nor do his anxieties, whatever their source or extent, seem to have exerted a large distorting influence on the actual contents of his thought.[14]

There remains, of course, the question of Darwin's physical health. Psychoanalytic writers have been eager to interpret Darwin's long illness as psychogenic. If it was so, we ought to consider the possibility that the source of strain lay not in his infantile relationship with his father but in the adult decision he made to keep his ideas secret.[15]

We are not wanting in evidence that an aura of fear and oppression surrounded scientific ideas challenging the literal interpretation of the Bible during the years when Charles Darwin was himself working out his ideas about evolution.

The most dramatic case is the *Vestiges of the Natural History of Creation*, an anonymous book printed in London in 1844. The book collected the evidence for the occurrence of evolution, advanced a

---

14 A prominent psychoanalyst, Phyllis Greenacre, who has written an orthodox psychoanalytic interpretation of Darwin's life, agrees on this point. She writes, in the course of discussing the hypothesis that Darwin was deeply neurotic, "He was able to keep the *content* of his work almost wholly free from neurotic inroads, although he was generally unable simply and directly to admit that his theories were such as to overthrow the Victorian belief in Divine Creation." Phyllis Greenacre, *The Quest for the Father: A Study of the Darwin-Butler Controversy as a Contribution to the Understanding of the Creative Individual* (New York: International Universities Press, 1963), pp. 90-1. The new material in our book, showing how sharp the distinction was between what Darwin would admit publicly and what he admitted to himself, may lead psychoanalysts to reconsider some of their interpretations.

15 Here we must let this question rest. The etiology of Darwin's illness remains a mystery. Medicine in those days was simply not far enough advanced to permit a diagnosis choosing among many possibilities: a tropical disease contracted during the voyage of the *Beagle;* a severe allergy, possibly to pigeons, with which Darwin associated much; or the strain of his work as discussed above. A profound neurosis, too, remains a possibility but seems unlikely in view of his happy and productive life. See Sir Gavin de Beer's biography, *Charles Darwin* (London: Nelson, 1963), for a good, brief discussion of Darwin's health.

theory of sorts, and covered the whole span of evolutionary possibilities: the evolution of the solar system, of the physical character of the earth, of organisms, and of man and his civilization.

Vestiges was severely criticized and widely read and discussed. By 1853 it had gone through eleven editions and sold nearly 24,000 copies. The identity of the author, Robert Chambers, was revealed after his death in a preface to the twelfth edition written by a friend, Alexander Ireland, who was in a position to describe Chambers' motives and the great lengths to which he had gone to conceal his identity. The motives were to avoid "bitter and probably painful personal disputes," and to avoid injury to his business: Robert and his brother William Chambers were very successful publishers in Edinburgh, in addition to Robert's extensive literary activities.

To preserve the anonymity of the book, Chambers had it transcribed in another's handwriting and sent it from Edinburgh to his friend, Mr. Ireland, in Manchester. From there it was forwarded with fresh covers to a publisher in London. The proofs were sent by the printer to Mr. Ireland, who returned them at last to Chambers. Thus, wrote Ireland in 1883, twelve years after the death of Robert Chambers, "all suspicion on the part of the printer and the publisher that the book emanated from Scotland was averted."[16]

Although the book was a highly successful popularization of what could then be said on behalf of an evolutionary world view, it had many scientific weaknesses. These need not detain us here. For Darwin, the key point is the identity of the leading and most ferocious critic of *Vestiges:* his teacher, Adam Sedgwick, Professor of Geology at Cambridge, the man whom Darwin had accompanied on his first geological field trip, just before the *Beagle* voyage.

Darwin's work was peculiarly effective because he was able to combine a lifetime of discovery with a realistic awareness of the intellectual forces arrayed against him. This achievement was not an accidental equilibrium but the outgrowth of the complex web of tradition from which Darwin stemmed. To understand Darwin's position, poised at the center of the struggle between conservative and progressive forces, we must look at his personal intellectual heritage, first his family and then his teachers.

---

16 Robert Chambers, *Vestiges of the Natural History of Creation*, 12th edition, 1884. Preface by Alexander Ireland. See also Milton Millhauser, *Just Before Darwin: Robert Chambers and Vestiges* (Wesleyan Universities Press, 1959) and Loren Eiseley, *Darwin's Century* (London, Gollancz, 1959), for good accounts of Chambers' work.

CHAPTER 3

A Family Weltanschauung

Then twitch, with fairy hands, the frolic pin—
Down falls the impatient axe with deafening din;
The liberated head rolls off below,
And simpering Freedom hails the happy blow!

From *The Loves of the Triangles,*
by Canning and Frere[1]

Erasmus Darwin is known as the grandfather of another famous evolutionist, as the author of an evolutionary theory quite similar to and fifteen years earlier than Lamarck's, as a founder of the Lunar Society, as a famous physician, and as the composer of thousands of lines of verse, mostly rhyming couplets popularizing quite accurately the scientific knowledge of his day.

The lines quoted above conclude a parody of one of Erasmus Darwin's poems, "The Loves of the Plants," which appeared in 1789. "The Loves of the Triangles" appeared in 1798 in the *Anti-Jacobin,* a weekly whose guiding spirit was the prominent conservative politician George Canning. He and his collaborators effectively, for a time, used the weapon of literary ridicule against those whose "new and liberal system of Ethics [serves] not to bind but to loosen the bands of social order,"[2] and on behalf of those who would "still contemplate the office and the person of a king with veneration, and . . . speak reverently of Religion. . . ."[3]

---

[1] Charles Edmonds, ed., *Poetry of the Anti-Jacobin: Comprising the Celebrated Political and Satirical Poems, Parodies, and Jeux-D'Esprit of George Canning, J. H. Frere, W. Gifford, W. Pitt, G. Ellis and others.* 2nd edition, enlarged (London: G. Willis, 1854) , p. 149.
[2] *Ibid.,* p. 6. From the "Prospectus" of *The Anti-Jacobin.*
[3] *Ibid.,* p. 10.

How does it happen that a botanical poem should be attacked in a parody directed against the French Revolution? Why should a government-inspired publication (Canning was then in the government and later became Prime Minister) give this much attention to the verse of a physician far from the capital? How can we understand the extraordinary fact that grandfather and grandson generated influential theories of organic evolution?

The basic answer is that the Darwins' evolutionary thought was not simply a special scientific hypothesis that happened to clash with accepted religious ideas on certain matters of fact. It was, rather, the product of, and an essential part of, a *Weltanschauung* closely linked to the making of the industrial revolution and the political revolutions, notably the French, those great historic currents spanning the years 1776–1848.[4]

The sense in which the struggle over evolutionary thought was part of a more general struggle between two world outlooks is neatly summarized in the preface to "The Loves of the Triangles," where the authors underscore a few points heavily in prose; they propose to attack those who believe that "Whatever is is wrong," those who believe in the "eternal and absolute perfectibility of man," and those opposed to "KING-CRAFT and PRIEST-CRAFT."[5] Or, as the parodists put it in one fine line of the poem itself, they mean to rebuke those who dare to speak of "The *wrongs* of Providence, and *rights* of Man."[6]

We fall back on the term *Weltanschauung* to mean something at once more general and less systematic than formal philosophic thoughts; we mean a general perspective composed as much of attitudes and feelings as of explicit thought; we mean an outlook expressed in work and play and action, whether or not in words. Men can share the same *Weltanschauung* without necessarily addressing themselves to the same problems or, when they do, immediately agreeing on the same solutions.

To clarify the frame of reference that Charles Darwin brought with him, first to his university education and later to his scientific work, would be conceptually simpler if this framework were complete prior to the intellectual developments it is intended to explain. The task is complicated by the fact that the framework evolves in the life history, and is changed by the very ideas we are trying to explain.

Charles did not begin his university education or his scientific career as a *tabula rasa;* he came with some family tradition, some

---

[4] See E. J. Hobsbawm, *The Age of Revolution: 1789–1848* (London: Weidenfeld and Nicolson, 1962) for an excellent account, considering both the industrial and political revolutions, together with a survey of corollary events in the fields of religion, philosophy, arts, and sciences.

[5] *Poetry of the Anti-Jacobin, op. cit.,* p. 120.

[6] *Ibid.,* p. 136.

conception of himself, and some ideas. To understand his beginnings, we need a social and intellectual history of the extended family and culture in which the young Charles Darwin moved: the Darwin-Wedgwood clan and their connections. This would take us back to the life of Charles' fascinating grandfather, Dr. Erasmus Darwin, to the ambiance of the Lunar Society, which Dr. Darwin founded, and to Charles' own complex life. We would then need to show how that tradition was passed on, perhaps altered, from one generation to another.

To catch hold of this complexity in a more direct way, we need as far as possible to step outside the theory of organic evolution whose construction we are trying to explain.

To that end let us turn our attention to a sketch of some ideas shared by grandfather and grandson. It is *not* my aim to show how their scientific ideas were identical or different, or to show that Erasmus Darwin anticipated everything Charles Darwin wrote, or that he did not. Rather than a comparative inventory of their two theories of evolution, my concern here is with the general point of view that generated two expressions of evolutionary thought in one corner of English society. In Chapter 7 I discuss more specifically the relations between their theories of evolution.

There are three main questions. The first deals with conceptions of nature: attitudes toward change, pansexualism, nature worship, conceptions of struggle, adaptation, and design. The second deals with questions of knowledge: the nature of scientific work, invention, and education. The third deals with social and ethical questions: happiness and humanitarian feelings; in dealing with this group we will have occasion to discuss Charles Darwin's politics and attitudes to some special questions, such as poverty, war, race, and slavery.

Mutaphilism. There are two rival perspectives, mutaphilia and mutaphobia: love and fear of change. The *mutaphilic* sees in variation and change the essence of nature; as a student of it he becomes its enthusiast. If he also loves nature, he will see progressive improvement as the consequence of change. Thus Erasmus in a stanza describing Nature's origination of life: "From embryon births her changeful forms improve, Grow, as they live, and strengthen as they move."[7]

In the *mutaphobic*, the same positive view of nature is associated with a belief in the perfection of things as they are and, wherever there is a choice, opposition to change. The relation of attitudes toward change in nature and society can be seen in a passage from Edmund Burke's *Reflections on the Revolution in France.* "A spirit of innova-

---

[7] Erasmus Darwin, *The Temple of Nature; or, the Origin of Society* (London, 1803), Canto I, "Production of Life," lines 225–226.

tion is generally the result of a selfish temper, and confined views. . . . By a constitutional policy, working after the pattern of nature, we receive, we hold, we transmit our government and our privileges, in the same manner in which we enjoy and transmit our property and our lives."[8] The whole essay is a panegyric on the virtues of hereditary monarchy, hereditary property rights, and a system of law that changes only enough to protect the established order.

Both Burke and Erasmus Darwin wrote enough on the question of aesthetic taste for us to discern their characteristic differences in point of view at work. Both begin with the topic of novelty. Burke dismisses it as "superficial," its effects easily dissipated by experience; Darwin expands on the theme, arguing that experience and intellect can increase our power of appreciating novelty, although he grants that this requires "some degree of mental exertion."[9]

In Charles' notebooks, of course, the welcoming of change is everywhere. Species must change to survive: "They die without [unless] they change, like golden Pippins; it is a *generation of species* like generation of *individuals*." (*B* 63, Darwin's italics)

And the closing lines of the *Origin:* "From so simple a beginning endless forms most beautiful and most wonderful have been, and are being, evolved." (*Origin,* 490)

Pansexualism. Not all change is progressive; *cyclic* change is common enough in nature, and the reproductive cycle of birth, growth, mating, and death is everywhere. In evolutionary theories, progressive change is composed of small deviations from exact repetition in the reproductive cycle of passages from one generation to another. Both Darwins saw that sexual reproduction was an important part of the evolutionary process, allowing as it does for stable transmission of hereditary characteristics coupled with room for some variation and recombination, room for evolutionary change. For them a theory of evolution was of necessity a theory of ubiquitous sexuality.

Sexual love is a pervasive theme in Erasmus Darwin's poetry. True, it is generally clad in botanical form, and his descriptions of "the loves of the plants" are scientifically accurate. They are, at the same time, completely personified and thoroughly erotic. Their poetic intent is not merely to inform but to arouse the reader. Nor would Dr. Darwin have missed the point that through emotional arousal lies the way to profounder intellectual grasp. He was not aiming only at an

---

8 Edmund Burke, *Reflections on the Revolution in France* (London: J. Dodsley, 1790).
9 Edmund Burke, *Philosophical Inquiry into the Origin of Our Ideas of the Sublime and Beautiful: with an Introductory Discourse Concerning Taste* (London, 1757). Erasmus Darwin, *The Temple of Nature, op. cit.,* Additional Notes, XIII: "Analysis of Taste."

M Notebook, p. 123. *Courtesy of Cambridge University Library.*

arid exploitation of erotic interest as a tool for the dissemination of knowledge. *The human value of sexuality* was in good part the message he wanted to convey.

The universal theme of physical attraction—gravitation, chemical bonds, electrical and magnetic polarity—is dealt with in sexual terms.[10] The idea that each living being, having enjoyed its term of life, dies and contributes its body to reconstruct the earth for those to come can be found prominently in both Darwins. Erasmus Darwin was interested in geology, and in the increasing knowledge of his day that much of the earth is composed of fossil remains; he wrote: "Thus the tall mountains . . . ARE MIGHTY MONUMENTS OF PAST DELIGHT."[11] In his discussion of aesthetic taste, he argues (citing Hogarth) that mature visual pleasure in rounded undulating forms is traceable to infant pleasure at mother's breast.[12] And to close the circle, the adult sexual attraction of the female breast is repeatedly stressed in his poetry. For Erasmus Darwin, both in his personal life and in his poetry, sexual reproduction was the "chef-d'oeuvre, or capital work of nature."[13] Well might he repeat the poetic refrain, "And hail THE DEITIES OF SEXUAL LOVE."[14]

---

[10] Erasmus Darwin, *Temple of Nature, op. cit., passim,* especially Canto III and Additional Note XII.
[11] *Ibid.,* Canto IV.
[12] *Ibid.,* Canto III.
[13] *Ibid.,* Additional Notes, p. 36.
[14] *Ibid., passim.*

In Charles Darwin's work most of these themes are repeated. The importance and ubiquity of sexual reproduction are reflected in his work on barnacles, where he was delighted to discover that an organism previously thought to be hermaphroditic actually possessed a microscopic male form. In his botanical work, he did much to elucidate particular sexual mechanisms. The way in which living organisms contribute their own bodies to making the earth is the central theme of his work on coral reefs. Erasmus' emphasis on the female breast receives only faint echoes in Charles' writings, perhaps because he had seen much more of non-European people and their bodies and knew first hand that breast worship is not so universal as Erasmus' theory would have it.

There are two aspects of the theme of pansexualism which are really transformed in Charles' treatment of them, because of his explicit and thorough development of the theory of natural selection. The first of these is the mechanism of sexual selection. Erasmus touched on it, and expressed the basic idea quite clearly. Having described the struggle among males for sexual access to the female in various species, he concluded: "The final cause of this contest amongst the males seems to be, that the strongest and most active animal should propagate the species, which should thence become improved."[15] In Charles' thought, sexual selection was one specialized aspect of the much more general process of natural selection. Systematically placed in this more general context, the concept gains much greater power and clarity. Charles Darwin dealt with it briefly in the *Origin* and in great and masterful detail in Part II of his work on man, whose full title is *The Descent of Man, and Selection in Relation to Sex.*

Finally, both men gave some attention to the theme of fertility. Erasmus, in a highly Malthusian passage, wrote of the explosive potential for population growth inherent in the reproductive mechanisms of all species, and concluded:

> —All these, increasing by successive birth,
> Would each o'erpeople ocean, air and earth. . . .
> The births and death contend with equal strife,
> And every pore of Nature teems with Life.[16]

Now, while it is true that this highly Malthusian passage laden with the notion of the struggle for existence antedates Charles' first

---

15 Erasmus Darwin, *Zoonomia; or, the Laws of Organic Life* (London: Johnson, Vol. 1, 1794; Vol. 2, 1796), Vol. 1, p. 503.

16 Erasmus Darwin, *Temple of Nature*, 1803 (posthumous), Canto IV. Malthus' *Essay on Population* was first published in 1798. Erasmus may have gotten some of his ideas from Malthus, but the fertility theme is also to be found in the work of Benjamin Franklin, whom Malthus cited and with whom Erasmus Darwin corresponded.

notes on the same subject by some thirty years, it would be going too far to argue that Erasmus was "the" author of the theory of evolution through natural selection. As with all preliminary gropings toward a great idea, one finds many precursor expressions of it. Typically, as in Erasmus' case, the idea in its earlier appearances is vaguely expressed and embedded in some context that conceals it from the author himself, not to speak of the reader. In that sense, we can find fully documented expressions of the theory of natural selection in Charles' notes months before he knew that he "had" the theory! Effective theoretical work consists in clarifying an idea, not in merely touching on it. The important point is not that Erasmus, like so many others, touched on the idea of natural selection. The more significant aspect of the intellectual relation between grandfather and grandson is that they shared a common outlook, that pansexuality was an essential part of it, and that the theme of the fertility of all nature was contained in their pansexualism.[17]

Adaptation, Design, and Invention. Mechanical inventions and biological adaptations have a number of points in common, among them the fact that in both cases a *set* of contrivances must operate harmoniously to carry out some function. Both Erasmus and Charles were fascinated by such creations, and both gave much of their attention to the details of adaptive mechanisms in living organisms. In this interest, they were expressing a preoccupation typical of their period. In burgeoning industrial circles, the deliberate control of the process of invention was just beginning. In theological circles, according to the "argument from design," the discovery in nature of beautiful and perfect adaptations was evidence for the existence of God. If, as Paley put it, we find a watch, we necessarily infer a watchmaker; therefore, the contrivances of nature are conclusive evidence for the existence of their Creator. This view of adaptation served as a vital link between science and theology. Whether it did more to justify the belief in God among those who loved nature, or to justify the pursuit of science by those who loved God, remains a question.[18]

For both Darwins, fascination with the inner workings of the contrivances of nature was a *leitmotiv* of their whole lives, but it took quite different forms. Erasmus was not particularly original or assiduous in

---

17 See Desmond King-Hele, *Erasmus Darwin* (London: Macmillan, 1963). King-Hele gives an amusing and informative account of Erasmus Darwin's life and work, but goes too far in the direction of attributing all of Charles' ideas to his grandfather.

18 William Paley, *Natural Theology; or, Evidence of the Existence and Attributes of the Deity Collected from the Appearance of Nature* (London, 1802). Topics taken up in this work include the geometric perfection of beehives, the optical perfection of the eye, the perfect operation of various instincts, and the Malthusian population principle—all dealt with by Darwin in the *Origin*. Paley also discussed the significance for natural theology of fossil remains. In that connection, as in many others, he referred to Erasmus Darwin's *Zoonomia*.

the scientific study of biological adaptations; he did know a great deal about them and gave this knowledge voice in his poetry. On the side of mechanical invention, he was always interested and had a number of inventions of his own to his credit.

DECLARATION AGAINST WAR.

" We believe that there has not existed during the past twelve months, and that there does not exist now, any justification whatsoever for a war between Russia and Great Britain, and we should hold our Government guilty of the greatest crime towards this nation should they lead us, or allow us to drift into war."—*(Signed)* WESTMINSTER, BATH, DUDLEY, SHAFTESBURY, CAMOYS, GIBRALTAR, COLERIDGE.

The following gentlemen will receive the names and addresses of all persons willing to sign this declaration. They will also receive contributions towards the necessary expenses :—

JOSEPH ARCH.
GEORGE ANDERSON, M.P., 13, Longridge Road, Earl's Court Road, S.W.
JACOB BRIGHT, M.P., 61, Onslow Square, S.W.
JOHN BROWNING, 63, Strand.
T. BURT, M.P., 3, Markham Square, Chelsea, S.W.
JOSEPH CHAMBERLAIN, M.P., 80, Wilton Place, S.W.
Rev. H. CROSSKEY, Birmingham.
CHARLES DARWIN, F.R.S., Down, Beckenham.
Rev. R. W. DALE, Birmingham.
Rev. W. DENTON, 22, Westbourne Square, W.
HENRY DUNCKLEY, Manchester.
J. A. FROUDE, M.A., 5, Onslow Gardens, S.W.
Rev. NEWMAN HALL, LL.B.

AUBERON HERBERT, 81, Queen's Gate, S.W.
T. HUGHES, Q.C., 80, Park Street, W.
BURNE JONES, The Grange, North End Road, Fulham.
HUGH MASON, Ashton-under-Lyne.
JOHN MORLEY, Brighton.
SAMUEL MORLEY, M.P.
W. MORRIS, 26, Queen Square, Bloomsbury.
HODGSON PRATT, 3, Lancaster Terrace, North Gate, Regent's Park.
FREDERICK PENNINGTON, M.P., 17, Hyde Park Terrace, W.
HENRY RICHARD, M.P., 22, Bolton Gardens, S.W.
Professor ROLLESTON, Oxford.
PETER RYLANDS, M.P., 78, St. George's Square, S.W.
Hon. C. WOOD, 10, Belgrave Square, S.W.

NAME.	ADDRESS.	OCCUPATION.

Anti-war petition signed by Darwin. *Courtesy of Cambridge University Library.*

Charles was no mechanical inventor. He liked good scientific instruments that were simple and well made. The main expression of his interest in the workings of contrivances came in his studies of many different living organisms. The extent of his contributions to the detailed knowledge of such adaptations is not even now fully recognized because much of his work remained scattered for many years in fragmentary articles.[19] Moreover, as part of an *oeuvre,* his attention to "inventive" detail is overshadowed by the evolutionary import he gave to it.

Both men were interested not only in the inner workings of the contrivances of nature, but in the way in which each organism fitted into the economy of nature. These concerns were by no means original, or uniquely characteristic of evolutionary theorists. But it is hard

---

[19] See *The Collected Papers of Charles Darwin,* edited by Paul H. Barrett (Chicago: University of Chicago Press, 1977).

to conceive of an evolutionist for whom the origin of adaptation and the appearances of design would not be a central concern.

Struggle. Charles Darwin is often, and I believe incorrectly, characterized as the biological theorist of struggle in the sense of hostile warfare among living beings. One even encounters the argument that the biological doctrine of survival of the fittest justifies war among nations. Nothing could be further from either Charles' or Erasmus' views. It is true that they both adopted the language of warfare from time to time, and in critical passages describing the struggle for survival. Nevertheless, it is clear that their usage was metaphoric and that the metaphor must be qualified in several important ways.

"War" was an imprecise anthropomorphization of the struggle for *existence*. Charles characterized living beings as struggling to survive, not to defeat each other. In some cases one organism's survival means another's extinction, but in the most general sense *survival depends on the organism remaking itself*—i.e., evolving—so that it can survive in the total complex of its ecological surround. There is no single enemy or group of enemies.

It would have been entirely out of character for Charles Darwin to develop a theory of struggle in the sense of confrontations between titanic forces. This is the very catastrophism he willingly abandoned, in its geological form, during the *Beagle* voyage. His imagery, his style of life, and his explicit scientific work all tell of a very different kind of struggle, that of the quiet action of a multitude of factors. He might as well have spoken of life as a changing balance of these forces as of a struggle among them.

There are different conceptions of struggle: between black and white polarized forces, where one or the other goes down to defeat and extinction; between approximately equal forces where the seemingly defeated contender influences the nature of the struggle and hence the evolution of the victor;[20] and between old and new, between established forms and new ones struggling to be born, where the emergent novelty represents a dialectical synthesis, the new in some sense containing the old. In different passages Charles characterized the struggle for existence in different ways, but I believe the less sharply polarized forms of struggle are closer to the main line of his thought.

Cooperation among members of the same species and symbiotic relationships among members of different species were as much a part of Darwin's thinking as direct competition. The particular means that would enhance the likelihood of survival always depends on the entire

---

20 See E. J. Hobsbawm, *op. cit.*, for a discussion of this process in the case of war among nations. Hobsbawm argues that the Napoleonic wars transformed all contenders because they were forced to adopt the revolutionary methods of warfare which grew out of the French Revolution.

set of concrete circumstances. Certainly, *within* a species cooperation is far more typical than destructive competition. Even among males contending for the same female, it is advantageous to the species if competition is muted, kept within bounds. The defeated stag does not die, he simply retires from the field of sexual combat and waits. Between parent and offspring, and between male and female, cooperation is the rule in the essential acts of nurturance and mating.

Any industrious reader can entertain himself by finding passages in Charles' work that will seem to contradict the above remarks. He used many metaphors, among them the metaphor of war among men. On balance, the metaphor of war was foreign to his mature view of nature, and insofar as it crept into his thought it may even have hindered him in the development of his more central theme of inventive variation and selection.

Darwin's great love of Milton's poetry at one period of his life seems to me to argue against the view of Darwin as reluctant to accept the notion of titanic struggle in nature. Darwin tells us that during the *Beagle* voyage Milton's *Paradise Lost* accompanied him everywhere, the only book so cherished. (*Autobiography,* 85) The core of *Paradise Lost* is the struggle between good and evil, and the fall of man. Assuming that Darwin took all this to heart (we ought at least to allow the possibility that he read Milton in a more recreational spirit), we can only guess what it meant in his life: perhaps the *Weltschmerz* of early manhood. The years of the voyage were enough to cure him of any predilection he may have had for this polarized view of reality. His own effort to assimilate Lyell's uniformitarian geology must have helped. Perhaps his prolonged contact with Captain FitzRoy, a man obsessed with questions of good and evil, was enough to convince Darwin of the craziness of this way of looking at the world. In any event, by 1837, when he began the transmutation notebooks, he cast the relation between life and death not as one of struggle, but as a cycle of growth and change and renewal.

In Erasmus I believe we can find essentially the same attitude to struggle as in Charles. He knew the value of cooperation, and he enjoyed the notion of dialectical resynthesis, as witness the already quoted passage in which he spoke of the present physical world as composed of organic remains, thus "mighty mountains of past delight." But there were three ways in which Erasmus' views may have differed from Charles'. First, he had not lived through the debate between catastrophist and uniformitarian geologists of the early nineteenth century, and so he was not as sensitive to the failings of the catastrophist position in geology. Second, he did live in the time of a really great social upheaval, the French Revolution, and he welcomed it; Charles was probably much more committed to the quiet evolution of established forms. Finally, the dramatic demands of Erasmus' poetry more often tempted him to use the metaphors of war and other cataclysms. His prose writings, including the extensive scientific notes accompanying the poetry, are in a much quieter vein.

A remark on the teaching of history by Thomas Huxley, made much later, captures the attitude toward history in an evolutionary, uniformitarian frame of reference as it might contrast with history in a creationist, catastrophist frame: "We must have History; treated not as a succession of battles and dynasties; not as a series of biographies; not as evidence that Providence was always on the side of either Whigs or Tories; but as the development of man in times past, and in other conditions than our own."[21]

Both Darwins, but especially the grandson, were deeply influenced in their view of change and struggle by the argument from design. The entire course of evolution was seen as a series of small readjustments on the part of a self-regulating system, nature as a whole. This teleological[22] view does not marry well with the image of destructive warfare.

Nature Worship and Natural Theology. The study of nature as a whole was common in the period of which we write. This cannot be explained away as the work of men of gigantic stature who could deal effectively with many domains of knowledge. Nor can it be explained simply as the obvious prologue to development of specialized knowledge requiring the paraphernalia of special disciplines. The fact is there were specialists in those days, and there were large accumulations of specialized knowledge in various subjects. But there were also generalists. Intellectuals were interested in nature as a whole, because they hoped to find some meaning in it, something about man's place in nature, man's relation with God.

It is difficult for the modern reader to imagine the importance in eighteenth- and nineteenth-century England of the subject called Natural Theology. It was both a subject of study—i.e., of nature as a whole in its theological setting—and a point of view. We deal here with only a few examples particularly pertinent to Darwin's work.[23]

The Zoological Journal was founded in 1824. In the opening issue, the editors' introduction describes the aims of the journal,

---

21 Cited by Donald G. MacRae in "Darwinism and the Social Sciences," a chapter in *A Century of Darwin*, edited by S. A. Barnett (London: Heinemann, 1958).

22 My use of the term *teleological* is non-pejorative in the same sense as a cyberneticist can speak of goal-seeking systems without any implication of extra-natural processes. Darwin accepted a characterization of himself as a teleologist in approximately this sense: see his letter to Asa Gray, *Life and Letters*, Vol. 3, p. 189. Biologists today sometimes prefer *teleonomy* to convey this meaning.

23 For a more comprehensive treatment of this subject, see Charles C. Gillispie, *Genesis and Geology: A Study in the Relations of Scientific Thought, Natural Theology, and Social Opinion in Great Britain, 1790–1850* (New York: Harper and Brothers, 1959).

invites contributions on zoological subjects, and stresses the idea that the study of natural history celebrates the wisdom of God; it concludes: ". . . at the head of all this system of order and beauty, preeminent in the domain of his reason, stands Man . . . the favoured creature of his Creator."[24] The first article in the journal, "An Inquiry Respecting the True Nature of Instinct, and of the Mental Distinction Between Brute Animals and Man," admits the *appearance* in animals of moral and intellectual qualities resembling man's, but the author goes on to argue at length that animals fail to meet certain metaphysical criteria, notably consciousness, and consequently man stands alone at the head of the Creation.[25]

The eight "Bridgewater Treatises on the Power, Wisdom and Goodness of God as Manifested in the Creation" all made their appearance between 1833 and 1836, the years of the *Beagle* voyage. Endowed and commissioned by the Earl of Bridgewater, and written by eminent men of the day, these books were very popular and went through many editions. Together, the authors covered a considerable part of the known science of the day, and did the best they could to square it with theology. There were important controversies, even within the context of Natural Theology, over the literal interpretation of the Bible, and over the continual intervention of Providence in the material world. But the main trend was clear: theological presuppositions set the stage for scientific investigation. Thus, in the seventh treatise, *On the Power, Wisdom and Goodness of God as Manifested in the Creation of Animals and in Their History, Habits, and Instincts,* the author, William Kirby, dealt with the question of geographical distribution of animals in the "postdiluvian" world. His problem was to understand "the means by which, after quitting the ark, they were conveyed to the other parts of the globe."[26] All sorts of evidence, geological, zoological, and Biblical, are marshaled to deal with the question.

Natural Theology could, from time to time, come remarkably close to Charles Darwin's thinking. For example, Kirby wrote a passage on the struggle for existence in which he borrowed from Thomas Malthus and Adam Smith. He is troubled by the "universal conflict" among living beings, ranging from wars among men to animals feeding on each other. But there is a higher Wisdom in all this, he concludes, for ". . . if we consider the present tendency to

---

24 *The Zoological Journal,* Vol. 1, March 1824–January 1825. The editors were Thomas Bell, John Children, James Sowerby, and George Sowerby.
25 The article was by John Oliver French, title as above.
26 Rev. William Kirby, *Seventh Bridgewater Treatise,* title as above (London: William Pickering, 1835) , Vol. 1, pp. 44 ff. Kirby was the most extreme "literalist" among the authors of the Bridgewater Treatises.

multiply, beyond measure, of all things that have life, we shall soon be convinced that, unless this tendency was met by some check, the world of animated beings would be perpetually encroaching upon each other, and would finally perish for want of sufficient food." Thus there is need for the intervention of a Providence who "proportions the demand to the supply" in a manner "beneficial to the whole system."[27]

Sometimes Natural Theology and natural science could come too close for comfort. Both Erasmus Darwin and Lamarck were deists, who believed that the Creator had set the world in motion according to certain general laws governing its operation and development. This was not enough for Kirby, who complained that Lamarck attributed "scarcely any thing to a metaphysical cause. Even when, in words, he admits the being of a God, he employs the whole strength of his intellect to prove that he had nothing to do with the works of creation."[28]

This complaint about Lamarck's materialism did not prevent Kirby from drawing heavily on Lamarck's scientific work, especially in the field of invertebrate zoology. In fact, Kirby hit the nail on the head: the line between Natural Theology and agnosticism was uncomfortably fine; studying nature could either celebrate the work of God or supplant the worship of Him.

In the case of the two Darwins, their emphasis was almost entirely on that part of Natural Theology which constitutes the celebration of nature for its own sake. In Erasmus we find fairly frequent references to God in the deistic sense of the originator who set the world in motion according to certain general laws, but not in the sense of a designing or intervening Providence. In Charles' published writing there is really almost no mention of a Creator, even in that deistic sense.

Although in Charles' time it had become impossible for theologians to yield on the ultimate question of man's unique place in nature, there was an earlier version of Natural Theology which took a somewhat different stand. John Wesley, the Protestant theologian, was a great popularizer of science. In his *Survey of the Wisdom of God in Creation* he wrote a passage on the scale of nature in which man's place was noticeably lower than other Natural Theologians would put us:

> The whole Progress of Nature is so gradual, that the entire Chasm from a Plant to Man, is filled up with divers Kinds of Creatures, rising one above another, by so gentle an Ascent that the Transitions from one Species to another are almost insensible. . . . Since we are

---

27 *Ibid.*, pp. 142–144.
28 *Ibid.*, Introduction, p. xxvii.

infinitely more remote from the All-perfect Creator than from the lowest of all the Works of Hands . . . is it not probable there are more Species of Creatures above than beneath us?[29]

Wesley was not writing as an evolutionist, but there is something of his thought in Charles Darwin's remark about the way in which living creatures fill up empty ecological niches, thus rising to an evolutionary occasion. In his first transmutation notebook he wrote: "If all men were dead, then monkeys make men.—Men make angels." (*B* 169)

The Darwins were not Natural Theologians, but they did try to study nature as a whole. And they both had an attitude toward nature that might be called worshipful—reverential, enthusiastic, and poetic. Both felt identification with, and love for, all living things. Both, although they tried to understand and reduce it, felt and enjoyed the mystery of nature.

This worshipful attitude toward nature cannot be separated from their attitude toward change. If nature is construed as all-that-is-becoming,. the worship of nature becomes the worship of change, and any god who may have set the universe in motion recedes increasingly into the background; as present reality becomes increasingly remote from the moment of creation, one might as well worship only nature.

We have seen that evolutionary thought, although it challenged accepted theological views, was ambiguous as to the relation between evolution, man, and creation.

One could believe that the order of nature is fixed; or that it varies slightly around a fixed average state; or that it evolves slowly for a time, then undergoes some convulsive reorganization before beginning to evolve again; or that it evolves endlessly and irreversibly through all of time.

One could believe that change in nature is non-progressive, or that it is progressive within set limits (e.g., up to the appearance of man, but not further) , or that *there is no set limit on the intelligence and complexity of evolving organisms.*

One could believe that the course of evolution is dictated by a continually superintending Providence; or that it is preordained by Providential fiat; or that it is predetermined by natural law; or *that it is forever emergent through the interaction of all natural forces.*

One could believe that man is at the pinnacle of God's creation; or that he is low in the scale of nature; or that it makes no sense to speak of such a scale and man is only one of many living creatures; or *that man is perhaps only temporarily the dominant organism on earth.*

---

29 John Wesley, *A Survey of the Wisdom of God in the Creation: or a Compendium of Natural Philosophy*, 3 vols., 2nd ed. (Bristol, 1770) , pp. 200–201.

Many different combinations of these beliefs were possible and did occur among nineteenth-century thinkers. Erasmus and Charles Darwin could be described as agreeing on the italicized points in the preceding paragraphs.

What little disagreement there was between Erasmus and Charles with respect to the points mentioned was more a matter of feeling than of belief. Erasmus believed in the eventual doom of our solar system, due to natural causes, and incorporated this fate in his view of a perpetually recycling universe. Charles, in discussing the slow decline of his religious views, made it clear that he felt reluctant to accept the eventual demise of our solar system and with it the obliteration of the more perfect species into which he believed man is evolving. (*Autobiography,* 92)

Education and the Sources of Knowledge. In the foregoing discussion we have been examining various conceptions of what was known or believed about the world itself. The *Weltanschauung* of the two Darwins had another side to it, an epistemological attitude toward the way in which we get knowledge of the world.

In spite of the evident differences between the evolutionary theories of Erasmus and Charles, there is one key respect in which they are alike: the implications of their ideas for the nature of knowledge. In both theories, the form and functioning of the organism represent the accumulated experience of the species in its evolutionary history; in both that experience has been tested and winnowed in the evolving organism's long interaction with its environment. Any theory which views this interaction as governing the course of evolution[30] contains an implicit conception of knowledge: Knowledge is not written down in a Book, waiting to be read; knowledge is *constructed* through the activity of the experiencing organism.

The emphasis in this view is on thought tested in action and on action reflected in thought. Sudden great insight in which the whole Truth is revealed at once smacks of Revelation. Sudden insight can have its place in this view of knowledge, but only as a moment in the cycle of thought and action.

Erasmus expressed this attitude in the conduct of the Lunar Society, in his views about education, and in his ideas about the nature of scientific work. The Lunar Society was an extremely influential group of inventors, scientists, and industrialists who met in the vicinity of Birmingham from about 1766 on, and numbered among its participants James Watt, Matthew Boulton, Joseph Priestley, and Josiah Wedgwood; Erasmus Darwin was its founder and chief inspiration.

---

[30] As compared with theories in which a preordained or predetermined series of forms simply makes its appearance by unfolding in the course of time.

The members of the Lunar Society, as individuals helping each other and in fuller collaboration, contributed to many subjects: the development of steam power, wheel and water transportation, the chemistry of water, the theory of heat, the discovery of oxygen, the manufacture of glass, geological subjects, the science of electricity, balloon design, and so on almost endlessly. Their activity, taken as a whole, epitomizes the ethos of advanced intellectual circles at the end of the eighteenth century in Britain. Their group efforts, their numerous international connections, and their political attitudes all underline the point that science and invention are intensely social processes. The most prominent feature of the Lunar Society's fascinating history was the interplay of abstract thought and practical activity.[31]

Erasmus' brilliant eldest son, Charles, died before the age of twenty, of an infection contracted while dissecting at the medical school of Edinburgh University. The bereaved father had gone up to Edinburgh in the crisis, and when his son died, he wrote a biography of him. This essay, printed as the introduction to the young man's dissertation, gives a good picture of Erasmus' philosophy of education. He attacks the verbalism of classical education; his son was "from his infancy accustomed to examine all natural objects with more attention than is usual: first by his senses simply; then by tools, which were his playthings. . . ."[32]

The important thing in education is to promote the "comparison of things with each other" and the examination of "ideas of causes and their effects. . . ." All this can be done while at the same time learning languages and mathematics. The dead Charles had learned his Latin and Greek "chiefly by reading books of useful knowledge, or which contained the elements of science. . . ."[33]

The purpose of a medical education in those days was far broader than preparation for medical practice. His son Charles had left Oxford because "the vigour of the mind languished in the pursuit of classical elegance . . . and sighed to be removed to the robuster exercises of the medical schools of Edinburgh."[34]

Erasmus, while he drew on the philosophy of the British empiricists, did not believe that knowledge was acquired simply by direct sensory experience: he emphasized the fusion of rational thought and

---

31 For a full and very enjoyable account, see Robert E. Schofield, *The Lunar Society of Birmingham: A Social History of Provincial Science and Industry in Eighteenth-Century England* (Oxford: Clarendon Press, 1963).
32 Obituary and biography of Charles Darwin (1758–1778), unsigned but presumed to be written by Erasmus Darwin; appears as an addendum to Charles Darwin, *Experiments Establishing a Criterion Between Mucaginous and Purulent Matter* (1780), p. 127.
33 *Ibid.*, p. 129.
34 *Ibid.*, p. 131.

concrete experience with poetic imagination; he wrote of the value of speculative thought: "Extravagant theories . . . in those parts of philosophy, where our knowledge is yet imperfect are not without their use; as they encourage the execution of laborious experiments, or the investigation of ingenious deductions to confirm or refute them."[35]

The grandson, not deeply involved in practical affairs connected with his scientific work, comes closer than his grandfather to our notion of the pure scientist. But their views of the nature of knowledge and how we get it were similar. Numerous remarks on education, scattered through Charles' letters, bring out his interest in individual activity and discovery rather than passive absorption of truths parceled out by teachers. Even the way he read a book—often annotating it heavily, preparing his own index of interesting passages, breaking it in half at the binding if it was too heavy, stopping to write about it in his notebooks—shows a man at work using books as tools for getting knowledge, not as exhibitions of knowledge already crystallized.

Charles did so much in the way of deductive theory construction, and so much in the way of assembling factual information, that it is possible to see him as working in an inductive fashion, from the facts "up" to the theory, or in a deductive spirit: first working out conclusions that follow from stated premises, then testing the conclusions by going "down" to the facts.

We can best catch a glimpse of Charles' notion of the proper relation between theory and experiment in his notebooks. From the opening pages of the transmutation notebooks onward, we see that he is always working within some theoretical framework, either trying to solve a problem generated by his own thinking, or choosing between alternative hypotheses, or disproving an idea running counter to his own views. Toward the end of the first notebook, he summarized the progress of his thought and the advantages of the theory of evolution he held at that point (not yet the theory of evolution through natural selection) . His theory connects known facts in an understandable way; it leads to predictions of discoveries as yet unknown—for example, "It leads you to believe the world older than *geologists* think." (*B* 226) His theory suggests directions in which one does *not* have to look; it leads to ever more profound questions about its own underlying premises: "We are led to endeavour to discover *causes* of changes." (*B* 227)

This passage is particularly interesting because it is so similar to what he said on the same subject in the *Origin*. (*Origin,* 484–488) In

---

[35] Charles Darwin, in his biographical sketch of his grandfather, cites this passage from the preface to Erasmus Darwin's *Botanic Garden*. See *Erasmus Darwin* by Ernst Krause, *with a Preliminary Notice by Charles Darwin* (London, John Murray, 1879).

other words, his views on the functions of scientific theory did not waver very much from a moment some six months before he thought of natural selection to a point twenty-two years later when writing the *Origin of Species*. A *Weltanschauung* is more persistent than the theories it embraces.

In some respects, Charles Darwin's greatest works represent interpretative compilations of facts first gathered by others. But he was no "mere" collector. He actively organized the search for information. In his long series of letters to Joseph Hooker and to many other scientists, we can see a guiding idea at work: facts are collected for some purpose, to help construct a theory or test a hypothesis. In addition to these letters, at least twice he sent out questionnaires widely to prospective ·informants. His first known printed questionnaire was sent out in 1839; it dealt with animal breeding and included questions about the inheritance of habits, and the effects of hybridity on behavior, as well as questions purely about physical form and about the effect of behavioral changes on inherited anatomical characters. In 1867 he sent out his more famous questionnaire, on the expression of emotions.[36]

When Darwin's short scientific papers are more fully studied, they will surely enrich our understanding of his view of the relation between theory and experiment, and his conception of the nature of scientific knowledge. In the nature of the case, he could not test his whole theory experimentally, because the theory dealt with the whole of nature, which could not all be brought into the laboratory. So his experiments dealt with issues that he deemed important enough and opportune for experimental attack by a scientific generalist such as he was.

One such question was the effect of prolonged soaking in sea water on the germination of seeds. He was interested in showing that many different kinds of seed could survive after such immersion and thus cross ocean barriers. That finding would support the hypothesis that a given species had arisen only once and then been dispersed in various natural ways to its far-flung habitats, as against the hypothesis of multiple creation. At the outset he had a hope somewhat higher than only to study the survival of seeds after immersion: "It would be a curious experiment to know whether soaking seeds in salt water &c has any tendency to form varieties?" (*B* 125) He could not bring the whole of nature into his laboratory—but he could dream about it.

Social and Ethical Outlook. In the civilized world as we have known it, man has always been wolf to man, nations have gone to war,

---

36 See R. B. Freeman and P. J. Gautrey, "Darwin's Questions About the Breeding of Animals, with a Note on Queries About Expression," *Journal of the Society for the Bibliography of Natural History*, 1969, 5 (3). Darwin's 1867 queries about expression are reprinted in his book *The Expression of Emotions in Man and Animals*.

men have been needlessly hungry and unjustly imprisoned, and civilized human beings have despoiled nature and enslaved each other. In one view, these are the evils we have always with us, to be borne if we must or used for gain if we can; in another view, these are the problems to be confronted on our way to making a better world. There is of course no simple logical connection between natural science and social thought. A person might, for example, believe in organic evolution and still think that the social order stands still, or that it ought to do so. But there is a psychological connection: it seems more plausible that belief in a changing natural order would be coupled with acceptance of social change, and belief in evolutionary progression with a hopeful desire for social progress.

Utilitarian Ethic. In a very general sense, both Erasmus and Charles accepted the utilitarian ethic. Actions were evaluated in terms of their actual consequences for living beings, not in terms of some supposedly timeless foreordained moral code. For Erasmus, as for others, "the greatest good for the greatest number" was translated into a "greatest happiness principle," about which he wrote on more than one occasion. In *Zoonomia* he expressed his belief "in the progressive increase of the wisdom and happiness" of the inhabitants of the earth, especially through their own exertions.[37] In the *Temple of Nature,* he wrote that "The sum total of the happiness of organized nature is probably increased . . . when one large old animal dies, and is converted into many young ones. . . ."[38] A few pages further on he gives a materialist theory of happiness: The "Bliss of Being" is measured by the amount of activity of the organs of sense and thought, and the actions these organs control.[39]

Charles discussed the sources of happiness in the M notebook. His argument there is similar to his grandfather's. Higher thought processes yield greater happiness; the conditions of life favorable to the greatest happiness—including physical and social conditions, satisfaction of the simpler bodily needs, and some sensual pleasures—are those which are conducive to these higher psychological processes. Although this passage was written before he had thought clearly about natural selection, it is evident that he is thinking of ethics as *evolving*—instincts having ethical import which might be serviceable to some animals would not be to others. Perhaps too hopefully, he writes of aggressive impulses that "with lesser intellect they might be necessary and no doubt were preservative and are now, like all other structures slowly vanishing." (*M* 123) He sounded the same note of evolutionary optimism in *Descent:* in discussing the conflict in each

---

[37] *Zoonomia,* section xxxix, 4.
[38] Erasmus Darwin, *Temple of Nature, op. cit.,* p. 162.
[39] *Ibid.,* Canto IV, both in verse, lines 429–456, and in prose notes.

individual between social and anti-social tendencies, he concluded that through natural evolutionary processes ". . . the struggle between our higher and lower impulses will be less severe, and virtue will be triumphant." (*Descent,* 125)

Compassion for All Living Things. While Erasmus came close to a pure utilitarian position, since he believed that the sum of happiness of all living creatures is the prime good, Charles, guided by the theory of natural selection, really substituted *survival* for happiness as the prime good. For him, happiness, or in lower organisms sensual pleasure, had adaptive value in that each species has evolved in such a fashion that the quest for happiness and pleasure contributes to its survival. Although the two positions are slightly different, both are based on a feeling of oneness with all of nature—all creatures enjoy and suffer; it is hard to imagine even an oyster or a plant as insensible.

In Charles' case, there was definitely a boyhood phase in which he loved to hunt, and ostentatiously counted his kill of birds. But he grew ashamed of his wantonness, and wrote in his *Autobiography:* "I must have been half-consciously ashamed of my zeal, for I tried to persuade myself that shooting was almost an intellectual employment; it required so much skill to judge where to find most game. . . ." (*Autobiography,* 55) In fact, it was good training for his later activities as a naturalist.

In the 1870s there was an attempt in England to carry through anti-vivisection legislation. Darwin appeared before the Royal Commission on Vivisection, opposing the bill. He worked hard behind the scenes, helping to draw up and rally support for an alternative proposal that would safeguard animals against needless suffering and at the same time protect the rights of scientists to pursue their research. The sense in which his feeling extended to all of life is caught in his son Francis' recollection: ". . . my father's strong feeling with regard to suffering both in man and beast . . . was indeed one of the strongest feelings in his nature, and was exemplified in matters small and great, in his sympathy with the educational miseries of dancing dogs, or in his horror at the sufferings of slaves." (*LL* 3, 199)

This sense of compassion emerged strongly during the *Beagle* voyage—that is, by the time he was twenty-one—and consistently characterized his behavior from then on.

Opposition to Slavery. In the long run every civilized society decides against slavery. Along with the rise of capitalism, the eighteenth century saw the beginning of the worldwide movement against slavery. In the nineteenth century, first the international slave trade and then, in most countries, slavery itself was abolished through a series of sharp struggles and international agreements.

Members of the Darwin circle were early opponents of slavery. In 1788 Charles' grandfather, Josiah Wedgwood the potter, manufactured hundreds of copies of a cameo showing a black slave in chains with the words: "Am I not a man and a brother." The cause Wedgwood celebrated in pottery Erasmus Darwin praised in poetry: in 1789 an anti-slavery stanza of the *Loves of the Plants* ended:

> . . . hear this Truth sublime,
> He, who allows oppression, shares the crime.[40]

The anti-slavery agitation of those years joined forces naturally with the movement across the Channel for "Liberty, Equality and Fraternity." To commemorate the fall of the Bastille, the Revolutionary Society of Birmingham arranged a dinner meeting for Bastille Day, July 14, 1791; members of the Lunar Society were active in the planning. The meeting was never held—the famous Birmingham Riot,

Wedgwood anti-slavery medallion. *Courtesy of Josiah Wedgwood and Sons Ltd.*

---

40 Erasmus Darwin, *The Botanic Garden; Part I, "The Economy of Vegetation"; Part II, "The Loves of the Plants"* (London: Johnson, 1789), Canto III. This is the work that drew the wrath of the anti-Jacobins and provoked their vengeful parody.

lasting three days, broke out, possibly encouraged and certainly not much discouraged by the conservative British government. Joseph Priestley's house was burned down, including his books, papers, and laboratory; he left Birmingham for London and then for America.[41]

Within Great Britain the struggle against slavery slowly succeeded. In 1811 participation in the slave trade was made a felony. By 1838 all slaves in British colonies were freed. After this history, one might think that steadfast opposition to slavery would have been a foregone conclusion among liberals. But John Stuart Mill, in writing about the American Civil War, described his own dismay at

> "the rush of nearly the whole upper and middle classes of my own country, even those who passed for Liberals, into a furious pro-Southern partisanship: the working classes, and some of the literary and scientific men, being almost the sole exceptions to the general frenzy."[42]

His compatriots had forgotten the discussions of the horrors of slavery which had prevailed in England only a generation before.

On slavery Charles never wavered. During the *Beagle* voyage he had an intense quarrel with Captain FitzRoy, who believed that some slaves they had seen in Brazil were as happy as they professed to be when asked by their master. (*Autobiography,* 74) Darwin often described the sufferings of slaves as he had witnessed them in South America. Some of his feeling was expressed in the 1839 edition of his *Journal* of the *Beagle* voyage, although this was a government document and still under FitzRoy's supervision. In the 1845 edition he added two pages describing the brutality of slaveholders he had seen, saying: "It makes one's blood boil, yet heart tremble, to think that we Englishmen and our American descendants, with their boastful cry of liberty, have been and are so guilty. . . ." (*Voyage,* 1845, 500)

In America the issues of slavery and evolution were fused in a striking academic confrontation. One of the major scientific opponents of evolutionary thought was Louis Agassiz, the Swiss biologist, who spent much of his life at Harvard. Agassiz believed that the races of man had been separately created by God and were meant to stay separate. In 1854 he wrote an essay for a pro-slavery book, the main aim of which was to prove that Negroes were a separate and inferior species.

One of the main scientific proponents of evolutionary thought was Asa Gray, the influential Harvard botanist. His thinking was close

---

41 See Schofield, *op. cit.,* for an account of the role of the members of the Lunar Society in events connected with the Birmingham Riots.
42 John Stuart Mill, *Autobiography* (London: Longmans, 1873).

enough to Darwin's that the latter confided in him about his theory of evolution two years before the publication of the *Origin,* in 1859. In 1860 there was a notable public debate between Agassiz and Gray, the former attacking and the latter defending Darwin's *Origin of Species.* Gray saw clearly that Darwin's theory, applied to man, "makes the Negro and the Hottentot our blood-relations." Gray did not mind these new cousins; he was anti-slavery and, when war came, pro-North.[43]

During the war Gray vainly tried to persuade his friends in the English upper class to give up their pro-Confederacy stand. By the end of the war Darwin was the only Briton with whom he could correspond about the war and slavery.

All men are brothers, they are descended from a common ancestor, and they therefore should not exploit and enslave each other; insofar as the war was a war against slavery, the cause of the North was just. So men like Darwin and Gray reasoned. Of course, not everyone was consistent. Among Darwin's friends there were those who opposed his theory of evolution but agreed with him about slavery. And that is just the point: Darwin came from a tradition which equipped him to express *consistently* an egalitarian and evolutionary point of view.

I must mention one more link between the lives of Charles and Erasmus Darwin. *Zoonomia,* the compendious medical treatise that included Erasmus' pioneering essay on evolution, was originally intended for posthumous publication. Erasmus delayed some twenty years before publishing his evolutionary and other unpopular views. But in 1792 he wrote to his son Robert (Charles' father), "I am studying my 'Zoonomia,' which I *think* I shall publish . . . as I am now too old and hardened to fear a little abuse." Charles, in telling this story, adds that the work "was honoured by the Pope by being placed in the 'Index Expurgatorius.' "[44] Half a century later the same honor was bestowed upon the grandson.

There are several important limitations on the subject of this chapter.

First, I speak of a *family* rather than a *class* outlook. Intuitively, I feel that a comprehensive group of ideas shared by a relatively stable group over a long period of time must certainly express some class position. But the structure of social classes and its relation to ideology are very complex subjects. The Darwin circle was only one part of the English *bourgeoisie;* there were other sectors who were orthodox in religion, conservative in politics, and antagonistic to the idea of an evolving universe. The task of disentangling and clarifying the rela-

---

[43] The Gray-Agassiz debate is described by A. Hunter Dupree in *Asa Gray* (New York: Atheneum, 1968). See also Edward Lurie, *Louis Agassiz: A Life in Science* (Chicago: University of Chicago Press, 1960).

[44] Charles Darwin in *Erasmus Darwin* by E. Krause, *op. cit.*

tions between science, class, and political outlook would be worth the trouble.

Second, when I touch on social and political questions, I speak of an *outlook and feeling,* rather than political *behavior.* Charles Darwin was not what you would call politically *engagé.* He did participate in public affairs from time to time and to a limited extent. But he chose to live the major part of his adult life in a quiet place, and he protected himself from becoming publicly embroiled in matters that would distract him from his vast scientific undertakings. There is no reason to believe that this outward detachment reduced the importance of his general outlook in shaping his scientific thought.

Third, when I speak of a family outlook, it does not mean that all members of the family shared the same ideas. There is really not much evidence on the subject. Charles' brother Erasmus may have been more radical or at least more atheistic—he was friends with people like Thomas Carlyle and Harriet Martineau who were outspoken in their anti-religious views. The ideas of any group can be described better as a *region* of some spectrum rather than as a point on it. The Darwin group occupied the region of the political spectrum which Charles described as "Liberal or Radical."[45]

The appellation *liberal-radical* probably meant then approximately what it would mean today—concerned more with the preservation and extension of individual liberty than with the preservation of hallowed social institutions; concerned more with human rights than with property rights; favorably yet cautiously disposed toward social change; unattached to any organized group that would pursue the desired aims in a manner disturbing to the comfort and tranquility of upper-middle-class life.

As to party politics, his son William said of Charles that "he was an ardent Liberal and had a very great admiration for John Stuart Mill and Mr. Gladstone. . . ."[46]

If there is a slight difference in shading between his son's and Darwin's own description of himself, it probably reflects both the shifting complexities of English political life and the fact that Charles Darwin was never systematically involved in political affairs.

It is essential to grasp how pervasive and ominous were the issues raised by the long struggle for a completely naturalistic account of all phenomena. Questions that seem to us "purely scientific" were heavily freighted with religious and political meanings. This was an age of revolutions: 1776, 1789, 1830, 1848. The *Origin* appeared just before

---

[45] This was the phrase he used about himself in answering one of Francis Galton's questionnaires. (*LL* 3, 177–179)

[46] Litchfield, editor, *Emma Darwin: A Century of Family Letters, op. cit.,* Vol. 2, p. 169.

the outbreak of the American Civil War, and, as we have seen, the biologists' debate over the brotherhood of man played its part in the fierce struggle to end the enslavement of some men and women by their brothers and sisters. *The Descent of Man* appeared in 1871, just after the crushing of the Paris Commune. Ideas become weapons in social struggles when they undermine established ways of thinking, especially ideas embracing a world in flux.

Natural theology was repeatedly exploited to justify the existing social order as part of a divinely created natural order. The Natural Theologians were by no means insensitive to the existence of widespread human suffering: it could only be justified as part of a universe superintended by a kind Providence if one invoked some larger Plan as yet unknown to man. It is this corollary of the argument from design which ought to be recognized as the mainspring of "social Darwinism" rather than Darwin's own egalitarian social philosophy.

Any intellectual tendency that removed Providence from contact with the contemporary human scene was taken as a threat to the established order. God was needed to keep man in his place. In this context, Darwin's use of the Malthusian principle of superfecundity expressed a radical social idea. The conservative Reverend Malthus had seen superfecundity as a threat to the established order, and as an answer he had urged chastity upon the poor. Darwin, in contrast, saw superfecundity as a creative principle, making possible the whole panorama of evolutionary change.

I do not mean to suggest that religious institutions formed one monolithic structure. The Tolpuddle Martyrs, for example, a group of workingmen who were deported to Australia for their efforts to organize, were all Wesleyans. Wesley's thought had encouraged these workers to believe that in the infinite chain of being they were no further from God than other humans. As one of them put it,

> England has for many years been lifting her voice against the abominable practice of negro slavery; numbers of her great men have talked, have laboured, have struggled, until at length emancipation has been granted to her black slaves in the West Indies. When will they dream of advocating the cause of England's white slaves? . . . But I am told that the working man ought to remain still and let their cause work its way—"that God in his good time will bring it about for him." However this is not my creed; I believe that God works by means and men, and that he expects every man who feels an interest in the subject to take an active part. . . .[47]

It is by no means an unimportant part of the story that these workingmen saw the Whigs as well as the Tories as their enemies. The

---

[47] George Loveless, *The Victims of Whiggery; Being a Statement of the Persecutions Experienced by the Dorchester Labourers,* a pamphlet published in 1873.

author lists the members of the minority in Parliament who voted to pardon the six exiles. In a House of 390 members, those 82 voting for mercy included 7 Whigs and 12 Tories, the rest being independent liberals and radicals. If at this crucial time in his life Darwin had been able to ally himself with the liberals and radicals, he might have profited from the philosophical help of men like John Stuart Mill rather than suffering silently under the yoke of Mill's antagonist in matters of logic and philosophy of science, the Reverend Professor William Whewell.[48]

When the *Origin* appeared, Marx and Engels, those apostles of a world in flux, greeted it enthusiastically. In 1860 Marx wrote to Engels, "Although it is developed in the crude English style, this is the book which contains the basis in natural history for our view." The crudity of which he complains may refer to Darwin's avoidance of any discussion of the philosophical issues related to his scientific thought. In a way, the criticism would be fair, since we now can see that Darwin really was aware of these issues, gave them considerable thought, and then covered his philosophical tracks in his published work.

Marx and Engels did not, of course, have to wait for the *Origin of Species* before deciding in favor of organic evolution. In a letter to Marx on July 14, 1858, reviewing the progress of science in the preceding decades, Engels writes: "comparative physiology gives one a withering contempt for the idealistic exaltation of man over the other animals. At every step one bumps up against the most complete uniformity of structure. . . ."[49] He goes on to remark that the Hegelian "qualitative leap" applies to evolution—i.e., evolutionary continuity does not exclude the emergence of special human characteristics.

As to the particular form of Darwin's theory of evolution, Marx and Engels were delighted with the fact that it bore such a striking resemblance to the economics of the capitalist market-place: "nothing discredits modern bourgeois development so much as the fact that it has not yet succeeded in getting beyond the economic forms of the animal world."[50]

In spite of its "English crudity," Engels wrote a long and spirited defense of Darwin's work, its originality, its scientific validity, and its philosophical value. The critic whom Engels was answering, Eugen Dühring, had claimed that Darwin's Malthusian image of nature brutalizes man. Engels grants the point that Darwin had blundered in accepting the special formula that food supply grows arithmetically while population grows geometrically; but Engels insists that the essential Darwinian idea is the struggle for existence. Moreover, he

---

[48] See Mill's *Autobiography* for a refreshing account of some of these issues.
[49] Karl Marx and Friedrich Engels, *Selected Correspondence, 1846–1895* (London: Martin Lawrence, 1934). Engels to Marx, July 14, 1858.
[50] *Ibid*. Engels to F. A. Lange, March 29, 1865.

reiterates Darwin's view of the manifold nature of this struggle: "not merely as direct bodily combat or devouring, but also as a struggle for space and light, even in the case of plants."[51]

In Darwin's library at Down House there is still a German edition of Volume 1 of *Das Kapital*. On the flyleaf is inscribed: "Mr. Charles Darwin on the part of his sincere admirer Karl Marx London 16 June 1873." In 1880 Marx offered to dedicate Volume 2 of the Bible of revolution to Charles Darwin; the latter replied, "I should prefer the part or volume not to be dedicated to me (although I thank you for the intended honour), as that would, in a certain extent, suggest my approval of the whole work, with which I am not acquainted."[52]

Darwin's caution and long hesitation—his non-polemic style, his efforts to propitiate his prospective opponents, his effort to avoid controversy by concealing his most inflammatory ideas—all failed. When he left man out of the *Origin,* his enemies immediately assumed that Darwin really included man, and attacked him for doing so.[53] Meanwhile, whether he wanted it or not, his allies included the most radical thinkers of his day.

---

[51] Friedrich Engels, *Herr Eugen Dühring's Revolution in Science (AntiDühring).* (London: Martin Lawrence, 1935). First published in 1878.

[52] H. E. Gruber, "Darwin and *Das Kapital,*" *Isis,* Vol. 52, 1961, p. 582. See also Keith, *op. cit.,* p. 234.

[53] Bishop Samuel Wilberforce, "Darwin's *Origin of Species,*" *Quarterly Review,* Vol. 108, 1860, pp. 225–264. Wilberforce wrote that Darwin "not obscurely . . . applies his scheme . . . to Man himself . . ." and that Christianity was "utterly irreconcilable with the degrading notion of the brute origin of him who was created in the image of God." (pp. 257–258) Incidentally, the Bishop quoted from Canning and Frere's parody of Erasmus Darwin's "Loves of the Plants."

CHAPTER 4

Darwin's Teachers

I remember one trifling fact which seemed to me
highly characteristic of the man: in one of the bad
years for the potato, I asked him how his crop had
fared; but after a little talk I perceived that, in fact,
he knew nothing about his own potatoes, but seemed
to know exactly what sort of crop there was in the
garden of almost every poor man in his parish.

Darwin's recollections of Professor John S. Henslow, in Leonard Jenyns, *Memoir of the Reverend John Stevens Henslow* (London: John von
Voorst, 1862)

We think of science as the fusion of two quite different things: an
existing body of knowledge and a set of methods for creating new
knowledge. Educating a scientist calls for teaching these things in such
a way that they become mutually supportive rather than antagonistic.

The working scientist cannot do without the disciplined ability to
assimilate what is already known. He needs this not only in order to
get started on his scientific career, but daily in the lifetime pursuit of
it. On the other hand, overgrown respect for what is now known and
too much time spent mastering it lead only to sterile pedantry.

Darwin wrote quite disparagingly about his own education. Answering Francis Galton's questionnaire directed to scientific men of
the day, he wrote that "I consider that all I have learnt of any value
has been self-taught," that his formal education had been "almost
entirely classical," and that the chief omission had been "No mathematics or modern languages, nor any habit of observation or reasoning." (*LL* 3, 177). A few years after Galton's questionnaire, Darwin
wrote, "I have always felt that I owe to the voyage the first real
training or education of my mind." (*Autobiography*, 77)

This picture leaves us with a puzzle: how could so unprepared a
young man have done so well? For Darwin did make wonderful use of
the five years of the *Beagle* voyage (1831–36, age 22–27), not only in

training himself, but in the production of significant scientific advances.

When we examine Darwin's education at Cambridge more closely,
even from his own account the picture is not really so bleak, particularly if we give adequate weight to his informal contacts with professors and fellow students, to many walks in woods and fields—
shooting birds, collecting insects, and discussing subjects ranging from
natural history to theology, subjects not so far apart then as they are
now. From numerous remarks it is clear that he much preferred
reading to listening to lectures.

The attitude toward nature Darwin shared with his friends and
teachers was at once playful, reverent, analytical, and acquisitive—in
short, enthusiastic. He hunted birds for pleasure, collected beetles
passionately, gloried in the anatomical structure of a flower, and
delighted in studying Paley's *Natural Theology* and Euclid's *Elements*. The Reverend Paley's argument sets the tone: all nature is the
handiwork of God, and the study of nature draws one closer to Him.
The distance between the two books was not great: Paley's argument
leans heavily on geometry. A substantial part of the argument from
design, as he presents it, rests on the geometrical perfection of a bee-
hive, from which he drew the conclusion that there must be a Divine
Artificer, otherwise one could not conceive of such a perfect construction.

Years later Darwin was to show that, through minor variations

Darwin as seen by a fellow student at Cambridge University. *Courtesy of Cambridge University Library.*

and natural selection, the evolution of the bee's cell-making behavior could be naturally explained. Today, with our knowledge of man-made teleological machines, we feel little need to invoke supernatural forces to explain such systems. But in Darwin's time the physical sciences were heavily mechanistic, and it may well be that the immersion in the Cambridge combination of theology and natural history served to deepen his awareness of the adaptive structures and teleological systems he was later to explain.

This connection was reflected even in his way of rejecting religion later on. In the midst of a passage condemning Christianity for its doctrine of eternal damnation, he stops to discuss various arguments for or against the existence of God—the occurrence of suffering as arguing against a beneficent and omnipotent God, the ubiquity of "endless beautiful adaptations" arguing for an intelligent Creator. He writes: "The old argument of design in nature, as given by Paley, which formerly seemed to me so conclusive, fails, now that the law of natural selection has been discovered. We can no longer argue that, for instance, the beautiful hinge of a bivalve shell must have been made by an intelligent being, like the hinge of a door by man." (*Autobiography*, 87)

The poetic vein in Darwin's approach to nature was nourished throughout his education. Poetry can be important in the development of a scientist: its content results from the poet's efforts to search out hidden meanings in the world around him; its form demands a similar effort of those who would enjoy it. Looked at in this way, Darwin even at his prosiest draws on the poetic mode of thought: "all true classification is genealogical; . . . community of descent is the hidden bond which naturalists have been unconsciously seeking." (*Origin*, 420) One does not have to look far in Darwin to find prose passages in which he is being more self-consciously poetic, striving to invoke in his readers something of his own feeling for nature.[1]

The structure of knowledge exemplified by Darwin's teachers and the authors he admired was one he emulated in combining geological and biological pursuits in his early career. The Rev. John Henslow was the man Darwin was closest to at Cambridge: he was a professor, a clergyman, and a botanist who did some work in geology. Darwin's first real hero, Alexander von Humboldt, was an indefatigable world traveler whose efforts took in geology, plant geography, and almost everything else in the *Kosmos*, which was the title of his twenty-volume final work. As already mentioned, Darwin had with him on board the

---

[1] For a full treatment of this subject, see Stanley Edgar Hyman, *The Tangled Bank: Darwin, Marx, Frazer and Freud as Imaginative Writers* (New York: Atheneum, 1962). The title comes from the closing passage of the *Origin*.

Beagle the first volume of Lyell's new *Principles of Geology.* The first sentence of the *Principles* defines geology as "the science which investigates the successive changes that have taken place in the organic and inorganic kingdoms of nature. . . ."[2] Darwin did not have to invent the grouping of interests he displayed on the *Beagle* voyage, which led him directly to his work on evolution. This grouping was almost a commonplace among his teachers. He had only to discover that it applied to him too.

The blend of observation and speculation exhibited by Darwin's teachers provided him with a useful set of models. British science, especially geology, was at that time beginning to come out of a period of intense hostility to theory making, a period in which science and fact gathering had been practically equated. The emerging attitude toward the relation between theory and observation, just at the time Darwin was starting out, gave him just about the amount of freedom he needed for creative work; it also imbued him with the zeal to overwhelm his critics with facts. During his Edinburgh days Darwin read *Zoonomia,* his grandfather's major scientific and medical work in which are expressed both a philosophy of nature and a theory of evolution. Recollecting this period, Charles wrote, "At this time I admired greatly the *Zoonomia;* but on reading it a second time after an interval of ten or fifteen years, I was much disappointed, the proportion of speculation being so large to the facts given." (*Autobiography,* 49) The balance that is best for clinching an argument is not the same as that for opening a mind.

A repertoire of techniques is essential to the working scientist. For the *Beagle* voyage Darwin needed those techniques useful on an extended field trip: observing carefully in an informed way based on significant hypotheses, collecting and preserving specimens (of rocks, animals, plants), and keeping good notes. He used his years at Edinburgh and Cambridge to develop skills such as shooting and stuffing birds, making collections of beetles, geological field work, broad-gauge natural-history walks, and extracting information from the writings of other travelers. Darwin as a student organized expeditions for collecting, and taught others what he knew; this ability to train his helpers stood him in good stead on the voyage and later.

It may have seemed to Darwin that all this was not part of his education, because it was not contained in the lectures he heard, nor was it covered in the examinations he wrote. But it was provided for in the ambiance of his universities, and encouraged and assisted by his professors. Darwin's emergence as a scientist was recognized by these same men, not because of any brilliance in his formal education but

---

2 Lyell, *Principles, op. cit.,* p. 1.

because he shared their passions and skills. Informal contact with some of his professors and some fellow students was the most important part of his education. Has it ever been otherwise?

Personal models he could draw upon in constructing his own style of work were provided by a few teachers and a few authors closely studied. And some of these models could be studied at very close range. In addition to his many walks and talks with Henslow, there were long evenings and excursions with other professors. Darwin got a large part of his early geological training from a three-week field trip through Wales, alone with Professor Adam Sedgwick.

These men also gave Darwin warm encouragement after he had left Cambridge. Henslow took care of the collections that Darwin sent back during the long voyage. Excerpts from Darwin's letters to Henslow were read to the Cambridge Philosophical Society and printed before his return from the *Beagle* voyage. The letters contained very little botany, but a great deal of vivid description of animals and insects, some youthful braggadocio and iconoclasm, and a steady thread of Lyellian geology. The last must have troubled Henslow, for he was a great friend of Adam Sedgwick's. Sedgwick, an eminent Cambridge geologist, believed in a nearly literal interpretation of the Bible, and therefore at first ardently opposed Lyell. Nevertheless, Henslow published Darwin's letters with their evidences of the great age of the earth, and of the uniformly operating material forces still at work, slowly shaping and reshaping the face of the earth. Even Sedgwick sat at these meetings, heard these letters, and later in 1835 called on Charles Darwin's father to praise the son and predict great things for him.

Darwin's *Autobiography* has a spontaneous quality and involves numerous memories long after the event. There are a number of small but interesting errors and contradictions. After describing the lectures he attended as "intolerably dull," with one exception, he concludes: "to my mind there are no advantages and many disadvantages in lectures compared with reading." (*Autobiography*, 47) But then he writes, ". . . I did not even attend Sedgwick's eloquent and interesting lectures. Had I done so I should probably have become a geologist earlier than I did." (*Autobiography*, 59–60)

If one lists all the remarks he ever made about lectures attended at Edinburgh and Cambridge, it appears that he commented favorably on three (Chemistry by Hope, Clinical Lectures by hospital staff members, I suppose, and Botany by Henslow) ; and *un*favorably on three (Materia Medica by Duncan, Anatomy by Monro, and Geology and Zoology by Jameson) . It would be easy to quote him on either side, as he was given to superlatives in both directions. The comments on individual lecturers in the letters he wrote at the time accord well with comments in the *Autobiography*.

He told his family that he didn't like all the lectures on his schedule. There is a letter from his sister Susan, March 20, 1826, to Edinburgh:

> . . . My reason for writing so soon is, that I have a message from Papa to give you, which I am afraid you won't like: he desires me to say that he thinks your plan of picking and choosing what lectures you like to attend not at all a good one; . . . as you cannot have enough information to know what may be of use to you, it is quite necessary for you to bear with a good deal of stupid and dry work . . . if you do not discontinue your present indulgent way, your course of study will be utterly useless. Papa was sorry to hear that you thought of coming home before the course of lectures were finished, and hopes you will not do so.[3]

Thus, Darwin liked some of the lectures he heard, disliked others. He may well have objected more to the necessity of attending courses of lectures unselectively, and to the paternal pressure on him to do so, than to the unrewarding lectures themselves. When he speaks of attending occasional lectures, as against courses, at the Edinburgh Royal Medical Society and the Wernerian Society (where he heard Audubon and liked him), he passes quickly over the fact that some were good and others not.

As for his reading habits, although it is true that he always read widely and was in a sense self-taught, it is also true that he read what he was required to read, and not always critically, at least according to his own account: "I did not at that time trouble myself about Paley's premises; and taking these on trust I was charmed and convinced by the long line of argumentation." (*Autobiography*, 59)

Most likely Darwin's intention to prepare for the clergy was lightly held, a sort of stopgap statement of purpose sufficient to tide him over the transition from the study of medicine at Edinburgh (a period he used more for the pursuit of natural history than for medicine) to a more definitely avowed intention to live on the means his father would allow him and spend his life as a scientist. For this interpretation of his early aspirations we have numerous lines of evidence in addition to those already cited.

Darwin makes it clear in his *Autobiography*, and other circumstances corroborate, that soon after he went to Edinburgh he was "convinced . . . that my father would leave me property enough to subsist on with some comfort . . . my belief was sufficient to check any strenuous effort to learn medicine." (*Autobiography*, 46) Although he leaves the implication hanging that the prospect of independent means led to idleness, all the facts show that he worked hard at what interested him, both at Edinburgh and at Cambridge.

---

3 Unpublished letter, Darwin MSS, Cambridge University Library.

From his letters written during his Cambridge days, especially those to his distant cousin William Darwin Fox, it is clear that he was very deeply ensconced in scientific work. After a trip to London in 1829, he wrote, "The first two days I spent entirely with Mr. Hope, and did little else but talk about and look at insects. . . ." (*LL* 1, 174) The following summer he began an "entomological trip" with Professor Hope which was to go all through North Wales, but Darwin had to quit after two days, due to illness. (*LL* 1, 178) He worked hard at entomology for at least a year, probably two or three. In the summer of 1830 he went back to North Wales, writing to Fox, after two weeks that he has been "working from morning to night . . . on the rainy days I go fishing, on the good ones entomologising." (*LL* 1, 182)

Too much emphasis has been placed on the fact that Darwin was not the first man approached for the post of naturalist on board the *Beagle* and that his father at first refused him permission to go, so that his going on the voyage seems a matter of chance rather than the product of a set purpose. On the contrary, he had been *for some time firmly set in his intention to engage in scientific travel,* emulating his hero at that time, Alexander von Humboldt. In the spring of 1831 he had a plan to visit Teneriffe in the Canary Islands. He studied Spanish for the purpose, looked into the cost of passage, recruited some of his friends for the venture, which was probably planned for the summer of 1832. In the summer of 1831, after his geological tour of Wales with Sedgwick, he got the *Beagle* offer and sailed the following winter. Considering the years he spent in South America, his study of Spanish was not wasted.

On Darwin's part, then, the *Beagle* voyage was not a lucky accident but the exploitation of an opportunity that fitted in perfectly with his own well-developed purposes.

There is one crucial aspect of Darwin's relations with his teachers to which we must now turn: their beliefs and behavior in matters connected with the subject of evolution. Even more broadly, however, we shall have to examine their feelings, as far as we can know them, about the discovery of genuine novelty, especially discovery that challenges fundamental presuppositions such as man's place in (God's?) nature. For it is in their *feelings* about such changes in thought, and in Darwin's *feeling* relation with these men, that we can find part of the answer to a great puzzle in his life, the long and tortuous path he chose in writing the *Origin of Species* and the *Descent of Man.*

There were four teachers with whom Darwin had an especially significant intellectual relationship. Robert Grant was probably the first outspoken evolutionist Darwin met, and the man who guided Darwin in his first original scientific investigation. John Henslow was his chief mentor at Cambridge and the man responsible for Darwin's selection as naturalist on board the *Beagle*. Adam Sedgwick, the professor with whom Darwin made his first serious geological field trip, later became something of a *bête noire*. Charles Lyell's *Principles of Geology* served as a guide during the voyage, and Lyell became his chief mentor on Darwin's return. These four I shall discuss in some detail. In his permanent cast of characters,[4] these men became colleagues to conjure with, to persuade, to ask questions of, to tell or not to tell one's bright ideas—*senior* colleagues.

To them should perhaps be added Alexander von Humboldt, whom Darwin hero-worshipped and strove to emulate before and during the early part of the voyage, but whom he met only briefly years later. We should also remember the black taxidermist in Edinburgh from whom Darwin learned that art, for, although his name is forgotten, the simple fact that Darwin had an early opportunity to study with a black man must have underlined a point which became essential in his thinking: the unity of man.[5]

Dr. Robert Edmund Grant was a zoologist in Edinburgh when Darwin was there. Grant, in his thirties at that time, seems to have spent a good deal of time in the company of students interested in science, especially Darwin. The two often went for walks along the shore together, collecting marine organisms which were later dissected and studied. Grant took Darwin, then sixteen and seventeen, to various scientific lectures. Darwin's two early discoveries about marine organisms grew out of this work with Dr. Grant. At the meeting of the Plinian Society, March 27, 1827, where Darwin communicated his discoveries, Grant was present and spoke after him, enlarging on the same subject from his more extensive knowledge.[6]

Immediately after Dr. Grant spoke, Browne gave his paper on the material basis of all life and mind. Grant is listed as participating in the discussion, which was, as recounted earlier, then expunged. What Grant said in public we do not know, but we may guess his thoughts from the appearance the year before of an article supporting the Lamarckian theory of evolution. The major evidence cited in the

---

[4] On the importance of the internal cast of characters for the creative person, see Jerome S. Bruner, "The Conditions of Creativity," in *Contemporary Approaches to Creative Thinking*, edited by H. E. Gruber, G. Terrell, and M. Wertheimer (Chicago: Atherton Press, 1962).

[5] ". . . he gave me lessons for payment, and I used often to sit with him, for he was a very pleasant and intelligent man." (*Autobiography*, 51)

All I have been able to learn about him is the following: A slave of a Mr. Edmonstone in Demerara, British Guiana, he was known as "John." His master took him to Scotland where, on gaining his freedom, he was employed as a taxidermist by the Edinburgh Museum. He had learned taxidermy while still in Demerara from Charles Waterton. See Charles Waterton, *Wanderings in South America*, 3rd edition (London: Fellowes, 1836), p. 158.

[6] Minute Book of Plinian Society, Edinburgh University Library.

article was the geological succession of fossil remains, lower organisms being found in older beds of rock and higher ones in more recent beds. The author made it clear that he intended to include "human remains" in this geological series, as occurring only in the most recent deposits. The article was anonymous, but Grant was almost certainly the author: years later Darwin told in his *Autobiography* how he had been dumbfounded by Grant's sudden confession of agreement with Lamarck, during one of their walks together.[7]

Something of the transitional state of affairs in British thought is suggested by the way in which Grant revealed his views. Not only did he feel free to tell young Darwin, but he did publish them somewhat more openly in one signed article, a paper on fresh-water sponges.[8] Presumably, the more general article was published anonymously to protect the author from attacks originating outside the scientific community, for at least one established scientist must have known his identity: Professor Robert Jameson of Edinburgh University, the editor of the magazine in which it appeared.

Professor Jameson gave the "intolerably dull" lectures on geology and zoology of which Darwin complained. One of the aims of his course was to "consider . . . the different theories of creation, and point out the agreement of the Mosaic account, in all its stages, with modern mineralogical discoveries." In spite of his own diluvial, or antediluvial, views, Jameson was tolerant enough to publish the anonymous Lamarckian paper, and the books he led his students to read included a fairly wide spectrum of opinion on the creation.[9]

Dr. Grant moved to London, where in 1827 he became the first professor of zoology at University College, London. After the *Beagle* voyage, he was one of the few scientists helpful to Darwin in arranging for the analysis of Darwin's fabulous collections; Grant himself did some of the work on classifying corallines when Darwin turned to that subject. Grant was not a productive scientist in later years, but he remained a staunch supporter of evolution and was remembered by Huxley as the only biologist he knew who would speak up for evolution in the decade preceding the appearance of Darwin's *Origin*.[10]

Professor John Stevens Henslow—botanist, geologist, and clergy-

---

7 The anonymous article attributed to Grant was "Observations on the Nature and Importance of Geology," *Edinburgh New Philosophical Journal*, Vol. 1, 1826, pp. 293–302.
8 Robert E. Grant, "Observations of the Structure of Some Silicious Sponges," Edinburgh, *Philosophical Tracts*, 1825, 1826.
9 Notes on Jameson's Lectures on Natural History, MS in Edinburgh University Library, by a student in 1818, William Damsey. Darwin's own student notes, although much briefer, suggest that the content of Jameson's course did not vary much.
10 Thomas H. Huxley, "On the Reception of the *Origin of Species*," *LL* 2, 188.

man, but most of all dedicated teacher—was a man thoroughly imbued with the idea of a university as a community of scholars. He himself made no great contribution to the progress of thought. But without a sufficiency of men like him, universities would be far poorer places to study in. He gave Charles Darwin the direction and help he needed at several crucial points in his life.

The struggle to change the social character of Oxford and Cambridge universities—to free them from religious domination, to give natural science and humanism their due places, and to admit students on the basis of merit rather than class or creed—has been going on for centuries. Henslow and his good friend and senior colleague Adam Sedgwick played a role in it, and at a time opportune for Darwin. It might be fairly said that they prepared Cambridge to give Darwin the education he needed.

In the spring of 1819, Adam Sedgwick, then a young professor of geology, took Henslow on a geological expedition to the Isle of Wight. Henslow, ten years his junior, was then a fellow of St. John's College, Cambridge. During their trip they discussed a project which they carried out soon after their return. They organized the Cambridge Philosophical Society "For the purpose of promoting Scientific Enquiries, and of facilitating the communication of facts connected with the advancement of Philosophy and Natural History."[11] This seems innocent enough to us today, but it was at its founding the only such society in Cambridge. To some, its purposes deviated from the essentially religious commitment of the university. Sedgwick was able to disarm the opposition, and the society was highly successful.

Henslow set about organizing the Zoological Museum, which led eventually to the formation of other scientific museums.

By the time Darwin arrived at Cambridge, Henslow had been elected professor of both botany and of mineralogy. Darwin remembered the lectures on botany as "clear as daylight" and popular both with students and faculty.

But the most important thing about Henslow was his continuous informal contact with everyone around Cambridge interested in natural history. He held open house once a week, bringing young students such as Darwin and learned professors such as Whewell together— "all undergraduates and several older members of the university, who were attached to science." (*Autobiography*, 64)

About once a month he took his botany class on an excursion, but they stopped to examine all sorts of natural objects, not only plants. Darwin was a particular favorite of Henslow's. In his *Autobiography*

---

11 John W. Clark and Thomas McK. Hughes, *The Life and Letters of the Reverend Adam Sedgwick* (2 volumes, Cambridge: University Press, 1890) , Vol. 1, p. 207.

Darwin says that he became known as "the man who walks with Henslow."

Henslow was included in Darwin's scheme for an expedition to the Canary Islands. In July of 1831, at the end of his Cambridge days, and just before he went off with Sedgwick on his three-week geological tour of Wales, Darwin wrote to Henslow, "I hope you continue to fan your Canary ardor." The mixture of plans, requests for information, and other commissions—including one about the purchase of a Stilton cheese—is very similar in tone to some of the letters Darwin later sent Henslow from the *Beagle*.[12]

Mrs. Henslow was probably relieved when, only six weeks after that letter, the proposal arose to send Darwin out as naturalist to the *Beagle*, thus extricating her husband from Darwin's Canary project.

Shortly before Darwin's embarkation, Henslow wrote him an avuncular letter, counseling him to accept the difficulties of the voyage, including the vulgarity of naval companions. Henslow, devoted to the ideal of a tranquil life, passes on his rule of conduct to Darwin: "I have ever found the advantage of accommodating myself to circumstances. It is wonderful how soon a little submission conquers an evil & then all goes on smoothly."[13]

During the voyage Henslow was enormously helpful to Darwin. Back in Cambridge, he received the boxes of specimens Darwin sent home, gave him advice on packing and labeling, sent him books as requested, and sang his praises. On November 16, 1835, four years after Darwin's departure, his teachers Henslow and Sedgwick arranged for the reading of extracts from Darwin's letters to Henslow before the Cambridge Philosophical Society.[14]

His circumnavigation completed in the fall of 1836, Darwin returned to Cambridge for the first two months of 1837. Henslow helped him get started on the arduous task of processing all the material he had sent or brought home. Government funding had to be secured, collaborators found with expertise in various fields; collections had to be unpacked and sorted out. Darwin spent two months in Cambridge, but when he really got under way he moved to London for three years and then to the little village of Downe, where he spent the next forty. The results, not finished until 1846, were the ten books: five volumes of zoology of the *Beagle* voyage, three of geology, the two editions of

---

12 Nora Barlow, editor, *Darwin and Henslow: The Growth of an Idea, Letters 1831–1860* (London: John Murray, 1967).

13 Henslow to Darwin, November 20, 1831. In Barlow, *op. cit.*

14 The extracts were printed as a pamphlet on December 1, 1835 and reprinted by Dr. Sydney Smith for the Cambridge Philosophical Society, 1960: *Extracts from Letters Addressed to Professor Henslow by C. Darwin, Esq.* The complete set of letters is included in Nora Barlow, *op. cit.*

the *Journal* of the voyage, as well as a number of articles on a variety of subjects.

Darwin did not see very much of Henslow from then on. Although they remained good friends and there is a long series of letters in the years from 1837 to 1860, a gulf had opened between them. Darwin knew that he could not share his ideas about evolution with Henslow without wounding his old teacher, and so in his letters he kept the peace by writing about everything else. He got Henslow's help with the nomenclature of cirripedes during his eight long barnacle years. And in 1855, when he was preparing to write his big book on evolution, he exploited Henslow's knowledge of botany. He needed an unbiased botanist to classify plants for him in a way designed to test a special hypothesis about variation. Henslow was the ideal candidate. He knew plenty of botany and nothing of Darwin's hypothesis.[15]

Finally, in 1859, Darwin sent Henslow a copy of the *Origin,* with a plea for mercy masked, in typical Darwinian fashion, as an invitation to criticize: "If you have time to read it carefully, and would take the trouble to point out what part seems weakest to you and what best, it would be a most material aid to me in writing my bigger book. . . ."[16]

In May of 1860 Sedgwick attacked Darwin at a meeting in Cambridge. Darwin, of course, was not there, but Henslow, himself not a full supporter of Darwin's views, managed to defend him, especially where Sedgwick had imputed an anti-religious animus to Darwin. Darwin learned about Henslow's defense of him from his close friend Joseph Hooker, who was by this time Henslow's son-in-law. In writing to thank him, Darwin spent about as much space on a request for more botanical information as he did on Sedgwick's criticisms. His questions were always very instructive, directing the other person's attention to some point which would help him to see the merit of Darwin's views at the same time as he collected information to help Darwin go further.

Given all this attention, his life of striving for toleration, and his affection for Darwin, who had once called him "my father in Natural History," it is not surprising that Henslow's views shifted toward support of his protégé.[17]

During his last year of life, Henslow was trying to assimilate his old student's disturbing ideas with a minimum of damage either to old friendships or to his long-standing views. In one of his last letters to Darwin, he complained of the vehemence of Richard Owen's attack on the *Origin of Species:* "I don't think it is at all *becoming* in one

---

15 Barlow, *op. cit.*
16 *Ibid.*
17 *Ibid.* Darwin to Henslow, July 24, 1834.

Naturalist to be bitter against another any more than for one sect to burn the members of another."[18]

Henslow was very much the man in the middle. At the Oxford meeting of the British Association for the Advancement of Science, he was chairman of the meeting at which Bishop Wilberforce and Thomas Huxley had their famous exchange. From his experience in Cambridge, Henslow was well prepared to continue his role as the voice of moderation. He managed to preside over the dispute without losing friends.

A few months later he described his own position. Man-made stone hatchets had just been found in geological formations far older than the Adam of 6,000 years of Biblical time. He admitted to having changed his conception of the age of the earth to conform with modern science. But where *man* was concerned he needed more evidence.[19] He was still prepared to change his ground in keeping with new facts, but only at a pace that gave tradition its due.

There wasn't time for Henslow to go all the way with Darwin. In April of 1861 he was in his last illness. Joseph Hooker, Darwin's great supporter, was at his bedside together with Adam Sedgwick, a savage critic.[20]

Adam Sedgwick was Professor of Geology at Cambridge University from 1818 to his death in 1873. When we see that his old friend, prudent, pious John Henslow, had to defend Darwin against Sedgwick in 1860, when we see Darwin reading Sedgwick's vicious attack on the *Vestiges of Creation* in 1845 and fifteen years later Darwin suffering from a similar Sedgwickian attack on the *Origin,* it is easy to imagine Sedgwick as the arch-enemy of scientific progress toward acceptance of evolutionary thought. But these matters are seldom so simple.

Sedgwick entered Darwin's life at several significant points. In the summer of 1831, just before the *Beagle* voyage, Darwin accompanied Sedgwick on the three-week geological tour of North Wales; this was Darwin's most important training in geological field work. In 1848 Darwin wrote a chapter on geological field work for an Admiralty manual; it was Sedgwick who suggested Darwin for the task, having refused it himself, and it was Sedgwick's style of work that Darwin described, as much as his own.[21]

During their 1831 field trip, Darwin learned something very

---

18 *Ibid.,* Henslow to Darwin, May 5, 1860.
19 *Ibid.,* Note by Barlow.
20 *Life and Letters of Sedgwick, op. cit.,* Vol. 2, pp. 370–372.
21 *Manual of Scientific Enquiry; prepared for the use of H.M. Navy: and adapted for travelers in General,* edited by Sir John Herschel (London, 1849) . See also Paul H. Barrett, "The Sedgwick-Darwin Geologic Tour of North Wales," *Proceedings of the American Philosophical Society,* Vol. 18, 1974, pp. 146–164.

general about scientific method from Sedgwick: facts do not speak for themselves. Sedgwick discounted as unreliable a finding that he believed to be in contradiction to his geological views at that time. Darwin remembered this incident: ". . . I was then utterly astonished at Sedgwick not being delighted at so wonderful a fact as a tropical shell being found near the surface in the middle of England. Nothing before had ever made me thoroughly realise . . . that science consists in grouping facts so that general laws or conclusions may be drawn from them." (Autobiography, 69–70)

Sedgwick, of course, was operating under one set of guiding preconceptions at that time, and Darwin was soon to abandon these for another. But in one sense the methodological lesson stuck. Years later Sedgwick, writing to the African explorer Dr. Livingstone, grumbled that the Geological Society was "in fetters . . . led by the nose in the train of an hypothesis—I mean the development of all organic life from a simple material element by natural specific transmutation, ending in the flora and fauna of the actual world with man at its head." Pricked by Lyell's conversion to Darwinism, he wrote of Lyell, ". . . he has never been able to look steadily in the face of nature except through the spectacles of an hypothesis."[22] Since the gist of his complaint was that Darwin had assumed the leadership of the scientific community, his rancor was directed not so much against Lyell as against his former student and companion. Darwin's teachers had wrought better than they wanted.

What really bothered Sedgwick throughout these decades was not the age of the earth, or even the stability of species, but the direction in which science was going. Geology could go as far as it liked, but some beginning had to remain veiled in the mystery of Creation, and, even more urgent, some crowning achievement of God's will must remain at the other mysterious pole.

> They may varnish it as they will; but the transmutation theory ends (with nine out of ten) in rank materialism; which is as pestilent in the investigations of material science, as is Popery in the discussions of religious truths, and the duties of a religious life. There is a world of mind, as well as a world of matter; and all the materialists on the earth will never bridge over the interval between the two.[23]

Sedgwick was for a while—as much as a geologist could be—a believer in a nearly literal interpretation of the Bible. He was confident that scientific truth and religious truth, both properly understood, could never really conflict.

---

22 Life and Letters of Sedgwick, op. cit., Vol. 2, pp. 410–412. Letter to Dr. Livingstone, March 16, 1865.
23 Ibid., p. 412.

He was also a man who could change his mind. His reaction to Lyell's *Principles of Geology*, the first volume of which appeared at the end of 1830, can be read in two ways. We can see him as defender of the faith, that faith being the general *idea* of Creation, a world with some beginning and undergoing some sporadic changes under the influence of Divine intervention. Or we can see him as man of science, open to new truths, making a major theoretical concession when forced to do so. For in 1831, in his presidential address to the London Geological Society, Sedgwick conceded much to Lyell. He publicly recanted his belief in Noah's Flood as the origin of important geological phenomena; he admitted that there had been a flaw in the argument in the first place, since there was no actual evidence of human remains in the geological deposits formerly ascribed to the action of the Flood. "Having been myself a believer, and to the best of my power, a propagator of what I now regard as a philosophic heresy . . . I think it right . . . thus publicly to read my recantation."[24]

The reader would be within his rights to pay as much attention to Sedgwick's choice of words, still the language of Inquisition—"heresy" and "recantation"—as to Sedgwick's announcement of a change in his views. Lyell had not been able to persuade men like Sedgwick to abandon their fundamental attachment to a cataclysmic creed. The key point for Sedgwick was not the occurrence of this or that geological convulsion, but the belief in forces, always at the disposal of Providence, which could when it pleased Him transform nature in ways and at rates transcending human experience and human understanding. On this point Sedgwick did not yield. For him, there had to be some line that men of science could not cross. On one side of this line—i.e., below it—were observable facts which could be gathered together in higher and ever higher laws.

But only so high. Above the line there was always man and his God-given mind and soul, there was always the possibility of humanly unfathomable Divine intervention.

Moving the line about a bit—to render unto science that which it had wrested back from Creation—cost Sedgwick some pain and even drew some attacks upon him and his like from sterner theological quarters. But he was a scientist, and up to a point open to scientific truth.

There remained the points on which he would not yield. In 1844, when Chambers published, anonymously as we have seen, the *Vestiges of Creation*, Sedgwick led the attack. Darwin felt its weight—Sedgwick was not only a man to conjure with in the scientific community, he

---

24 *Ibid.*, Vol. 1, pp. 370–371.

had also been one of Darwin's mentors. Unknown to Sedgwick, he still was—for Darwin read and thought about every page of Sedgwick's critique of *Vestiges* until he had satisfied himself that *his* theory of evolution could meet all the criticisms.

Sedgwick's 85-page critique of. *Vestiges of Creation*[25] was later widely admitted to be vicious and unfair. But at the time, Darwin went over it with extreme care, and concluded with relief that he could meet Sedgwick's onslaught. In a letter to Lyell he wrote, after reading Sedgwick's endless review, "I think some few passages savour of the dogmatism of the pulpit, rather than of the philosophy of the Professor's Chair. . . . Nevertheless, it is a grand piece of argument against mutability of species, and I read it with fear and trembling, but was well pleased to find that I had not overlooked any of the arguments. . . ." (*LL* 1, 344)

While Darwin's private notebooks have a spontaneous, sometimes slapdash quality, his published writings were produced with extreme care and attention to all possible criticisms. Much good his caution did him in this case. He took fourteen years to perfect his arguments after reading *Vestiges* and Sedgwick's critique. When the *Origin of Species* finally made its appearance, Sedgwick hauled Darwin over the coals just as mercilessly as he had done for Chambers. Darwin wrote to his friend, the American biologist Asa Gray, at Harvard, "Sedgwick . . . has reviewed me savagely and unfairly . . . my dear old friend Sedgwick, with his noble heart is old, and is rabid with indignation." (*LL* 2, 296)

The change in tone from "fear and trembling" to "noble . . . old . . . rabid" is notable. By 1860 history had moved a little. The publication of *Vestiges* had helped it; the arguments against evolution were a little tired, just as Sedgwick had aged; and even the Church had moved a little further toward making an accommodation with the doctrine of perpetual change.

There was an older generation whom Darwin regarded as beyond his reach, but to whom he could be, generally speaking, moderate and kind. It stung him, no doubt, when Sedgwick wrote him in a private letter about the *Origin*, "Parts of it I admired greatly, parts I laughed at till my sides were almost sore; other parts I read with absolute sorrow, because I think them utterly false and grieviously mischievous." (*LL* 2, 247–250)

But Darwin looked mainly to the young to embrace the view of a

---

25 *Edinburgh Review*, July 1845. Sedgwick later expanded this into a book-length attack on *Vestiges: Discourse on the Studies at the University of Cambridge*, 5th ed. (London, 1850). See also *Life and Letters of Sedgwick, op. cit.*, Vol. 2, p. 84, for a striking letter from Sedgwick to Lyell in which he describes at length his "inexpressible disgust" on reading the "foul book."

world evolving: ". . . I by no means expect to convince experienced
naturalists whose minds are stocked with a multitude of facts all
viewed, during a long course of years, from a point of view directly
opposite to mine . . . but I look with confidence to the future, to
young and rising naturalists, who will be able to view both sides of the
question with impartiality." (*Origin*, 481–482)

In spite of these words, Darwin did not give up hope of convincing the older generation of scientists, or at least propitiating them. In
1859 the flyleaf of the *Origin of Species* carried two quotations. Both
were obviously chosen to persuade religious men that they could
accept a causal theory of evolution without giving up their religious
views; or, as Darwin quoted Francis Bacon, men need not refrain from
either "divinity or philosophy [i.e., science]; but rather let men endeavor an endless progress or proficience in both."

The other quotation was from William Whewell's 1833 Bridgewater Treatise, one of the series of eight works by eight authors "on
the power, wisdom, and goodness of God as manifested in the Creation." The passage Darwin chose summarized a particular view of
theology that would leave it relatively intact but relieve it of the
responsibility of intervening in scientific matters: "But with regard to
the material world, we can at least go so far as this—we can perceive
that events are brought about not by insulated interpositions of
Divine power, exerted in each particular case, but by the establishment of general laws." The reservation that this rule of general laws
applies only to "the material world" was intended by Whewell to
exclude the province of mind from the domain of science.

There is something not quite straightforward in Darwin's use of
these quotations, since he almost certainly did not share the views they
stated. They were not his ideas but a possible bridge between himself
and some of his contemporaries; Darwin did not make this distinction
clear.

In his student days Darwin had known Whewell as one of
Henslow's distinguished friends, a fine "converser on grave subjects."
In 1859, when the *Origin of Species* was published, Whewell was
Master of Trinity College, Cambridge. Darwin's attempt to mollify
Sedgwick and Whewell and others of their persuasion had only limited
effect. In a letter to Darwin, Whewell expressed some respect for and
much disagreement with the *Origin*. The disagreement won out:
Whewell would not give the *Origin* a place on the shelves of the
Trinity College library. (*LL* 2, 261)

Charles Lyell was one of the really great geologists of the nineteenth century. Reading his *Principles of Geology*, just published, was
a crucial event in Darwin's life. Not just reading, of course, but

circumnavigating the globe, conducting geological studies wherever he went, using Lyell's books as a guide, taught Darwin the *kind* of geology he needed to know in order to become Charles Darwin, evolutionist.

For the present, our interest is in Lyell's view of the relation between science and religion, the particular style of his stand on controversial matters—in short, the things he taught Darwin about the proper behavior of a man of science possessed of dangerous ideas.

When straightforward matters of science, uncluttered by religious sentiment, were involved, Lyell knew how to be open and bold and generous. For example, when young Darwin returned from the *Beagle* voyage with a new theory of the formation of coral reefs, a theory that contradicted Lyell's own published views, the latter was delighted, and entirely open in his admiration. He was glad to have a colleague and supporter like Darwin. In 1837 he wrote to Sedgwick: "It is rare even in one's own pursuits to meet with congenial souls, and Darwin is a glorious addition to my society of geologists. . . ."[26]

But Lyell could sense the temper of his opposition, and he knew how to trim his sails. His aim was not to assert but to persuade, and he knew that this would take time, much time. He and Darwin became close friends, and from Lyell's own behavior in writing and publishing the *Principles of Geology* we can gather the kind of advice he must have given Darwin.

The first five chapters of Lyell's *Principles* were specifically intended as a review of the history of geology in such a form as to combat the "physico-theological" point of view in which all scientific thought had to be reconciled with religious teachings and often with a literal interpretation of the Bible. Lyell wished to show the harm this approach had done, or, as he put it in a letter to a colleague, to "free the science from Moses." This letter, addressed to another geologist, George Poulett Scrope, and dated June 14, 1830, advises Scrope how he should handle a review he is about to write of Lyell's *Principles,* to gain the maximum advantage for their cause, including the suggestion that it would help if Scrope were to attack Lyell on certain points. Lyell then goes on with his suggestions:

> If we don't irritate, which I fear that we may (though mere history) , we shall carry all with us. If you don't triumph over them, but compliment the liberality and candour of the present age, the bishops and enlightened saints will join us in despising both the ancient and modern physico-theologians. It is just the time to strike, so rejoice that, sinner as you are, the Q[uarterly]. R[eview]. is open to you. If I have said more than some will like, yet I give you my word that full *half* of my history and comments was cut out, and

---

even many facts; because either I, or Stokes, or Broderip, felt that it was anticipating twenty years of the march of honest feelings to declare it undisguisedly. Nor did I dare come down to modern offenders.[27]

Not only did Lyell soften his critique of the history of Mosaic geology for prudential reasons, as shown in his letter to Scrope. Even in his treatment of one crucial geological issue he pulled his punches: on the question of geological time scale, including the age of the earth, although it is very clear that he is referring to periods of many many millions of years, he remains comfortably vague, using such terms as "20,000 years or more" when he has aeons in mind. To us, 20,000 years seems ridiculously short for discussing events on the scale of geological time, but seen in a certain human perspective it was more than enough time: it was more than three times as long as the then widely believed 6,000 years of Biblical time since the Creation.

Lyell was adept at avoiding unnecessary public bitterness in scientific controversy. The tone of his critical review of the history of geology is very moderate and, as he wrote in his letter to Scrope, intended to persuade his contemporaries rather than offend them. In the main he succeeded, although there were a few years of sharp controversy in British geological circles, years when Darwin was away on the voyage of the *Beagle,* convincing himself of the correctness of Lyell's views, and adding greatly to the evidence for them.

In retrospect, it is difficult to see how a man as careful as Lyell, marking as he did the culmination of a major theoretical development rather than its inauguration, need have worried so much about the public reception of his views. But in understanding Lyell's anxiety we should bear in mind how quickly we may be induced to forget certain social realities. Thomas Huxley, in 1888, described well this process of softening harsh memories. Huxley was discussing the furor surrounding the appearance of the *Origin of Species,* as contrasted with the calm way the world, theologians included, could accept the existence of such ideas only a quarter of a century later; "the contrast," he wrote, "is so startling that, except for documentary evidence, I should be sometimes inclined to think my memories dreams." (*LL* 2, 181)

In many ways Lyell was a great supporter of Darwin's. It was he who urged Darwin, in 1856, to write out his views on evolution for publication lest someone else anticipate him, and he was one of a small group (chiefly Hooker, Huxley, and Lyell) who shepherded Darwin through the travails of writing and publishing the *Origin.*

Before the book actually appeared, in his capacity as president of

---

[27] *Life, Letters, and Journals of Sir Charles Lyell, edited by his sister-in-law Mrs. Lyell* (London: Murray, 1881) , Vol. 1, p. 271.

the geological section of the British Association, he gave a very enthusiastic announcement of the forthcoming work. But he was a little slow in publicly announcing his support for Darwin's views. In fact, on September 20, 1859, in his letter thanking Lyell for his announcement, Darwin writes, "I am foolishly anxious for your verdict. . . . I remember the long years it took me to come round." (*LL* 2, 167) Two months later Hooker, an ardent supporter of Darwin's, writes that Lyell has been reading the book: "Lyell, with whom we are staying, is perfectly enchanted, and is absolutely gloating over it." (*LL* 2, 227)

Darwin then writes to Lyell, "I rejoice profoundly that you intend admitting the doctrine of modification in your new addition." (November 23, 1859, *LL* 2, 229). When Lyell's book *The Antiquity of Man* appeared in 1863, Darwin was bitterly disappointed. Lyell did not take a clear stand on the crucial questions. His book included a very able review of the history of evolutionary thought, and Darwin certainly got very fair coverage. In a letter to Hooker, Darwin wrote, with perfect justice, "I am deeply disappointed . . . to find that his timidity prevents him giving any judgment. . . . The Lyells are coming here on Sunday evening to stay till Wednesday. I dread it, but I must say how much disappointed I am that he has not spoken out on species, still less on man. And the best of the joke is that he thinks he has acted with the courage of a martyr of old." (*LL* 3, 8–9)

Darwin wrote and spoke frankly with Lyell of his disappointment, and the two men remained good friends. Lyell may not have gone nearly far enough for Darwin, but *The Antiquity of Man* did suffice to elicit another recantation from Adam Sedgwick. The book may have been pusillanimous with regard to the theory of evolution and conciliatory toward those who still needed to lean on the myth of Creation, but in one respect it was very clear. It made it impossible to go on believing that man had made his appearance on earth only 6,000 years ago.

By the time Lyell wrote *Antiquity*, the time scale of scientific geology was widely accepted, but even eminent geologists still held out for the view that man could be exempted. Lyell's cautious book carried just the right message to persuade scientists still clinging to Biblical time scale as applied to man.

By 1868 Adam Sedgwick, then aged eighty-three, gave his fiftieth annual course of lectures, and announced his conversion, not to the theory of evolution, but to his antagonist Lyell's views on the antiquity of man. He was now "bound to admit that I can no longer maintain the position which I have hitherto held. I must freely admit that man is of a far higher antiquity than that which I have hitherto assigned to him. But, Gentlemen, I shall always protest against that degrading hypothesis which attributes to man an origin derived from the lower animals."[28]

The year 1868 was just the moment when Darwin was coming to terms with the fact that there was no one but himself to write a book like the *Descent of Man*. Lyell's *Antiquity of Man* had fallen far short of Darwin's hopes, and Wallace had made it clear that he did not include man's mind among the natural products of evolutionary processes. Sedgwick's blast confirmed Darwin's knowledge that the threat of harsh criticism came not only from strangers or from an impersonal and abstract public opinion, but also from scientists with whom he had enjoyed a personal bond.

The foregoing examination of Darwin's heritage helps us understand the pattern of his life. From his family tradition and his teachers he took both the corpus of knowledge and the world outlook that determined the main directions of his thought. From the voyage of the *Beagle* he gained the unique breadth of experience and opportunity for self re-education that permitted him so quickly to transcend the thinking of his teachers and contemporaries on such a wide front. But from his grandfather's experience with ridicule and from the cautious attitudes of his teachers toward intellectual progress he formed the basis for his strategy of delayed expression of his ideas. Lyell's prudence on the left, Henslow's moderation, and Sedgwick's thunder on the right all worked together to confirm him in his double delay, first in postponing the publication of his evolutionary ideas, and second in eliminating from the *Origin* his views on man.

These were some of the external sources of Darwin's strength and some of the constraints within which he operated. Now I shall examine the actual workings of his mind as he shaped his life's work and as he pursued his chosen tasks.

---

[28] *Life and Letters of Sedgwick, op. cit.*, Vol. 2, p. 440.

PART II

The Development of
Darwin's Evolutionary Thinking

Charles Darwin in 1854, showing the strain of the long years of delay. *Courtesy of Nora Barlow.*

CHAPTER 5

The Construction
of a New Point of View

Love of the deity effect of organization, oh you materialist! . . . Why is thought being a secretion of the
brain, more wonderful than gravity a property of
matter? It is our arrogance . . . our admiration of
ourselves.

Charles Darwin, C notebook,
p. 166, about May 1838

The ability to look at a situation from more than one point of view
and form a coherent impression synthesizing the results of these different perspectives is not something to be taken for granted. Only rudiments of it can be found in other animals, as in a chimpanzee standing
off from a situation and deciding upon a wholly new and indirect path
to some desired goal. The high development of this ability is an out-
standing characteristic of the human animal. We help ourselves with
all sorts of tools—models, books, conversations—all of which free the
individual from the prison of his own immediate here and now by
bringing to life the perspectives of other times, places, people.

Young children, as Piaget has shown, do not automatically take
the point of view of another. A child looking at a scene, such as a
model of some geographical terrain, believes that another person,
viewing it from a different angle, sees it in the same way as the child
himself. Only by about the age of seven or eight can most children
reliably take the point of view of another in such simple situations.

The study of history is one of mankind's major ways of getting a
fresh perspective on itself. There may still be room for argument as to
whether some species commit suicide, make war, exploit others of their
own kind, marry, cooperate, or speak. But it is safe to say that only one
species on earth studies its own history.

We can look at the development of Darwin's thought from varying time perspectives; for example, we can take a close look at him
struggling with the nuances of a single idea within a brief span of
time, or we can look at the changing interrelations in a wider structure
of ideas over longer spans.

It is important that we vary our perspective. The thinker's pains-
taking attention to the details of one idea may seem like mere fussiness
in a short view; it gains in significance as we understand its relationship with other ideas, possible for us only if we take the longer view.
On the other hand, taking only the long view is like sketching with a
broad brush. Too much detail is lost, and in seeing the specific relation between detail and the general composition of ideas lies our
chance to grasp the individuality of the creative person.

The present chapter runs rather quickly over some of the major
features of Darwin's thought during the eight-year period 1831–39—
the *Beagle* voyage and the period following. In the chapters that
follow we will look more closely at Darwin's thinking in the years
1837–39, the period of both the transmutation notebooks and the
notebooks on man and mind.

While Darwin was circumnavigating the earth during the years
1831–36 a protracted theoretical struggle in geology was drawing to a
close. His own intellectual growth during the voyage must be understood in the light of these theoretical developments back home. As
geological knowledge grew it became increasingly difficult to reconcile
it with the story of Genesis interpreted as one Creation in six days, one
Flood, and a subsequent human history of only a few thousand years.
Among the various proposals that had been advanced to deal with this
dilemma, one approach, catastrophism, was the prevailing idea in
European geological circles during the 1820s. If one Flood could not
account for the geological findings, many floods might: "Life in those
times was often disturbed by these frightful events. Numberless living
things were victims of such catastrophes: some, inhabitants of the dry
land, were engulfed in deluges; others, living in the heart of the seas,
were left stranded when the ocean floor was suddenly raised up again;
and whole races were destroyed forever, leaving only a few relics which
the naturalist can scarcely recognize."[1]

This view was explicitly intended as a new reconciliation of Scripture and Science. Its great exponent in England, Professor William
Buckland of Oxford University, insisted that in two essentials catastrophism confirmed Scripture: the very recent appearance of mankind

---

[1] Georges Cuvier, *Recherches sur les ossemens fossiles,* Vol. 1, pp. 8–9, cited in and
translated by Charles Ç. Gillispie, *Genesis and Geology* (New York: Harper Torch-
books, 1951), p. 100.

on earth and the occurrence of a universal deluge in the not very remote past. In 1824 Buckland was President of the London Geological Society.

Criticism of this diluvial theory mounted rapidly from about 1825. By 1830 the first volume appeared of Lyell's *Principles of Geology, Being an Attempt to Explain the Former Changes of the Earth's Surface, by Reference to Causes Now in Operation*. The title of the book explains the name the theory acquired; *uniformitarianism*, or the insistence that the same natural laws have always operated, are operating, and will operate through all eternity.

Lyell drew charges of heresy from Adam Sedgwick, severe attacks from the pulpit, and some threats of ostracism. In 1831, when he was a candidate for professor of geology in King's College, London, the decision lay in the hands of an archbishop, two bishops, and two laymen. There were some objections to Lyell because of his unorthodox views. But he was appointed.

For several reasons, acceptance of Lyell's views came relatively peacefully. Lyell's synthesis of geological knowledge had been ably foreshadowed by an earlier generation of geologists. There were large classes of geological facts that could not be successfully interpreted within the catastrophist framework. Lyell, as I have discussed in Chapter 4, was both a prudent and a pious man. His theory left room for the occasional intervention of Divine Providence to effect the successive creations of new populations of organic beings to inhabit the earth.

Lyell denied the occurrence of grand physical catastrophes that would suddenly depopulate the earth. But he recognized that even the slow geological changes he insisted upon would gradually reduce the fitness of species which were perfectly adapted to a limited range of milieux. Since he believed that species were mutable only to a very limited degree, he had to invoke the idea of multiple creations to deal with the otherwise inevitable mismatch of organisms and their environments. Such multiple creations also seemed to accord with the growing knowledge of fossil organisms unlike living species.

Lyell's *Principles* included an attack on existing theories of evolution, using a severe criticism of Lamarck as his main object lesson.[2] In 1835 Lyell was elected President of the London Geological Society. In short, Darwin came home from his voyage to a scientific community in which geological uniformitarianism had prevailed but not its theoretical twin, biological evolutionism.

Because it insists upon a steady state universe, uniformitarianism

---

[2] This material was included in Volume 2 of the *Principles* (1832). Darwin's copy of Volume 2 is inscribed, "Charles Darwin. M. Video. Novem. 1832."

might seem to be the antithesis of an evolutionary point of view. Similarly, catastrophism and creationism seem to emphasize change, and might therefore seem to favor evolution. But the central point is that in one view stability is achieved through the uniform operation of natural law, while in the other view change is achieved through Divine intervention. Lyell's approach emphasized long reaches of geological time, complex balances of subtle forces, and a world in perpetual flux. Only over incredibly long periods of time could the world be seen as maintaining a steady state in which change is made and unmade.[3] It was not a very great transformation from Lyell's steady state geological world to Darwin's steadily evolving natural order. Making that small shift and expunging the Creator from the process of change were the twin tasks that were to become Darwin's life work.

The Beagle Voyage: A Journey Through Space and Time. There seems to be little doubt that Darwin hit on the idea of organic evolution through natural selection sometime *after* the five-year voyage of the *Beagle,* but the question remains: when did Darwin first become convinced of the mutability of species and the possibility of evolution? Was it a sudden access of insight on seeing the peculiar variations in the species of the Galapagos archipelago, or was it the result of a slow, stepwise growth of ideas about the whole field of natural history?

Part of the answer to these questions can be found in a study of the neglected scientific notes kept by Darwin during the voyage of the *Beagle.* In addition to the smaller field notebooks that have been described by Nora Barlow,[4] there are 1,383 pages of geological notes and 368 pages of zoological notes, written on large sheets, most of them about 9 by 11 inches. These were generally written shortly after the event. Some are mere transcriptions of field notes and catalogues of specimens. Others are speculative jottings and a few connected essays, especially on geological subjects. One twenty-page essay contains his theory of coral reefs, much as it was later published.

Darwin's major theoretical preoccupations throughout the voyage, including the Galapagos visit and the period following it, were geological rather than zoological. In his geological thought during the first two years of the voyage, Darwin vacillated between catastrophism and uniformitarianism. As he became convinced that Lyell's uniformitarian views were correct, not only did he come to recognize the occurrence of gradual geological change in accord with principles still

---

3 See Martin J. S. Rudwick, "The Strategy of Lyell's *Principles of Geology,*" *Isis,* Vol. 61, 1969, pp. 5–33; Leonard G. Wilson, editor, *Sir Charles Lyell's Scientific Journals on the Species Question* (New Haven: Yale University Press, 1970).
4 Nora Barlow, *Charles Darwin and the Voyage of the Beagle* (London: Pilot Press, 1945).

operative, but he expanded his conception of the time scale on which the history of the earth has unfolded from the Biblical base of 6,000 years to some indefinite number much greater than 20,000 years.[5]

Of special interest is an ornithological notebook in which Darwin, referring to the birds and tortoises of the Galapagos, suggests that the small variations in species from island to island in an archipelago shake his belief in the immutability of species. It would be helpful to know the date of this passage, as it shows Darwin beginning to draw evolutionary inferences from his own field observations. It was probably written in 1836 on the last leg of the voyage home, when Darwin was writing up notes and surveying his experiences as a whole. I should add that even this passage mentions only *mutability*, which is something short of evolution.[6]

Although there is almost nothing of directly evolutionary import in the scientific notebooks, four themes recur often: the difficulty of using a pre-established system of classification to include new species found in new geographical domains or in earlier geological strata; the ecological relations among living organisms; the pleasure of finding new species; and reflecting on the peculiarities of the geographical distribution of species. On the whole, the zoological notes are concerned with cataloguing, classifying, and describing.

All in all, then, it would be a mistake to interpret the few faint suggestions of organic evolution in these notebooks as signifying the important part of Darwin's intellectual development during the *Beagle* voyage. He was during this period first and foremost a geologist—as indeed he wrote repeatedly in his letters home. And at that time geology to him chiefly meant the history of the earth's surface, not of its inhabitants.

Coral Reefs: A Model Theory. If we wish to find the beginning of Darwin's evolutionary thought in the voyage of the *Beagle,* there is something far more interesting than a few vague hints of organic evolution. Darwin worked out a theoretical model that bears a striking *formal* resemblance to his later work on organic evolution. I refer to his theory of the formation of coral reefs, worked out in 1835 when he was still on the west coast of South America. Just as he had speculated on the geology of the west coast while still on the east coast, he now continued to extrapolate westward. Concomitant with the general elevation of the level of the continental land mass, he believed that there must have been a general subsidence of the ocean floor. His

---

[5] For a general discussion of the contents of these notes see H. E. Gruber and Valmai Gruber, 1962, *op. cit.* The MSS are in the Cambridge University Library.

[6] "Darwin's Ornithological Notes," edited by Nora Barlow, *Bulletin of the British Museum (Natural History)*, *Historical Series*, Vol. 2, London, 1963, pp. 203–278. These notes will be discussed in greater detail in the next chapter.

theory of the formation of coral reefs by "the upward growth of the corals during the sinking of the land"[7] is really an extension of this idea.

The two theories (organic evolution and coral reefs) display several basic similarities:

1. Both theories contain a principle of population growth—in the case of coral reefs, the assumption is that the coral organism does not grow beyond some limiting distance from the surface of the sea. In both cases the principle of population growth is described by Darwin as struggle—in the case of coral formations the struggle is, he said, "between the two nicely balanced powers of land and water."[8]

2. Both theories employ a general approach to physical geology, taken together with the principle of population growth, to explain the major facts of geographical distribution. In the case of coral reefs, the hypothesis of a general subsidence of the Pacific floor determines the places in which the coral organism can grow and form reefs.

3. Finally, both theories are capable of generating a continuous series of forms where direct experience had previously revealed only a few classes. In Darwin's words, summarizing his theory: "On this view, the three classes of reefs ought to graduate into each other. Reefs having intermediate character . . . do exist."[9] And later, "Fringing-reefs are thus converted into barrier-reefs; and barrier-reefs, when encircling islands, are thus converted into atolls, the instant the last pinnacle of land sinks beneath the surface of the ocean."[10]

Developing the theory of coral reefs may well have provided Darwin with a simplified model on which to frame his later evolutionary ideas. By the same token, it may explain his preoccupation with a creative geological idea to such an extent that he cast a blind eye at first to the importance of the biological phenomena he observed in the Galapagos and elsewhere during the last year of the voyage.[11]

Oddly, Darwin's first theory of evolution did not parallel his already devised coral-reef theory as closely as did his later ideas. It was as though he had had a deep view of nature, but only in one corner, and needed a few years before he could understand how the same approach applied to the whole.

---

7 *Voyage*, 1845, p. 475.
8 Charles Darwin, *On the Structure and Distribution of Coral Reefs; also Geological Observations on the Volcanic Islands and Parts of South America* (London: Ward, Lock, Bowden, 1890) , p. 24. Originally published 1842–1846.
9 *Ibid.*, p. 78.
10 *Ibid.*, p. 109.
11 For a fuller discussion of Darwin's scientific development during the voyage, and the role of his theory of coral reefs, see H. E. Gruber and Valmai Gruber, 1962, *op. cit.* For the complete text of an early essay giving this theory in its essentials, written during the voyage, see Charles Darwin, *Coral Islands*, transcribed and edited by D. R. Stoddart (Atoll Research Bulletin No. 88, 1962, published by the National Academy of Sciences) .

Monads: Darwin's First Theory of Evolution. These are the essential points in Darwin's first theory of evolution as he wrote it down in the opening pages of his first transmutation notebook in July of 1837: In a changing world, species must change in order to remain adapted; when new species appear, old ones must die out if the number of species is to remain approximately constant. The first requirement would be satisfied if *monads*—i.e., simple living forms—appeared through spontaneous generation from inanimate matter and evolved as the result of direct environmental influences. The second requirement would be satisfied if, in a manner analogous to the death of individual organisms, the monad had a limited life span. Then, when a monad "died," all the species into which it had evolved would die—i.e., become extinct—thus making room for the progeny of new monads.

Darwin soon gave up the monad theory and eventually gave up attempts to speculate about the origins of life, including the reliance on spontaneous generation involved in his monad theory. But that theory led him to formulate one conclusion which remained a hallmark of his thought, the image of the irregularly branching tree of nature.

Perpetual Becoming: Darwin's Second Theory. This was a revision of the monad theory. Darwin gave up the notion of a fixed monad life span and substituted the idea that a species, like an individual, survives in its progeny. Thus, a species lives on if, and only if, it gives rise to other species—that is, if it changes. If not, it dies. Darwin never quite abandoned this view. Rather, it led him on in his persistent search for the causes of change.

The Causes of Variation. From about the fall of 1837 to the fall of 1838 Darwin remained on a plateau, making little apparent progress in theory construction. He was searching assiduously for the causes of heritable variation and seemed to think that the elucidation of those causes would be the essential feature of a theory of evolution. Among various hypotheses that he examined was the view, reminiscent of his grandfather's *Zoonomia,* that hybridization might sometimes cause heritable variations.

His interest in hybridization led him to study the literature of plant and animal breeding. Darwin neither found the causes of variation nor added much to our understanding of hybridization. But his interest in plant and animal breeding led him to deepen his knowledge of artificial selection; eventually this helped him to see the very useful analogy between artificial and natural selection, which formed one of the cornerstones of the *Origin of Species.*

Hereditary Habit. As his search for the causes of variation continued, sometime in about March or April of 1838 Darwin began to think seriously about the possibility that functional changes might precede and induce structural changes. Thus, habits acquired in the life of the individual might be transformed into heritable changes in structure which would become part of the evolutionary course of events. Darwin had always been a keen observer of animal behavior; he now had a profound theoretical motive for pursuing this interest. The second transmutation notebook has many entries on this and related subjects.

Man, Mind, and Metaphysics. By July of 1838 Darwin's interest in the role of behavior in evolution had grown to the point where he began the new set of notebooks dealing chiefly with this question. The initial intent of the M and N notebooks seems to have been to study the inheritance of habits, diseases, and other characteristics acquired during the life of the individual. Darwin's hope was that he could in this way elucidate the causes of heritable variation. But Darwin's interest in mental functions grew and the notebooks became a repository of ideas and information on behavior, memory, emotions, and thinking—in short, the entire gamut of psychological functions as understood by Darwin.

Materialism. When Darwin addressed himself to the evolution of mental functions, he soon became aware that his approach to the relation of mind and body was leading him into philosophic materialism. His awareness of this tendency in his thought, and his fear of the social consequences of it, became explicit by about April of 1838, when he wrote in quick succession: "Mention persecution of early Astronomers . . ." (*C* 123) and "It is of the utmost importance to show that habits sometimes go before structure. . . ." (*C* 124; "go" here means "change.")

Darwin would probably have liked to limit the meaning of his materialism. At one point he wrote, "By materialism, I mean, merely the intimate connection of kind of thought with form of brain.—Like kind of attraction with nature of element."[12] This formulation was not absolutely incompatible with the idea of a designing Creator who had intended the brain to act as the organ of thought. But Darwin knew that even the more restricted form of materialism was a dangerous idea, and he would have quickly sensed that it was leading him toward a more thoroughgoing philosophic materialism.

These themes recur repeatedly in the M and N notebooks. Darwin's fear of persecution because of his ideas is reflected in the dream he recorded on September 21, 1838. Although in 1837–39 Darwin seems to have intended to take a more forthright stand, he never did "mention persecution" in his published writings.

Natural Selection. As a conservative force in nature, working

---

12 Marginal note in Darwin's handwriting in his copy of John Abercrombie, *Inquiries Concerning the Intellectual Powers and the Investigation of Truth,* 8th edition (London: Murray, 1838) , p. 28.

against change, the idea of natural selection was well known before Darwin. The idea crops up repeatedly in his notes, beginning with his remark written in July of 1837 on the role of predators in keepihg a population small and thereby leading to in-breeding within the preyed-upon species. (*B* 7) But it was not until September 28, 1838, that he read Malthus' *Essay on Population;* this prompted him to recognize that natural selection, although it might work against mal-adaptive variants, could also work in favor of occasional variants which were better adapted than their ancestors to the prevailing conditions under which they must survive.

Since Darwin had been exposed to the idea of superfecundity many times before this moment of insight, we must ask: in what way had his thinking changed so that he could now make use of the prin-ciple? The full answer is extremely complex. Some of its main features are as follows. Darwin had abandoned the monad theory and its attendant assumption of continuing spontaneous generation, which was in effect a superfecund alternative to the Malthusian superfecun-dity principle; he had become acquainted with the dramatic rate of reproduction in certain micro-organisms, and was thus better prepared to appreciate the force of Malthus' claim that population growth would be geometrically explosive were it not for the "checks" of war, predation, disease, etc. Finally, Darwin, in his assiduous search for the *causes* of variation, had become deeply acquainted with the *fact* of its ubiquity.

Completion of the Theory. Darwin was now armed with the prin-ciples of superfecundity and ubiquitous variation, and their combined outcome: natural selection. Except for a few passing references he does not, during the period of the notebooks, seem to have made much of the analogy between artificial and natural selection. If he had, he might have appreciated even more fully the explanatory power of the principle of natural selection. As matters stood, he believed that a theory of evolution, to be truly explanatory, must include an account of the causes of variation, and he continued his search. Consequently, the contents of the E notebook, written after the Malthus insight, resemble the notes written before it. Interspersed with a productive exploration of the principle of natural selection and other topics, one finds the same groping, essentially ineffectual search for the causes of variation.

Darwin's dissatisfaction with his theory was reflected in three main ways: the long delay in publishing his work on evolution; an inadequate, faltering attempt to deal with the causes of variation in the opening chapter of the *Origin;* and his unsuccessful theory of pangenesis, advanced in 1863, in which he tried to deal with the genetical problems left unsolved in his theory of evolution.

From 1838 onward, explaining as much of nature as possible by means of the theory of evolution through natural selection remained the central task of Darwin's life. Although it made him extremely uncomfortable, he managed to construct a theory in which heredity and variation operated as essential but unexplained premises. This was a difficult and unstable posture to maintain. There was always the possibility that, if only one did know the causes of variation and the mechanism of genetic transmission, such knowledge would indeed explain evolution and render the process of natural selection secondary or even superfluous. Even in his most concise statements of his theory where he was most successful in keeping heredity and variation in the role of unexplained premises, there is an obvious yearning to go further, to clear up the mystery.

The *Origin,* even in the first edition, begins with a discussion of heredity and variation. In one sense, this is the weakest and vaguest part of the book, largely a confession of ignorance: "The laws governing inheritance are quite unknown . . ." (*Origin,* p. 13) "Variability is governed by many unknown laws, more especially by that of correlation of growth. Something may be attributed to the direct action of the conditions of life. Something must be attributed to use and disuse. The final result is thus rendered infinitely complex." (*Origin,* p. 43)

Given this unresolved group of problems, Darwin always wavered, or better, wobbled a bit. Heredity, variation, and evolution per se were like three components of a system, held together by steel springs. It took strength to keep them apart. In some moods he weakened. The last edition of the *Origin* (1872) is, consequently, a slightly inconsistent book. In some passages Darwin seems to treat both natural selection and the inheritance of acquired characteristics as causes of evolution. In other passages he clearly separates the issues of variation and evolution, but admits that inheritance of acquired characteristics may play a more important role than he formerly thought as a cause of variation. In still other passages, he questions the occurrence of Lamarckian inheritance even as a cause of variation.

The punishment for pioneering is that you can never know exactly where you are. But you must sometimes act as though you think you do. In the main, Darwin's position remained remarkably stable, as given in the last paragraph of the *Origin:*

"It is interesting to contemplate an entangled bank, clothed with many plants of many kinds, with birds singing on the bushes, with various insects flitting about, and with worms crawling through the damp earth, and to reflect that these elaborately constructed forms, so different from each other, and dependent on each other in so complex a manner, have all been produced by laws acting around us. These laws, taken in the largest sense, being Growth with Reproduction; Inheritance which is almost implied by reproduction; Variability from the indirect and direct action of the external conditions of life, and from use and disuse; a Ratio of Increase so high as to lead to a Struggle for Life, and as a consequence to Natural Selection, entailing Divergence of Character and the Extinction of less-improved forms. Thus, from the war of nature, from famine and death, the most exalted object which we are capable of conceiving, namely the production of the higher animals, directly follows. There is grandeur in this view of life, with its several powers, having been originally breathed into a few forms or into one; and that, whilst this planet has gone cycling on according to the fixed law of gravity, from so simple a beginning endless forms most beautiful and most wonderful have been, and are being, evolved." (*Origin*, pp. 489–490) [13]

Darwin's Double Task. In his life work Darwin carried forward two distinct but closely related aims: first, to propose a theory that would explain how evolution occurs; and second, to marshal the evidence that evolution had in fact occurred. The *Origin of Species* is organized in a way that reflects these twin themes. The first five chapters give the basic theory. The topics dealt with are variation under domestication and under nature, the struggle for existence, natural selection, and the laws of variation. The next four chapters deal with difficulties confronting the theory. One of these difficulties was the enormous strain placed on nineteenth-century thought by the proposal that mental functions had evolved in a thoroughly natural fashion; in the *Origin* Darwin treated only the subject of instinct, leaving the higher mental functions for his later works. The next four chapters marshal the evidence for the occurrence of evolution: "the geological succession of organic beings, geographical distribution, mutual affinities of organic beings, morphology, embryology, rudimentary organs."[14]

Beyond a doubt, the *Origin* is a master work precisely because of Darwin's beautiful orchestration of these two themes. For those who were not entirely persuaded by Darwin's theory of natural selection, the fact that *any* reasonably plausible theory could be advanced gave weight to the evidence that evolution occurs. For those who saw gaps in the factual evidence, the theory explained just why such gaps must necessarily occur, so that they almost became evidence for the theory rather than reasons to doubt it.

The construction of the theory and the marshaling of the evi-

---

13 See Peckham, *op. cit.*, especially pp. 422, 747, and 758–9. The only substantial changes in the final paragraphs of the *Origin* were the deletion of the word "external" before the phrase "conditions of life" (5th edition, 1869) , and the insertion of "by the Creator" (2nd edition, 1859) . Regarding the latter, see Chapter Ten, below.

14 These phrases are from the chapter headings of the *Origin*.

dence entailed somewhat different activities on Darwin's part. Theory construction is a matter of rumination and schematization; it is primarily an internal effort, involving play with ideas—information and generalizations—already incorporated in existing schemes of thought; its end product is the alteration of those schemes.

The marshaling of evidence and the construction of general laws from particular facts is largely a matter of observation and data collection, the noting of similarities among events, and the drawing of general conclusions. But this marshaling of evidence is not simply "induction" if that term means a theoretically neutral activity or an activity preceding the construction of a theory. The whole point is that information can *only* be incorporated in existing schemes of thought. When we notice a similarity between events or processes that seem superficially different, we are being guided by a point of view that makes some characteristics important, certain comparisons possible and meaningful. This is what Hanson meant when he wrote, "Observation is a theory-laden undertaking."[15]

The two kinds of task, theoretical and evidential, entail different activities, and in the long run they may yield distinguishable products for our consideration. But *in vivo*, in the life of the thinking person, they are thoroughly intertwined. The most speculative "castle in the air" is triggered off by a simple observation or a friend's remark about his dog. Hard work amassing the facts on a special point is guided by a long theoretical argument with which it may have only a tenuous logical relationship: the theory does not absolutely depend on the facts, nor could the facts ever guarantee the theory. The relation of theory and evidence is not simply logical but psychological.

For example, Darwin's experimental work on the germination of seeds in sea water, mentioned above in Chapter 3, clearly did *not* bear a relationship of necessity and sufficiency to any theory of evolution. He wanted to show that some facts of geographical distribution could be harmonized with the idea of evolution—i.e., a widespread species of plant might have had a single origin and then become diffused if its seeds could have been floated across the sea. This argument requires that certain seeds soaked in sea water must then germinate. But if the seeds do not germinate, Darwin can find other mechanisms of diffusion—indeed, there are many. If the seeds do germinate, it increases the plausibility of the notion of a single origin—but only to someone who is already prepared to reject the notion of creation. To another, an undoubting believer in God's power to create the same species in as many places as He wishes, the appearance of the same creature in widely separated loci presents no special problem, and the germination of sea-soaked seeds is only an isolated curiosity.

---

15 N. R. Hanson, *Patterns of Discovery* (Cambridge University Press, 1958) .

The relation between theory and experiment would be somewhat different if the entire debate were public. After all, a theory is not simply an argument of one man with nature; it is an argument *among* men *about* nature—or, in Darwin's case, about the relation of God and nature. If Darwin had shown how the theory of evolution had led him to the experiment on sea-soaked seeds, his positive results might have changed the structure of the public debate. From the private 1837–39 notebooks we know how theory led to experiment. But in his published papers on this subject, begun in 1843 and printed in 1855 and 1857, Darwin restricted himself to the bare facts, biding his time until 1859 before revealing the full connection of these facts with his evolutionary theory.

He did, however, indicate that the facts bore on "a very interesting problem, . . . whether the same organic being has been created at one point or on several on the face of our globe." He ended the same article on the successful generation of seeds after floating across a salt-water barrier: "But when the seed is sown in its new home then as I believe, comes the ordeal; will the old occupants in the great struggle for life allow the new and solitary immigrant room and sustenance?"[16]

The sense in which experiments form part of an argument among people is neatly conveyed in a letter Darwin wrote to his close friend, the botanist Joseph Hooker. Hooker was one of the very few who knew all along about Darwin's theories and the complex interrelationships among Darwin's many projects and varied levels of thought. In 1855 the two men had been corresponding about the seed-soaking experiments. In answer to a letter from Hooker, Darwin wrote, "You are a good man to confess that you expected the cress would be killed in a week, for this gives me a nice little triumph. The children at first were tremendously eager, and asked me often, 'whether I should beat Dr. Hooker!' The cress and lettuce have just vegetated well after twenty-one days' immersion." (*LL* 2, 155. Letter written April 14, 1855)

Darwin was certainly thinking not only of seeds but of the unity of man, his single origin, and his subsequent dispersal through countless small migrations. In his account of the *Beagle* voyage he alluded to the similarity between seeds and canoes washed up on shores far from their origins. (*Voyage*, 1839, p. 542) Just a few pages before his first mention of the "curious experiment" of soaking seeds in sea water (*B* 125e), he wrote of human migrations, "In first settling a country, people very apt to be split up into many isolated races!" (*B* 119) He, of course, had first-hand knowledge of the sea-faring exploits of the

---

16 Charles Darwin, "Does Sea-Water Kill Seeds?" *Gardeners' Chronicle and Agricultural Gazette*, 1855. Darwin's papers on the germination of sea-soaked seeds are reprinted in Barrett, *op. cit.* The *Origin* has several pages summarizing these experiments.

creature he described as "the most dominant animal that has ever appeared on this earth"; in his survey of human inventions he wrote, "He has made rafts or canoes for fishing or crossing over to neighboring fertile islands." (*Descent,* 48) Even in the *Origin,* one chapter of his lengthy treatment of geographical distribution closes with an analogy between man and other sea-borne creatures carried from one habitat to another: "The various beings thus left stranded may be compared with savage races of man, driven up and surviving in the mountain-fastnesses of almost every land, which serve as a record, full of interest to us, of the former inhabitants of the surrounding lowlands." (*Origin,* 382)

In the present volume I have concentrated almost entirely on Darwin's first strategic aim, theory construction. This leads to an oversimplification which may make it appear as though Darwin's thought was a purely endogenous process. But during the summer of 1837 he was engaged in a great variety of activities related to the subject of the notebooks. Most of his time was probably spent in writing the *Journal of Researches* describing the voyage of the *Beagle.* This work required him to go over his notes and specimens in all fields of natural history. He also completed the practical arrangements for government support of the *Zoology of the Voyage of the Beagle,* which eventually ran to five volumes. The B notebook, for the period from July to September 1837, refers to at least seven conversations, twenty-one books and twenty scientific articles—all used in thinking through the problem Darwin had set himself.

From a methodological point of view, as we have already seen, facts are ambiguous unless linked by a plausible and coherent theory; a theory is weak and empty if it does not unite many important facts; and a new theory is pointless if it does not do its appointed job better than its predecessors.

From a psychological point of view, the individual's engagement in more than one enterprise permits him to continue productive work on one front when he is forced to a halt on another. When these enterprises are related, continued progress in one of them may eventually permit him to move forward in the others. Let us see how this feature of the total economy of thought worked out in Darwin's case.

When he began the transmutation notebooks, clearly he was aiming at a theory that would explain evolution. At the same time, he believed that evolution taken as a *premise* could explain many of the peculiarities of geographical distribution and taxonomic relationships he had come to know so well.

After a few months of hard theoretical work, Darwin had given up the monad theory and had come to doubt the effectiveness of the theory of perpetual becoming. At about the same time, he began to see that if he could not advance on the theoretical front, it was still extremely useful to group facts together under general empirical laws which could best be accounted for by assuming that evolution had occurred. Darwin had actually begun to do this work much earlier, but his first explicit statement of this methodological goal is the remark: "Absolute knowledge that species die and others replace them.—Two hypotheses: fresh creations is mere assumption, it explains nothing further; points gained if any facts are connected." (*B* 104)

Accordingly, the notebooks devote much attention to the searching out of these empirical connections. But Darwin leaves no doubt that his ultimate goal is the construction of an explanatory theory, a theory having the same universality and deductive structure as Newtonian physics.

In a passage summarizing the progress he has made by January or February of 1838, the entire weight of emphasis is on the variety of facts that will be explained if one assumes the correctness of the concept of an irregularly branching tree of nature. But he concludes that all these studies of special groups of facts will "lead to laws of change, which would then be main object of study. . . ." (*B* 228)

As Darwin searched vainly for the causes of variation, he began to think that if he did not find them, his theory of evolution might not get much further than a clear organization of the many facts that the assumption of branching evolution could explain. If so, his theory would be only a small advance over previous efforts. Although he is aware of many differences between himself and Lamarck, now he likens himself to his precursor: "What the Frenchman did for *species* between England and France I will do with *forms*." (*C* 123)

A few months later, on September 7, 1838, just three weeks before his recognition of the evolutionary significance of natural selection, he wrote: "Seeing what Von Buch (Humboldt) G. St. Hilaire, & Lamarck have written I pretend to no originality of idea— (though I arrived at them quite independently & have used them since) the line of proof & reducing facts to law only merit if merit there be in following work." (*D* 69)

By-productive Thinking. In his beautiful book *Productive Thinking,* Max Wertheimer, founder of Gestalt psychology, focused his attention on the kind of direct thinking that goes to the heart of the problem under attack. In Darwin's long and twisting path, however, there are several striking examples of important steps toward the theory of evolution through natural selection being taken as by-products of efforts that seemed to move in other directions. Let us review briefly some of these by-productive moves.

The theory of coral reefs was based on an extrapolation from what

Darwin had learned about the formation of continental mountain chains; if mountains are up-raised, he reasoned, the adjacent sea bed must sink; from this slow subsidence of the sea bed, the coral-reef theory followed. That theory does not deal at all with organic evolution, but it does provide a formal model quite analogous to Darwin's eventual theory. Darwin did not have a five-year *plan* to move through this important sequence of ideas. It evolved.

The monad theory, itself short-lived in Darwin's thought and not entirely original, led him to his branching model of evolution. This became a cornerstone of his thought. During the difficult months when he had dropped the monad theory without yet discovering the natural-selection theory, the branching model guided him in a searching critique of the Quinarian system of classification. The essence of this mystical approach to taxonomy was the notion that there are five major groups of animals, that each group has five subgroups, etc., and that at all levels of classification the groups are ordered in perfect circles of affinity—in other words, a closed arrangement in which each group could be placed between two neighboring groups most resembling it.[17]

It was, of course, important for Darwin to reject the mystical insistence on fives. But more fundamental was his criticism of the closed, regular system of nature. Darwin's system was irregular, open-ended, uncertain in number. His critique of Quinarianism and his development of the branching model stimulated him to organize his ideas about taxonomic affinities, and to reinterpret much of the information then known.

The branching model contains within it the very same formal structure which is the kernel of the Malthusian idea of explosive population growth. The branching diagram depicts an exponential growth function because it shows a series of successive branchings with an increasing number of possible branches as distance from the origin (measured in number of generations) increases. Darwin never explicitly used this way of showing exponential population growth; rather, he used the branching model to show that most of the species that were in some sense possible did not in fact exist—either they were extinct or they never had existed. Thus, although its substance was entirely different, the form of Darwin's early image of the irregularly branching tree of nature foreshadowed his use of the Malthusian principle over a year later.

Darwin's long wrestling match with hybridization did not lead him to a clear explanation of the causes of variation, as he hoped it would. But it did serve to acquaint him with the field of plant and animal breeding and thus with artificial selection, which gave him the

---

[17] See below, Chapter 9, for further discussion of Quinarianism.

nearest thing he had to an experimental version of natural selection.[18]

Similarly, Darwin's abiding preoccupation with the influence of function on form was also part of his search for the causes of variation. It led him to the study of behavior and mind, and the marshaling of the material which gave him the confidence to write his chapter on "Instinct" in the *Origin,* and later the *Descent of Man* and the *Expression of Emotions.* In short, by-productive thinking led him in 1838 to begin the notebooks on man and mind.

I do not intend to suggest that the concept of "by-productive thinking" contradicts Wertheimer's major thesis, which is not so much that thinking is direct as that it is *organized.* This chapter and those that follow are intended to explore just how thinking is organized, and in that sense they carry out part of the program Wertheimer had in mind. But something does emerge in this picture which Wertheimer neglected. Thinking about complex subjects is *organized over time,* over long periods of time; it is organized in major sub-groupings or enterprises; at any given moment, any one of these may wholly occupy the consciousness of the thinking person. Holding the entire complex together, disciplining oneself so that every by-productive moment does not threaten the integrity of the larger structure of enterprise—this struggle for coherence and identity does not come simply from direct perceptual contact with the materials of nature. On the contrary, those materials are so fascinating, and at each moment they lead to such engrossing thoughts and so many enchanting tangents, that we need to introduce another conception to explain how the individual maintains his sense of direction.

That other concept is the individual's sense of purpose: his ability to imagine himself outside the perspective of the moment, to see each sub-task in its place as part of the larger task he has set himself. This abstract purposefulness and perspective, this *standing outside,* is an activity undertaken in quite a different spirit from that in which the creative person immerses himself, loses himself in the material of nature. To accomplish his great synthesis Darwin had to be able to alternate between these two attitudes. To see more deeply into nature, he needed the perceptual, intuitive direct contact with the material. To understand what he had seen, and to construct a theory that would do it new justice, he had to re-examine everything incessantly from the varied perspectives of his diverse enterprises.

---

[18] See Robert M. Young, "Darwin's Metaphor: Does Nature Select?" *The Monist,* Vol. 55, 1971, pp. 442–503. In Young's view Darwin began his studies of domestic breeding in order to demonstrate the tenuousness of the distinction between species and varieties. Young bases his account on Darwin's recollections as given in the *Origin.* The interpretation given above is based mainly on Darwin's early notebooks. While the two views differ, they are not mutually exclusive. In any case, Darwin's knowledge of artificial selection was a by-product of other theoretical interests.

CHAPTER 6

Identity and the Rate of Cognitive Change

This multiplication of little means & bringing the
mind to grapple with great effect produced is a most
laborious & painful effort of the mind . . .

Charles Darwin, C notebook,
p. 75, about March 1838

When we try to understand any process, some conception of the rate at
which it occurs, the range of possible rates, and the relation of rate to
other factors is usually an intimate part of our conception of the
process itself. Many important landmarks in the history of science are
concerned with questions of rate and its inseparable partner, time: the
acceleration of falling bodies, the speed of light, the velocity of the
nerve impulse, and the age of the earth together with its implications
for possible rates and modes of evolution—these are some of the
fundamental notions of science in which rate, time, and the nature of
process are inextricably intertwined.

The stream of thought is incredibly swift, but the emergence and
solidification of new ideas is a relatively slow process. Creative thinking is often treated as an isolated act, but if instead it is treated as a
growth process it may be easier to understand why progress is slow.

To understand the rate of change of scientific thought we need to
consider many things, among them the factors inhibiting change, the
relation between method and rate, and the identity of that which is
changing. This last point inevitably refers to groups of ideas which are
not changing, or which are changing much more slowly than the
change process under scrutiny. Most important of all, a full discussion
of rate of change in a system must take into account the new problems

the system confronts, by virtue both of its own inner development and of its interaction with the larger milieu in which it functions.

Any special system of ideas undergoing change is at all times part of some larger system with which it is interacting, and in such a fashion that change often inhibits further change. Examples of this kind of relationship are the following:

Communication. As the individual departs from accepted patterns of thought, he becomes less capable of communicating with others who have not. But such communication is both the instrument and the goal of change, so that the increase in intellectual distance inhibits further change.

Definition of Problems. As the individual departs from accepted patterns of thought, he moves into areas where basic premises defining soluble problems are less and less clear. Ill-defined problems are hard to solve, and some of them, when clarified, turn out to be insoluble. The time devoted to such matters may be not only unproductive but disruptive as well. Normally, one works within a context that defines soluble problems, and provides methods for solving them and criteria for recognizing solutions.[1] The further one moves from this complex norm, the less likely one is to arrive at an effective solution: change inhibits further change.

Interpretation of Observations. The two examples above illustrate ways in which the very process of change inhibits further change. The existing structure of ideas also protects itself more directly from new elements which might lead to change. Observations which might require change are either neglected or assimilated into existing structures. Thus, even in the face of objective novelty, the existing structure inhibits its recognition, inhibits change. Psychologists have drawn attention to the occasional *non*-perception of anomaly, but have done little to clarify the conditions under which anomaly will be perceived.

Memory. Similarly, a novel achievement is often unstable simply because there exists as yet no structure into which it can be assimilated. It is therefore neglected or even forgotten—but since some change is eventually engendered, the meaning of the term *forgotten* must be considered carefully.

Psychologists have been peculiarly silent on the rate of growth and change of cognitive structures. Gestalt psychology, identified with the notion of sudden insight, seems to suggest that rapid change is characteristic: in *Productive Thinking*, Wertheimer does not actually discuss the velocity of thought, but his illustrations are presented *as though* it occurs directly and quickly.[2]

---

[1] See Thomas S. Kuhn, *op. cit.*

[2] Max Wertheimer, *Productive Thinking*, enlarged edition (London: Tavistock Publications, 1961).

Piaget's studies of the slow growth of cognitive structures in the child have been greeted with several varieties of skepticism, all ·linked to some conception of growth rate. On the one hand, it is said that the child does not reason in a manner qualitatively different from adults: he simply invests his premises with different meanings, so the conclusions are different. This argument, separating form from content, implies that the actual mental structures necessary for logical reasoning are present very early in the life history (i.e., are inborn or grow rapidly), while only the content of adult thought or the language necessary to express it takes long to develop.

On the other hand, it is said that Piaget's results do indeed express the actual course of events, but that the slow development of the concepts Piaget has studied simply reflects the properties of one particular social milieu.

Thus, the first criticism questions the *reality* of Piaget's results, while the second questions their *necessity*. I believe that understanding the complexity and slow tempo of cognitive change in an adult thinking creatively may increase the credibility of Piaget's findings among children.[3]

In the pages that follow I take up the rate of growth of ideas in what may be deemed a "limiting case"—the growth of a new point of view in a highly intelligent individual who is also highly and specifically motivated to change his thinking in a certain direction, and who has had a long and excellent preparation for this task. In his twenty-eighth year Darwin was at the height of his young manhood. He was thoroughly committed to a scientific career. He had all the self-confidence and professional encouragement merited by his magnificent work during the five-year voyage of the *Beagle* (1831-36). He was not yet afflicted by the illness that sapped his energies in later years. Most important of all, he had deliberately set out to develop a theory of evolution.

During the voyage Darwin had had prolonged experience with two conceptual conflicts which prepared him to think about organic evolution. In the first years of the voyage he had assimilated uniformitarian geology; we may assume at least a tacit conflict between this quasi-evolutionary point of view concerning the physical history of the world and his relatively static picture of the organic world as a stable, harmonious order created by Divine Providence. In addition to this disparity between his geological and his biological viewpoints, we find another prolonged conflict—his repeated encounters with anomalous species and peculiarities of geographical distribution that did not fit in with then prevalent ideas of systematic biology.

---

[3] For a compact summary of an immense work, see Jean Piaget and Bärbel Inhelder, *The Psychology of the Child* (London: Routledge and Kegan Paul, 1969).

Let us now look briefly at three incidents in the life of Darwin bearing on the rate of change of ideas.

Darwin in the Galapagos Archipelago. In various writings Darwin emphasized the importance of his experiences during the voyage of the *Beagle* in eventually leading him to think about evolution. In his *Journal* for 1837 he wrote, "In July opened first notebook on 'Transmutation of Species'—Had been greatly struck from about Month of previous March on character of S. American fossils—& species on Galapagos Archipelago. These facts origin (especially latter) of all my views." But he was not *immediately* struck by the small variations in species found in the Galapagos as one moves from island to island. Indeed, if he had been, he might then have assimilated these variations from island to island to a system of ideas in which a Divine Providence would provide slightly different creatures for slightly different milieus. He was struck by his observations only in March of 1836 (or 1837, depending on how one interprets the phrase "previous March"), although he had visited those islands in October of 1835. It therefore required either five months or one year and five months for his thinking to evolve to the point where he could see some significance for evolutionary thought in his Galapagos experiences.

Darwin's Image of the "Tree of Nature." Darwin worked out the branching model, together with many of its implications, early in his 1837–38 notebooks. The irregularly branching "tree of nature" is discussed verbally and illustrated diagrammatically in 1837 and in 1859. It is, indeed, the only illustration Darwin used in the *Origin*. But toward the end of the notebooks the branching model is given much less attention. Two essays, written in 1842 and 1844, sketched his theory of evolution in some detail: the branching diagram is absent.

In his *Autobiography,* written thirty years later, Darwin describes himself as having had the fundamental insight about the nature of evolutionary divergence sometime *after* 1844 (*Autobiography*, 120–121)—yet this was an insight achieved much earlier, in 1837. One plausible conclusion is that Darwin had the same insight *at least twice.* Sir Gavin de Beer has given another interpretation of these facts, but I believe he overlooks the fact that the diagram of the branching model is missing from the 1842 and 1844 sketches: Darwin, in writing the never published treatise "Natural Selection," *inserted* in the chapter on natural selection a long essay on divergence, complete with diagram almost exactly as it appears in the *Origin*. The fact that this is an insertion, written after the rest of the chapter (i.e., after the second occurrence of the insight?), can be clearly seen from the pagination of the manuscript.[4]

Why this lapse? The branching model and the principle of diver-

---

4 Darwin MSS, Cambridge University Library.

gence are mainly concerned with large-scale evolutionary dynamics. The "tree of nature" scheme is exploited to clarify the genealogical relations among many species, both extinct and extant. The principle of selection, on the other hand, is mainly concerned with local forces—what Haldane has called evolutionary statics, or the way in which nature remains at all times in a state of approximate equilibrium.[5] Although the two ideas, divergence and selection, are closely linked, they involve two quite different styles of explanation. In October of 1838 Darwin did not simply discover how to apply the principle of selection. This step, important as it was, formed only part of his development of a broader style of thought in which he focused his attention increasingly on the local "factors" of evolution.

This change in style is reflected in changes in Darwin's imagery. In the notebook passage where he first refers to Malthus he likens selection to "wedging." The wedge image appears in the essays of 1842 and 1844: the struggle for existence is likened to "ten thousand sharp wedges packed close together," splitting the surface of nature. This image persists in the first edition of the *Origin*, then is dropped. In short, Darwin swung over for a time to a one-sided emphasis on local processes, and in so doing actually neglected the existence of the problem of divergence and even his own solution of it. The *Origin* is a more coherent whole than these early efforts, and manages to coordinate both kinds of explanation.

Darwin's Development of the Principle of Natural Selection. Darwin has described the way in which the idea was illuminated for him by his reading of Malthus' *Essay on Population.* Yet the idea occurs in various forms in his notebooks *before* he read Malthus; moreover, he had numerous encounters with it in his reading of other authors, and he had paid considerable attention to domestic breeding and artificial selection before he read Malthus. He was even aware of the analogy between artificial and natural selection. It may be that Malthus' presentation was particularly helpful because of its quasi-mathematical form, or because of its emphasis on the enormous over-productivity of nature without checks upon fecundity, or because of its dramatization of the struggle for existence in his long account of the depopulating effects of human warfare. But none of these aspects of Malthus' thought would have meant anything special to Darwin if his thinking had not developed to the point where he was prepared to assimilate them.

The key psychological point is not so much the moment at which Darwin happened to read Malthus, perhaps quite purposefully or

---

[5] J. B. S. Haldane, "The Statics of Evolution" in *Evolution as a Process,* edited by J. Huxley, *et al.* (London: Allen and Unwin, 1954) .

perhaps for "amusement" as he wrote nearly forty years later, but rather the fact that it took Darwin many years from the time he was first exposed to these ideas to the point in his development when he could use them in an evolutionary theory.

The above interpretation of the role of Malthus in Darwin's thought is borne out by reference to the development of Alfred Russel Wallace's ideas. He too stressed the influence of Malthus in helping him suddenly to grasp the idea of natural selection. But, unlike Darwin, Wallace was *not* reading Malthus at the critical moment. He had read Malthus *fourteen years before*. Thus, Wallace remembered Malthus only when his thinking about evolution had matured to the point where the Malthusian principle could be assimilated into the system he was constructing.[6]

This example illustrates the way in which novel ideas can be forgotten until the structure of which they are to become a part is sufficiently complete to stabilize them. But there is another point as well. Let us take seriously these two coincidences in the lives of Darwin and Wallace: both men were stimulated to think about evolution through their contacts with an archipelago—in which a small-scale model of evolution is nearly visible; and both ascribe a significant part of their solution of the theoretical problem to their reading of Malthus. In both cases we see a synthesis of something immediate and something remembered. Wallace was actually in his archipelago when he had his great insight, but he had read Malthus fourteen years before. Darwin was far from his archipelago, but he was reading Malthus at the time of his insight.

In Darwin's case we have positive evidence that the same, or nearly the same, thought had occurred to him before, but less forcibly, not with the subjective quality of a "Eureka!" experience. Wallace too went through a long growth process, during which he was searching for an evolutionary theory, probably over a longer period of years than Darwin.[7] In both cases, then, we see that the external stimulus is

---

[6] A. R. Wallace, *My Life: A Record of Events and Opinions* (London: Chapman and Hall, 1905), Vol. 1, pp. 232, 240, and 361. In one place Wallace gives twenty years as the interval between reading Malthus and having the insight as to its relevance for evolution; in another place twelve years. From the fact that he describes his reading of Malthus as occurring in 1844 and his insight as occurring in 1858, fourteen years seems to be correct.

[7] In 1955 Wallace wrote and published a paper in which he concluded: "Every species has come into existence coincident both in space and time with a pre-existing closely-allied species." See A. R. Wallace, "On the Law Which has Regulated the Introduction of New Species," *Annals and Magazine of Natural History*, 1855; A. R. Wallace, *My Life*, Vol. 1, p. 355. In retrospect, we can say that this paper was part of Wallace's long, groping search. For a good account of Wallace's efforts during the years 1845–58 see H. L. McKinney, "Alfred Russel Wallace and the Discovery of Natural Selection," *Journal of the History of Medicine and Allied Sciences*, 1966, Vol. 21, pp. 333–357.

effective in shaping the development of thought, but it can be effective only in ways that are constrained by the developing thought process itself.

This picture suggests a circle in which the new evidence cannot develop until the evidence has been perceived. In some respects this is true, but it is not a *vicious* circle. Thought, like all other biological processes, must strike an effective balance between adaptive stability and adaptive variation. There is nothing necessarily creative in being immediately trapped by every original thought one has. There is something to be said for holding it in a kind of neutral storage for a while, and using it if and when it becomes assimilable to some valid structure. This restraint might be likened to the maintenance of a reservoir of variability in the gene pool of a population, in the form of recessive mutants. Although they are often harmful when they first appear, the population is protected from them by their recessivity; when the milieu changes so that they are now favorable, individuals displaying the deviant characteristic may multiply rapidly. Moreover, changes in the gene-complex may permit the initially recessive gene to evolve toward dominance.

Just so, forgotten ideas are not really lost: they are reactivated when useful. Similarly, an intellectual achievement even when half forgotten may help to change the intellectual system of which it is a part so that the next time the same insight occurs it has a better chance of solidifying. Isolated ideas of considerable originality may be emitted fairly rapidly. The reconstruction of a coherent system of ideas is probably a much slower process. Effective creative thinking requires a balanced relation between these two kinds of process.

Like any other growing thing, a system of thought must change and yet retain its identity. Like any other life process, creative thinking depends on a delicate balance among many factors, organized as a functioning whole. What we too easily call "scientific method" is actually a repertoire of methods for optimizing the growth of ideas about nature. To do this, the scientist or, better, the scientific community must satisfy a number of criteria. The new ideas being developed must be substantiated and applied in solving both old and new problems; they must be successfully communicated and eventually accepted as superior to competing ideas; they must expand our vision of nature, and give greater coherence to our appreciation of the world.

Not all novelty is good. A scientific way of thought is a way of generating and testing novel ideas, and of assimilating them into the corpus of human knowledge. Granting all this, there is nevertheless considerable room for debate about the optimal strategy for advancing knowledge in a particular domain of nature at a particular moment in human history. The subject is made more difficult by the fact that the individual thinker can rarely give a correct account of his own thought processes, and, as the present state of Darwin studies shows, it may take a century or more even to attempt a thorough examination of a well-documented discovery. To make matters even more confusing, the individual scientist may react defensively if he senses a discrepancy between the way he actually works and the ways considered proper by his contemporaries.

Especially in Darwin's day, before the advent of our present emphasis on wholistic, unconscious, and intuitive ways of knowing, the only legitimate choices available to the empirical scientist seemed to lie between straightforward movement from facts to simple laws and from simple laws to more general laws, or, on the other hand, movement along the same continuum but in the opposite direction.

The relation between legitimate scientific method and acceptable rate of change in thought was expressed quite clearly in 1845 in John Herschel's presidential address to the British Association for the Advancement of Science. Herschel was an important figure, as one of the most influential scientists of his day, and as a middle-ground person receptive both to Whewell's *a prioristic* logic and Mill's newer radical empiricism. He played a role in Darwin's life. His book *A Preliminary Discourse on the Study of Natural Philosophy*[8] is one of two works (the other being Humboldt's *Personal Narrative*)[9] which most inspired Darwin toward a scientific career during his final year at Cambridge. (*Autobiography*, 67) Darwin met Herschel in South Africa during the *Beagle* voyage, and later on saw him in London.

In his address Herschel spoke of the need to keep ultimate principles of religious faith "sacred from question," and to combine "working our way *upwards towards* those principles as well as *downwards from them*. . . ." He also cautioned against too rapid a movement away from the accepted idea that science is the discovery of objective truth and toward the positivistic view of scientific knowledge as nothing but a provisional human construction: too rapid change in this direction would lead to "a kind of intoxication, which precludes all rectilinear progress. . . ." He objected strenuously to the positivistic rejection of the idea of *cause* and the substitution of the idea of *law*. He objected to theories of evolution which express a general law of development because a truly causal explanation could not be offered. Without such

---

[8] Sir J. F. W. Herschel, *A Preliminary Discourse on the Study of Natural Philosophy* (London: Lardner, 1831) .

[9] Alexander von Humboldt and Aimé Bonpland, *Personal Narrative of Travels to the Equinoctial Regions of the New Continent, 1799–1804,* 6 vols. (London, 1819) . See also Paul H. Barrett and Alain F. Corcos, "A Letter from Alexander Humboldt to Charles Darwin," *Journal of the History of Medicine and Allied Sciences,* Vol. 27, pp. 159–172, 1972.

an explanation, the transition from inanimate matter to evolving living matter is "as *miraculous* as the immediate creation and introduction upon earth of every species and every individual would be."[10]

The pandemonium of Darwin's notebooks and his actual way of working, in which many different processes tumble over each other in untidy sequences—theorizing, experimenting, casual observing, cagey questioning, reading, etc.—would never have passed muster in a methodological court of inquiry among Darwin's scientific contemporaries. He gave his work the time and energy necessary to permit this confusion to arise, at the same time persistently sorting it out, finding what order he could. It was an essential part of this "method" that he worked at all times within the framework of a point of view which gave meaning and coherence to seemingly unrelated acts.

Insofar as he said anything publicly on the subject of method, Darwin presented himself in ways that are not supported by the evidence of the notebooks. In the *Origin* he wrote that, after becoming interested in the subject of evolution, "it occurred to me, in 1837, that some thing might perhaps be made out on this question by patiently accumulating and reflecting on all sorts of facts which could possibly have any bearing on it. After five years' work I allowed myself to speculate on the subject, and drew up some short notes. . . ." (*Origin*, 1)

In *The Expression of Emotion in Man and Animals,* published in 1872, he also described himself as having conformed to the accepted canons of inductive science, withholding larger judgments until justified by a fullness of observation: "I arrived, however, at these three Principles only at the close of my observations." (*Expression,* 1) Actually, they all occur in the M and N notebooks, written in 1838–39.

Some interpretations of Darwin's views on method may result from a schoolmasterish desire to use Darwin for a simplistic cautionary tale, aimed at persuading restless young spirits to look before they think (better described as the rule of "listen, look, and stop"). And some of the confusion results from the fact that Darwin never wrote a systematic treatise on method, so that his stated views are only scattered comments on varying aspects of a very complex process. But some of the misunderstanding arises from Darwin's desire to defend his unpopular views by suggesting that he had been driven to them by a mass of unassailable evidence, rather than the less acceptable reality that much of his evidence had been indeed patiently assembled, but only after his views were quite well developed.

---

10 John F. W. Herschel, "The Logic of Scientific Endeavor," Presidential Address to the British Association for the Advancement of Science, 1845; reprinted in *Victorian Science: A Self-Portrait from the Presidential Addresses of the British Association for the Advancement of Science,* edited by G. Basalla *et al.* (Garden City, N.Y.: Anchor Books, 1970).

Hints of the pressures under which Darwin labored may be gleaned from his letters. In 1861 he wrote to a Cambridge political economist, Henry Fawcett: "About thirty years ago there was much talk that geologists ought only to observe and not theorise. . . . How odd it is that anyone should not see that all observation must be for or against some view if it is to be of any service!" (*ML* 1, 195) In 1863 he wrote to an Edinburgh botanist, John Scott: "*let theory guide your observations,* but till your reputation is well established be sparing in publishing theory. It makes persons doubt your observations." (*ML* 2, 323)

Darwin's granddaughter Nora Barlow has given an excellent summary of Darwin's remarks on method, but on one point I disagree with her. She suggests that in early life there was a closer intertwining of theory and observation in his work, and that later on he accepted their partial separation and was more inclined toward "speculation." (*Autobiography,* 149–166) It seems to me that even in these early notebooks, which form the main material of the present work, he delighted in far-ranging speculations and saw himself as creating ideas of the same grandeur and cosmic scale as the "early astronomers" to whom he likened himself.

If scientific thought moved more swiftly, perhaps we could single out a characteristic type of sequence of great creative import, such as "first theorize, then observe"—or the reverse. But in a long process, carried out by a living person, many different sorts of acts occur repeatedly in different sequences, and, since each act may itself be prolonged and interrupted by other acts, important acts sometimes occur in parallel with each other, extended over the same period of time.

When we speak of a complex system, such as a person or other organism, maintaining its identity while undergoing change, we have in mind certain invariants, important aspects of the system that do not change during the period in question. In developing a clear picture of the amount of change that does take place in a system of ideas, we need to have some idea about what it is that does not change. This is a difficult question to tackle because in a mature person the inventory of things that are *not* fundamentally changed is very long. Indeed, the list would be a good description of the person's cultural heritage, and also of those skills and concepts which are well nigh universal in the human repertoire, such as certain elementary ideas about objects, space, time, and causality.

In discussing Darwin's "family *Weltanschauung*" I dealt with some of these issues, but there I was primarily concerned with ideas shared by Charles and Erasmus Darwin. Some of these ideas were so general that they can hardly be said to enter directly into a scientific theory, forming, instead, the background for it. Now I want to review briefly a group of ideas which formed an explicit part of his eventual theory and which can be identified in the forefront of his consciousness at some specifiable moment early in his development. These ideas appear not in isolation from each other but in closely organized groups. These remain more or less intact even though the larger system of which they are a part changes appreciably; I therefore call them *invariant groups.*

I have already discussed the image of the irregularly branching tree of nature, which appeared in his first notebook on evolution in 1837 and survived as the only diagram in the *Origin.* A closely related idea is the "conservation principle." In its first form, as I shall discuss in greater detail in the next chapter, what Darwin presumed would be conserved is the approximate *number of extant species;* in his eventual theory this version was supplanted by the idea that what is generally conserved is the approximate *number of individuals of one species.* We can choose to focus our attention on the fact that something in Darwin's thinking changed, or that something remained invariant. In either form, the link between the branching image and the conservation principle is accomplished through some scheme for the reduction of number. Since the branching model is an image of exponential increase, if number is to be conserved something must be eliminated. Darwin wove these elements together in different ways at different times, but they remain an invariant group which may be called the "conservation schema": irregular branching with potential for rapid increase, reduction of number leading to conservation of number. The conservation schema, of course, expresses a commitment to search for continuity in nature—continuity of space, time, form, and cause. But continuity is a vaguer idea. After all, we can think childishly of continuous growth and change, without facing the question: what is conserved?

There is a second invariant grouping which appeared somewhat earlier in his thinking, the concept of adaptation as a steady state linked with the concept of adaptive change to compensate for environmental change. Its first clear-cut appearance was in the coral-reef theory. The coral organism is adapted to flourish within a certain distance of the surface of the ocean; as the ocean bottom sinks, the coral organism flourishes at a new level. The interplay of these factors accounts for the varying forms of coral reefs. Some change in the form of that living entity which is adapting necessarily results from all such interactions of mutually compensating forces. Since the forces in question are thought of as changing smoothly rather than in sudden steps, the production of a continuous series of adaptive forms is implicit in this interplay. This invariant group may be called the "equilibration schema": adaptation, adaptive change, and continuous series of forms. Although this group made its first coherent appearance as a group in

Darwin's creative thought in his coral theory in 1835–36, some of its components were important to him earlier.

The idea of adaptation as such is something which flows all through the thought of Paley, whom Darwin admired so much, and permeated the thinking of everyone studying natural history during Darwin's Cambridge days. As I have discussed, it was the central theme of the argument from Design.

The idea of continuity in nature occurs in many places in the history of human thought. *Natura non facit saltum*—nature makes no jumps—was a guiding motto for generations of evolutionists and proto-evolutionists. But Darwin encountered it in a sharp and interesting form, posed as an alternative of terrible import: nature makes no jumps, but God does. Therefore, if we want to know whether something that interests us is of natural origin or supernatural, we must ask: did it arise gradually out of that which came before, or suddenly without any evident natural cause?

We can, of course, ask this question about anything in the natural world. We can also ask it about the very idea of God. And it was in this form that Darwin encountered the question, while a student at Cambridge. Among the pages of his student notes that survive, there are a few sheets outlining the argument of *The Evidence of Christianity Derived from Its Nature and Reception* by John Bird Sumner, then Bishop of Salisbury, later to become Archbishop of Canterbury.

Sumner wanted to deal as logically and factually as possible with the question of the origin of Christianity. Was Jesus divine and were his teachings of divine origin, or was Jesus human and were his teachings merely human inventions, either his own or his followers? Sumner's central argument rests on a simple proposition cast in a specific logical form: nature makes no jumps, therefore if something is found in the world that appears suddenly, its origins must be supernatural. The argument for the divine origin of Christianity, then, requires examination of the historical evidences for its sudden appearance without apparent cause in the motives of people as they were known to be at the time of its origin. Sumner argued that the character of Christian morality represented a sharp discontinuity with its Jewish and all other predecessors, that the rapidity of the spread of Christianity was unprecedented: "If Christians were known as a tangible body in Rome, upon whom a popular stigma might be attached, within thirty years of the death of Jesus . . . it is quite clear that the system was not gradually formed, but regular and authoritative from the first."[11]

Darwin made a chapter-by-chapter outline of Sumner's *Evidence*.

---

11 John Bird Sumner, *The Evidence of Christianity Derived from Its Nature and Reception* (London: Hatchford, 1824), p. 20. Darwin paraphrased this passage quite closely in his notes.

Among his notes there is the following passage: "When one sees a religion set up, that has no existing prototype, demanding such a life as is held in the lowest esteem, and yet most suitable to its object it gives great probability to its divine origin."[12]

In other words, sometime in his Cambridge years, 1827-30, Darwin took cognizance of the proposition that in order to show something is of natural origin it must be shown that it evolved gradually from its precursors, otherwise its origins are supernatural. This formulation of the choices open to rational men remained a *leitmotif* throughout his life. The particular choice he made changed drastically, as did the content with which he invested the logical structure of the proposition. But the structure of choice remained invariant.

The passage just quoted is interesting for another reason. It contains a clear reference to the argument from Design.[13] Obviously, the "argument from discontinuity" would lose its force if the entity whose sudden origin or creation is to be explained did not exhibit beauty or ingenuity adapted to some purpose, the hallmarks of Design. Darwin's life work became the demonstration that adaptation could be demonstrated without discontinuity.

To sum up, it took Darwin his adolescent years to assimilate the family *Weltanschauung* that led him from Edinburgh to Cambridge, where he became "the man who walks with Henslow." It took him the five years of the *Beagle* voyage to revise his thinking about nature,

---

12 Darwin MSS, Cambridge University Library. This passage is very similar in wording to Sumner, *op. cit.*, p. 164, in his chapter on the "Originality of the Christian Character."

13 Sumner was among those who attempted to link Natural Theology and the Malthusian principle of population with a moral justification of the class structure of society, not excepting the existence of poverty and starvation. In an earlier work Sumner included a chapter entitled "On the Principle of Population, and its Effects: intended to show that Man is inevitably placed in that Condition which is most calculated to improve his Faculties, and afford Opportunities for the Exercise of Virtue." The same volume had one appendix entitled "That the Mosaic History is not inconsistent with geological discoveries," and another, "On the Descent of Mankind from a single Pair." In the latter Sumner drew on the evidence of artificial selection in plants and animals, "selection of the subjects most remarkable for the quality which it is desired to improve." But he used this evidence only to establish the plausibility of human races widely different in appearance originating from a single pair. Concerning the origin of human races he spoke only of a universal "tendency to variety in the midst of general uniformity, and some secret law of nature by which accidental varieties become permanent and hereditary." John Sumner, *A Treatise on the Records of the Creation, and on the Moral Attributes of the Creator; with particular reference to the Jewish History, and to the Consistency of the Principle of Population with the Wisdom and Goodness of the Deity*, 2 volumes (2nd edition, London: Hatchard, 1818). There is no record of Darwin's having read this book, but its content, written by an author whom Darwin did read and pay attention to, shows how much of his thinking comprised an argument with his contemporaries, in which the same general ideas were worked and reworked in different patterns.

assimilate Lyell's ideas, and develop one highly original theory in which one of these invariant groups, the equilibration schema, played a central role. By the end of that period he was also able to see the dilemma posed by the conception of a changing world populated with well-adapted but unchanging organisms. In the fifteen months from the time he posed this issue sharply to himself, he was able to utilize the combination of the conservation schema and the equilibration schema to generate the main outlines of his theory of evolution through natural selection.

A. 1832 and before: The Creator has made an organic world (*O*) and a physical world (*P*) ; *O* is perfectly adapted to *P*.

B. 1832–1834: The physical world undergoes continuous change, governed by natural laws as summarized in Lyell's *Principles of Geology*. In other respects, *B* resembles *A*.

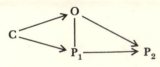

C. 1835: The activities of living organisms contribute to the evolution of the physical world, as exemplified by the action of the coral organism in making coral reefs. In other respects, *C* resembles *B*.

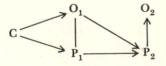

D. 1836–1837: Changes in the physical world imply changes in the organic world, if adaptation is to be maintained; the direct action of the physical milieu induces the appropriate biological adaptations. In other respects, *D* resembles *C*.

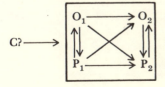

E. 1838 and after: The physical and organic worlds are both continuously evolving and interacting with each other. The Creator, if one exists, may have set the natural system in being, but He does not interfere with its operation, standing *outside* the system.

Darwin's changing world view.

It would be good to know how these invariant groups arose. About the best I can do at the moment is to say that they were all present very early in Darwin's thinking and that they remained a part of him throughout his lifetime.

To understand how he spent this time, one must come to see that these invariant groups are very general, flexible structures. They can encompass more than one theory, depending in part on factual issues and in part on the particular way in which they are interwoven. It is time now to see what Darwin did when he constructed his first theory of evolution.

CHAPTER. 7

Darwin's First Theory of Evolution: Monads

Tempted to believe animals created for definite time: —not extinguished by change of circumstances.

Charles Darwin, "R.N." notebook, p. 129

This is a notebook of uncertain date, but perhaps stretching from a period somewhat before the B notebook to sometime late in 1837. It is mainly on geological subjects, including plans for some of Darwin's early papers. But Darwin's geological thinking touches on fossils and extinction, which probably accounts for the intrusion of an idea from his monad theory in this notebook. Physically similar to the BCDE notebooks and the M and N notebooks, it is kept at Down House.

In the discussion up to this point we have been dealing mainly with the movement of individual ideas: archipelagoes as micro-evolutionary systems, the branching model of evolution, and the principle of natural selection. We have looked at each idea as it waxed and waned over fairly long time periods, ranging from months to years. Even in order to do this much, we have had to consider each idea in relation to its place in some more general set of Darwin's ideas.

To examine more closely the relation of an idea to the structure of the argument of which it is a part, one must look at the structure of that argument—i.e., what Darwin thought at a moment in time. It is difficult enough, as any student of logic knows, to grasp the interrelationship among a stable group of ideas. Here the difficulty is compounded because we are dealing with a creative thought process, a changing structure of ideas. We can simplify somewhat by neglecting certain features of the argument, but too much simplification will destroy the argument itself. If the reader wishes to go further into the creative growth process, he must wrestle with some complexity at this point.

My *intent* is to describe the structure of an argument at one moment in time, including its unstable and changing features. The *method* of relying on whatever Darwin made explicit in his notes and published writings sometimes requires me to look beyond the moment of thought I am trying to describe: by seeing where someone has been before and after the moment in question, we get a better picture of where he is going at that moment.

To understand Darwin's first theory of evolution, it is important first to have as clear as possible a grasp of the progress he had made toward becoming an evolutionist during the voyage of the *Beagle*. I have referred before to a passage in his ornithological notes. In discussing the fauna of the Galapagos archipelago, 500 miles west of Ecuador, he draws attention to the slight variations between closely related forms found on neighboring islands, especially the different kinds of tortoise and finch:

> In each Isld. each kind is *exclusively* found: habits of all are indistinguishable. When I recollect, the fact that the form of the body, shape of scales & general size, the Spaniards can at once pronounce, from which Island any Tortoise may have been brought. When I see the Islands in sight of each other, & possessed of but a scanty stock of animals, tenanted by these birds, but slightly differing in structure & filling the same place in Nature, I must suspect they are only varieties. The only fact of a similar kind of which I am aware, is the constant asserted difference between the wolf-like Fox of East & West Falkland Islds.—If there is the slightest foundation for these remarks the zoology of Archipelagoes—will be well worth examining; for such facts would undermine the stability of Species.[1]

Nora Barlow has urged the view that the ornithological notes were all "written with the red-hot memory of the living bird,"[2] representing a sudden insight soon after the material encounter. Gertrude Himmelfarb, on the other hand, has argued that the retrospective character and certain internal evidences of the ornithological notes suggest that "the whole was composed after Darwin's return from the voyage."[3] Gavin de Beer has also singled out this passage for attention. He does not question Nora Barlow's dating of the passage, but he does recognize its ambiguity: "It was in this condition of doubt about the fixity of species that Darwin returned to England. . . ."[4]

---

[1] *Darwin's Ornithological Notes, op. cit.*, p. 262. The Falkland Islands are 500 miles northeast of Cape Horn. The *Beagle* had sailed there twice during the voyage, in 1833 and in 1834.

[2] *Ibid.*, p. 204.

[3] Gertrude Himmelfarb, *Darwin and the Darwinian Revolution* (London: Chatto and Windus, 1959).

[4] De Beer, *op. cit.*

Despite the apparent differences among these authors, they resemble each other on two related points: their idea that Darwin's conversion to the theory of evolution, whenever it did occur, was relatively sudden, and their failure to pay attention to the character of Darwin's first theory of evolution. When both points are examined carefully, the appearance of sudden insight gives way to a more gradual reorganization of thought. Michael Ghiselin has also discussed this passage, and has come to a conclusion similar to mine about Darwin's development during the voyage. But, in the interest of examining Darwin's life work as a whole and his role in the history of ideas, he skips quickly over the years 1837–39, and therefore blurs the distinction between Darwin's early ideas about evolution and his ideas as expressed in the *Origin*.[5]

How much the meaning of an idea depends on the whole argument of which it is a part can be seen well in Captain Robert Fitz-Roy's published account of the voyage of the *Beagle*.[6] FitzRoy was a moody, difficult person with whom Darwin and everyone else quarreled occasionally. But FitzRoy was Darwin's messmate for five years, named a mountain and a sound in Tierra del Fuego after him, praised him for his courage, and urged him to publish his *Journal of Researches*.

In his book FitzRoy touched on many of the issues that Darwin thought about, used some of the same evidence, and proposed some of the same ideas. But he wove it all together in an entirely different argument. He wrote two concluding chapters, one "on the origin and migration of the human race," and the other on the "Deluge." He defended an absolutely literal interpretation of the Bible: creation in six twenty-four-hour days, one and only one Creation, the Flood and the Ark, and the subsequent dispersal of the survivors to repopulate the earth after the waters had subsided. He was a dogmatic zealot but he respected learning. Indeed, Darwin's copy of Lyell's *Principles* carries a pencilled notation inside the front cover of Volume I: "Given me by Capt. F. R. C. Darwin."

FitzRoy saw Darwin's fossils, read some geology, and in general felt a need to cope with the evidence of change. To account for the evidence of extinction, he believed that not all kinds had gotten into the Ark. To account for the existence of a greater variety of creatures than seemed a plausible number of occupants of the Ark, FitzRoy

---

5 Ghiselin, *op. cit.*
6 Captain Robert FitzRoy, *Proceedings of the Second Expedition, 1831–1836*, which is Volume II of the *Narrative of the Surveying Voyages of His Majesty's Ships Adventure and Beagle Between the Years 1826 and 1836, Describing Their Examination of the Southern Shores of South America, and the Beagle's Circumnavigation of the Globe*, 3 vols. (London: Colburn, 1839).

proposed that the species had altered since the Flood: "There is abundant proof that animals have changed their habits, shape, coat, colour, or size, in consequence of migration, or transportation to different climates; therefore we cannot tell, from what is now seen, what alterations have taken place since their second dispersion."[7]

In his view, mankind was "created perfect in body, perfect in mind."[8] To account for the "degraded condition" of the primitive people encountered during the voyage, he believed in a gradual deterioration of some of the descendants of Abraham in their troubled wanderings after the Flood. And so on and on—every evidence of adaptive change could be incorporated within the story of Genesis and its foreordained aftermath.

To understand the possible meanings of Darwin's phrase "such facts would undermine the stability of species," we must now do our best to place it in its context by examining his thinking as a changing, coherent structure.

In order to reconstruct some of Darwin's thinking toward the end of the voyage, we need a few clear benchmarks. While he was in the Galapagos, and shortly after, he was not nearly so "struck" by their fauna as he was in retrospect. Both his geological notes and his zoological notes for that period were more copious than his average for the voyage as a whole. But the geological notes on the Galapagos are more than three times as long as those on zoology. Darwin, on first viewing those islands, was far more interested in their peculiar volcanic formations than he was in the peculiarities of their organic forms.[9] His preoccupation with the geology of archipelagoes had a direct connection with his theory of the formation of coral reefs. Indeed, he mentions this point in his first essay on reefs, written between December 3 and 21, or two months after leaving the Galapagos.[10]

On January 18, 1836, while still in Australia, he made an entry in his diary which shows him reflecting on the following matters: that the fauna of Australia is so unusual; that, as everywhere else in the world, the adaptation of each organ to its function and each organism to its circumstances is so beautiful; and that, in spite of the differences, there are striking similarities between creatures to be found in widely separated places. These reflections tempt him to conclude that there must have been separate creations, that there must have been one Creator—and, from the geological evidences, he would add that the separate

7 *Ibid.*, p. 672.
8 *Ibid.*, p. 650.
9 Darwin MSS, Cambridge University Library. See H. E. Gruber and Valmai Gruber, *op. cit.*
10 Darwin, *Coral Islands, op. cit.*

creations must have occurred at different times: "The one hand has surely worked throughout the universe. A Geologist perhaps would suggest that the periods of Creation have been distinct & remote the one from the other; that the Creator rested in his labor."[11]

These are the ideas of a *non*-evolutionist thinking about some of the facts that would later lead him to become an evolutionist. More exactly, these are the ideas of Charles Lyell, who endorsed the hypothesis of multiple creations in order to avoid taking the evolutionary high road.

Theoretically, as Darwin became converted to Lyell's geology, he must have felt the tension between two contradictory ideas, a slowly evolving physical world and an unchanging, well adapted creation of species inhabiting it. If the world changed, how could its inhabitants remain both unchanged and well adapted? Empirically, Darwin's extensive encounters with fossil remains of extinct organisms bespoke earlier "creations," presumably adapted to their physical world. For such reasons Lyell had adopted the hypothesis of multiple creations, in which the earth was repeatedly repopulated with creatures adapted to their stations. In the passage quoted, we see Darwin accepting the same idea.

While still in Australia, in January 1836, Darwin wrote a letter to Henslow which reflects his preoccupations as I have described them, devoting twice as many lines to the geology of the Galapagos as to their fauna and flora. It is true that he alludes to questions about the archipelago that were later to become part of his evolutionary argument, writing, "I shall be very curious to know whether the Flora belongs to America, or is peculiar. I paid also much attention to the Birds, which I suspect are very curious."[12] But we can now see that these curiosities at that time seemed to him to support the hypothesis of multiple creation rather than evolution. In a later letter, July 9, 1836, discussing the island of St. Helena, lying midway between Africa and South America, he again uses the idea of a "centre of a distinct creation."[13]

To sort out the fauna and flora indigenous to one place, the biologist must take account of migration. In St. Helena he showed himself to be keenly aware of this question, and even wrote about the struggle for survival between native and migrant forms: "These numerous species, which have been so recently introduced, can hardly have failed to have destroyed some of the native kinds." (*Beagle Diary*, 410) With enough hindsight, such a sentence can be inter-

---

[11] *Beagle Diary*, p. 383; see below, Book Two, for the whole passage.
[12] Barlow, *Darwin to Henslow, op. cit.*
[13] *Ibid.*

preted as showing Darwin at last beginning to think as an evolutionist. But if we go even further back into Darwin's thought we can find the same idea expressed over and over throughout the voyage: the frequent success of migrant forms, imported by Europeans, over native forms. He, like many before him, was impressed with the astounding spread of horses and Europeans over the Americas in only a few centuries.

Here, then, are some of the steps Darwin may have taken on the way to becoming an evolutionist. Abandoning the view of a single Creation, with each species forever in its appointed place, he concedes with Lyell that one may invoke the idea of multiple creations; this accounts for the facts of extinction as exhibited in fossil remains, and copes with the contradiction between an evolving physical milieu and unchanging yet well-adapted organisms. But even multiple distinct creations will not account very well for all of the facts. Some of the contemporary similarities between species in different places can better be accounted for by migration from a single point of origin. Some of the differences, especially between the species of adjacent islands, can better be accounted for by invoking the idea of a limited instability of species.

None of these steps takes the theorist all the way to evolution. Lyell had gone this far without becoming an evolutionist, and waited years for Darwin to convince him. Why, then, must we suppose that an isolated remark by the young Darwin meant more to him than the same remark would have meant to the man who was at that time his chief theoretical guide?

Since Darwin had been for so long acquainted with the existence of theories of evolution, since he had been circumnavigating the globe with Lyell's book, which gives a masterful account of Lamarck's theory and then criticizes it mercilessly, we must suppose that Darwin thought about evolution from time to time throughout the voyage. Some of the major facts that he discovered about extinction, geographical distribution, and taxonomy were all highly suggestive that some new way of looking at the organic world was needed. Finally, the whole geological aspect of Darwin's work during the voyage constituted an excursion into an evolutionary way of looking at the physical character of the earth. Darwin *must* have thought about evolution.

Perhaps we need to ask a new question: when is a hypothesis a hypothesis? Not: when did he first entertain the hypothesis? Not: when did he become a convinced evolutionist? Instead: when did the idea of evolution begin to govern his behavior and thought in a systematic way? The answer to that question is reasonably clear now: sometime between March and July of 1837, when he gathered enough momentum to begin his transmutation notebooks.

Darwin may well have written the passage in the ornithological notes questioning "the stability of Species" on the last leg of the voyage, as Lady Barlow believes. This would have been anywhere from three to twelve months after sailing from the Galapagos. In that case, it does not represent "red-hot memory" but variation recollected in tranquility.

As I shall discuss below, when Darwin wrote down his first theory of evolution it was permeated with the image of a branching tree of nature. We cannot find any evidence of a rush toward evolutionary thought in Darwin's first reflections on his Galapagos experiences. But perhaps his encounters with archipelagoes helped him begin to clarify the branching image. Typically, an archipelago near a continental land mass has fauna and flora quite similar to but not identical to those of the continent. The fact of this similarity, coupled with the small differences from island to island, can be translated quite directly into a taxonomic tree which looks a lot like a fragment of Darwin's image.

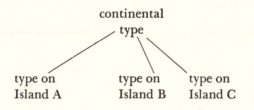

Darwin's first transmutation notebook was begun about July of 1837 and ended early in February of 1838. Pages 1–136 were written before September 25, 1837. They can be treated as a unit, albeit a unit with internal structure and exhibiting definite changes during the ten to twelve weeks in which they were written. To simplify the reader's task, the table of ideas on pages 136–37 provides a sketch of the main features of Darwin's theory in July 1837.

The opening pages consist of notes for a reasonably coherent essay. (*B* 1–22)

The first passage questions the meaning of the whole life cycle. Why this ubiquitous pattern of birth, maturing, and death? Why is life short? Why is the reproductive cycle an essential part of life? The answer lies in a principle of adaptive equilibrium and a principle of numerical conservation.

Changes in the physical environment provoke and require changes in the organisms that inhabit it. The function of the life cycle is twofold. On the one hand, immaturity provides a period in which the organism is plastic, modifiable. On the other hand, death "destroys the effect of accidental injuries, which if animals lived for ever would be endless." (*B* 5) Thus, the life cycle as a whole serves to permit adaptive variation, but at the same time to stabilize the living world by limiting the effects of accidents.

If species are being constantly created, they must constantly be destroyed: "this tendency to change . . . requires deaths of species to keep numbers of forms equable." (*B* 21) Elementary forms of life, "monads are constantly formed . . ." (*B* 18) and these have a definite life span. While a monad lives, it undergoes evolution: "the simplest cannot help becoming more complicated. . . ." (*B* 18) When the monad's life is over, it dies, and with it must die all the species that it has become.

Darwin's First Theoretical Model
July 1837

1. *Adaptive equilibration*

Organisms are adapted to their environment. A changing environment necessitates changing organisms.

2. *Physicalism*

Changes in the physical environment are probably the direct cause of changes in organisms.

3. *Numerical conservation*

The number of species must be approximately constant. When a new species appears, an old one must become extinct, or "die."

4. *Monadism*

Simple living particles, or "monads," are constantly springing into life. They have their origin in inanimate matter and are produced by natural forces.

5. *Progress*

Simple things, when they change, tend to become more complex.

6. *Monad life span, species life span*

A monad's life cycle is in part analogous to that of an individual organism. It begins simple, differentiates, matures, reproduces, and after some relatively fixed life span it dies. The phases of differentiation, maturation, and reproduction in individual organisms correspond to the evolving of new, more complex species from simple monads. When a monad's life is spent, all the species it has become must die.

7. *Irregularly branching tree of nature*

The cause of evolutionary change lies in the *accidental* encounters of organisms and their environments. Such occasions lead to the branching off of new evolutionary lines. Not everything that could conceivably happen actually does happen. Consequently, there is no necessary continuous gradation among all living species; continuity can be found only by tracing contemporary species back to one or a few common origins. The course of evolution is erratic, and the "tree of nature" is irregular. Missing links are evidence not against evolution but for the branching model.

8. *Man*

Man is an animal included in the tree of nature. Mental functions are to be treated on a par with other evolutionary problems.

Darwin used his physicalist principle of adaptive equilibration to account for the production of new species and his monadist principle of numerical conservation to account for the corresponding "death" (i.e., extinction) of old ones.

The major mechanism by which equilibrium is maintained is the system of sexual reproduction. Darwin asks: given the widespread tendency to vary, "why are species all constant"? (*B* 5) He answers immediately that there is a "beautiful law" of blending inheritance: offspring derive their characters from both parents, and through widespread interbreeding, variations are averaged and diffused, and species are preserved.

But this stabilizing mechanism must be partially circumvented if adaptive variations are to be the point of departure for an evolutionary theory. Darwin accomplishes this by introducing the idea of isolating mechanisms: if circumstances "separate a pair and place them on fresh island, it is very doubtful whether they would remain constant." (*B* 6) Such geographical separation, he proposes, works in three ways: first, physical conditions of the isolated pair are likely to be different from the habitat of the species as a whole; second, in-breeding provokes rapid variation; and third, the fact of separation permits a variant to become established.[14]

Darwin put himself in a delicate position by his double-edged use of the system of sexual reproduction sometimes to blend variations and sometimes to avoid blending. He immediately senses this weakness and remarks that to avoid the problem he "must suppose the change is effected at once . . . every grade . . . surely is not produced?" (*B* 8) This proposal, quantal change, was actually antithetical to Darwin's search for continuity, and it received no further attention from him at this time. Instead, in the following pages he frequently turns his atten-tion to the invention of other isolating mechanisms to supplement geographical separation: hybrid sterility is first mentioned on page 10, and interspecific sexual aversion on page 24. Both of these have the advantage of permitting species that have descended from a common ancestor to occupy the same terrain without mixing. Thus, in the unfolding of geological processes, when an area undergoes subsidence, hilltops become islands, giving rise to the isolation necessary for evolv-ing new species; when the area is rejoined by a subsequent elevation, the species can remain distinct: "Species formed by subsidence. Java and Sumatra. Rhinoceros. Elevate and join keep distinct, two species made: elevation and subsidence continually forming species." (*B* 82)

From a modern perspective, Darwin's use of monadism in his early theorizing seems bizarre. But in its historical context it was not so strange.[15] Recurrent spontaneous generation of living from non-living matter was an acceptable scientific idea until Pasteur's experi-ments in 1861. Lamarck, in 1809, had expressed the view that the evolutionary process was everywhere continuous, receiving daily re-invigoration from the production in nature of the simplest forms.[16]

Spontaneous generation of simple forms might well seem prefer-able to the Divine Creation of complex ones as called for in the theory of multiple creations.

As I have mentioned, the latter theory had been developed in response to the rapid growth of knowledge about extinct organisms. Lyell, whose influence on Darwin was so profound, expressed the view that "species may have been created in succession at such times and in such places as to enable them to multiply and endure for an appointed period, and occupy an appointed space on the globe."[17] Lyell's view

---

14 These points are discussed in greater detail in Chapter 8.
15 Dr. Harriet Barr has pointed out to me that there was another influential theory in which the quantity conserved was the number of species rather than the number of individual organisms—namely, the story of the Flood and the Ark.
16 Jean-Baptiste de Lamarck, *Philosophie Zoologique* (Paris, 1809) , p. 65.
17 Lyell, *Principles, op. cit.,* pp. 26–27.

did not exclude some mutability of each created species—i.e., some adaptive variation—but he vigorously attacked the notions of progressive change and common descent of all species from one or a few ancestors.

Thus, components of the monadism found in the opening pages of Darwin's first notebook can be found in the thought of two of his major precursors: Lamarck believed in the recurrent production of simple living forms from non-living ones, and Lyell believed in the limitation of each species to a definite species life span, a notion quite similar to Darwin's monad life span. Darwin merged these components in a novel way, formulating a theory of evolution that incorporated the facts of extinction.

Lamarck's position on extinction is ambiguous. At one moment he proposes that the lost species may yet be found somewhere, as our knowledge grows. At the next, he argues that extinction does not occur because the species that disappears *becomes* the one which replaces it.[18]

Stated in the second form, Lamarck's thought is in some ways close to Darwin's. But it clearly lacks an element that was essential in Darwin's thinking, the principle of the conservation of the number of species. For Lamarck, this would have been a meaningless number, since the classification of organic beings into separate species was "the part of art"—i.e., a set of arbitrary human decisions. Darwin too recognized an arbitrary element in the human decision as to which organisms can be classed together as one species, but he believed in the reality of species and supported this belief with the whole paraphernalia of isolating mechanisms and the theory of divergence. If species are real, the question of their number is meaningful, and the idea that the number is conserved may be a useful guide in the construction of an evolutionary theory.[19]

In spite of these historical roots, it is not immediately clear why Darwin resorted to the idea of the monad life span to explain extinction. Just a few pages earlier he had explained the production of new

---

18 Lamarck, *op. cit.* pp. 75–81.
19 It should be mentioned that many points of the monad theory were also jotted down in the small pocket books that Darwin had carried with him during the voyage. Darwin habitually used any available blank paper to record his thoughts; judging from the great similarity of the wording of these notes and those of the first transmutation notebook, it seems certain that they were written at almost the same time. One plausible guess would be that he began to develop these ideas about March 1837, and jotted them down in the pocket books because he happened to be going through the latter at the time; then, when he began the first transmutation notebook, he transferred his notes from one book to the other. Nora Barlow has given some of the relevant excerpts in an addendum to her transcription of the *Ornithological Notes, op. cit.*, pp. 276–277.

forms as the result of changes in the physical milieu: why could not the same changes account for extinction? One reason is given quite clearly in his account of the voyage of the *Beagle*, written in 1837 and published in 1839. There he goes to some pains to reject the notion that extinction is due mainly to massive environmental changes, even in the tempting case where a large number of mammalian forms disappeared from the fossil record at the same time. He had rejected the whole thesis of geological catastrophism, which in his thinking was merely the complement of another equally unscientific idea, creationism. This opposition led him to look for a non-environmental cause of extinction; hence his willingness to borrow Lyell's idea of a species life span. This idea was easily extended to account for simultaneous extinction of numerous related species, on the assumption that they have evolved from the same monad. He concludes this published discussion: ". . . as with the individual, so with the species, the hour of life has run its course, and is spent." (*Voyage*, 1839, 212)

This was the only echo ever to appear in print of Darwin's monad theory. The sentence quoted was deleted in the 1845 edition.

But why did not Darwin try immediately to conceive of extinction as a gradual process at once consistent with the principle of adaptive equilibrium and the idea of continuity in nature? There were probably several reasons. There was some paleontological evidence suggesting that species—indeed, whole groups of species—had disappeared suddenly.[20] Darwin needed a theory that could assimilate this discontinuity without invoking the notion of a worldwide catastrophe reminiscent of the Flood of Genesis. In 1837 he was not so well equipped as later to appreciate the extremely fragmentary character of fossil remains. It was therefore easier for him to entertain the idea that sometimes the absence of a species from the known fossil record implied its non-existence and sudden extinction at the corresponding geological moment. By the time he wrote the *Origin* he knew enough to include a whole chapter "On the Imperfection of the Geological Record," to which such apparent discontinuities could be attributed.

There was some recent embryological evidence of fundamental discontinuities between certain great classes of living things. Darwin's brief use of spontaneous generation to account for such systematic discontinuities resembles the embryologist Baer's thinking on this matter. Darwin needed to construct a theory that could assimilate whatever impassable discontinuities might be discovered. Darwin's

---

20 I know of no definite evidence that in 1837 Darwin had read Agassiz' work pointing in this direction. But he had read the fourth, 1835, edition of Lyell's *Principles of Geology*, throughout which Agassiz' findings are scattered. The idea of wholesale disappearances and replacements of species fitted in with Lyell's hypothesis of multiple creation.

early difficulty with this point is reflected in a revision he later had to make in the *Origin*. In 1859 he wrote, "Thus, community in embryonic structure reveals community of descent. It will reveal this community of descent, however much the structure of the adult may have been modified and obscured." (*Origin*, 449) In 1866 he altered this to read, "Thus, community in embryonic structure reveals community of descent; but dissimilarity in embryonic development does not prove discommunity of descent, for in one of two groups all the developmental stages may have been suppressed, or may have been so greatly modified as no longer to be recognized. . . ."[21]

Finally, Darwin's own theoretical position did not permit him to use the principle of adaptive equilibrium in a perfectly symmetrical way. If adaptation to environmental change could just as easily erase a variant as it could produce one, there would be no cumulative change. He wanted to construct *a theory in which change would be conserved.* In short, he was hunting for a theory that would permit as much continuous and progressive change as possible while retaining the ability to assimilate whatever discontinuities it became necessary to admit. It is interesting to note that his key principle of adaptive equilibrium gives the initiative entirely to the environment. The organism quite passively responds to changes in its physical milieu by its own adaptive variation. But the process by which adaptive variation is produced and conserved depends upon the system of sexual reproduction, and thus in a way expresses Darwin's later point of view, stated even in the Table of Contents of the *Origin of Species:* "The relation of organism to organism the most important of all relations."[22] And the process by which the number of species is conserved involves the principle of monadic life span which is independent of the pressures of the environment: "The absolute end of certain forms . . . (*independent of external causes*) does appear very probable." (*B* 35)

The position-as-a-whole, once taken, became the basis for further growth. In the *Origin of Species* there is only one diagram, one guiding image—the "tree of life," depicting the theoretical model of branching evolution referred to repeatedly throughout the *Origin*. The first intimation of this tree occurs on page 21 of the 1837 *B* notebook. In Darwin's first use of the tree image, both the principle of monadism and the principle of adaptive variation are thoroughly intertwined. "Organized beings represent a tree, *irregularly branched;* some branches far more branched,—Hence Genera.—As many terminal buds dying, as new ones generated. There is nothing stranger in

---

21 Charles Darwin, *The Origin of Species: A Variorum Text,* edited by Morse Peckham (Philadelphia: University of Pennsylvania Press, 1959) , p. 703. I quote from the fourth edition, 1866; some further changes were made subsequently.
22 *Origin,* p. vi, outline of Chapter 3, "Struggle for Existence."

Darwin's first attempt to sketch the idea of the irregularly branching tree of nature. *Courtesy of Cambridge University Library.*

death of species, than individuals." (*B* 21–22) Thus he sees the point of origin of the tree—or perhaps each tree, since he is not yet committed to a single origin of all life—as the monad with its tendency to vary adaptively, hence branch. He adds: "Would there not be a triple branching in the tree of life owing to three elements—air, land and water, and the endeavour of each typical class to extend his domain into the other domains. . . ." (*B* 23) The last remark is interesting because Darwin had just a few pages earlier denied Lamarck's theory of the will as a factor in evolution: "Changes not result of will of animals, but law of adaptation. . . ." (*B* 21) Thus, although the principle of adaptive variation is implicated in the tree image in a thoroughly physical manner (three elements—air, land, and water), the initiative is beginning to pass from the environment to the organism.

From the notes immediately following, it is apparent that Darwin was able to use even his first crude version of the tree schema to produce further deductions. He sees immediately that the branching model accounts for certain observed discontinuities in nature: "The tree of life should perhaps be called the coral of life, base of branches dead, so that passages cannot be seen." (*B* 25) Later on he will see that the branching model accounts for discontinuities so well that it presents an alternative to monadism, but at this moment branching is only the expression of monadism.

Soon he realizes that the coupling of monadism and the branching model *requires* the simultaneous extinction of many related species, not as an occasional event but as a regularly recurring phenomenon. The evidence patently does not support this deduction. (*B* 35) But he does not immediately abandon either idea. Instead, he goes on to develop the branching model with much greater precision and detail, stresses the point that conserving the number of species *requires*

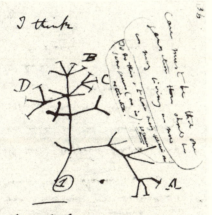

Darwin's second attempt to sketch the idea of the irregularly branching tree of nature. *Courtesy of Cambridge University Library.*

extinction, and explores in a quasi-mathematical form the amount of divergence that the branching model can permit him to imagine.

He redraws his sketch of a tree; where the first two sketches were rough, mainly intended to show the idea of a dead base and consequent discontinuities, the second sketch is cleanly drawn and more abstract, with a definite symbol used to distinguish between extinct and living forms, so that the number of each is actually countable.

Almost immediately Darwin reformulates the branching model in terms of human survival and descent, as though the ordinary form of a genealogical family tree were inherent in his idea from its conception. (B 40–41) In this early treatment of the subject, the idea of selective survival in order to keep the number of species constant is clearly stated. But at this time he applies the idea only to extinction, not to the production of new species.

Even going this far was a subtly original step. Others had seen natural selection as a conservative force, but their focus had been either on the elimination of maladaptive mutant forms within species or on limiting the total population of living organisms. Darwin, with his interest in keeping the number of species constant, made a population principle a natural part of his irregularly branching tree elucidating relationships among species.

As his scheme clarified, it expanded, permitting him to imagine how the branching model could account for an "immense gap of relation" between descendants from the same ancestor. Previously he has used rather prudent examples of discontinuities between relatively similar forms. Now he writes of the "great gap between birds and mammalia, still greater between vertebrate and articulata, still greater between animals and plants" (B 43) —all to be accounted for in the branching model.

As already mentioned, Darwin has by now encountered one major source of evidence against the principle of monadism. But he cannot discard it directly, as it still provides him with his only mechanism of extinction. He begins to play with the possibility that the factor of environmental change can be used to account for extinction, but this idea does not work very well, for reasons given above, especially as he is still thinking in terms of widespread simultaneous extinction: "some great system acting over whole world, the period of great quadrupeds declining as great reptiles must have once declined." (B 53)

Then he hits on a new device. He modifies the monadic principle so that it can account for simultaneous extinctions when the evidence suggests that they have occurred, or for their absence when the evidence suggests that they have not. (B 61) He now proposes that the monad has a *variable* life span, depending on whether or not it evolves. Just as the individual dies without a trace unless he leaves progeny, the species dies unless it produces offspring. The offspring of one species is another species: "it is a *generation of species* like generation of *individuals*." (*B* 63) In its own uneasy way, this formulation handles the problem of extinction. Although still closely tied to the idea of monadism, in its logical form this solution resembles an important part of Darwin's ultimate solution of the problem: in many cases the species extinguished becomes the species that extinguished it. But the keynote of struggle which informs the *Origin* is not yet present.

In this modified form the principle of monadism has become truly superfluous: the major discontinuities it was invoked to explain have been treated without monads. The systematic discontinuities follow directly from the branching model. The temporal discontinuities—i.e., extinction—have been transformed into the idea of *becoming*. Once it is admitted that the monad's life span is proportional to the amount of change it undergoes, it should follow that perpetual adaptive variation means unbroken continuity among living forms, and the monad life span disappears.

But Darwin does not deny the outgrown concept so much as cease to use it. On pages 71–73 and 78 the modified form of the monadic principle is recapitulated and developed a little further. On pages 95–100 some facts are asserted that seem to argue against monadism, or against some deductions that would follow from it, but the argument is not made explicit. On page 135 there appears a last, sporadic attempt to use the species life-span idea in accounting for some new facts of geographical distribution, followed by the remark: "Weakest part of theory death of species without apparent physical cause." Almost immediately after writing this passage, sometime in September of 1837, Darwin went off on a four-week trip, visiting family and friends. When he returned, he continued the notebooks for many hundreds of pages—four notebooks in all. In a summary of his position toward the close of the first notebook, pages 224–229, there is no trace of the monadic principle, nor does it reappear in the later notebooks, not even as the object of criticism.

In sum, Darwin's monadism was probably born sometime in the year preceding the summer of 1837; it flourished in July of that year, evolved rapidly in August, and disappeared in September. But we cannot say it died without progeny, for monadism played a key role in the birth of Darwin's branching model of evolution. What of the other parent of the branching model, Darwin's physicalist principle of adaptive variation? Throughout the notebooks, and throughout the rest of Darwin's life, that principle can be found, waxing and waning in importance but never completely forgotten. Try as he might, Darwin never succeeded in developing a satisfactory way of accounting for the source of variation. He had to build his theory of evolution around the fact of ubiquitous variability taken as an unexplained premise. His vacillation about the role of the environment in producing variations shows that he was never happy with this gap in his theory. Nevertheless, it seems to me that the most valuable and the most heroic thing he ever did was to go ahead with his work founded on that premise. Even today we have no satisfying unitary theory explaining the immediate cause of variations. But we have a powerful theory of evolution which serves as the unifying idea of biological science. Ignorance is not the hallmark of science, but the disciplined recognition of it is indispensable for scientific progress. As the slow growth of Darwin's thinking shows, that disciplined ignorance is hard won.

It has been suggested that essentially the whole of Darwin's mature point of view is reflected in his earliest remarks on evolution, as though his ultimate theory sprang forth at once the moment he turned his thoughts to the matter. Nothing could be further from the truth. Darwin had to go through many stages of intellectual growth. To become the author of the *Origin of Species* he had to modify his principle of adaptive equilibrium so that it stressed relations among organisms rather than relations between each organism and its physical milieu; he had to eliminate completely the concept of monadism and monad life span. Working from his starting point, he had to develop the model of branching evolution first in a formal way, and then to transform it by suffusing it with the idea of struggle and selection. Although there are occasional moments of sharp insight, these moments are only nodal points in a slow growth process.

The picture of scientific thought is often painted as being carried forward by the construction of alternative hypotheses followed by the rational choice between them. Darwin's notebooks do not support this rationalist myth. Hypotheses are discovered with difficulty in the activity of a person holding *one* point of view, and they are the expression of that point of view. It is hard enough to have one reasonable hypothesis, and two at a time may be exceedingly rare. In Darwin's case, when he is forced to give up one hypothesis, he does not necessarily substitute another—he sometimes simply remains at a loss until his point of view matures sufficiently to permit the expression of a new hypothesis.

The concept of trial and error would be very difficult to apply to this case. Was Darwin's monadism an error? Surely it was wrong from the point of view of modern biology; and it was wrong from Darwin's point of view in September of 1837, when he abandoned monadism. But in July of 1837 monadism was not an error, for we can recognize in Darwin's July monadism the fruitful source of the branching model of evolution.

In key respects Darwin's first theory resembled Lamarck's, while his eventual theory was more like Erasmus Darwin's. It is well known that both Erasmus Darwin and Lamarck believed in the inheritance of acquired characteristics and in the role of the organism's own activity in determining what is to be acquired. But there were also important differences between the two theorists. Lamarck believed in multiple origins of life, or ongoing spontaneous generation, an idea contained in Charles' first theory; for Erasmus a cardinal metaphysical point was the single origin of all living things from one great first cause, one original "living filament." Charles learned to avoid trying to explain the origin of life; nevertheless, his later theory was imbued with the idea of a single origin.

Lamarck recognized that the inheritance of acquired characteristics was inadequate to explain evolution, and used it only as a secondary principle. The more important idea for him was a metaphysical law of progress. There are traces of this belief in progress as an explanatory principle in Charles' first theory; he was later careful to avoid it. In this respect his later theory more closely resembled his grandfather's; Erasmus was vaguer than Lamarck on the question of progress and anyhow preferred to emphasize an endlessly re-cycling evolutionary process, "world without end."

Erasmus, like Lamarck, avoided exclusive reliance on acquired characteristics. For him, perhaps a more important cause of evolutionary change was hybridization: once a few simple forms have evolved by growth and differentiation, much further change can be accounted for by postulating a profusion of new combinations among these forms. Erasmus introduced a sort of selection principle at this point in his theory: many hybrids would be immediately eliminated because of imperfections in their reproductive organs. Charles' knowledge of the limitations of hybrid fertility greatly surpassed his grandfather's. But as he gradually surrendered the monad theory, he went through a long period of searching for a way of making use of hybridization as a key principle.[23] This approach was finally obviated by his use of the principle of natural selection.

Each of the three theories under discussion had different implications for the eventual construction of a theory of evolution through natural selection. Charles Darwin's first theory, by its emphasis on branching, extinction, and conservation of number of species, strongly implied a principle of selection. Lamarck's theory denied extinction and selectivity altogether: everything that develops has a place in the natural order. Erasmus Darwin's theory, as expressed in *Zoonomia*, did in fact include many hints of selection, but these are scattered and,

---

[23] This theme is particularly prominent in the C notebook.

more significantly, for Erasmus the construction of a theory of evolution was not his central aim. Rather, he was interested in expressing a general world view which might be called "pan-transformism." For him, the process of species evolving was simply a special case of the changefulness of all living things in a Heraclitan world of perpetual change. *Zoonomia* devotes far more attention to the transformations of individual growth than to the transmutations of species. This embryological rather than evolutionary perspective is expressed in Erasmus' choice of metaphor; he concludes the scientific exposition of this theory by evoking the image of the "first great egg . . . animated by . . . Divine Love; from whence proceeded all things which exist."[24] His embryological perspective explains how selection could be only an incidental idea, while growth through addition of parts, re-combination, re-organization, and differentiation are far more urgent themes.

It would be a great psychological mistake to interpret this complex pattern of similarities and differences among theories merely as the evidence for the borrowing of isolated ideas by later theorists from earlier ones. Rather, each thinker must be seen as struggling in the course of his own life and in his own historical circumstances to develop a coherent argument, or structure of ideas. The more important positive contribution of earlier theories to later ones may be that they provide the thinker with a challenge: can he develop a theory more coherent, more plausible, and more powerful than did his predecessors?

The theory of evolution through natural selection is subtle and elusive. It eluded Darwin the first time he seemed to have had it in his grasp. When he constructed his first theory of evolution, he had already, in 1835, developed his theory of the formation of coral reefs. As we have seen, there is a close formal analogy between the two theories. There were two supplementary points of contact between them. Darwin, of course, did not in 1837 see the analogy between the one theory he had already developed and the other theory which was to take him one more year to devise. But he did see the analogy between his irregularly branching image of nature and the irregular branching growth of a coral mass. His coral-reef theory, moreover, made use of the concept of differential survival of species, depending on the conditions of life. Among the species of coral there were some that flourished in wild surf, others in quieter waters. Each could carry on its reef-building activities under circumstances best suited to its own survival, thus accounting for some of the details of reef formation.

---

[24] Erasmus Darwin, *Zoonomia; or, the Laws of Organic Life*, 2 Vols. (Dublin: P. Byrne, 1800), Vol. 1, p. 599.

The question strikes one forcibly: given this seemingly opportune point of departure, why did Darwin not proceed more directly to formulate the theory of evolution through natural selection? How did the monad theory attract him so much?

When he began his transmutation notebooks he had not yet recognized that a theory of evolution could be constructed without reference to the origin of life. The monad theory contains the principle of spontaneous generation. When he began his transmutation notebooks, being reasonably certain that the appearance of new variants could be explained as direct adaptations to changes in the physical milieu, he was chiefly concerned with searching for a mechanism of extinction of the old forms; the kernel of the monad theory was the species-life-span idea. In 1837 natural selection looked like a conservative principle. Before he could see it as an innovative one, he had to re-situate it within the branching model. The monad theory helped him to develop the branching model. From there it took him another year to transform the entire structure of his argument so that he could see the creative power of natural selection.

CHAPTER 8

The Changing Structure
of an Argument

No doubt it is often *convenient* to formulate the
mental facts in an atomistic sort of way, and to treat
the higher states of consciousness as if they were all
built out of unchanging simple ideas. [But] . . . A
permanently existing 'idea' or 'Vorstellung' which
makes its appearance before the footlights of consciousness at periodical intervals is as mythological an
entity as the Jack of Spades.

William James, The Principles of Psychology, Vol. 1
(London: Macmillan, 1890).

What makes an effective theory, one with real striking power? It must
persuade; it must be superior in some distinct fashion to theories its
author proposes to supplant; it must deal somehow with its own difficulties, which it will surely have since it is a human invention and
neither nature nor man's knowledge of it is ever finished; it must give
guidance to future work.

To accomplish these complex ends, a theory must have a clear
structure. An assemblage of vague or disjointed ideas, no matter how
original or correct, is not an effective theory.

Darwin had to go through many steps in moving from his early
monadism toward an effective theory of evolution. These were not
accomplished one at a time, each step once and for all, followed by the
next. He was moving on a number of fronts all at once; a good idea
might be dimly seen and then held in abeyance while some other
matter was taken up, clearing a way for the former's further clarification and utilization.

The main point to be considered now is the changing structure of
an argument and the way in which a given idea changes its significance as its role in an argument evolves. There are two sorts of error to
be avoided. On the one hand, the atomistic fallacy that an idea simply

retains its identity as a sort of hard, unaltering atom, regardless of the context in which it is used. From this atomistic point of view, there really is nothing new under the sun; everything can be explained as a "mere" borrowing from somewhere else, and the glimmering of any great idea can always be found in the work of some minor figure whom the biographer or critic has chosen to exalt. If, however, what exists and what evolves are structures and *only* structures, there is nothing "mere" about such reorganization: *every* idea must be seen as gaining its significance from its role in a structure of ideas, an argument.

The atomistic approach deprives us of historical and developmental perspective because it is too analytical. The opposite error, the wholistic fallacy, also prevents us from seeing development clearly. If each structure is a law unto itself, entirely determining the function of each of its parts, it is difficult to see how one structure can pass into the next.

The solution to this apparent dilemma is to maintain a shifting perspective. The ideas of which we speak are not hard, impenetrable atoms; they are organized structures in their own right, each one a subunit that can retain its identity—i.e., its basic form—through a considerable range of transformations and at the same time change its role in an argument. Whether in the long run a particular sub-structure can be said to disappear—to have been reorganized, reduced, and relocated until it is in no sense the same idea—need not concern us here. In following a continuous thought process we need deal at first only with those ideas which do in some sense retain their identity but change their function. This focus of attention will give us scope enough for the moment.

I turn now to an examination of several different ways in which an idea's position in the structure of an argument can change. The examples chosen form a group connected with a significant step in Darwin's development, the reorganization of his thought in ways that permitted him to recognize the evolutionary significance of natural selection, the events surrounding his moment of Malthusian insight.

Expunging a Problem from Consideration: The Origin of Life. In one important respect, the *Origin of Species* is a modest book. Darwin makes no claim that his theory of the origin of *species* says anything about the origin of *life*. His is a theory of continual change in an ongoing system, not an explanation of the origins of that system.

In his historical introduction to the *Origin* (added in the second and subsequent editions), Darwin points out that the logic of Lamarck's position had required the assumption of the continuing origin of life—that is, spontaneous generation of simple forms—in order to account for the existence of such forms in the contemporary world. This was necessary for Lamarck because his cardinal principle of evolution was an inherent tendency of *all* living things to become progressively more complex; therefore, without the fresh generation of simple forms, after the passage of time none would exist.[1]

Regarding the origin of life, Darwin made no claim for his theory. His settled view was that life had originated through the operation of entirely natural physical and chemical forces, and that it had probably originated only once, in which case all living beings would be the descendants of the same original living form.

To the theory that spontaneous generation continues today, he had two main objections. First, postulating *many* origins of life would weaken his main empirical argument—that the ensemble of similarities among all organisms is due to their common origin. Secondly, the very emergence of life alters the conditions under which that event occurred: the first primordial living things consume the complex but non-living molecules from which they evolve, so that, once done, the deed becomes forever impossible. The first point is implicit in the whole argument of the *Origin;* the second, a speculation with a very modern ring, occurs only in a private letter. (*LL* 3, 17–18)

By avoiding the issue of the origin of life, the *Origin of Species* gains in simplicity what it loses in scope. Unless there is life, it obviously makes no sense to speak of adaptation. By avoiding the issue, Darwin was able to remain within the compass of the equilibration schema: adaptation, adaptive change, and the generation of a continuous series of forms. Even though the step is one of omission and restraint, some effort was involved in taking it.

The opening pages of Darwin's first transmutation notebook are written in an expansive, confident mood. Darwin thinks he has a theory that will deal with the origin of life, the causes of variation and heredity, *and* the transmutation of species; he does not even consider separating these issues—as we have seen, they are all bound up together in Darwin's monad theory of evolution, which he formulated and then discarded in the summer of 1837. The heart of the monad theory was the premise that the spontaneous generation of simple living forms continues now and forever, so long as life exists and evolves.

When Darwin gave up the theory of monads, he did not all at once give up hope of saying something about the origin of life. Throughout the transmutation notebooks the question arises in various ways. First of all, how *many* beginnings has life had? Must a coherent theory of evolution postulate only one? Does the science of taxonomy, describing the distribution of similarities and differences

---

[1] The inheritance of acquired characteristics, widely thought to be the essence of Lamarck's theory, was only a secondary principle.

among all organisms, force the conclusion that there are some unbridgeable gulfs in the natural order?

Of course, Darwin wanted to reduce the occurrence of origins to a number far fewer than the number of species; otherwise the theory of evolution would be formally indistinguishable from the theory of creation. But at first he was neutral as to the choice between one or several points of origin. Only as the structure of his argument became clearer did he seem to realize that, from his point of view, one origin is by far preferable to several.

In several passages he cites evidence suggesting seemingly unbridgeable gaps, the most extreme being that between animals and plants. Always he has available to him the argument worked out earlier in his branching model of evolution: the passages between remote forms are no longer visible—they go back through aeons of geological time, and the geological record is incomplete. The outermost branches of a large tree may seem disconnected from each other until we trace them back to their trunk and root. But he senses the weakness of this purely formal method of accounting for the observed discontinuities in nature. About February or March of 1838 he writes: "Extreme difficulty of *tracing* change of species to species although we see it effected tempts one to bring one back to distinct creations." (*C* 64)

Tempted he may be, but not fallen. For the doctrine of distinct creations is without any factual foundation, endows the hypothetical Creator with no powers of establishing general laws, and requires Him to pause in His celestial rounds to make "a long succession of vile molluscous animals." (*D* 37, August 16, 1838) At one point he exclaims, "Has the Creator since the Cambrian formation gone on creating animals with same general structure.—Miserable limited view." (*B* 216, about January 1838)

A crucial empirical finding for Darwin was Ehrenberg's then very recent discovery of fossil unicellular organisms identical with extant forms. This showed Darwin that there was no need to assume that *all* simple organisms become more complex: some could remain simple, undergoing no progressive evolution. This discovery eliminated the necessity of introducing the idea of spontaneous generation to explain the present existence of unicellular organisms. A single origin of life, very remote in time, might suffice: ". . . we know from Ehrenberg there are . . . Tertiary fossil Infusoria of same forms with recent & we have nothing to do with CREATION." (*C* 146)

Apart from the problem of seemingly unbridgeable gulfs between species, and the existence of extant simple organisms bearing on the *number* of "fresh creations," there is the question of the *order* in which different kinds of organisms appeared in the evolutionary series. This too is a question that derives from a concern for the origin of life, for if we could trace the sequence back to its beginning we would have described that origin.

At several points in the notebooks Darwin expressed a hope that such a reconstruction of the past would be possible. For example:

> There must be progressive development; for instance none ? of the vertebrata could exist without plants & insects had been created; but on the other hand creations[2] of small animals must have gone on since from parasitical nature of insects & worms . . . we may say that vegetables & most insects could live without animals but not vice versa. (Could plants live without carbonic acid gas. Yet unquestionably animals most dependent on vegetable of the two great kingdoms. [B 108–109]

In this passage we see something that occurs often in Darwin's thinking. He begins on a very definite note, then questions arise, and the thought trails off (even the parenthesis is unclosed), to be resumed days or months later.

He goes on to worry that placing the plant and animal kingdoms in the same evolutionary network imposes a heavy burden on him in his search for similarities of structure among widely disparate forms: "The existence of plants and their passage to animals appears greatest argument against theory of analogies." (B 110) Darwin's concern for this argument undoubtedly helps to explain his enduring interest in plant behavior, which resulted in his later works on insectivorous plants and on the movements of plants.

There are a few other efforts in the notebooks to reconstruct specific parts of the order of succession of evolution, but by and large he did not pursue this line of inquiry very far; in the *Origin of Species* there are no explicit genealogies. Only in very abstract and general terms did he develop the argument that "From the first dawn of life, all organic beings are found to resemble each other in descending degrees, so that they can be classed in groups under groups."[3]

During the gradual demise of Darwin's monad theory after the first thirty-five pages of the B notebook, there are only a few direct references to spontaneous generation or the origin of life. He became increasingly aware that ultimate origins are obscure: "We need not

---

2 In this passage Darwin probably used the word *creation* to mean *origin* or *appearance in an evolutionary series*. He never quite got over that unfortunate usage, which was in harmony with his abiding desire to placate his religious critics. Considering the early date of the passage (about October 1837) the ambiguity of the term may have reflected his own religious doubts.

3 *Origin*, 411. Darwin's careful avoidance of the issue of the origin of life is reflected in his revision of this sentence in the fifth and sixth editions. In the last, it reads, "From the most remote period in the history of the world . . .," etc. *Origin, Variorum Text*, edited by M. Peckham, *op. cit.*, p. 646.

expect to find varieties intermediate between every species.—Who can find trace or history of species between Indian cow with hump and common [cow];—between Esquimaux and European dog?" (*B* 154-155) A little later on, in a passage about the appearance of the great classes of vertebrates, he wrote, "it is useless to speculate not only about beginning of animal life generally, but even about great division. Our question is not how there come to be fishes & quadrupeds but how there come to be many genera of fish &c. &c. at present day." (*C* 58, about March 1838)

When he did refer directly to spontaneous generation, it was, during these months, in a vacillating way. Thus, in the spring of 1838: "The intimate relation of Life with laws of chemical combination, and the universality of latter render spontaneous generation not improbable." (*C* 102, about April 1838) Toward the end of this period he seems to have grasped quite fully the sense in which he must deal with an ongoing system of evolutionary change, rather than with the system's origins. He quotes from an author of the day, " 'in fact in all reasonings of which human nature is the object, there is really no natural starting place, because there is nothing more elementary than that complex nature itself with which our speculations must end as well as begin' etc. etc. *Their centre is everywhere & their circumference nowhere as long as this is so—!! Metaphysics!!!*"[4] Darwin's own remark is reminiscent of Nicolas of Cusa, who had the same thought in the fifteenth century, when men were beginning to think seriously about the possibility of an infinite universe.

By the summer of 1838 his position has become firmer; he speaks in the imperative: "In my speculations, must not go back to first stock of all animals, but merely to classes where types exist, for if so, it will be necessary to show how the first eye is formed,—how one nerve becomes sensitive to light, (Mem. whole plant may be considered as one large eye . . .) & another nerve to finest vibration of sound, which is impossible.—" (*D* 21, about July 1838)

The rejection of spontaneous generation is implicit but complete when he uses the term in a sense quite different from its ordinary meaning: "My view would make every individual a spontaneous generation: what is animalcular semen but this—the living nerve massed in mould." (*D* 132) Here, in a sort of play on words, he is using the term *spontaneous generation* to mean that every newly conceived individual is a new beginning, and a recapitulation of the course of evolution.

---

[4] The quotation is from Lord Francis Jeffrey's book *Memoirs of the Life of the Right Honourable Sir James Mackintosh* (London, 1836). Italics mine; exclamation points double and treble, Darwin's. (*C* 218)

These lines were written shortly before Darwin's first clear application of the Malthusian principle in the theory of evolution through natural selection. Later on, when the outlines of his theory were becoming much clearer to him, he had a clearer sense of what he did *not* have to say. In a series of remarks specifying those demands which his theory must satisfy and those which it need not, the following sentence lays the matter to rest: "My theory leaves quite untouched the question of spontaneous generation." (*E* 160, May 1839)

Shifting a Proposition from Conclusion to Premise: Variation. It is a serious error to suppose that the main features of a complex idea are adequately characterized by the more elementary ideas which make it up. If that were the case, the discovery of a new component idea and its introduction into a theoretical structure would always be the most prominent kind of event in the growth of the complex structure.

In fact, however, very profound changes in the nature of a complex idea may depend mainly on the rearrangement of its components to form a new structure. I turn now to such a case: changes within the equilibration schema making for a deep change in the role of adaptive variation in Darwin's conception of evolution.

When he began the evolution notebooks in July of 1837, Darwin treated adaptive variation as the necessary *conclusion* of two lines of argument, and as the central explanatory concept in his monad theory of evolution. In his finished theory, by contrast, variation was one of several *premises* which, if properly combined, could explain evolution.

To discuss this change in some detail it will be helpful to look first at a moment in time when Darwin's views had clarified and simplified in a form quite like the position taken in the *Origin*.

In a passage written between November 7 and December 1, 1838, Darwin wrote:

> Three principles will account for all
> (1) Grandchildren like grandfathers
> (2) Tendency to small change especially with physical change
> (3) Great fertility in proportion to support of parents [*E* 58]

In other words, the *conclusion*, evolution, follows from three *premises:* heredity, variation, and great fertility. The first premise is not especially Darwinian—hereditary transmission and the consequent resemblance of generations was widely accepted. The third premise, which modern biologists might call *selection pressure,* is the key point that Darwin had gotten from Malthus—any one generation is fertile enough to produce offspring in far greater numbers than itself, thus engendering the process of competition and selection for the best-adapted individuals.

The second premise, variation, is here stated in a complex form.

The main point is "tendency to small change," but a clause is attached, "especially with physical change." In other words, even in this passage Darwin does not feel entirely free of the necessity to *explain* variation. Nevertheless, he is free enough to recognize that the three premises, whether or not any of them can be explained, taken together can generate his theory of evolution through natural selection.

To move from his starting point in the monad theory to the natural-selection theory, Darwin had to alter his conception of variation in a number of ways. Initially, he postulated adaptive variation with an inherent tendency to progress; he came to see that this would be tantamount to a bald statement that evolution occurs because it occurs, and not at all an explanation of it. In the final version, variations are not necessarily adaptive—some are useful to the organism and favor its chances of survival, others may be useless or harmful, as circumstances dictate. In the final version, to account for evolutionary progress, variation alone is not enough: it must be coupled with selection.

Initially, Darwin felt that he had a definite explanation for adaptive variation. First, variation is necessary if the organism is to remain well adapted to its circumstances, because those circumstances keep changing; secondly, variations are direct, adaptive responses to the changes in the physical milieu. In the final version, although Darwin still felt a need to explain variation, he was not at all sure of his various attempts to do so; yet he was willing and able to treat variation as a *premise,* as one of the three principles that would "account for all."

This step was not easy. There was some novelty in the idea that the fact of variation was insufficient to account for evolution; this idea represents one of Darwin's criticisms of Lamarck. Moreover, the *amount* of variation in nature had not been fully recognized before Darwin. In good part, the notebooks are a catalogue of variations collected by Darwin in his omnivorous search of the literature of science and plant and animal breeding, in his many conversations with all sorts of experts, and in his own travels.

As we move back and forth through the notes, we see that Darwin is often preoccupied with the causes of variation, and his first effort to explain it within the framework of his monad theory is closely linked to his experiences on the *Beagle* voyage. He puts great stress on geographical isolating mechanisms, which he thinks have two related consequences. First, if we begin with members of the same species and transport some of them to different places, their environment will be different, and this will directly induce adaptive variations. Secondly, if the variants are restricted to a confined area, there will be in-breeding; in-breeding contributes to the process of variation in two somewhat contradictory ways. On the one hand, it stabilizes any change due to environmental factors by disseminating it within the in-breeding population; on the other hand, in-breeding may, he thinks, directly induce variations. All of this rich collection of ideas is contained within the opening passage of the B notebook. Thus: "According to this view animals on separate islands ought to become different if kept long enough apart, with slightly different circumstances.—Now Galapagos tortoises, mocking birds, Falkland fox, Chiloe fox.—English and Irish hare." (B 7) The Galapagos, Chiloe, and Falklands are all islands he had visited during the voyage.

In a euphoric passage on the operation of natural law, he suggests that the *amount* of variation is proportional to the amount of environmental change. As compared with the idea of continual divine intervention, "how much more simple and sublime" to create a world obeying certain general laws: "let animal be created, then by fixed laws of generation, such will be their successors. Let the powers of transportal be such, and so will be the forms of one country to another.—let geological changes go at such a rate, so will be the number and distribution of the species!!" (B 101–102)

God, I suppose, and people playing God can vacillate: Darwin did. Only a few pages later he wrote in quite a different vein, emphasizing the view that organic variations do not, and ought not from the standpoint of evolutionary theory, match too closely the changes in their physical milieu: "It is a point of great interest to prove animals not adapted to each country.—Provision for transportal otherwise not so numerous" (B 115) ; and "A race of domestic animals made from influences in one country is permanent in another.—Good argument for species not being so closely adapted." (B 130)

At this point, as I have shown in my discussion of the monad theory, about three months after beginning the notebooks he was seriously reconsidering his first view that organic variations are direct adaptive responses to environmental changes.

One Miltonic passage, reflecting his thoughts about ecological niches, brings home the point that he has begun to abandon the idea that adaptive variations stem directly from physical changes in the milieu. The notion of an ecological niche really puts the emphasis on the organism's capacity to vary to exploit new environmental opportunities, and therefore implies a more clearly interactionist view than the simple physicalism with which Darwin began: "If all men were dead, then monkeys make men.—Men make angels." (B 169)

The mysterious reference to angels leads us on. Darwin liked the monkey-into-man-into-angel transformation.[5] It crops up a few months

---

[5] Not only Darwin liked to speak of angels. Herschel mentioned them in his 1845 address. Speaking critically of the evolution hypothesis, he suggested that it included "an unbroken chain of gradually exalted organization from the crystal to the globule . . . up to the monkey and the man (nay, for aught we know, even to the

later, in a passage criticizing the notion that exactly the same species may evolve more than once: unless *"two* species will generate common kind, which is not probable, then monkeys will never produce man, but both monkeys and man may produce other species." In the next sentence he makes it reasonably clear that "angels" are not supernatural, but simply his optimistic shorthand for the unpredictable outcome of man's possible evolution. (*B* 215)

In this passage we can almost see Darwin giving up the remnants of his hopes for a strictly causal, deterministic theory. He is saying that there is far more than one possible adaptive variation for any available ecological niche; the exact form that will emerge and survive depends on many factors, not just the shape of the niche: variation is unpredictable, incessant, protean, and non-repeating.

And here the matter comes almost to rest, in an unstable equilibrium. Although Darwin never quite gave up the search for the causes of variation, he managed very well without knowing or even feeling that he knew them. Neither did he quite give up his sometime belief that variations were direct adaptations to changes in the physical milieu, but from this time forward he was extremely cautious about relying on direct environmental influences. Evolution through natural selection *means* that variations are not necessarily adaptive, so that variation must be coupled with selection if adaptive change is to occur.

At a critical moment in his thinking, on September 23, 1838, five days before the Malthus insight, we see Darwin struck, with new force, by the sheer magnitude of the number of variations: "Saw in Loddiges garden 1279 varieties of roses!!! proof of capability of variation.—Saw his collection of Hummingbirds, saw several greatly developed tails & one with beak turned up like Avocette. here is what . . ."[6]

Thus, when we say that Darwin shifted variation from a conclusion to a premise of his argument, we mean more than a mere rearrangement of sentences. In the final version, variation was at once something less and something more than in the original. It was less in the sense that it was no longer *adaptive* variation; the task of ensuring that only adaptive variations find an enduring place in the pantheon of nature was left to the process of selection. It was more, simply in its numbers; there was far more for selection to work on when the fact of variation was freed from the restraint of being only a response to environmental change: arising from forces within each individual

---

angel)." (*Loc. cit.*) Disraeli indignantly repudiated evolution. "The question is this: is man an ape or an angel? I am on the side of the angels." (Speech, Oxford, November 25, 1864) Darwin could not be so sure. For him the "if" was all important. Only *if* there were no man would the monkey evolve into a man-like creature, and likewise for man into angel.

[6] *D* 118. The page ends here and the next seven pages are missing.

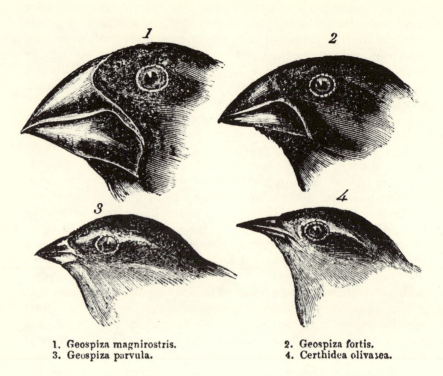

1. Geospiza magnirostris.   2. Geospiza fortis.
3. Geospiza parvula.   4. Certhidea olivaʒea.

Each species of finch found in the Galapagos has a beak adapted to its particular feeding habits. Darwin found thirteen species, of which the four major
types are shown.

organism, the number of variants from which nature could select was
plentiful—almost unlimited.

It is worth reflecting a moment on Darwin's situation when he
advanced a theory which depended on ubiquitous variation without
having any satisfactory explanation of it. Why did he not simply
accept this premise and go on to use it? Why did he constantly search
for the cause of variation, both throughout these notebooks and in
much of his later work?[7] We ought to recognize that it was conceivable
that the actual cause or causes of variation might, for all Darwin knew,
indeed turn out to be identical with the causes of evolutionary
progress. Even if Darwin could invent a plausible theory which did
not depend on his knowing the causes of variation, that would not
guarantee its correctness. Plausible theories are often wrong.

---

[7] See, for example, numerous passages in the *Origin of Species* and his two-volume
work *The Variation of Animals and Plants Under Domestication* (London: John
Murray, 1868). It cannot be said that Darwin found the causes of variation or that
he solved any other of the puzzles of genetics; but all his life he kept on trying.

Darwin would have been far more comfortable if he could have based his theory of evolution on a satisfactory science of genetics, including an understanding of the causes of variation. Without such knowledge, a theory of evolution is a leap into the dark, and it took Darwin even more courage than it might have taken others to make it—he was not a leaper. In public, he liked to be on solid ground; speculation was best done in private notebooks. As I shall discuss in the next chapter, the search for the cause of variation took him deeply into the study of the evolution of behavior, and led to his notebooks on man and mind.

Increasing the Importance of a Variable: Superfecundity. A complex theory is a structure composed of a number of ideas. Important changes in such a structure can stem from the simple realization that some phenomenon is significantly greater than previously recognized. Our conception of the structure of the universe would be entirely different if the attraction of gravity varied inversely with the cube of the distance, or if $E = mc^4$. Cyrano without an especially large nose would not be Cyrano de Bergerac.

A key point in the development of Darwin's thought concerns his recognition of the magnitude of two variables: *variation,* which I have just discussed, and *superfecundity,* the extent to which each organism tends to reproduce far more of its own kind than the number alive in any given parent generation. It is this superfecundity which leads to competition for the means to survive, or the struggle for existence, and thus to natural selection.

From the entry Darwin made in his evolution notebook on September 28, 1838, it is clear that his reading of Malthus' *Essay on Population* had at last stimulated his conscious recognition of the implications of superfecundity for evolutionary theory.

But this was by no means the first time Darwin had been exposed to the fact of great fertility in nature. During the period of these notebooks the work of the German biologist C. G. Ehrenberg (mentioned above in my discussion of spontaneous generation) on fossil and living micro-organisms was becoming well known. One of Ehrenberg's most dramatic findings was the incredible rate of reproduction of such organisms. As Darwin jotted down in his notes on Ehrenberg's work, "One invisible animalcule in four days could form 2 cubic stone."[8]

---

[8] D 167. This passage was definitely written on or after September 25, 1838. The pagination of the end of the D notebook is confusing, because Darwin skipped some pages and began a separate series of entries, so that page 95 and page 152 are both dated September 11. From the context, I believe that page 167 was written *before* the Malthus passage of September 28—i.e., between the 25th and the 27th—but the exact date remains in doubt. In any case, Ehrenberg made several appearances before British scientific gatherings earlier that year, and Darwin was well aware of his work.

Darwin did not at first attend mainly to this feature of Ehrenberg's work. His first mention of the latter appears early in the B notebook, while he was still working through the monad theory of evolution. It seemed to him then that Ehrenberg's micro-organisms might be the monads of his first theory: "If we suppose monads are constantly formed, would they not be pretty similar over whole world under similar climates and as far as world has been uniform at former epoch. How is this Ehrenberg?" (*B* 18–19)

Six months later, about February 1838, Darwin had apparently read a paper by Ehrenberg describing silicious rocks composed entirely of billions of these organisms, but he was not yet interested in superfecundity, and his note deals with the relation of living and extinct infusorians, one of the types of micro-organism Ehrenberg studied. (*C* 16)

In a note written about April or May of 1838 he is suddenly very much aware of the great reproductive powers of micro-organisms. But this does not lead him to see that the general notion of superfecundity might be useful in his own theory. Rather, he is troubled again at the possibility of a large number of points of origin for the tree of evolution; in that case, similarities among species that his theory would attribute to common descent might instead be described as mere analogies, due to different monadic lines following similar evolutionary paths: "When one reads in Ehrenberg's Paper on Infusoria on the enormous production—millions in few days—one doubts that one animal can really produce so great an effect—the spirit of life must be everywhere ambient and merely determined to such points by the vital laws.—So that all characters originally may must have had the character of analogical." (*C* 143) This passage is virtually the last gasp of Darwin's early belief in spontaneous generation and the monad theory of evolution. The great effect he is doubting is for one single individual organism to be the ultimate ancestor of all living things.

Now we come to the passage already mentioned, of uncertain date but probably written just before Darwin's Malthusian insight. When Darwin says, almost in passing, that "one invisible animalcule in four days" could manufacture a sizable stone, he *is* talking about the geometrical rate of population increase in a very pure and evident case. Nevertheless, he does not yet transform this awareness of great fertility in nature into the superfecundity principle. For that step he was now well prepared, but he needed the hint and the stimulus he drew from Malthus' *Essay*.

It is not easy to understand why Darwin had to wait so long before recognizing the evolutionary significance of the Malthusian principle. As we have seen, Darwin had been exposed to the Malthusian idea over and over. It occurs in the works of authors with whom he was very familiar and for whom he had the highest regard: Erasmus Darwin, Charles Lyell, Alexander von Humboldt, and William Paley. It was widely discussed during his whole life up to the period of the notebooks. Malthus died in 1834; in 1837 a review of his life and work appeared in the *Edinburgh Review,* a magazine which Darwin read. Certainly we can reject the notion that to construct a theory of evolution there was one simple step to make, and that by reading Malthus Darwin was enabled to make the step. We have seen that Wallace, although he attributed much to Malthus, took over a decade after reading the *Essay* to make the step. As for Darwin, we have just been tracing some of the complex moves that preceded his moment of insight.

Nor is it easy to understand just what remained for Darwin to do in September of 1838. In what sense had he *not* already grasped the principle of evolution through natural selection?

Transforming the Significance of a Process: Natural Selection. As a *conservative* force in nature, the idea of natural selection had a long history before Darwin, both as "nature's broom" and as "nature's policeman." It was long known that deviants from a species norm— sports, or monsters, or mutants, depending on the historical context— tend to be *less* fit than their more typical brothers and sisters. In the struggle for existence, natural selection, "nature's broom," operates to remove these weaklings and ugly ducklings. It was also recognized that there exists a balance of nature, and that various natural mechanisms of population control, "nature's police," operate to maintain it. Predating Malthus by some forty years, Linnaeus had emphasized these points and had seen that man was part of the balance of nature. He wrote, in his essay on the *polity of nature:*

> . . . I know not by what intervention of nature or by what law man's numbers are kept within fitting bounds. It is, however, true that the most contagious diseases usually rage to a greater degree in thickly populated regions, and I am inclined to think that war occurs where there is the greatest superfluity of people. At least it would seem that, where the population increases too much, concord and the necessities of life decrease, and envy and malignancy toward neighbors abound. Thus it is *a war of all against all.*[9]

---

[9] From Knut Hagberg, *Carl Linnaeus,* translated by Alan Blair (London: Jonathan Cape, 1952) , p. 183. I have not seen the original, but quote from an excellent article by Robert S. Stauffer, "Ecology in the Long Manuscript Version of Darwin's *Origin of Species* and Linnaeus' *Oeconomy of Nature," Proceedings of the American Philosophical Society,* Vol. 104, 1960, pp. 235–41. Among numerous accounts of the prehistory of the idea of natural selection, see Conway Zirkle, "Natural Selection Before the *Origin of Species*," *Proceedings of the American Philosophical Society,* Vol. 84, 1941, and Loren Eiseley, *Darwin's Century* (London: Gollancz, 1959).

All that Darwin had to do was to see that, although most mutants are at a disadvantage, some few are better adapted to their environment, and that over the long haul of geological time the perpetual struggle for existence permits these few to leave their marks on the course of evolution. That was "all" the change Darwin had to make.

As we inspect the numerous appearances and disappearances of the idea of natural selection in Darwin's notebooks, we can see that his problem was not so much to discover the idea as to discover its significance for evolutionary theory—to rescue it from its concealment in a variety of hiding places.

Early in the first notebook, as Darwin was thinking over the interplay of geographical isolation and in-breeding within the framework of his monad theory, he wrote: "is it not said that marrying-in *deteriorates* a race, that is alters it from some end which is good for man." (*B* 6) Here we see that Darwin has caught a key question: the value of a variation depends on the standpoint of the judge. But he is not quite saying what he must eventually: that a particular variation may be either good or bad even from the standpoint of the varying organism itself.

In the next sentence he uses the idea of struggle: "Let a pair be introduced and increase slowly, from many enemies, so as often to intermarry—who will dare say what result." (*B* 7) Here competition between species is used in two ways. It is a conservative force in limiting the population growth of a species newly arrived (on the hypothetical island); it is a force for change because it accentuates inbreeding among the new arrivals.

Thus we see that in its first appearance in Darwin's notes on evolution the idea of natural selection occurs with its two main components, variation and struggle, explicitly stated and closely linked. But the whole point is embedded in an argument about the cause of variation, drawing upon his own experiences in the islands the *Beagle* had visited.

The trick of permitting a whole species to change at once by isolating it on an island was neat but costly—it missed the point that, to be successful, variations must survive and spread *within* a larger population. Darwin eventually had to give up his one-sided focus on a *species* changing all at once and concern himself with the variation, survival, and reproduction of deviant *individuals* within a relatively stable larger population. An essential part of his first theory of evolution was the notion that the *number of species* remains approximately constant[10]; since monads were perpetually forming and evolving, old

---

10 As compared with the Malthusian idea that factors limiting the growth of populations keep the *number of individuals* approximately constant. In an excellent article Sandra Herbert has drawn attention to the importance in Darwin's thinking

forms had to vanish in order to make room for new ones. In the monad theory, then, extinction was accomplished by drawing an analogy with the life cycle of the individual: "There is nothing stranger in death of species, than individuals." (*B* 22)

As we have already discussed, Darwin soon gave up his monadic theory in favor of a theory of perpetual "becoming" in which the very fact of the organism's changing was the guarantor of its survival, in the sense that a species must have progeny in order to survive, and *the progeny of a species is a new species,* just as the progeny of an individual is a new individual. It is in this context that we must understand the question Darwin asks himself, "Whether every animal produces in course of ages ten thousand varieties (influenced itself perhaps by circumstances) and those alone preserved which are well adapted?" (*B* 90, about September or October 1837) Without the context it might seem as though Darwin already had the core of his ultimate theory of evolution. But at this point his theory of becoming, or necessary change, uses as its unit of analysis the species and not the individual. This is a far cry from the opening phrase of the *Origin,* "When we look to the individual. . . ."

About a month later he has serious misgivings: "Weakest part of theory death of species without apparent physical cause." (*B* 135) But he wants to insist that species do die—that is, extinction does occur. He works out in some detail the number of human individuals who would, after a lapse of 400 years, have no remaining progeny, assuming the population remains constant and not all family lines survive indefinitely. His aim is not to explore selection ratios of individuals within a species, but to examine more thoroughly the process of divergence by which species with a common origin become more and more remote from each other. This discussion of the fate of individual human families is intended only as an analogy to clarify the fate of species, but dwelling on the mathematics of populations as applied to individuals may have had its effect on Darwin's implicit unit of analysis. A few pages further on, in a peculiar and perhaps unwitting reversal of his usual way of stating the point, he writes, "There is no more wonder in extinction of individuals than of species." (*B* 153)

At about this time Darwin became increasingly concerned with a number of problems related to genetics—the causes of variation, the consequences of hybridization, the inheritance of acquired character-

of the transition from using species as the unit of analysis to using individuals. She places great weight on Malthus' contribution to this change in Darwin's approach. I believe it is true that reading Malthus helped Darwin to clarify his thinking on this crucial point, but the evidence below suggests that the change in choice of unit was a protracted process, stretched over a year or more, and linked to other aspects of his thought. See Sandra Herbert, "Darwin, Malthus and Selection," *Journal of the History of Biology,* 1971, Vol. 4, pp. 209–217.

istics, the contributions of the two sexes to their offspring. There is correspondingly less in the notes about divergence and the branching model of evolution, population dynamics, and similar topics that might have led him on more directly to the theory of natural selection.

One of the key metaphors in the *Origin of Species* is the parallel between artificial and natural selection. Darwin devoted many years to the study of plant and animal breeding, and nine years after the *Origin* he published his large work *The Variation of Animals and Plants Under Domestication*. Chapter 1 of the *Origin* is entitled "Variation Under Domestication." He chose to introduce the concept of natural selection by first describing plant and animal breeding by man as an unintentional large-scale experiment which could compensate for Darwin's inability to bring the process of natural selection into the laboratory. To understand the development of Darwin's idea of natural selection it is therefore essential to examine his use of knowledge about artificial selection.

In connection with his interest in these genetical questions Darwin had begun to steep himself in the literature of plant and animal breeding. Throughout the first notebook there are scattered remarks on this subject, mainly centered around hybridization. It is not until the second notebook that we find any remarks suggesting his eventual use of the human experience of controlled plant and animal breeding as providing an analogy with natural selection. The following sentence was written in February of 1838, or some seven months before he discovered the theory of evolution through natural selection: "The changes in species must be very slow owing to physical changes slow & offspring not picked.—as men do when making varieties." (*C* 17)

The same idea is reiterated a few pages further on. From the two passages we can see clearly that Darwin is somehow *aware* of the analogy between natural and artificial selection, but he is not *using* it. Rather, he is contrasting the two kinds of selection in order to attack a genetical problem. He knows that varieties produced by artificial selection can be hybridized; if this were true of natural varieties, permanent differences might not have a chance to evolve because they would be averaged out. This is the problem of blending inheritance which remained unsolved and with which his critics troubled him in later years.

At this point, the winter of 1838, he believed he had a solution. Variations which are produced gradually by slowly acting natural forces will have the strongest and most enduring hereditary effects: "varieties produced by slow causes, without picking become more and more impressed in blood with time." (*C* 34) Variations produced by faster-acting artificial selection will have weaker effects. Natural hereditary differences are stable and guarantee the main effect in question, hybrid sterility—i.e., the permanence and integrity of newly evolving species.

Of course, Darwin cannot carry this argument too far or he will have constructed a theory that argues against all natural change. To avoid this difficulty, he relies on the effects of geographic isolation and other isolating mechanisms, to ensure some in-breeding and stabilization of a new variant. These complexities are expressed succinctly in the following passage: "The infertility of crosse [sic] & cross is method of nature to prevent the picking of monstrosities as man does.—One is tempted to exclaim that nature conscious of the principle of incessant change in her offspring has invented all kinds of plan to insure sterility, but isolate your species her plans are frustrated or rather a new principle is brought to bear." (*C* 53)

The way Darwin ran animals and "other people" smoothly together in his thoughts is shown in a passage bearing on the role of isolation: "Animals having wide range, by preventing adaptation owing to crossing with unseasoned people would cause destruction.— Simile man living in hot countries, if continually crossed with people from cold, children would not become adapted to climate." (*C* 60)

It would be useful to be able to date some of the pages in the C notebook. Unfortunately, there are no dated entries except a reading list for a later period in the back pages. It is likely that the first 50 pages or so were finished by the end of March and the next 100 pages written in April and May.

The timing is of interest because there is a brief emergence of remarks bearing both on artificial and natural selection, somewhat freed from the confusing context of hybrid sterility. Then the idea of selection seems to go underground again, as Darwin continues with his earlier concerns and becomes increasingly preoccupied with another approach to the causes of variation, the idea of hereditary habit.

In its nascent form, the idea of natural selection is suffused with the special notion of sexual selection; this contradicts the suggestion that Darwin in later life felt impelled to introduce sexual selection to bolster a weakened case for the more general idea. He asks, "Whether species may not be made by a little more vigour being given to the chance offspring who have any slight peculiarity of structure. Hence seals take victorious seals, hence deer victorious deer, hence males armed & pugnacious all orders. . . ." (*C* 61)

He is struggling to separate the effects of selection from other factors: "Two grand classes of varieties; one where offspring picked, one where not—the latter made by man & nature, but cannot be counteracted by man.—effect of external contingencies & long bred in." (*C* 106) In other words, selection is *un*natural and its effects are ephemeral, not the real basis of evolution. To the modern reader, this may seem like an unproductive idea; for Darwin it may well have been a "good error"[11] one reflecting an increased grasp of the structure of the problem. At least he was beginning to see that selection could be separated from other factors; eventually this move would permit him to take a longer look at it.

A reminder: we need to work hard to avoid misusing our historical hindsight. The following passage seems to express one form of the Darwinian idea of natural selection, the notion of an evolutionary blind alley: "Changes in structure being necessarily excessively slow they became firmly embedded in the constitution. . . . The constitution being hereditary & fixed, certain physical changes at last become unfit, the animal cannot change quick enough & perishes." (C 153) Actually, Darwin is referring to an idea previously stated by Lyell, who granted that species vary somewhat and understood that the uneven relation between the rate of biological adaptation and the rate of change of the physical world could sometimes lead to *extinction* of species. This is not necessarily an evolutionary idea.

In the main, then, during this period Darwin used the idea of selection in its conservative sense, although he had occasional glimpses of its evolutionary power. The last 100 pages of the second notebook (in other words, probably part of May, June, and the first half of July) have almost nothing on the subject of selection. He seems to have had the thread and lost it.

Darwin's concerns, as discussed up to this point, continued without any remarkable change for the last 100 pages of the second or C notebook and up to the point of the Malthus insight.

The "naturalness" of selection is again denied in the following passage: "The varieties of the domesticated animals must be most complicated, because they are partly local & then the local ones are taken to fresh country & breed confined to certain best individuals.—scarcely any breed but what some individuals are picked out,—in a really natural breed, not one is picked out." (D 20, about the beginning of August 1838) Although the naturalness of selection is denied and the whole idea is buried in a thought about the complexity of variation under domestication, there is something else. The notion that a variety arises in one place and is then removed elsewhere for further breeding resembles his remarks about the importance of geographical isolation in nature, written about a year earlier. Even though he is now contrasting artificial breeding with natural variation, the form of his thought and even the language are very close to a point he has already expressed and assimilated, in which the

---

11 See Wolfgang Köhler's profound and delightful book *The Mentality of Apes* (London: Routledge and Kegan Paul, 1973), for a discussion of the idea of "good errors".

naturalness of geographical isolation and its effects was embraced rather than denied. Perhaps a transition to the recognition of natural selection as analogous to artificial breeding has already begun.

During this period Darwin remained aware of the role of adaptation and selection in extinction. On August 19, 1838, he jotted down a note applying the idea to the varieties of man (*D* 37–38) ; on September 7 he wrote more generally: "It is important with respect to extinction of species, the capability of only small amount of change at any one time." (*D* 69) This is a repetition of Lyell's point that the physical changes of the environment sometimes proceed at a rate exceeding the capacity of organisms to adapt; Lyell applied the idea only to explain extinction, and he rejected the idea of evolution. Darwin, of course, embraced evolution, but he did not in early September see how a small adjustment of Lyell's statement could lead to an explanation of the making of *new species.*

It is well to stress the fact that at this moment only a few weeks before the Malthus insight Darwin was really very vague as to the actual mechanism of evolution. On September 8, the day after the above passage on extinction, he wrote: "When I show that islands would have no plants were it not for seeds being floated about,—I must state that the mechanism by which seeds are adapted for long transportation, seems to imply knowledge of whole world—if so doubtless part of system of great harmony." (*D* 74) The uncertain and risky teleology in that note is not spoken in the voice we know as Darwin's; as he clarified his views on adaptation, "final causes," and teleology, he developed a point of view that made it possible to explain harmoniously acting, goal-seeking systems without appeal to the supernatural[12]—but on September 8, 1838, he definitely did not have the cybernetic system of variation and selection in mind.

On September 14 he notes several conversations about animal breeding, leading to the conclusion that through artificial selection man can breed "monsters"—that is, distorted varieties "which could not have been persistent in nature." (*D* 108) On either the 15th or 16th he asks, "How long will the wretched inhabitants of N.W. Australia go on blinking their eyes without extermination, & change of structure." (*D* 111)

We are now at last coming up to the moment of the Malthus

---

[12] It eventually became possible for some thinkers to incorporate the idea of evolution through natural selection in their conceptions of a designing Providence: It takes as much ingenuity to devise a natural order that will evolve according to a few fundamental laws as it does to accomplish the Creation in six days. In 1872 Charles Lyell put the matter succinctly: "When first the doctrine of the origin of species by transmutation was proposed, it was objected that such a theory substituted a material self-adjusting machinery for a Supreme Creative Intelligence." Charles Lyell, *Principles of Geology*, 11th edition, 2 vols. (London: Murray, 1872) , Vol. 2, p. 500.

insight. There are no further notes on selection until then, but around this time there are two entries dealing with population dynamics and sex ratios. On September 11 there is a bibliographical note indicating that he has been looking at a statistical paper on human sex ratios by Quetelet, a pioneering Belgian statistician.[13] On September 17 there is a brief allusion to the superfecundity idea, though only in a restricted sense: "wasps breed many females, but almost all die—bees breed but few, because they are kept in security." (D 116) Had this been written *after* the Malthus insight, we could say that Darwin now sees that sex ratios evolve in compensating relationships with other characteristics: if an insect does not breed many females, natural selection favors the survival and evolution of mechanisms for protecting the few. But the passage in question was written before September 28, and we can only say that Darwin was taking an interest in some new questions and unwittingly sensitizing himself to appreciate the value to him of the Malthusian argument.

Finally, September 28, 1838, the great Malthusian moment of truth arrives. Does it strike Darwin with the sudden force of a thunderbolt? Is it an Archimedean "Eureka" experience? Does it transform his thinking from that moment forward and for all time to come?

We have reproduced pages 134–135 of the third or D notebook, so the reader may judge for himself. Notice the disjointed format full of long insertions, the vigorous and elevated prose style, the use of metaphor, the triple underlining. Surely, this is not merely a great moment in the history of science but also a great culmination, a peak experience for the man Charles Darwin?

Not really. The insertions, the metaphors, the occasionally high-flown style, the underlining—these traits can be found all through the notebooks. As it happens, the crucial passage does not even contain a single exclamation point, although in other transported moments he used quite a few, sometimes in triplets.

More significantly, he does not drop all his other concerns and questions in a manner suggesting that he now feels he has the answer of answers to the "question of questions." The next day, September 29, we find a long entry on the behavior of various primates, much of it about their sexual curiosity. (D 137–139)

Because Darwin skipped some pages and some are still missing, the next definitely datable entry we can study begins on page 4 of the fourth or E notebook, dated October 4, six days later. In that entry, and in the one just preceding (E 3), Darwin is certainly discussing the theory of evolution through natural selection, and he refers to it

---

13 D 152, written in the back section of the D notebook to which Darwin had skipped, accounting for some peculiarities of pagination.

D Notebook, p. 134. *Courtesy of Cambridge University Library.*

D Notebook, p. 135. *Courtesy of Cambridge University Library.*

fondly as "my theory." But the reader should bear in mind that Darwin uses the phrase "my theory" liberally throughout the notebooks, to refer to whatever idea happens to have caught his enthusiasm at the moment, especially when he is thinking of his ideas in relation to those of others.

As we read on through the E notebook, we see that Darwin is not vacillating about natural selection. He remains convinced that this is a theory that works. But he has good reason to continue asking all his old questions. He does not know the cause of variation or the mechanism of hereditary transmission. A theory of evolution without a science of genetics seemed a shaky structure. And so, although the E notebook contains much about the new theory, the questions of the previous months still haunt him. It is not until six or eight weeks after the first Malthus insight that he is able to sum up the theory succinctly in the passage discussed earlier, beginning: "Three principles will account for all. . . ." (E 58, written sometime between November 7 and December 1, 1838)

Darwin had come to the summit. After a hard climb, the summit is not a simple achievement. It is no longer clear which way is up or down. Getting down is still a problem, and other peaks have become visible. Nor is the summit a sharp point, but rather a broad field with subtleties and ambiguities all its own.

The links between Darwin's concepts of the nature of variation, of the amount of variation, and of the superfecundity principle are intricate. So long as variation was conceived of as directly adaptive, there need be only one appropriate modification for each change of the environment. Only *after* he had given up the idea that variations are necessarily adaptive would it become imperative to have many variations for selection to choose among. But the moment the number of variations required by the theory becomes large, the superfecundity principle .comes to the foreground of attention. There must be many individuals to serve as "carriers" of the many variations. Variation and selection may be separate principles, but they are both aspects of the same reality, a large and varying number of individuals.

In his *Autobiography* Darwin gives his recollection of the Malthus insight:

> In October 1838, that is, fifteen months after I had begun my systematic enquiry, I happened to read for amusement Malthus on *Population,* and being well prepared to appreciate the struggle for existence which everywhere goes on from long-continued observation of the habits of animals and plants, it at once struck me that under these circumstances favourable variations would tend to be preserved, and unfavourable ones to be destroyed. The result of this

would be the formation of new species. Here, then, I had at last got a theory by which to work. . . . [*Autobiography*, 120]

This paragraph follows shortly after a statement about his method:

My first note-book was opened in July 1837. I worked on true Baconian principles, and without any theory collected facts on a wholesale scale. . . . [*Autobiography*, 119]

Taken together, these statements give an extremely misleading picture. Darwin certainly began the notebooks with a definite theory, and when he gave it up it was for what he thought was a better theory. True, when he gave up his second theory he remained in a theoretical limbo for some months. But even then he was always trying to solve special theoretical problems, such as those related to hybridization, and he almost *never* collected facts without some theoretical end in view. It was not simply from observation but from hard theoretical work that he was so well prepared to grasp the significance of Malthus' essay.

A quick résumé of this effort will help to establish the point. Darwin had worked his way through and then abandoned the monad theory with its attendant premise of spontaneous generation; the ubiquitous transformation of inanimate into animate matter was a principle that competed with the superfecundity idea implicit in natural selection. Darwin had then surrendered his theory of perpetual becoming—that is, he had seen that variation by itself could not explain progressive evolution. He had begun at least to doubt that variations are directly adaptive responses to environmental forces; if they were, there would be no need for selection. He had seen that the amount of variation in nature was very much greater than previously realized. He had become aware of Ehrenberg's work showing the dramatic superfecundity of micro-organisms. He had searched valiantly for the causes of heritable variations, and although he had not given up the search, he had become better prepared to treat variation not as the conclusion of a satisfying argument but as an unexplained premise. Although he had attended to the subject of domestic breeding mainly with the intent of contrasting artificial and natural selection, it seems plausible that this effort may have prepared him to see the useful analogy between them.

But the way was neither straight or narrow. We do come to an apparent paradox. He still had to take the crucial step of *combining* the premises of ubiquitous variation and Malthusian superfecundity in an argument that leads logically to the conclusion of natural selection and progressive evolution. This means that he must have already successfully disembedded the idea of natural selection from the conservative matrix in which, as we have seen, it had been previously utilized. Are we saying that restructuring the argument depends on seeing the principle of natural selection, while at the same time seeing the principle depends on restructuring the argument?

Yes. This is a circular argument or, better, a helical process. Understanding the structure of Darwin's argument as a growth structure helps to explain why the path to the moment of insight seems so tortuous, repetitive, cyclical. A path of such shape is the only way in which you can construct an argument out of parts which depend for their significance on the structure of the whole. The developed whole *must* be foreshadowed or prefigured at earlier and more primitive steps in the process of creative development.

There is one last point which expresses the same apparent paradox, resolved only through a thoroughly developmental approach. As we have seen, Darwin had been through so much by the time he read Malthus' *Essay,* what could possibly have remained for him to glean from the *Essay* itself? To see the full force of this question, the reader should remember Erasmus Darwin's poetic expression of the Malthusian idea, from which we have already quoted a little (see page 51). Erasmus Darwin did not leave much out. His poem applied the superfecundity principle to a wide variety of species—oak, poppy, aphid, snail, worm, frog, herring, and man. He wrote, "So human progenies, if unrestrain'd . . . would spread. . . . But war, and pestilence, disease, and dearth, Sweep the superfluous myriads from the earth."[14]

In the growth of thought a given idea may move from an early phase in which it is implicit in the structure of an argument to a later phase in which it becomes explicit, consciously recognized, and deliberately expressed. As the thinking person becomes more aware of the idea, he can begin to use it more actively and purposefully. Eventually, his feeling of personal connection with it fades. He can look at it with detachment, see some of the unexpected possibilities the idea now generates, and some of the problems it raises.

What then could Malthus give Charles Darwin that he did not already have? Two things. First, a clear statement of the superfecundity principle, in its well-known, quasi-mathematical form. Secondly, a *re*-reading of the superfecundity principle at just the right moment: when Darwin's thought had at last grown to the point where, having met natural selection so often, he could finally recognize it.

---

14 Erasmus Darwin, *Temple of Nature, op. cit.,* Canto IV. In an earlier passage in the same canto, he called up a global vision: "From Hunger's arm the shafts of Death are hurl'd, And one great Slaughter-house the warring world!"

PART III

Darwin on Man, Mind, and Materialism

CHAPTER 9

Man's Place in Darwin's Argument

Arguing from man to animals is philosophical . . .
[Man is] a "frontier instance . . ."

Charles Darwin, N notebook,
p. 49, about December 1838

Psychologists interested in thinking rarely consider the general archi-
tecture of a person's ideas; implicitly, they often write as though its
structural form is a set of problems, perhaps organized in a hierarchy
of importance, or even just one central problem. Another way of
conceiving of this structure is to imagine a network of enterprises.
Each enterprise is far more inclusive than a problem; it is, rather, one
domain within which the person works. If the recognizable problems
within that domain were ever all solved, the thinker might well invent
new ones in order to keep the enterprise alive. The enterprises composing the network are mutually supportive, yet in some ways they
have an existence independent of each other, very much as the strands
of a net. And since it is a living network, new relationships are constantly appearing.

In this chapter I examine Darwin's thought about a crucial issue,
the evolution of man and mind, with special regard for the period in
his life when he explicitly decided that this subject was an enterprise
worth differentiating from the rest of his work.

To anticipate, my examination of Darwin's notes leads me to
believe that he first took up the evolution of mental processes because
these seemed to be the most rapidly modifiable of all biological func-

Jemmy Button in 1833 after a few years among Englishmen; in 1834, a few months later, after his return to Tierra del Fuego.

tions, and therefore the most useful for testing the "Lamarckian" idea of the inheritance of acquired characteristics. Examining Darwin's hypothesis of "hereditary habit" therefore requires consideration of the relation of his ideas to Lamarck's.

In short, I deal first with man's place in Darwin's general argument about the evolution of all organisms. But the premise underlying this discussion is the idea that man has evolved according to the same natural laws as other organisms. Accepting this premise had special significance, treatment of which I reserve for the following chapters.

On July 15, 1838, one year after beginning his first notebook on transmutation, Darwin began the third notebook, which he labeled "D." On the very same day he began another notebook. Skipping some letters of the alphabet, he labeled it "M," which may have meant Man, or Morals, or Mind, or may have been merely mnemonic. This new enterprise was begun while he was staying at his father's house, after a two-week geological expedition in Scotland: ". . . reached Shrewsbury July 13th. Very idle at Shrewsbury, some notes from my Father. Opened notebook connected with metaphysical enquiries." (*Journal*) Sometime later he wrote on the cover, "This book full of Metaphysics on Morals and Speculations on Expression." Perhaps because of the label, students of Darwin's biological thought have neglected this document. On laboring through it, deciphering Darwin's difficult handwriting, one realizes that these notes served as the point of departure for *The Descent of Man*, which he wrote and published thirty-three years later (1871), and for *The Expression of Emotions in Man and Animals* (1872).

Why did Darwin begin a new set of notes about a subject on which he had not done any previous systematic work? As his journal entry suggests, the idleness of a vacation away from London may have provided a convenient setting, and the opportunity to question his father about various medical subjects related to mental processes may have served as a further invitation to embark on the study of man. But such accidental reasons hardly seem sufficient to explain the M and N notebooks, which continued for well over a year and which contain so much hard thinking. During the months before and after July 1838 he was engaged in processing the materials of the *Beagle* voyage, he had begun some new geological work, and he was secretary of the London Geological Society, not to mention his work on evolution. He did not lack projects or need a new one to fill a vacuum.

A second possible reason for his beginning the new notebooks might have been a desire to separate the question of man's origins from his other inquiries. Speculations on man and mind intruded constantly into his evolutionary notebooks. Possibly he wanted to put man to one side, devoting a little time to the subject as a special pursuit, in order to give more focused attention to the main question, the search for a workable theory of evolution of all other organisms. Separating man from the rest of creation would have been entirely consonant with the thinking of most of his contemporaries. But, as we shall see, even at this point in his thinking such a cleavage would have been quite un-Darwinian.

A careful reading of the two parallel sets of notes, the D notebook and the M notebook, and the B and C notebooks preceding them, suggests a third explanation: that Darwin began his systematic study of man and mind because he hoped to find in that direction answers questions that went right to the heart of his search for a theory evolution. For other evolutionary theorists man and his intellect mig pose special problems. But Darwin treated man as a unique *opp tunity* for the biologist, an opportunity to study intelligence central feature of adaptive change, and to study it in that organis which it is most prominent, man.

The preceding chapters dealt with a group of questions constitute the genetical problem: how do variations arise? variants are heritable? which survive crossing between di strains? how does hybridization work and when does it fail? ally, Darwin had to admit defeat; a complete theory of e might explain variation and the hereditary transmission of v but Darwin would have to accept these steps as premises, in th unexplained. In July 1838, however, it seemed to him of th importance to solve this group of related problems. Withou no matter how well he might marshal the evidence for the of evolution, he would not have a truly explanatory theory o

It is in this context that we must consider the meaning of Darwin's beginning the M notebook. The first six weeks of those notes represent an effort to collect all sorts of ideas and information that might bear on the inheritance of acquired characteristics. His basic hypothesis is that an often repeated act may lead to a structural change, which in turn may be inherited.

The belief that habits change slowly fitted in with Darwin's idea that only slowly acquired changes can be transmitted. He rejected the Lamarckian notion that "willing" produces changes. Darwin insisted that it is the real action which must be the prime mover, but then this is moderated by his belief in the efficacy of mental acts of various kinds.

The M and N notebooks had a second function, to serve as a repository for observations and reflections on the continuity between man and other animals. In this connection, Darwin made many notes on animal intelligence, animal language, and animal emotions—all aimed at showing that the gulf between man and other animals is not unbridgeable.

But Darwin could hardly go this far into the subject of the origin of man without, as he put it, attacking "the citadel itself": man's mind and the way it works. In his day no one could make the effort to develop a scientific psychology without at the same time taking a stand on a fundamental issue in philosophy, the relation of mind and body. In the M and N notebooks we see Darwin's growing awareness that his evolutionary theorizing opened the way for a thoroughgoing philosophical materialism, with all its painful consequences.

The third major function, then, of these notebooks was to explore the possibility of developing a scientific psychology and the relation of that effort to materialist philosophy. Taking that stand, albeit in private, may well have strengthened Darwin for the long struggle that lay ahead. In a sense, these notebooks have not only an intellectual function, the exploration of questions and issues, but an emotional and expressive function, the making of a private commitment. Even as he began to realize that he might not want to say certain things aloud, he felt a need to say them as clearly as possible to himself.

As we shall see, the path he took included a great deal of highly personal introspection. Far from impoverishing the inner life, as some theologians feared, Darwin himself is a case in point for the view that the act of divesting oneself of the protective coat of conventional religion can serve as the point of departure for a deeper examination of oneself.

In short, the M and N notebooks represent the interweaving of three themes in Darwin's thought: searching for the source of heritable variation and testing the hypothesis of habits becoming hereditary; marshaling the evidences for psychological continuity between man

and other animals; bringing a variety of methods—introspective, pathological, experimental, and developmental, as well as comparative—to bear on the effort to construct a scientific psychology. Underlying this systematic effort lay Darwin's rapid movement toward a firm decision that only a materialist philosophy of biology could support the whole enterprise.

Are We Not Brothers?

Although the M notebook represents Darwin's first systematic attack on the question of man, it was hardly his first expression of interest in the subject. Indeed, the organization of the manuscript notes during the *Beagle* voyage parallels and foreshadows the later notebooks. On the voyage he kept several sets of scientific notes (in geology and in various fields of biology) and a large diary. The latter was used for general descriptions of scenery, for recording the main events and adventures of the voyage, and for many interesting observations on the different sorts of human being he encountered in his scientific circumnavigation.

From his very first remarks on encountering Negroes on the island of St. Jago, off the coast of Africa, it is clear that he is interested in the issue of race differences. His description of the behavior of the people he met is sympathetic and emphasizes their intelligence. (*Beagle Diary*, p. 27, January 20, 1832)

Six months later he describes the black men, both slave and free, whom he met in Brazil, in laudatory terms:

> I cannot help believing they will ultimately be the rulers. I judge of it from their numbers, from their fine athletic figures, (especially contrasted with the Brazilians) proving they are in a congenial climate, & from clearly seeing their intellects have been much underrated; they are the efficient workmen in all the necessary trades. [*Beagle Diary*, 77, July 3, 1832]

In many anecdotes he stresses the essential humanity of the black people he meets, not only in regard to intelligence but in moral qualities as well. For example, he writes of the recapture of a group of runaway slaves from a cliffside retreat: "excepting one old woman, who sooner than be again taken, dashed herself to pieces from the very summit. I suppose in a Roman matron this would be called noble patriotism, in a negress it is called brutal obstinacy!" (*Beagle Diary*, 51, April 8, 1832)

As we have seen, members of the anti-slavery Darwin family circle were well prepared to accept the idea that all men are brothers, sharing both a common fate and a common origin. From the early appearance in Darwin's travel diary of such egalitarian expressions of feeling it seems clear that he shared the family point of view.

His sympathetic acceptance of the people of another race and approximately his own civilization stands in sharp contrast to the profound shock of his first encounter with a truly primitive group, the Indians of Tierra del Fuego. On December 18, 1832, he wrote, while still in Tierra del Fuego: "I would not have believed how entire the difference between savage & civilized man is. It is greater than between a wild & domesticated animal, in as much as in man there is greater power of improvement." (*Beagle Diary*, 119, December 18, 1832)

To his teacher Henslow he wrote in the same astonished vein:

> I do not think any spectacle can be more interesting than the first sight of man in his primitive wildness. . . . I shall never forget this when entering Good Success Bay—the yell with which a party received us. They were seated on a rocky point, surrounded by the dark forest of beech; as they threw their arms wildly round their heads, and their long hair streaming, they seemed the troubled spirits of another world." [*LL* 1, 243, April 1833]

Over a year later, writing to a friend at Cambridge:

> But I have seen nothing which more completely astonished me than the first sight of a savage. It was a naked Fuegian, his long hair blowing about, his face besmeared with paint. There is in their countenances an expression which I believe, to those who have not seen it, must be inconceivably wild. Standing on a rock he uttered tones and made gesticulations than which the cries of domestic animals are far more intelligible.[1]

Darwin's amazement may have been heightened by the dissimilarity between the primitive people of Tierra del Fuego and the Fuegians he had known on board the *Beagle*. On a previous voyage the *Beagle* had brought to England a party of four Fuegians, three of whom were now being returned to their native country. (The fourth had died of smallpox.) In their year abroad these individuals had learned some English and grown accustomed to wearing European clothes and other manners. It was these three whom Darwin had in mind thirty-five years later when he wrote of the

> numerous points of mental similarity between the most distinct races of man. The American aborigines, Negroes and Europeans are as different from each other in mind as any three races that can be named; yet I was incessantly struck, whilst living with the Fuegians on board the "Beagle," with the many little traits of character, shew-

---

[1] Letter to C. Whitley, written from Valparaiso, July 23, 1834. (*LL* 1, 255)

ing how similar their minds were to ours; and so it was with a full-blooded negro with whom I happened once to be intimate. [*Descent,* 178]

Anti-slavery medal, 1838. *Courtesy of Emma and Sidney Kaplan.*

Robert FitzRoy, captain of the *Beagle,* had succeeded in some degree in educating the transported Fuegians in "English, and the plainer truths of Christianity, as the first object; and the use of common tools, a slight acquaintance with husbandry, gardening, and mechanism, as the second."[2] His success may have gone much farther than he intended. He himself was an professed Christian, a believer in every word of Scripture, and a natural enemy of all evolutionary thought. But the transformation he helped produce in the three Fuegians must have also had a transforming effect on Charles Darwin's thinking, helping him to see the similarities among different sorts of men, and the continuity between the most urbane, devout Englishman and all other animals.

Contrary to Darwin's earlier remark, the language of the Fuegians, their social system, and their mores were all entirely human. His remarks about the Fuegians vary in tone, reflecting the fact that there are two different truths at stake, the unity of humankind and man's relation with other animals. Simply as a good Christian, Darwin could

---

2 FitzRoy, *op. cit.,* p. 12.

adhere to the first point, although there was still room for Darwin's comparisons of various human groups to strengthen his belief in the unity of man.

With regard to the second point, man's place in nature, the *Beagle* experience was more important. Not only did Darwin have the occasion to see primitive men whose manner of life dramatized for him the animal nature (and eventually animal *origins*) of man. By seeing European man under a great variety of circumstances, he was able to shed all illusions that there is any group of human beings exempt from animal impulses.

As he moved over the face of the earth Darwin took advantage of his many opportunities to compare human groups with each other. Often he seems to be forming a scale along which different groups can be ranged. Such efforts appear especially in the later years of the voyage when he had acquired sufficient breadth of experience to warrant such comparisons. For example, he looked with disfavor on the aggressiveness of the New Zealanders (i.e., Maori) as compared with the mildness of the Tahitians:

> Looking at the New Zealander, one naturally compares him with the Tahitian; both belonging to the same family of mankind. . . . If the state in which the Fuegians live should be fixed on as zero in the scale of government, I am afraid New Zealand would rank but a few degrees higher, while Tahiti, even as when first discovered, would occupy a respectable position. [*Beagle Diary*, 363–364, December 22, 1835, while in New Zealand]

Darwin consistently took these differences to be the products of history, culture, education, and habitat, rather than the reflection of a fixed inheritance of psychological traits. One passage makes this point very succinctly. Landing on the island of Chiloe, off the coast of Chile,

> we saw a family of pure Indian extraction; the father was singularly like to York Minster; some of the younger boys, with their ruddy complexions, might be mistaken for Pampas Indians. Everything I have seen convinces me of the close connection of the different tribes, who yet speak distinct languages. . . . It is a pleasant thing in any case to see the aboriginal inhabitants, advanced to the same degree of civilization, however low that may be, which their white conquerors have attained.[3]

But a belief in the educability of primitive people (either through the spontaneous development of their own culture, or through the ministrations of more "civilized" conquerors) has no necessary connection with evolutionary thought. Only if the products

---

[3] *Beagle Diary*, 251, written November 26, 1834, on the island of Chiloe. York Minster was one of the educated Fuegians on board the *Beagle*.

of experience are passed on through heredity can they be thought to play a direct role in organic evolution.

Do Habits Become Hereditary?

Several passages in the *Beagle Diary* tempt one to believe that Darwin was, during the *Beagle* voyage, already examining the hypothesis that habits may become hereditary. For example, in discussing the seemingly miserable existence of the Tierra del Fuegians, living as they did in hard country at the end of the world, he concludes:

> There can be no reason for supposing the race of Fuegians are decreasing, we may therefore be sure that he enjoys a sufficient share of happiness (whatever its kind may be) to render life worth having. Nature, by making habit omnipotent, has fitted the Fuegian to the climate & productions of his country. [*Beagle Diary*, 213, February 24, 1834]

Although Darwin speaks of the importance of "habit" at many different points in his notes, what he means by the term is shifting. In the *Beagle Diary* the term *habit* refers to a behavior pattern, without always distinguishing learned from hereditary patterns. This is not an unusual usage; even today naturalists informally describing the "habits" of an animal may mean simply its characteristic behavior patterns, without regard to their genesis.

As the *Beagle* drew near England, in a retrospective passage Darwin wrote of himself,

> It has been said that the love of the chase is an inherent delight in man—a relic of an instinctive passion: if so, I am sure the pleasure of living in the open air, with the sky for a roof, and the ground for a table, is part of the same feeling. It is the savage returning to his wild & native habits." [*Beagle Diary*, 429, sometime between September 24 and October 1, 1836]

Even in the *Origin* Darwin used *habit* in a number of different senses. In the chapter on "the laws of variation" there is a section entitled "Effects of Use and Disuse" in which, in a representative sentence, he writes, "We may imagine that the early progenitor of the ostrich had habits like those of a bustard. . . ." (*Origin*, 135) In the same chapter, in a section entitled "Acclimatisation," he begins, "Habit is hereditary with plants, as in the period of flowering, in the amount of rain requisite for seeds to germinate, in the time of sleep, &c. . . ." (*Origin*, 139) The point is not so much that Darwin applied the term *habit* to plants, since we know that he believed that plants engage in behavior—in the present context, the significant point is that he uses *habit* in a way that makes it sometimes hard to tell whether he is speaking of a learned or an unlearned pattern of behavior.

An early expression in Darwin's notes of the hypothesis of habits becoming hereditary occurs in a quotation from F. Cuvier about "one of the most general laws of life—the transmission of a fortuitous modification into a durable form, of a fugitive want into a fundamental propensity, of an accidental habit into an instinct." Darwin adds, "I take higher grounds and say life is short for this object and others, viz. not too much change." (*B* 118, about October 1837) He means to say that if such changes accumulate indefinitely in an individual organism, it will lose its identity as a member of a species, and so will its progeny if the changes are heritable. Consequently, the process of death serves the adaptive function of limiting change and maintaining the integrity of species.[4] The changes in question are all the psychological developments that occur in the life of an individual.

Evolutionary Change Must Be Selective

Darwin was searching for a theory that would account for evolutionary change without postulating the destruction of the natural order in which species retain their identity over very long stretches of time. At one extreme, the process of change might be too chaotic or be carried too far if characteristics acquired in the individual's life history are too readily incorporated in its bequest to posterity. At the other extreme, if acquired characteristics are too readily inherited, changes in one direction achieved by one generation might be as readily unmade by the next: a facile mutability of species might operate against evolution rather than favoring it.

For these reasons, Darwin was on the alert for selective or damping mechanisms that might reduce change and stabilize its products without obliterating it. But the boundary of death was not a sufficient limitation on the acquisition of heritable change, because the process of changing would be simply taken over by the succeeding generation. He was therefore led to search further for principles of selection.[5]

---

4 This is an expansion of an earlier idea that death prevents the endless accumulation of the effects of accidents suffered by the individual. (*B* 4)

5 These two paragraphs involve considerably more interpretation on my part than most of my efforts to trace Darwin's thought. There is clear evidence that he was trying out various selective mechanisms that would have the effect of limiting change. But his reasons for doing so are not made explicit in his notes. There is, obviously, room for error in "filling in" for Darwin.

Selective Breeding

The mechanisms for moderating change that Darwin considers fall under two general headings, those concerned with keeping sorted out changes that have already occurred, and those concerned with ensuring that the changes that occur are in themselves stable. Keeping existing differences sorted out means preventing wholesale interbreeding among all manner of unlike creatures. If such interbreeding could occur, and if the progeny inherited something from each parent, the number of new combinations constantly arising would be very large, the amount of change occurring in a single generation might be very great, and the distinctions among species would disappear entirely.

Cropping up repeatedly in Darwin's notes are the subjects of hybrid sterility and sexual isolating mechanisms that prevent crosses between unlike creatures. Of course, some of these mechanisms depend on details of the structure of the sexual organs, and in later life Darwin made major contributions to our knowledge of this subject in plants. At this time, however, he was more interested in a psychosexual isolating mechanism, the repugnance of unlike creatures for each other:

> There is in nature a real repulsion amounting to impossibility holds good in plants between all different forms; therefore when from being put on island & fresh species made parents do not cross—we see it even in men; thus possibility of Caffers & Hottentots coexisting proves this. [*B* 189, about December 1837]

This passage recapitulates his earlier idea that geographical isolation, as on an island, would lead to variations and the beginning of new species. The question then arises: how will the new variants endure? His answer is that the backcross does not occur: the new variants, being alike, breed with one another. In other words, he starts with the plausible idea that "The dislike of two species to each other is evidently an instinct; & this prevents breeding"—and extends it to mean dislike between a new variant and the original species. (*B* 197)

Although in the passage quoted above he mentions an example of members of different human groups failing to interbreed, more generally he is aware of the fact that some interbreeding does occur. Since in his view sexual repugnance is instinctive, man, being a creature of reason rather than instinct, is freer to make choices governed by his ideas of beauty, which may or may not lead him to choose a partner from his own group. This line of thought stems from Darwin's steady belief that human beings form a single species. Thus, "Man has no *hereditary prejudices* or instinct to conquer or breed together.—Man has no limits to desire, in proportion instinct more, reason less, so will aversion be." (*B* 93)

But this possibility of interbreeding among human groups, while it contributes toward preventing divergence and maintaining mankind as one species, poses a problem for Darwin. The same catholicity of sexual taste might lead to the incorporation of monstrous variations into the heritable characteristics of our species. Having eliminated instinctual repugnance as a selective mechanism in man, he must propose an alternative. Accordingly, he considers social arrangements to prevent the propagation of undesirable human variants: exile. From an article about Ava, the ancient capital of Burma, he cites an

> account of HAIRY (because ancestors hairy) man with one hairy child, and of *albino* DISEASE being banished, and given to Portuguese priest. —In first settling a country, people very apt to be split up into many isolated races! are there any instances of peculiar people banished by rest?—.˙. Most monstrous form has tendency to propagate as well as diseases. [*B* 119]

The last sentence seems to mean that the existence of the practice of banishing monstrous variants would suggest that the community in question knows that such individuals do indeed propagate their own kind, and this folk knowledge is in itself useful evidence on that unsettled point.

The idea of selective sexual repugnance implies its obverse, sexual attraction. Darwin in 1837 stated the negative side more explicitly: "Animals have no notion of beauty,—therefore instinctive feelings against other species for sexual ends, whereas man has such instincts very little." (*B* 161, about November 1837) Less than a year later he would have been quite willing to grant a sense of beauty to animals, and by the same token its role in the process of sexual selection. It is interesting that the idea of sexual selection makes its first appearance in these notes in a negative form. Perhaps as he approached marriage (he became engaged to Emma Wedgwood on November 11, 1838) the positive virtues of sexual attraction found their way more explicitly into his biological theorizing.

Two Mechanisms for Selecting among Acquired Characteristics

In parallel with his reflections on selective mating as discussed above, Darwin was beginning to consider another type of mechanism for moderating change: selective processes ensuring that some but not all changes or adaptations will become part of the heritable material of the species. The central idea takes two forms, one that might be labeled "biogenetic," the other "psychogenetic."

In its biogenetic form, the idea runs about as follows: those characteristics will be a stable part of the organism's heritable material which have been acquired slowly, which involve small changes, and which were acquired long before the moment of reproduction; "long before" may mean either early in the life history of the individual or in previous generations.[6]

During the summer of 1838, just when he was beginning the M notebook, Darwin was interested enough in this idea to state and restate it three times in succession, striving for greater clarity, concluding:

> Same Prop. better enunciated.—An animal in either parent cannot transmit to its offspring any change from the form which it inherits from its parents stock without it being small & slowly attained. N.B. The longer a thing is in the blood the more persistent any amount of change. . . . Hence mutilations not hereditary, but size of particular muscles . . . expression of countenances, organic diseases, mental disposition, stature, are slowly obtained & hereditary. . . . [*D* 17]

How could a change be "long in the blood" only after it had occurred in several generations, unless some change was transmitted from one generation to another? Presumably, Darwin intended that a change which could not yet be transmitted in a detectable form nevertheless in some way altered the heritable material. This would imply the distinction geneticists made much later between "phenotype" and "genotype." Only in this way can we make sense of the proposal that changes can occur in several generations without being transmissible and then, as a result of this history, become transmissible. In Darwin's thinking, the sequence might have run: the conditions of life (both the external milieu and the activity of the individual) produce acquired changes in the individual; these in turn produce changes in the underlying heritable material; these in turn accumulate over several generations to produce detectable changes.[7] I do not mean to

---

6 A similar idea is expressed in the *Origin*, in the chapter on "Hybridism." But the causal relationships are shifted in the later version. In these notes he is saying that old characteristics will be inherited *because* they are old; in the *Origin* the argument runs that, through the agency of evolution and natural selection, those characteristics which have adaptive value *become* a stable part of the organism's inheritance—i.e., "old."

7 Darwin retained the same line of thought in the *Origin*, where he wrote: "When a character which has been lost in a breed, reappears after a great number of generations, the most probable hypothesis is . . . that in each successive generation there has been a tendency to reproduce the character in question, which at last, under unknown favourable conditions, gains an ascendancy." (*Origin*, 160–161)

suggest that Darwin had an explicit grasp of the distinction between phenotype and genotype, but only that it was implicit in his thinking. As we have seen over and over, making implicit ideas explicit is no small matter.

While the long-in-the-blood hypothesis plays a prominent role in the C and D notebooks, it makes its first appearance earlier in Darwin's notes. We can see it happening in two steps. First, in about October 1837 he writes, "A Race of domestic animals made from influences in one country is permanent in another.—Good argument for species not being so closely adapted." (*B* 130. The same idea is also stated on *B* 115.) He was beginning to see that he needed to find ways of dealing not only with change, but with *permanent* change, and that this imposes special demands on theory.

This realization set the stage for his interest in the long-in-the-blood hypothesis. He writes, "Mr. Yarrell says that old *races* when mingled with newer, hybrid variety partakes chiefly of the former." (*B* 138, about October 1837) He cites Yarrell, an ornithologist, to the same effect repeatedly. (*B* 140, *B* 171) By about April of 1838, however, he writes, "I am sorry to find Mr. Yarrell's evidence about old varieties is reduced to scarcely anything,—almost all imagination." (*C* 121)

In spite of this disappointment, Darwin finds the long-in-the-blood hypothesis promising and continues throughout the notebooks to record facts related to it.

He could expect to find direct evidence for the hypothesis only in domestic breeds, since the history of crosses of wild animals cannot be known accurately; and, in any event, in wild animals the principle of repugnance operates to prevent crosses that would test the hypothesis. Darwin believed that in domestic animals the conditions of confinement and artificial breeding are conducive to crosses that would not occur in the wild state.

Despite such weaknesses and some doubts, Darwin gave credence to the hypothesis long after he had discovered the principle of natural selection. On March 11, 1839, he wrote, "Yarrell's law must be partly true, as enunciated by him to me, for otherwise breeders who only care for first generations, as in horses, would not care so much about breed." (*E* 112)

We turn now to a psychogenetic hypothesis that parallels the biogenetic long-in-the-blood hypothesis. It runs about as follows: the behavior and mental activity of the organism may produce changes in its structure; structural changes can be inherited; but not every transient act produces inheritable structural changes, only those which are often repeated over long periods of time. This idea, that old habits become hereditary, is a major theme of the M and N notebooks. It is foreshadowed by only a few vague remarks in the B notebook, but by about March 1838 it appears fairly clearly. It is an idea of some significance, because it bears on any discussion of the relation between Darwin and Lamarck, and, more generally, demonstrates how deeply Darwin was imbued with the view that function determines form.

In a passage reflecting a terminological confusion to which we have already referred, he writes, "Instinct goes before structure (habits of ducklings & chickens young water ouzels) hence aversion to generation, before great difficulty in propagation." (*C* 51, about March 1838) This most probably means: if evolutionary changes in instinctual attraction and repugnance precede structural changes in sexual organs, this would account for the absence of interbreeding, between closely related species ("aversion to generation") in cases where there is not sufficient structural difference to prevent interbreeding.

A few pages farther on he writes, "All structures either direct effect of habit, or hereditary and combined effect of habit,—perhaps in process of change.—Are any men born with any peculiarity, or any race of plants." (*C* 63)

He cites his old teacher at Cambridge: "Whewell in comment few will dispute says civilisation hereditary." (*C* 72) He notes several examples of "hereditary habits" in birds. (*C* 105–107) In some of these first expressions of this idea it is reasonably clear that he simply means inherited behavior patterns and is not singling out for attention the point that they are learned behaviors. Gradually, the weight of emphasis shifts to the latter point. In about May 1838 he writes, "Hereditary ambling horses (if not looked at as instinctive) then must be owing to hereditary power of muscles.—Then we SEE structure gained by habit." (*C* 163)

Up to this moment he was still thinking about the heritability of *all* habits. Only when he has this idea fairly explicitly stated does he go on to raise the problem of *selection:*

> Reflect much over my view of particular instinct being memory transmitted without consciousness, a most possible thing see man walking in sleep.—an action becomes habitual is probably first stage, & an habitual action implies want of consciousness & will & therefore may be called instinctive.—But why do some actions become hereditary & instinctive & not others.—We even see they must be done often to be habitual or of great importance to cause long memory,— structure is only gained slowly, therefore it can only be those actions which *many* successive generations are impelled to do in same way. [*C* 171]

In its formulation of the "old habits become hereditary" hypothesis, and in its freely ranging psychological thought, this passage resembles very much the character of the M notebook, which Darwin was shortly to begin.

Darwin and Lamarck

Two closely related points have emerged from our examination of Darwin's idea of hereditary habit: the fact that he was in 1837–38 a "Lamarckian" in the sense that he believed in the inheritance of acquired characteristics, and the fact that for him this belief did not so much solve the problem of evolution as intensify the problem of selection.

Probably most biologists would grant that function is more protean than form, since it is in the functioning of the organism that it adapts to every transitory shift in the conditions of life, while its "essential" structure remains unchanged. Consequently, if one entertains the view that function determines form, a serious problem arises. If form varies as much as function, there will be no fixed categories of form, no species. Lamarck and Lyell both saw this point and took different positions on it. Lamarck believed that there were indeed no fixed categories, that species were merely "the part of art," or entirely artificial categories invented by man. Lyell believed that species were real and hence mutable only within very limited bounds. Darwin's solution, entirely different, was to introduce selective mechanisms: let function determine form, let species be real, let change be perpetual—selection is the device for moderating change, permitting it to occur endlessly without at any given moment in evolutionary time destroying the reality of species.

As we have just seen, many months before Darwin consciously grasped the principle of natural selection, he was preoccupied with the *problem* of selection and considered various ways in which it might occur. His view of adaptive change as selectively buffered meant that the organism might be only imperfectly adapted to its external milieu, but it had the great virtue of preserving the sexual system of reproduction in which the mating individuals must be drawn from a population which remains in some sense the same.

It has been suggested that Darwin fell back on Lamarckian inheritance after publishing the *Origin* when he was subjected to criticisms that caused his faith in the explanatory power of natural selection to wane. Such an interpretation rests on the assumption that he saw the inheritance of acquired characteristics as a principle of evolution, complementing the principle of natural selection. This misses the main point, that for Darwin the inheritance of acquired characteristics was a mechanism for dealing with the *genetical* problem of how variation is introduced into the system and says nothing about evolution *per se*. In his main argument, about evolution, Darwin was able to "bracket" variation—that is, to treat it as an unexplained premise.

Lamarck too believed that the inheritance of acquired characteristics could not explain evolution. He relied on a "law of progressive development" inherent in all life. After the brief period in 1837 when Darwin entertained the monad theory, he considered such a law to be an unjustified metaphysical assertion. After that time he consistently rejected such ideas as having no explanatory value.

For these reasons it is too simple to say that Darwin became a Lamarckian under the pressure of criticism. He was in one sense always a Lamarckian, in another sense never. It should be added that Darwin was uncomfortable with the idea of the inheritance of acquired characteristics because he knew of so many exceptions to it, as well as the theoretical difficulties we have already discussed.

Like Darwin's, Lamarck's ideas formed a system, or a structured argument. Darwin gave a good account of some of its features:

> With respect to the means of modification, he attributed something to the direct action of the physical conditions of life, something to the crossing of already existing forms, and much to use and disuse, that is, to the effects of habit. To this latter agency he seems to attribute all the beautiful adaptations in nature;—such as the long neck of the giraffe for browsing on the branches of trees. But he likewise believed in a law of progressive development; and as all the forms of life thus tended to progress, in order to account for the existence at the present day of very simple productions, he maintained that such forms were now spontaneously generated.[8]

In his notebooks Darwin objected several times to Lamarck's other notion that organisms modify themselves by willing to do so, but in his published comment Darwin omitted this point. Perhaps he recognized that Lamarck's meaning was not entirely clear, or that it was a secondary and non-essential point; perhaps he did not want to expose his great predecessor to further ridicule by so much as mentioning his seemingly most implausible idea.[9]

---

[8] *Origin*, 3rd edition, 1861, p. xiii. In this edition Darwin added the historical review of evolutionary theories, which was reprinted in all subsequent editions. Darwin's marginal notations in his various volumes of Lamarck's works show that his recognition of the complex relationships between his ideas and Lamarck's came quite early. Many of these marginalia date from the period of the 1837–39 notebooks.
[9] See C. H. Waddington, "Theories of Evolution" and Donald Michie, "The Third Stage in Genetics" in *A Century of Darwin*, edited by S. A. Barnett (London: Mercury, 1962). Also C. C. Gillispie, "Lamarck and Darwin in the History of Science," in *Forerunners of Darwin*, edited by Bentley Glass (Baltimore: Johns Hopkins University Press, 1959). From these sources one can begin to get a picture of a modern re-evaluation of Lamarck's great achievements.

We have seen now how, at two early points in Darwin's thinking, aspects of Lamarckian theory captured his interest: during the period of his monad theory of evolution and during his exploration of the idea of hereditary habit. In both instances, besides the similarities there are fundamental differences between the two men.

Darwin's monad theory had the fact and the idea of extinction at its core. Spontaneous generation to fill up the gaps left by extinction was an idea Darwin entertained only briefly and reluctantly. The idea of perpetual becoming, which might have left no gaps in nature, was a theory *faute de mieux* which he considered for a short while when the monad theory failed him. For Lamarck, on the other hand, extinction played no part, and spontaneous generation to fill up gaps by organisms that have evolved into higher forms was a necessity.

There is an essential difference between the two theorists in their views of nature, for Darwin an irregularly branching tree, for Lamarck at once a network everywhere dense and a ladder always ascending. "Network" expresses Lamarck's implicit faith in the continuity and completeness of the natural order—everything that might be is, somewhere; "ladder" expresses his faith in the metaphysical law of universal progress. The "ladder" idea is thoroughly explicit in Lamarck. The "network" idea is an implication, I suggest, for the following reason: if spontaneous generation is constantly occurring, then there are *many* points of origin for the evolutionary ladder—i.e., many more or less parallel ladders; if, due to circumstances and the law of use, each unbroken vertical ascent up the ladder of progress is typified by horizontal deviations from the main axis of a ladder, then the only way such a deviant can continue its upward ascent is along a new line; this is enough to suggest a network. The further notion that it must be everywhere dense follows from Lamarck's rejection of any gaps in nature, either in biological or in chemical series.

Even *before* Darwin became preoccupied with problems of selection in the sense that we have been discussing it in the present chapter, his point of view embraced a selective image of nature. For what is Darwin's irregularly branching tree of nature but a selection from among the possibilities? What is the premise of extinction as a commonplace in nature? Many different creatures *might* evolve and survive, but only some do. Before being able to propose any satisfactory mechanism to account for it, Darwin began with a presupposition of selectivity.

Something else lies behind this presupposition: the particular character of the presumed interaction of organism and environment. For Lamarck, what the organism becomes is *in essence* independent of the environment because the general direction of its development is given in the law of progress; *in transitory details* what it becomes is a direct reflection of its own active response to the immediate circumstances of life. Darwin is much more the interactionist, believing that the course of evolution depends on the character of the encounter between organism and environment. The organism as Darwin conceives it is in a sense separate from the milieu, resistant to environmental pressures, and by the same token not always perfectly adapted; circumstances propitious for change arise only occasionally, and the course of evolution is contained not in any *a priori* law of progress but in the unpredictable intersection of these two partially independent systems, organism and milieu.[10]

As I hope I have made clear, before Darwin had gotten a good grasp of the principle of evolution through natural selection, the differences between himself and Lamarck, while profound, entailed quite subtle shadings in the structure of their arguments. They are often implicit rather than explicit differences, and Darwin may have been unaware of some of them. Quite rightly, he felt the weight of the similarities. A few weeks before picking up Malthus' *Essay on Population,* his reading of which led to the definitive restructuring of his ideas around the principle of natural selection, Darwin wrote the lines already quoted: "Seeing what Von Buch (Humboldt) G. St. Hilaire, & Lamarck have written . . . I pretend to no originality . . . in following work." (*D* 69, September 7, 1838) On September 7 he might well wonder whether or not the "following work," the treatise he imagined himself writing, would contain an original theory.

Darwin's originality lay neither in his espousal of the general idea of evolution, nor in his collection of supporting facts, but in his persistent search for a theory of evolution consonant with his underlying image of nature as an irregularly branching tree, an image deeply imbued with the idea of selectivity.

The Argument from Continuity and the System of Nature

Grasping the importance for Darwin of this image of nature is essential for understanding the second theme of the M and N notebooks, his approach to the problem of continuity between man and other animals, to which I now turn.

---

10 There is another aspect to Darwin's conception of the interaction of organism and milieu—the way in which the former changes the latter. This was expressed in his theory of the formation of coral reefs, and in his work on the action of earthworms in forming the soil. It is remarkable that he gave papers on both these subjects before the London Geological Society in 1837. His later recognition that spontaneous generation of new life could not continue because life itself would obliterate the conditions permitting its origin was, it appears, not a passing thought but a reflection of a deeper conviction about the relation between organism and milieu.

We must bear in mind three different types of image of the system of nature, three arrangements of organisms in schemes of classification: the linear model, the branching model, and the "circular" model. As we have already seen, it was possible for either an evolutionist or a non-evolutionist to embrace a linear model.[11] The upward-ascending unbroken chain or Scala Naturae was a widespread image in pre-Darwinian thought. Unfortunately, it left little room for biological systematists to maneuver when they wanted to work out systematic arrangements among related organisms. Lamarck's "ladder image" utilized a second dimension, the horizontal rungs of the ladder, and was somewhat more flexible, but could not do justice to the complexities of the known facts. Lamarck as a systematist certainly could not stick to the simple ladder image employed by Lamarck as an evolutionist.

There was another approach to the issue of continuity in nature, non-evolutionary to the core, with which Darwin had to contend. This was the Quinarian system of William Sharp MacLeay, forgotten now but influential at the time Darwin was thinking things through. It was a "mystical system of classification built on the supposition that at all levels the animal kingdom is based on five groups arranged in a circle, each with affinities to its neighbors on both sides, each containing five sub-groups arranged in a comparable manner with affinities to their neighbors, and so on."[12]

Demonstrations of continuity in nature were, evidently, necessary but by no means sufficient for Darwin's argument. There were two strongpoints in non-evolutionary images of nature that Darwin had to attack. He had to show that it was unnecessary to assume a fundamental discontinuity between man and other animals that could be accounted for only by the hypothesis of supernatural fiat. And he had to show that the natural order did not exhibit a mystical and miraculous regularity and perfection but was instead an irregularly branching system.[13]

---

11 Lamarck is the evolutionist to whom we have referred on this point in the preceeding pages; Wesley is the non-evolutionist.

12 Sir Gavin de Beer in his introduction to *Darwin's Notebooks on Transmutation of Species, Bulletin of the British Museum (Natural History) Historical Series*, Vol. 2, No. 2, 1960, p. 29.

13 This second point of attack led him eventually to his own major systematic work, on barnacles. In that work he showed how MacLeay's mystical system of perfection and continuity in nature fell short in a specialized application, and how a detailed examination of one group of organisms revealed the irregularly branching, almost haphazard character of taxonomies produced by all the accidents of evolutionary change. When Darwin wrote his four-volume work on barnacles, which remains a classic in its field, he had not yet publicly confessed his evolutionary views. I am indebted to Dr. Sydney Smith for illuminating discussions on this subject; in a brilliant zoological detective story he revealed the hidden relations among Darwin,

Taxonomic tree showing hypothetical relation of man to other primates. Drawn by Darwin on April 21, 1868. *Courtesy of Cambridge University Library.*

The tree model saved Darwin the trouble of looking for the "missing link" between man and other primates. If his theory was true, these extant animals represented distinct branchings from a common progenitor, so that the search for living intermediate forms would be misguided: continuity could be found only by looking backward in evolutionary time to that long-past branching point. He writes, "My theory drives me to say that there can be no animal at present time having an intermediate affinity between two classes—there may be some descendant of some intermediate link." (*C* 201)

MacLeay, evolution, and barnacles. See "The Darwin Collection at Cambridge with One Example of Its Use: Charles Darwin and *Cirripedes*," by Dr. Sydney Smith in *Actes du XIe Congrès International d'Histoire des Sciences*, 1965, pp. 96–100.

His struggle with the Quinary system is exhibited repeatedly in the transmutation notebooks. He needed to satisfy himself that the appearance of a jewel-like perfection in the natural order, as expounded by MacLeay, was a contrivance of man and not of God, that such a system concealed a rampant irregularity beneath the surface, and that this was true at every level of classification, species, genera, orders, families, and classes. Thus he wrote, "Organized beings represent a tree, *irregularly branched;* some branches far more branched,—hence genera." (*B* 21)

In spite of the early appearance in Darwin's notes, both in words and in diagrams, of the branching model, there was probably an important shift in his thinking on this score. At first he was quite wedded to the idea of a deterministic universe, and he was looking for natural laws that would produce necessary results, not only plausible ones; specifically predictable evolutionary sequences, not just viable ones:

> Astronomers might formerly have said that God ordered each planet to move in its particular destiny.—In same manner God orders each animal created with certain form in certain country, but how much more simple and sublime power let attraction act according to certain law, such are inevitable consequences—let animal be created, then by fixed laws of generation, such will be their successors.
>
> Let the powers of transportal be such, and so will be the forms of one country to another.—let geological changes go at such a rate, so will be the number and distribution of the species!! [*B* 101–102]

There is a certain contradiction between this hope for lawfulness and Darwin's image, so consistently held, of an irregularly branching tree. Accordingly, he had two sorts of critique of MacLeay's Quinarian system, an earlier one which was more deterministic and a later one which was more probabilistic. In the earlier version he seems to be groping for a way of explaining how it might have come about that there would be five major groups within each class, hoping to explain the Quinarian appearance of nature on deterministic grounds:

> Would there not be a triple branching in the tree of life owing to three elements—air, land and water, and the endeavour of each typical class to extend his domain into the other domains and subdivisions, three more—double arrangement? If each main stem of the tree is adapted for these three elements, there will be certainly points of affinity in each branch. [*B* 23–24, written about July 1837]

Here we see Darwin relying on a definite feature of the physical environment, its provision of three main sorts of habitat, to produce quite directly three major groupings of the five needed; the remaining two[14] might well arise out of a process of further variation, "the endeavour of each typical class to extend his domain."

Later on, he was less impressed with the direct effects of the environment in producing change. Rather than trying to account for the appearance of a definite number of groups, he tries to explain the more general point, the appearance of circularity in systems of classification:

> Argument for circularity of groups. When a group of species is made, father probably will be dead—hence there is no central radiating point . . . now what is group without centre but circle, two or three lines deep—with respect to MacLeay's theory of analogies—when it is considered the tree of life must be erect not pressed on paper, to study the corresponding points. [*D* 58–59, September 2, 1838; "dead" means extinct.]

This is a nice passage, incidentally, because it shows how clearly Darwin was aware that he was adding a new dimension to the study of classification, the dimension of time. By the time he wrote the *Origin* Darwin was freed, partly by his own work, of the necessity of contending with mystical, numerological systems of classification. But a trace of his early struggle remains, in another passage I have always liked because it also shows Darwin's sensitivity to unconscious mental processes: ". . . all true classification is genealogical; . . . community of descent is the hidden bond which naturalists have been unconsciously seeking, and not some unknown plan of creation, or the enunciation of general propositions, and the mere putting together and separating objects more or less alike." (*Origin,* 420)

With its major circles and osculant or joining smaller circles carefully contrived to make a perfect fit between adjacent major groups, the Quinarian system was quite reminiscent of the Ptolemaic cosmology with its major orbits and epicycles to account for the apparent irregularities of planetary movements employing no other image than the perfect circle. Darwin was sensitive to the analogy between himself and the great cosmologists; he thought of himself as building a new world system, and he enjoyed the thought:

> Before attraction of gravity discovered it might have been said it was as great a difficulty to account for movement of all [planets] by one law, as to account for each separate one; so to say that all mammalia

---

14 Or is it three or four? Darwin might well have attempted to show how his system of nature could be related to a system in which a given class is divided into a fixed number of major groupings without worrying too much about the exact number; he knew of at least one variation on the Quinary theme, a proposal to substitute the number 7 for 5. See de Beer, *loc. cit.,* and the B notebook, p. 46, where Darwin asks, "what subject has Mr. Newman the (7) man studied?"

were born from one stock, and since distributed by such means as we can recognize, may be thought to explain nothing. [*B* 196]

Or, more briefly, in a remark we are already familiar with in another context: "What the Frenchman did for *species* between England and France, I will do with *forms.*—Mention persecution of early Astronomers. . . ." (*C* 123)

In spite of some similarities between Darwin and other system builders, there was one terribly important difference. The astronomers had constructed orderly orbits which would account for the appearance of irregularity in the wandering of the planets without having to concede that such irregularity in fact marred the face of nature; the physicists had worked out universal laws to explain the orbits. Darwin's task was the reverse. He had to show that the appearance of order, which had been so carefully worked out by MacLeay and other systematists, could be explained as resulting from a random process producing an irregular result; and furthermore that his hypothesis was not only tenable but more plausible than the hypothesis of a supernaturally created order.

A key feature of the M and N notebooks follows from this aspect of Darwin's approach. If he had been attempting to reconstruct a realistic series of organisms showing the structural and mental continuity between man and other closely related organisms, he would have had to organize his search and record his findings in a way appropriate to that task. The scattered, ancedotal character of Darwin's evidence seemed useful to him only because his guiding image was that irregularly branching tree, because he could not hope to reconstruct it in any detail, and because his aim was limited. He wanted to show that if less-developed forms of a variety of human mental functions could be found in other animals, it was then plausible that such functions evolve according to the same laws as other biological functions, whatever those laws might turn out to be.

In the long run, it was the chanciness and irregularity of Darwin's system of nature that proved to be the most difficult point in his theory for the religious community. Opposition to the idea of evolution slackened at least a decade before opposition to Darwin's theory of evolution as the resultant of a conglomeration of chance events.[15] God, thought the modern theologians of that day, might choose to operate through natural laws rather than by fiat, but his regime would be more orderly than is provided for by the laws of chance!

---

15 Alvar Allegård, *Darwin and the General Reader: The Reception of Darwin's Theory of Evolution in the British Periodical Press, 1859–1872*, Acta Universitatis Gothoburgensis, Göterborgs Universitats Årsskrift, Vol. 64, 1958.

CHAPTER 10

The Citadel Itself

> By materialism, I mean, merely the intimate connec-
> tion of kind of thought with form of brain.—Like
> kind of attraction with nature of element.
>
> Charles Darwin, margin note on p. 28 of John
> Abercrombie, *Inquiries Concerning the Intel-
> lectual Powers and the Investigation of Truth*,
> 8th edition (London: Murray, 1838)

One day when the world and my family were agog with the subject, I
asked my children, then aged nine and eleven, how they felt about
heart transplants. Would they be willing to be recipients? Hesitantly
but without too much doubt, they answered yes. Then I asked: "How
about a brain transplant? Suppose the only way you could go on living
was to have someone else's brain transplanted into you. Would you be
willing?" Firmly, without any hesitation, they both answered NO.
"Why not?" One said, "I wouldn't be me."

The relation of mind and body is not only an abstract philosophical question. It impinges on a very personal matter, the nature and
locus of the self. The third theme of Darwin's M and N notebooks, the
mind-body problem—his early explorations of the possibility of a
scientific human psychology and its relation to philosophic materialism—brought into play Darwin's awareness of himself as a very
human animal.

There is a puzzle that harks back to issues raised in the opening
chapters of this book. In a way, the ground had been very well prepared for someone who wished to advance a theory of evolution. Why,
then, did Darwin wait so long to publish his evolutionary ideas? Why,
when he finally published the *Origin* in 1859, did he remain so

circumspect about man and mind? Were his fears and hesitations justified?

Darwin was the beneficiary of a line of distinguished attempts to create an evolutionary theory. Among non-evolutionists like Lyell the known fact of a succession of organic beings in successive geological strata had forced many into a revised interpretation of Genesis and toward the hypothesis of successive creation. Among Natural Theologians there were at least some who, like John Wesley, had already taken the dramatic step of dethroning man by recognizing man's place in the great chain of animate beings and by suggesting the possibility of organisms unknown to us and still higher. In 1844 *Vestiges,* Robert Chambers' evolutionary book, appeared. That was the year Darwin wrote his *second* long essay summarizing his views.[1] In 1856 he finally sat down to write his massive treatise on evolution, "Natural Selection," never finished because of Wallace's interruption in 1858. But by 1856 *Vestige* had gone through ten editions, clearly demonstrating the possibility of publishing an evolutionary theory and commanding wide attention of both the general and the scientific publics. True, *Vestiges* was severely criticized, but Darwin could hardly have intended to wait until all his potential critics were disarmed.

Does all this mean that Darwin's fears were groundless or that he was a cowardly man who retreated in the face of danger? To understand his predicament and his strategy of delay and concealment, a closer look at the subject is required. His theoretical efforts must be seen not only in the context of the search for a theory of evolution, but also in relation to the problem of materialism.

Darwin realized that it would weaken his whole argument if he permitted his account of evolution to stop short of the highest forms of intelligence. Once he admitted that God might have intervened in an act of special creation to make man's mind, others might argue, "In that case, why not also invoke the aid of God to explain the worm?"

There was an inherent weakness in the empirical approach of collecting instances pointing to the mental similarities of man and other animals. This fragmentary, anecdotal approach would be limited in much the same sense that any purely inductive theory must be. Given the indisputable fact of a considerable difference between man and other animals, Darwin might point to the similarities and assert the plausibility of the evolution of mind; others could point to the differences and cleave to their belief in special creation.

Moreover, Darwin sensed that some would object to seeing rudiments of human mentality in animals, while others would recoil at the idea of remnants of animality in man; he eventually divided the whole

---

[1] Darwin, *Foundations, op. cit.*

subject in two parts, corresponding roughly to these two aspects of the problem. *Descent of Man* deals mainly with the first issue, *Expression of Emotions* with the second. At the time of the M and N notebooks, however, he thought another approach might be possible. If only one could construct a scientific psychology at the human level itself, satisfying the demands of argument and evidence to which the natural sciences are subject, this achievement in itself would constitute evidence for the "naturalness" of mind.

It must be remembered how bitter and pervasive the struggle against philosophical materialism was in those days, and how much of the argument against it rested on the belief that the human mind was not subject to natural law. The intellectual story has been well told by academic historians of psychology, but the venom has been drawn in the telling.[2]

In an earlier chapter I dealt with the threat of persecution and ridicule of scientists in a general way. As I now examine the controversy over materialism and mind, my primary aim is to see how the significance for Darwin of his ideas about evolution was affected by his view of their place in a still larger argument. But it is not possible to divorce the discussion of the philosophical and scientific issues from the threat of persecution. In countries dominated by an alliance between state and church aimed at maintaining a threatened social order, the allegation that a particular idea was materialistic or tended to materialism or atheism constituted a very serious attack.

In virtually every branch of knowledge, repressive methods were used: lectures were proscribed, publication was hampered, professorships were denied, fierce invective and ridicule appeared in the press. Scholars and scientists learned the lesson and responded to the pressures on them. The ones with unpopular ideas sometimes recanted, published anonymously, presented their ideas in weakened forms, or delayed publication for many years. The known examples are not very numerous, nor need they be to make the point. Probably one striking case per decade was enough to keep the lesson fresh. If the progress of thought is slowed down enough, any establishment can incorporate new ideas without losing power.

The influential Scottish philosopher-psychologist Thomas Reid, in a letter "on the materialism of Priestley and the egoism of French philosophers" written in 1775, summarized Priestley's view that all "powers that are termed mental [are] . . . the result of such an organical structure as that of the brain," and its corollaries that "the whole man becomes extinct at death," and that the "lower animals

---

2 See especially E. G. Boring, *A History of Experimental Psychology* (New York: Appleton-Century-Crofts, 2nd edition, 1950).

. . . differ from us in degree only, and not in kind." Reid went on to express his disgust:

> I detest all systems that depreciate human nature. If it be a delusion, that there is something in the constitution of man that is venerable and worthy of its author, let me live and die in that delusion, rather than have my eyes opened to see my species in a humiliating and disgusting light. Every good man feels his indignation rise against those who disparage his *kindred* or his *country;* why should it not rise against those who disparage his *kind?*

Reid thought that Priestley's views of human nature "tend more to promote atheism, than to promote religion and virtue."[3]

The proposition that the brain is the organ of all mental functions received its first great modern impetus from Franz Joseph Gall. Today his name is associated with the discredited notions of phrenology, his misguided but once enormously popular doctrine of a strict relation between the exterior form of the skull and the psychological functioning of the brain within, so that individual character could be "read" from the bumps on the head. It was not, however, Gall's scientific errors but his insistence on a materialistic formulation of the relation between mind and body, as well as the ethical conclusions he drew from his materialism, that led in 1802 to the proscription of his lectures in Vienna as dangerous to religion. Gall migrated to Paris in 1807. There the cautious scientists of the institute were under considerable political pressure; they did not give his works a fair hearing or elect him a member. His books were eventually placed on the Index Librorum Prohibitorum, and he was forbidden a religious burial, although he was actually orthodox in his own religious beliefs.[4]

There was a strange law in England dealing with the property rights of authors. The law stemmed from the Star Chamber of Charles I, acting in 1637; in its interpretation in the 1820s, if a work was held to be blasphemous, seditious, or immoral, its author had no property rights in it. A publisher could ask for a ruling, and if the work fell under the disfavor of the court, the publisher could then issue a pirate edition without the consent of the author and without paying him.

Lord Byron was twice a victim of such suits. Another was William Lawrence, an eminent surgeon and for a time lecturer in the Royal

3 Thomas Reid, *Philosophical Works, with Notes and Supplementary Dissertations by Sir William Hamilton,* with an Introduction by Harry M. Bracken, 2 vols. (Hildesheim: Georg Olms Verlagsbuchhandlung, 1967) , Vol. 1, p. 52.
4 See Robert M. Young, *Mind, Brain and Adaptation in the Nineteenth Century: Cerebral Localization and Its Biological Context from Gall to Ferrier* (Oxford: Clarendon Press, 1970) .

College of Surgeons. In 1819 Lawrence published his *Lectures on Physiology, Zoology, and the Natural History of Man.* When the book first appeared, there was such fierce public objection to it that Lawrence had it withdrawn. When the pirate edition appeared, in 1822, he brought suit against the publisher and lost.

Lawrence was an advanced biological thinker for his day. He believed that living organisms obeyed natural laws of higher complexity than the simpler physicochemical laws necessary to account for inanimate phenomena. But he argued against any "vital principle" that could exist apart from the functioning organism, against any life function that could be understood without reference to a bodily organ that carried it out, and consequently against any mental function independent of the highly organized matter constituting the organ of mind—namely, the brain.

When Lawrence first delivered the lectures on which the book was based, in 1816–17, there was considerable controversy, which remained within a small circle of scientists and students. But immediately after the publication of the book he was attacked for materialism and atheism, both from the podium and in the press. The *Quarterly Review* condemned this expression of "the doctrine of materialism, an open avowal of which has been made in the metropolis of the British Empire in the lectures delivered under public authority by Mr. Lawrence. . . ."[5] The *Quarterly Review* demanded that the offending passages be purged from his book. Lawrence withdrew the book and resigned his post as lecturer. He was thus able to continue a brilliant medical career, but at the cost of his scientific freedom.

Lawrence, then, was in Darwin's day a living document of the price of dangerous ideas. Darwin owned his book, marked it up with marginal strokes, and referred to it in his transmutation notebooks and later on in the *Descent of Man.*[6] Huxley knew Lawrence and mentioned the story of his near-ostracism. Darwin probably knew him too; in any event, he could not have avoided knowing all the circumstances of the case. Lawrence lived until 1867. In the Darwin circle he was not a forgotten man.

In 1826, less than a decade after the suppression of Mr. Lawrence, young Charles Darwin attended the meeting of the Plinian Society in

---

[5] *Quarterly Review,* July 1819. Quoted in June Goodfield-Toulmin's article "Some Aspects of English Physiology: 1780–1840," *Journal of the History of Biology,* Vol. 2, 1969, pp. 283–320. Most of the information in the above account is taken from Dr. Goodfield-Toulmin's article. I am indebted to her and to Dr. Stephen Toulmin for illuminating discussions about these matters.

[6] *C* 204, about June 1838. There are several references to Lawrence's work in the *Descent of Man.* Charles Lyell also read Lawrence and referred to him in his notebooks. Alfred Russel Wallace mentions Lawrence in his autobiography.

Edinburgh and witnessed the expunging of his fellow student's paper, Mr. Browne's argument that "mind is material."

In 1830–33 the volumes of Charles Lyell's *Principles of Geology* appeared, just in time to play a major part in shaping Darwin's intellectual growth during the *Beagle* voyage. In Chapter 4 we discussed Lyell's policy of caution in expressing himself on geological matters that contradicted accepted interpretations of Scripture. This policy was related to his views on creation and on the relation between mind and matter. To account for the fossil evidence of innumerable extinct creatures, Lyell supported the hypothesis of successive creations extending into an indefinite past, repeatedly repopulating the globe with new sets of organisms. For Lyell, this view harmonized perfectly with an extended version of the argument from Design. As the physical state of the globe was altered ". . . the species likewise have been changed; and yet they have all been so modelled, on types analogous to those of existing plants and animals, as to indicate throughout a perfect harmony of design and unity of purpose."[7]

As early as 1841, while going through the sixth edition of Lyell's *Principles of Geology*, Darwin took cognizance of the latter's position on man. As was his habit, he used the back flyleaf of the book for notes and comments, among them: "Lyell always considers that there is *saltus* between man & animals."[8]

Much later, after Darwin had published the *Origin*, in *The Antiquity of Man* Lyell addressed himself both to the argument from Design and to the mind-body question. On Design he concluded, "The whole course of nature may be the material embodiment of a preconcerted arrangement; and if the succession of events be explained by transmutation, the perpetual adaptation of the organic world to new conditions leaves the argument in favour of design, and therefore of a designer, as valid as ever." He went on: "As to the charge of materialism brought against all forms of the development theory . . . far from having a materialistic tendency" the evolution of mind culminating in ". . . Man himself, presents us with a picture of the ever-increasing dominion of mind over matter."[9]

The emphasis I have placed on Lyell's prudence should not be taken to mean that he was given to making statements in which he did not believe. His private notebooks, only recently published, show that the thoughts expressed above reflected his real thinking. On December 6, 1859, after he had read the *Origin*, he wrote in his notes, "May not

7 Lyell, *Principles, op. cit.*, Vol. 4, p. 401.
8 See Sydney Smith, "The Origin of 'The Origin,'" *The Advancement of Science*, No. 64, 1960, pp. 391–401.
9 Charles Lyell, *The Antiquity of Man* (London: John Murray, 2nd edition, 1963), p. 506.

creation consist of four powers or principles," variation, natural selection, inheritance of acquired characteristics, and "The progressive tendency to more complex organizations, both physical & spiritual, material & immaterial."[10]

The essential point is that Lyell could easily compromise with religious believers in matters of phrasing and timing because he was himself a believer. To the extent that Darwin was an agnostic and a materialist, he was far more isolated in the scientific community, and his compromises would be harder to make.[11]

While it is often said that evolution was "in the air" in Darwin's time, not enough attention is paid to the crucial differences between Darwin and other evolutionists. Robert Chambers' *Vestiges* appeared anonymously in 1844. Although it was published after Darwin had worked out his main ideas, *Vestiges* is worth dwelling on because it was the most popular and immediate precursor of Darwin's published work. The differences between himself and Chambers help us to understand how Darwin might feel a wide gulf between himself and his potential audience, not simply because he espoused an evolutionary theory but because of its utterly materialistic tone.

The title of Chambers' book, *The Vestiges of the Natural History of Creation,* was well chosen. The whole tenor of the book is a continuation of the tradition of Natural Theology. The author pauses repeatedly and lengthily to expound his fundamental theme that "the Divine Governor of the world conducts its passing affairs by a fixed rule, to which we apply the term natural law. . . ."[12]

Chambers was not content with a Creator who set the world in lawful motion and then abandoned it to the operation of natural law, nor did Chambers' God leave anything to chance:

> . . . God may be presumed to be revealed to us in every one of the phenomena of the system, in the suspension of globes in space, in the degradation of rocks and the upthrowing of mountains, in the development of plants and animals, in each movement of our minds, and in all that we enjoy and suffer, seeing that, the system requiring a sustainer as well as an originator, He must be continually present in every part of it, albeit He does not permit a single law to swerve in any case from its appointed course of operation. Thus we may still

10 *Sir Charles Lyell's Scientific Journals on the Species Question,* edited by Leonard G. Wilson (New Haven and London: Yale University Press, 1970), p. 327. These notebooks record Lyell's ideas during the years 1855–61.
11 See Martin Rudwick's paper "The Strategy of Lyell's *Principles of Geology,*" *op. cit.,* for a very subtle discussion of the interplay between Lyell's scientific epistemology and his theistic ontology.
12 Preface to the 10th edition of *The Vestiges of the Natural History of Creation* (London: John Churchill, 1853). It was not until the 12th edition, published posthumously in 1884, that Chambers was revealed as the author of *Vestiges.*

feel that He is the immediate breather of our life and ruler of our spirits. . . .[13]

Chambers was aware that postulating a world in flux implied imperfection at any given moment. Moreover, he was concerned with the meaning of human suffering, war, and death and the questions they raised about the benevolence of God. He wrote, "To reconcile this to the character of the Deity, it is necessary to suppose that the present system is but a part of the whole, a stage in a Great Progress, and that the Redress is in reserve."[14]

Like Darwin, Chambers insisted on the continuity of human intelligence with "the lower animals." But their theological conclusions from this continuity take entirely different directions. Chambers, after expatiating on the gulf between humans and lower animals, especially with regard to human powers of "veneration . . . hope . . . reason . . . conscientiousness and benevolence," concludes that our belief in God is evidence for His existence. "The existence of faculties having a regard to such things is a good evidence that such things exist. The face of God is reflected in the organization of man, as a little pool reflects the glorious sun."[15]

Darwin's treatment of the origins of religious belief was, by contrast, entirely naturalistic. He likens primitive interest in the inexplicable to a dog's disturbance at some unfamiliar event; he assumes that sophisticated human theologies evolve from a general belief in "spiritual agencies" to account for inexplicable events; he repeatedly emphasizes the continuity of human religious beliefs with tendencies to be found in other animals, citing one author who claimed that "a dog looks on his master as on a god." (*Descent*, 96)

Like Darwin, Chambers drew on a human invention for an analogy to clarify his theory of evolution. Darwin drew the analogy between natural and artificial selection; at the heart of his thinking lay a probabilistic conception of the process of evolution. Chambers drew on an entirely different sort of invention, Charles Babbage's celebrated calculating machine. What is significant about the analogy is that Chambers treats the machine as operating in an entirely deterministic way: in a very long series of numbers generated by the machine, increasing regularly by steps of one, eventually a seeming irregularity appears; if we understand the machine fully, we know that the change is not an irregular violation of its laws, but expresses the fact that the machine is pre-set to generate numbers according to a more complex or "higher" law than first appeared to be the case.

---

13 *Ibid.*, p. 323.
14 *Ibid.*, p. 324.
15 *Ibid.*, p. 299.

Chambers quotes Babbage to the effect that both the simple numerical series, analogous to inheritance without evolutionary change, and the apparent irregularities, analogous to such change, were "as necessary a consequence of the original adjustment, and might have been as fully foreknown at the commencement. . . ."[16]

Was Darwin a materialist? We cannot quite say. Wherever he included a reference to the Creator or creation, one reader may claim that Darwin was really a believer, another that he was only propitiating prevailing opinion or, as he put it himself, "truckling."

In the *Origin,* Darwin was repeatedly explicit on one point: the hypothesis of independent creation of each species explains nothing. He went further, attacking the idea that there is a Natural System which "reveals the plan of the Creator"; because of the vagueness of such an idea, "nothing is thus added to our knowledge." (*Origin,* 413)

Publicly, on two points he conceded something, leaving some room for a Creator. First, on the origin of life, he wrote, "There is grandeur in this view of life, with its several powers, having been originally breathed by the Creator into a few forms or into one; and that . . . from so simple a beginning endless forms most beautiful and most wonderful have, and are being evolved."[17]

Second, his printed words admit the possibility that the whole lawful system of material nature might have had a supernatural Creator, a First Cause, who then left all else to "secondary causes." (*Origin,* 488)

How seriously should we take these occasional allusions to creation? A careful reading shows that they do not permeate the *Origin* in the way that the argument from Design permeated Chambers' *Vestiges.*

Privately, in a letter to his close friend Joseph Hooker, Darwin confesses, "I have long regretted that I truckled to public opinion, and used the Pentateuchal term of creation, by which I really meant 'appeared' by some wholly unknown process."[18]

Apart from the concluding passage of the *Origin* discussed above,

---

16 Chambers, *op. cit.,* p. 160. Chambers was quoting from *The Ninth Bridgewater Treatise* by Charles Babbage (London: John Murray, 2nd edition, 1838), p. 838. Uninvited, Babbage appropriated the title of the series of volumes on Natural Theology and added his own reflections on the subject. I do not think that Chambers was distorting Babbage's own meaning; both men believed that a changeful natural order could be understood as expressing the will of a designing Providence.
17 *Origin,* 490. The words "by the Creator" were added in the 2nd and all subsequent editions. Peckham, *Variorum Text, op. cit.,* p. 759.
18 *LL* 3, 18, letter to Hooker, March 29, 1863. However much he may have regretted his compromise, he did nothing to strengthen his stand in the three editions of the *Origin* which appeared after 1863: 1866, 1869, 1872.

the chapter in which concessions to creationism are most marked is Chapter 6, "Difficulties on Theory." Darwin saw the immense difficulty for his contemporaries of believing that an organ so wonderful and perfect as the human eye could have evolved by the haphazard process of evolution proposed in his theory. He devoted eight pages to the problem posed for his theory by "organs of extreme perfection and complication." Reminding his readers of the argument from Design, he agrees that it is natural to infer that the eye was made by a process analogous to that of a skilled human making other optical instruments. He asks, "But may not this inference be presumptuous? Have we any right to assume that the Creator works by intellectual powers like those of man?" (*Origin*, 188)

This is one of the more heavily revised sections of the *Origin*. From the third to the sixth edition, 1861–72, Darwin kept on adding new information about the eye, to bolster his contention that even an organ so marvelous might have evolved by natural selection. One year after his last revision of the *Origin*, a lecture on vision by Hermann von Helmholtz, the German man-of-all-science, appeared in English translation. Darwin marked up his copy of the lecture in a way that reveals how much he was troubled that the marvelous perfection of the eye might provide an opening for those who still wished to defend the argument from Design.

Helmholtz was a master physicist, mathematician, and biologist, the author of a great treatise on physiological optics. He was also devoted to a completely materialistic biology. Indeed, as a young man in 1845 he was a member of a group of physiologists who formed a pact to struggle against vitalistic theories and for the view that "No other forces than common physical chemical ones are active within the organism." Helmholtz's famous paper on the conservation of energy (1847) actually grew out of an effort to show the physical transformations of energy involved in muscular activity.[19]

In the lecture that Darwin read, "The Recent Progress of the Theory of Vision," almost every passage that Darwin marked dealt with defects of the normal eye as an optical instrument. After a discussion of the psychological complexities of vision, Helmholtz concluded:

> The inaccuracies and imperfections of the eye as an optical instrument, and those which belong to the image on the retina, now appear insignificant in comparison with the incongruities which we have met with in the field of sensation. One might almost believe that Nature

---

[19] See E. G. Boring, *op. cit.*, p. 708; and Howard and Valmai Gruber, "Hermann von Helmholtz: Nineteenth-Century Polymorph," *Scientific Monthly*, Vol. 83, 1956, pp. 92–99.

here contradicted herself on purpose, in order to destroy any dream of a pre-existing harmony between the outer and the inner world.[20]

Darwin also marked some of the passages in which Helmholtz explicitly drew the connection between the peculiarities of the visual system and the Darwinian theory of evolution. How could he have failed to appreciate the support of a great physicist who concluded that "Darwin's theory contains an essentially new creative thought. It shows how adaptability of structure in organisms can result from a blind rule of a law of nature without any intervention of intelligence"?[21]

Although Darwin did not make it easy for us to say exactly where he stood on certain philosophical matters, we can profitably ask what role these issues might have played in his argument. In rephrasing the question—was Darwin a materialist?—it is important to distinguish the concept of a Creator as a First Cause and the concept of God as omniscient and omnipresent in the universe. Darwin's theory of evolution dealt only with the laws governing the ongoing operation of the organic world; he had expunged the question of origins from his theory, which in its developed form said nothing about the origin of life or of matter and energy and the universe. Consequently, his theory could not be affected either favorably or adversely by the introduction of a supernatural Creator as First Cause.

On the other hand, the idea of either a Planful or an Intervening Providence taking part in the day-to-day operations of the universe was in effect a competing theory. If one believed that there was a God who had originally designed the world exactly as has come to be, the theory of evolution through natural selection could be seen as superfluous. Likewise, if one believed in a God who intervened from time to time to create some of the organisms, organs, or functions found in the living world, Darwin's theory could be seen as superfluous. Any introduction of intelligent planning or decision-making reduces natural selection from the position of a necessary and universal principle to a mere possibility.

Something of Darwin's agnosticism appears in various letters and in his *Autobiography*, all posthumous. The only publication in his lifetime expressing these ideas was the concluding passage of *The Variation of Animals and Plants Under Domestication*. There Darwin stated the issue badly, but left something for each reader to decide for himself:

---

20 H. Helmholtz, *Popular Lectures on Scientific Subjects*, translated by E. Atkinson (London, 1873), p. 219 ff. Darwin read Helmholtz's essay on the imperfection of the eye in time to use it in his second edition of *Descent*, 1874, p. 441.
21 *Ibid.*

If we assume that each particular variation was from the beginning of all time preordained, the plasticity of organisation, which leads to many injurious deviations of structure, as well as that redundant power of reproduction which inevitably leads to a struggle for existence, and, as a consequence, to the natural selection or survival of the fittest, must appear to us superfluous laws of nature. On the other hand, an omnipotent and omniscient Creator ordains everything and foresees everything. Thus we are brought face to face with a difficulty as insoluble as is that of free will and predestination.[22]

In this passage, published in 1868, Darwin went almost as far in public as he had gone in private many years before. Either the theory of evolution through natural selection or the idea of an omnipotent and omniscient Creator is superfluous. Even when he put the matter this bluntly, Darwin was carefully leaving room for those who wished to believe in an initiating Providence who had created a world that would operate according to natural law.

Using the idea of God merely to get the whole system of nature started puts God permanently outside the system and in a very real sense reduces his importance. This accords well with what Darwin has told us about the development of his religious views. "Quite orthodox" as a young man, his faith faded gradually and, as he remembered it, painlessly. He became an agnostic in a dual sense: he had no reason to believe in God, and no desire to disprove His existence.[23]

The fact that Darwin seemed to vacillate on certain philosophical issues, and that he was willing to be conciliatory in his eventual public posture, might conceivably mean that he had adopted a definite, subtle, middle-ground position. More likely he decided that these were secondary questions on which he could afford to be conciliatory because they did not affect his ruling passion, the theory of evolution through natural selection. Whether God had created the universe a long time ago, whether it had always been there with God standing by, or whether God was an outmoded hypothesis—none of this really mattered to Darwin, so long as the world of nature operated according to discoverable natural laws. If Darwin had been willing to compromise on questions he deemed fundamental, he would not have been the great Darwin we know. Strangely, the decision that God's existence was not a fundamental question for his purposes may have been a much more profound change in Darwin's ideas than for him to have

[22] Darwin, *Animals and Plants, op. cit.*, Vol. 2, p. 432.
[23] See the unexpurgated version of his *Autobiography*. For many years his family permitted the publication only of a version in which his views of religion were severely censored. This reduced version was included in the *Life and Letters of Charles Darwin*, edited by his son Francis. The unexpurgated version was published by his granddaughter, Nora Barlow, in 1958, seventy-six years after his death.

adopted the view that He did not exist, but that the question remained fundamental.

The rejection of the idea of a Planful or Intervening Providence carried with it an important implication for Darwin's ideas about man. Without such a Providence there was nothing except the laws of nature, including the principle of evolution through natural selection, always governing the entire natural order. There was absolutely no reason to exempt man, in either his past or his future evolution, from the Darwinian mill. Regarding man's past, Darwin's views are plain enough, all the way from the M and N notebooks to the *Descent of Man*.

As for man's future, I have previously mentioned an idea that Darwin reiterated at least six times in his early notebooks: "If all men were dead, then monkeys make men.—Men make angels." (*B* 169)

This is an idea that must be read at two levels. He is saying that organisms evolve in such a manner as to fill up ecological niches, and there is a place in the world for an intelligent, manlike creature. If chance had not brought forth *Homo sapiens,* a progenitor similar to ours would have evolved into an intelligent hominid, because the evolutionary conditions would have favored it. By emphasizing the point that this hypothetical creature would not have been the species *man* as we know it, Darwin brings home the idea that chance plays a large part in evolution. Whatever total set of conditions happens to prevail will determine the outcome.

On another level, Darwin means to say something about evolution as an ongoing process applicable to man today. At first he seems optimistic: man will evolve into something still higher, "angels." Later on he is not so definite. Of man, he writes, "he is not a deity, his end under present form will come. . . ." (*C* 77)

Darwin realized that he was dethroning man from his boasted place at the pinnacle of Creation in at least three senses: past, penultimate and ultimate futures. Man would no longer have the divine right of Kings; he was born not of God, but of the lower animals. Worse, future evolution might put man in the shade, inferior even in intelligence to some new species that would evolve, probably out of man. Worst of all, whatever man becomes, Darwin believed that in the end the sun and all the planets will grow too cold to support life: "Believing as I do that man in the distant future will be a far more perfect creature than he now is, it is an intolerable thought that he and all other sentient beings are doomed to complete annihilation after such long-continued slow progress." (*Autobiography,* 92) An intolerable thought it may have been, but Darwin thought it: the "angel" that man is becoming will be annihilated.

The question *Was Darwin a materialist?* has one other important side to which we must attend, the issue of *vitalism*. Granted that all organismic phenomena have a material basis in that they consist of highly organized forms of matter in motion and of specialized energy transfer systems. Is there not, in addition, something else, some "vital principle" necessary to account for the special properties of living things? One might believe that there are such special "vital" properties and suppose that they derived from non-natural or super-natural sources. Alternatively, one might interpret the "vital principle" as a qualitative leap, a group of emergent properties inherent in the very nature of matter and energy when they occur in the highly organized forms we label "alive." In the latter case one would be a sort of materialist, believing that life and mind are "nothing but" matter and energy, but the sting of nothing-but-ness, so painful to the faithful in Darwin's time, would be lessened. Perhaps this second position might be labeled *naturalistic vitalism*.

Today we seem very close to synthesizing simple forms of life in the laboratory, to controlling precisely the pattern of development of more complex forms, and to simulating thought process in cybernetic machines; but we have also come to recognize that there is nothing at all simple about the whole subject. As we come a little closer to this godlike control over nature, our respect for its enormous complexity grows again. But in the nineteenth century there was far greater uncertainty as to the distance to be traveled from inanimate matter to complex living forms. The very effort to understand the innermost secrets of life and thought seemed to set the scientist against the gods. As Thomas Huxley put it, probably with relish, "Most of us are idolators, and ascribe divine powers to the abstractions 'Force,' 'Gravity,' 'Vitality,' which our own brains have created."[24]

By dint of some effort, as we have seen, Darwin managed to place the question of the origin of life outside the scope of his theory. In that way he avoided dealing with the nature of life insofar as that phrase means understanding the differences between inanimate and animate matter and the transition from one to the other. Logically, and therefore publicly, he could exclude the origin of life from his theory. But psychologically the preservation of his intellectual comfort required that he arrive at some understanding with himself on the answer to these ultimate questions.

With respect to the emergence of all the major forms and functions of living things, of course Darwin's main theoretical life task was to show that these could be accounted for in an entirely natural way. But that left one crucial question hanging, and to Darwin it felt like a

---

[24] *Life and Letters of Thomas Henry Huxley*, edited by his son Leonard Huxley, 3 vols. (London: Macmillan, 1908), Vol. 2, p. 358, letter written in 1884.

hanging matter: with the evolution of complex nervous systems, does there at last appear in the pantheon of nature a type of process, mind, which can no longer be thought of as natural?

In all the manuscript material Darwin wrote most fully and openly on these questions in the bundle of papers he later labeled "Old and USELESS Notes about the moral sense and some metaphysical points . . . " written between 1837 and 1840. The date is important because it shows that he immediately felt the need to resolve these metaphysical questions which were thrown open by his theoretical work in biology. True, in his eventual published work very little of this "useless" thought appears. But in his private intellectual economy it did not seem to him at all useless to speculate on such ultimate questions as the nature of life, purpose, and mind.

On the whole, his position is clear. He is drawn to a relatively straightforward materialism: "Sensation is the ordering contraction . . . in fibres united with nervous filaments. . . ."[25] From the simplest sensations to the most complex thoughts, mental processes can be explained as the activity of the nervous system. He cites experiments done with planaria (a simple flatworm, not to be confused with the earthworms which Darwin also studied). By their adaptive, seemingly purposive behavior, planaria display the rudiments of consciousness; we can split one planarian and produce three functioning organisms, and the adaptive behavior or consciousness of the resulting individuals is "multiplied with the organic structure. . . ." For Darwin it follows that consciousness is the effect of "sufficient perfection of organization" of bodily structure.[26]

In the *Origin,* by limiting his treatment of the evolution of mental functions to the subject of instinct, Darwin essentially side-stepped the problem of purposeful behavior and motivation. But in the "Old and Useless Notes" he deals with it forthrightly. "Every action whatever is the effect of a motive. . . . Motives are units in the universe. . . . The general delusion about free will [is] obvious. . . ."[27] As human beings, we *feel* as though there is some incorporeal self controlling the actions of our bodies, but in fact even the mechanism of control represents the functioning of a part of the body, the brain.

At least transitorily, Darwin entertained the possibility that there

---

25 Old and Useless Notes, #9.
26 "Old and Useless Notes," #16. Psychobiologists are still interested in the redistribution of planarian intelligence, although modern efforts, rather than splitting the whole organism, involve the injection into untrained individuals of RNA extracted from planarians trained in a simple conditioning task. Planarians are interesting because they are among the simplest organisms in which the transition from a nerve net to a central nervous system occurs.
27 "Old and Useless Notes," #25-28.

are emergent levels of organization, that life may display properties not predictable from any knowledge of inanimate matter, that it may represent "matter united by certain laws different from those that govern in the inorganic world. . . ." But he goes on immediately to ask, "Has any vegetable or animal *matter* been formed by the union of *simple* non-organic matter without action of vital laws?"[28] We can see here how, at every turn, Darwin was concerned to keep his speculations as clearly as possible within the domain of natural phenomena. From the sequence of these notes, we can also see how his botanical work, done much later in life, was guided by a philosophy of biology. Darwin wanted to show that seemingly purposeful acts in plants as well as in primitive animals could be explained according to the same general laws as the voluntary behavior of more complex animals, and, consequently, that the simplest forms of mind, such as the photosensitivity of plants, are parts of the same evolutionary net as the more obviously purposeful acts of human beings.

The title of this chapter has been drawn from the N notebook, where Darwin wrote: "To study Metaphysics, as they have always been studied appears to me to be like puzzling at astronomy without

N Notebook, p. 5. *Courtesy of Cambridge University Library.*

---

28 "Old and Useless Notes," #34. In 1828 Friedrich Wöhler had synthesized urea from potassium cyanate and ammonium sulphate. This step is often regarded as the first laboratory production of an organic compound and as a great blow against vitalism. Perhaps Darwin did not yet know about Wöhler's work; more likely he did not regard it as decisive, since the substances with which Wöhler began were not exactly "simple."

mechanics.—Experience shows the problem of the mind cannot be solved by attacking the citadel itself.—the mind is function of body.— we must bring some *stable* foundation to argue from." (*N* 5, October 3, 1838) Just as we cannot directly see the full nature of the stars but only points of light, we cannot study the mind directly. Just as Newton was able to solve astronomical problems by applying to celestial motions a deep understanding of terrestrial mechanics, so we may be able to come closer to understanding the mind and solving the profoundest philosophical and psychological problems if we . . . what? Darwin does not quite say what this "stable foundation" might be.

To the modern reader, knowing about recent great advances in neuropsychology and computer science, these might seem to provide the foundation for understanding the mind, by giving us knowledge of the structures which carry out mental processes. Perhaps Darwin thought something similar, but his actual work never took him in that direction.[29] Instead, he addressed himself to the task of understanding how evolution might proceed in such a manner that the changing structures can perform the adaptive functions we wish to understand, including the functions called *mind*.

---

[29] For a good discussion of the history of the relation between evolutionary theories and neuropsychology, see H. W. Magoun's chapter, "Evolutionary Concepts of Brain Function Following Darwin and Spencer," in *Evolution After Darwin*, Vol. 2, *The Evolution of Man*, edited by Sol Tax (University of Chicago Press, 1960).

CHAPTER 11

Darwin as Psychologist

. . . the more one examines the mechanism of life
the more one discovers that love and altruism—that
is, the negation of war—are inherent in the nature
of living beings. . . . To struggle against war is therefore to act according to the logic of life against the
logic of things, and that is the whole of morality.

Jean Piaget, "La Biologie et la Guerre," *Zofingue*,
No. 5, 1918, pp. 374–380

The very sweep of Darwin's enterprise determined both his achievements and his omissions as a psychologist. Darwin had a major
influence on the growth of psychology, both by his work as an evolutionary theorist and by his pioneering work in psychology itself. The
main themes he wove together in his general theory of evolution each
had their counterparts in psychology.

His materialist approach to biology helped lay the basis for a
modern view of the brain as the organ in which mental functions are
centered. His insistence on the intellectual continuity of man and
other animals speeded the rise of comparative psychology and the
study of animal behavior. His study of the emotional continuity of
man and other animals provided Freud with a valuable springboard
for the development of psychoanalysis. His concern for the adaptive
significance of all biological functions helped in the construction of a
functional psychology focussed on the interplay and utility of psychological processes, as compared with a structural psychology preoccupied with the discovery of the static elements of experience. His
interest in variation led quite directly to an upsurge of interest in
individual differences in psychological functioning, as compared with
the search for the laws of a generalized mind. The synthesis of embryology and evolution provided a point of view for the emerging field of

child psychology. The idea of superfecundity provided an important antidote to the lean rationalism of scholastic psychology. Not only those acts occur which are logically necessary and sufficient; the mind, like nature, is prodigal, and this very prodigality imposes upon the individual the task of choice and selective growth.

In reconstructing the private path Darwin took to his theory of evolution, we have used as our guideposts the rich manuscripts he left, and as our clearly visible beacon the theory at which he indubitably arrived. In the case of his psychological thought, we must be either prudent or more speculative. The manuscripts available are fewer and the ultimate extended public statement is almost entirely lacking. In short, Darwin, by choosing to remain a biologist, "failed" to become a systematic psychologist. At the same time, the needs of his evolutionary theory required him to be steadfast in his treatment of the evolution of intelligence. This ambivalence toward psychology is reflected in the sequence of his last major works.

He disposed of man in *Descent* (1871) and *Expression* (1872). These works are an attempt to understand how some psychological functions might have evolved. Rather than moving "up" to a systematic human psychology, Darwin then moved to a more detailed exposition of some very primitive psychological functions. He produced a series of works which continue his demonstration that the evolution of mind through natural selection is a plausible hypothesis. In 1875 he published *Insectivorous Plants,* a book in which the subject of plant behavior figures largely. In the same year he published an improved version of an earlier monograph, *Climbing Plants.* This work was done in good part to refute the belief that plants do not have the power of movement. "It should rather be said that plants acquire and display this power only when it is of some advantage to them. . . ."[1]

These ideas were foreshadowed by remarks in his early notebooks—for example, "have plants any notion of cause & effect. they have habitual action which depends on such confidence. when does such notion commence?" (*N* 13)

In the same decade there were other botanical works, and in 1880 Darwin completed *The Power of Movement in Plants,* a long work in which he dealt with twining and climbing movements, sensitivity to light and to gravity, and plant "sleep." After a detailed technical treatment of these subjects, Darwin summarized his views on the "mental powers" of plants: sensitivity to stimulation, transmission of information from one part of the organism to another, and movement

---

[1] Charles Darwin, *The Movements and Habits of Climbing Plants* (London: John Murray, 1875) , p. 206.

which is variable, adaptive, and coordinated in response to changing circumstances. These powers, he writes, resemble ". . . many of the actions performed unconsciously by the lower animals."[2] He concludes, "It is hardly an exaggeration to say that the tip of the radicle . . . having the power of directing the movements of the adjoining parts, acts like the brain of one of the lower animals; the brain being seated within the anterior end of the body, receiving impressions from the sense-organs, and directing the several movements."[3]

In his last scientific book Darwin moved a long step up the evolutionary scale, from climbing plants to burrowing worms. The main body of his book on the earthworm deals with the action of worms in churning up the soil, resulting in improved fertility for higher forms of plant life. In other words, the book bore mainly on the ecological relationships among organisms. But there was a second theme on which Darwin expended considerable effort, the behavior and intelligence of worms. There was a 32-page section, beginning with a discussion captioned "Intelligence Shown by Worms in Their Manner of Plugging Up Their Burrows."[4] This section concludes with an argument against the hypotheses that the adaptive behavior of worms can be ascribed either to blind trial-and-error, or to "specialized instincts" for each case of adaptive behavior:

> To sum up, as chance does not determine the manner in which objects are drawn into the burrows, and as the existence of specialized instincts for each particular case cannot be admitted, the first and most natural supposition is that worms try all methods until they at last succeed; but many appearances are opposed to such a supposition. One alternative alone is left, namely, that worms, although standing low in the scale of organization, possess some degree of intelligence.[5]

The ecological functions and the intelligence of earthworms were, of course, not new targets of Darwin's curiosity. His first paper on the subject[6] was written in 1837 as an almost immediate sequel to his paper on the formation of coral reefs. Together, the two papers form

---

2 Charles Darwin, assisted by Francis Darwin, *The Power of Movements in Plants* (London: John Murray, 1880) , p. 571.

3 *Ibid.*, p. 573. The radicle is the rootlet of the embryonic plant. It emerges from the seed, makes contact with the soil, and finds a way to penetrate it.

4 Charles Darwin, *The Formation of Vegetable Mould Through the Action of Worms with Observations on Their Habits* (London: John Murray, 1904) , p. 61. First published 1881.

5 *Ibid.*, pp. 92–93.

6 Charles Darwin, "On the Formation of Mould," read November 14, 1837, published in *Transactions of the Geological Society of London* (Second Series) , Vol. 5, 1840, pp. 505–509. Reprinted in Barrett, *op. cit.*

his early statement of the way in which organisms change the world in which they live. He maintained an interest in worms throughout his life. In some ways it was an easy subject for him, a relaxation from more strenuous efforts. In what became a cooperative effort with his children, he made a forty-year study of the sinking of pebbles, large stones, and other objects due to the action of earthworms in bringing up the soil.

In the M and N notebooks reproduced below, we can see the wide range of psychological topics Darwin touched upon in the years 1837–39: memory and habit, imagination, language, aesthetic feelings, emotion, motivation and will, animal intelligence, psychopathology, and dreaming. We can get another estimate of the scope of his early hopes for the construction of a scientific psychology by surveying the impressive variety of methods he used in his first studies of man and mind. In general, his method was to search for mental resemblances between animals and humans, to look for ways of testing his hypothesis of hereditary habits, and to sketch very briefly the direction in which a fully developed system of psychology might go in dealing with a given issue. In support of these pursuits, he used a number of more specific methods.

Observation of behavior was the most important of these. The *Beagle Diary* is rich in descriptions of human behavior. During that period Darwin did not devise any systematic method of collecting behavioral data, relying on a keen eye and a questioning mind. But as the voyage progressed, his assiduous note-keeping, coupled with his love of comparing different ethnic groups, went a long way toward providing the thoroughness which is one of the chief advantages of a formal method.

The same combination of persistent observation, note keeping, and thoughtful comparison characterizes the M and N notebooks. In addition, especially in his visits to the zoo, he occasionally devised a special test which had some of the character of a genuine psychological experiment. Later on, in his work on insects, worms, and plants, he conducted many systematic, controlled observations which amounted to behavioral experiments in the full sense.

Questionnaires, for better or worse, are today among the best-known instruments of social scientists. Darwin's early use of questionnaires, in contrast to modern methods, was aimed not at collecting self-reports from his respondents but at assembling wide-ranging surveys of observations on the behavior of individuals other than the person answering the questionnaire.

As early as May 1839, as we have seen, Darwin circulated his printed questionnaire, "Questions About the Breeding of Animals." This small pamphlet consisting of twenty-one questions, or more properly groups of questions, dealt with hybridization, variation, artificial selection, sexual selection, permanence of new varieties, in-breeding, and susceptibility to disease. Much of the information requested dealt with psychological matters: sexual preferences, the manner of inheritance of various psychological traits after crossing or in-breeding, and the inheritance of acquired characteristics. Darwin's experimental turn of mind can be seen from the seventeenth group of questions: Are the effects of special training in one individual passed on to its progeny? Do animals "removed early from their parents" display habits which, it might then be inferred, must have been inherited? Although he did not actually conduct the corresponding experiments, his style of assembling the facts through questions that play on systematic variation of relevant conditions in order to test a hypothesis comes very close to a *bona fide* experiment.[7]

In the same year, 1839, Darwin attended the meeting of the British Association for the Advancement of Science, in Birmingham. The association voted the sum of five pounds for printing and circulating an anthropological questionnaire, and appointed a committee to prepare it. Darwin, by then an esteemed scientific traveler, experienced in observing people all over the world, was a member of the committee. The questionnaire was presented to the association the following year under the title "Queries Respecting the Human Race, to be Addressed to Travellers and Others." This title actually takes a stand on an important issue, the unity of the human species, for it speaks of *the* human race. In those early days of anthropology it was not at all clear that the diverse kinds of men newly becoming known to European travelers were members of a single species.[8]

The questionnaire covered the topics of physical anthropology, language, family life and education, art and technology, law and social structure. Many of the questions were related to matters of special concern to Darwin: infanticide (with its bearing on selection), "craniology" (the term used in the questionnaire for "phrenology"—i.e., the relation between variations in the outer form of the cranium and variations in psychological traits), variation, interbreeding between different human groups, the inheritance of psychological characteristics as reflected in the results of interbreeding, the domestication of animals and the consequent production of new varieties, fluctuations

---

[7] Some copies of the original questionnaire have survived and are kept in the Cambridge University Library, together with some of the answers Darwin received. See Freeman and Gautrey, *op. cit.*

[8] This insistence on the unity of man was a tradition from which Darwin never wavered. As we have seen, it was reflected in the medallion manufactured by his maternal grandfather, Josiah Wedgwood, which showed a Negro slave and bore the inscription, "Am I not a man and a brother?" And it was expressed clearly in Charles Darwin's scientific treatment of the subject of race differences in *Descent.*

in population and the causes of any such changes, religious beliefs, and educability of the people observed.[9]

It remained, however, for Darwin's cousin Francis Galton to adapt the questionnaire for the purpose of collecting self-reports. In 1874 Galton circulated a questionnaire to assemble biographical data on eminent men; in 1879 he circulated a list of "Questions on the Faculty of Visualising." Darwin was a respondent to both of these sets of questions. The one on visual imagery is probably the first use of a questionnaire to amass numbers of genuinely introspective reports of inner experiences.[10]

Introspection, the process of examining the operations of one's own mind, has always been an indispensable tool of serious psychologists. Even the most adamant behaviorist comes to his subject armed willy-nilly with guilty (from his point of view) knowledge of himself. Psychologists of other persuasions make full and explicit use of various forms of self-examination, and also systematically collect and analyze the self-reports of other individuals.[11]

In his published writings Darwin was the least subjective of authors. He wrote at length on psychological topics in *Descent* and in *Expression,* both of which covered such a wide field that they gave ample room for the use of his own mental life as a means of elucidating general psychological phenomena. But he remained highly objective, relying almost entirely on outwardly observable behavior for his materials. Even his *Autobiography* and his biographical sketch of his grandfather,[12] for all their intelligence and charm, have a cool, impersonal air. His *Autobiography* was neither very concerned with the examination of his inner life nor on that score very revealing.

All the more interesting, then, to discover in the M and N notebooks so much material of a highly personal and sometimes emotionally charged nature. These notes were not written in the spirit of a

---

9 See the *Reports* of Ninth, Tenth, and Eleventh meetings of the British Association for the Advancement of Science, 1840, 1841, and 1842 (each one year after the meeting itself). Apparently, J. C. Prichard, author of *The Physical History of Mankind,* was the moving spirit behind the formation of the committee. Another member was William Yarrell, to whom Darwin often referred in his notebooks, especially on questions relating to animal breeding and the inheritance of acquired characteristics.

10 See Francis Galton, *Inquiries into Human Faculty and Its Development* (London, 1883). Darwin's responses to both of Galton's questionnaires are reproduced in *LL* 3, 177–180 and 238.

11 Even the psychophysical methods for studying basic sensory processes do not involve direct observation of the perceiving individual; rather, they present him with a stimulus of known physical properties and require him to report on whether he has or has not sensed it—in other words, to report his private experience.

12 Ernst Krause, *Erasmus Darwin, with a Preliminary Notice by Charles Darwin* (London: John Murray, 1879). This is a 127-page biography by Charles Darwin and an 85-page discussion of Erasmus Darwin's scientific work by Krause.

confessional. They were devoted to the scientific tasks Darwin had before him. Because he took the task of clarifying the relation between mind and body very seriously, he examined his own inner life.

In the notebooks, Darwin draws in every possible way on his own experiences to nourish his scientific thought. He moves fluently from creatures observed during the *Beagle* voyage to those read about in the works of others, and then to some imaginary "angels." When he thinks of such psychological matters as the nature of memory, dreams, and creative thinking, he talks frankly in the first person—what other beginning is there for a good psychologist? When he discusses sexuality, he draws on his own psychosexual life, although in this area there is a slight effort at concealment. Darwin thought relatively freely about himself, and he drew useful scientific conclusions from the process of self-examination.

Child biography, observing and recording the development of a single child, seems so obvious that it may appear strange to classify it as a "method" of psychological research. And yet, when Darwin's article "A Biographical Sketch of an Infant" was published in 1877, it was an unusual piece of work. There had been earlier efforts at child biography published before Darwin's, but not many. In 1787 Tiedemann, a German, brought out the first known European account of early childhood. In 1798 Itard began his famous study, *The Wild Boy of Aveyron,* an effort to educate a ten-year-old boy who had been found abandoned in a French forest. There were few other published accounts of early childhood until 1876, when Taine published an account of the development of his daughter in the first eighteen months of her life. Taine's article appeared in translation in *Mind,* the first psychological periodical, then only a year old. Reading Taine reminded Darwin of a journal he had kept, thirty-seven years earlier, on the development of William, his newborn first child. A few years later, in 1882, Wilhelm Preyer's *The Soul of the Child* became the first book-length treatment of this subject and is widely regarded as the foundation of modern child psychology.[13]

Incredibly, then, Darwin's article, published in 1877 after a thirty-seven-year delay, could still be a seminal, pioneering work and has been so regarded ever since. Of course, the sense in which the keeping

---

13 For brief historical sketches of child psychology, see E. Claparède's *Experimental Pedagogy and the Psychology of the Child* (1911; 4th edition); William Stern's *Psychology of Early Childhood up to the Sixth Year of Age* (1923, 3rd edition). Hippolyte Adolphe Taine, an influential French liberal intellectual, was the author of "Theorie de l'Intelligence" (1870). His article, which first appeared in *Revue Philosophique,* Vol. 1, pp. 5–23, 1876, was partially translated in *Mind,* Vol. 2, pp. 252–259, 1877, under the title, "Taine on the acquisition of language by children." Darwin's response, published in *Mind* the following year, is reprinted in the present volume.

of a journal is a scientific method depends entirely on the questions the investigator uses as his guide.[14] Darwin, when he kept his record of the first months of his son's life, was mainly interested in the expression of emotions. Thus, the originality of his work stemmed from its origins in his thinking about evolution.

Although Darwin makes very few interpretative remarks in this article, these few, together with the sequence and organization of the observations he reports, permit a plausible account of his general meaning.

Several different psychological functions appear in rudimentary form, develop in parallel with each other, and then fuse to give rise to new functions. In the domain of action the newborn infant displays a variety of reflexes over which he gains increasing command: clearly intentional acts with simple examples of rational problem solving (e.g., sliding his hand down his father's finger so that the hand will not interfere with sucking the finger) appear by the age of four months. During the same period, emotional development also proceeds, moving from simple indications of discomfort and startle reactions to a full range of emotional response (such as angry passion) by the age of four months.

At about that time the child begins to display "associations." Darwin uses the term to mean the anticipation that one event will lead to another. The child's associations are indicated by his emotional expressions. For example, if he has been dressed to go out but there is a delay in taking him out, he gets cross (five months).

The three functions already developed—intentional action, emotional expression, and association—now fuse to produce the first signs of language. At about four months there are the first traces of imitation of sounds, but without any apparent meaning. At about seven months the child begins to recognize names and other words, as indicated by his emotional expressions and his actions. At about twelve months the child invents his first word (*mmm* for food) and uses it in a variety of contexts. It is striking how much initiative Darwin gives to the child: first he invents words, then he begins to imitate the words he hears.

Darwin seems to carry the same general pattern further. The growth and fusion of earlier functions give rise to later ones. Thus, the

---

14 For the modern reader this is most strikingly brought home by Jean Piaget's trilogy, based on the first two years of life of his three children: *The Origins of Intelligence in Children*, *The Construction of Reality in the Child*, and *Play, Dreams and Imitation in Childhood*. By the time Piaget began this work there had of course been accumulating a long bibliography of research in child psychology. He used a plain and rough method—observing children and keeping notes—but he asked original questions.

rudiments of morality appear at about the age of six months, and continue to develop throughout the second year of life. Always interested in variation, Darwin stresses the point that children vary a great deal in the rate of their development.

In his evolutionary writings, Darwin made cautious and qualified use of the embryological idea that ontogeny recapitulates phylogeny. The same idea receives reasonably clear expression in this paper on psychological development. Darwin used this paper to suggest the way in which evolutionary theory might expand into the field of child psychology.

Taine had placed great emphasis on the child's creativity in constructing his own language. In his view, the initiative lies with the child, both in making new sounds or gestures and in discovering new meanings in the world around him; the adult's role is only to help select those reactions and meanings which conform with conventional language. Taine went as far as to suggest that the child could construct an entire language: ". . . if language were wanting, the child would recover it little by little or would discover an equivalent."[15]

Darwin, without contesting Taine's facts as to the child's constructive efforts in the development of language, briefly pointed out that this creativity does not arise *de novo* in the child, but is preceded by an earlier phase in which the child shows capacities more like those of non-human species: understanding precedes invention. "He understood one word, namely his nurse's name, exactly five months before he invented his first word *mum;* and this is what might have been expected, as we know that the lower animals easily learn to understand spoken words."[16]

Taine emphasized inborn reflexes combined with random variation and selection through trial and error in the development of the infant's expanding control of his own behavior. Darwin, seemingly in response, wrote, "The perfection of these reflex movements shows that the extreme imperfection of the voluntary ones is not due to the state of the muscles or of the co-ordinating centres, but to that of the seat of the will."[17] The notion of trial-and-error and selection seems Darwinian, but it is Taine who uses it.

Darwin was not especially interested in drawing a direct analogy between the evolution of species and individual psychological development. Variation and selection were essential in Darwin's theory of evolutionary change, but he did not conceive of individual behavior as arising mainly out of random variation or groping trial-and-error. In his view, the basic pattern of individual psychological development is

---

[15] Taine, *op. cit.*, p. 258.
[16] Charles Darwin, "A Biographical Sketch of an Infant," *Mind*, 1877, Vol. 2, p. 294.
[17] *Ibid.*, p. 285.

an orderly growth process, the product of aeons of evolutionary trials; only heritable *deviations* from this pattern would arise out of variation and selection. Moreover, as we have seen, even in his discussion of the lowly worm Darwin seems to have believed that most individual variations in behavior are intelligently adaptive. Only their incorporation in the web of evolutionary change was dependent on random events.

Why was the systematic study of the child so long in coming? The Renaissance, with its upsurge of interest in the human individual, might seem to have been the right time. But there were various theoretical burdens to be lightened before the child could be recognized as an important subject of scientific study. On the one hand, a *prioristic* rationalism ran counter to looking at the actual development of an individual child. On the other hand, psychological empiricism, by ascribing all of development to the direct influence of the external world, turned its vision away from the child and toward his environment. Only a genuinely interactionist point of view provides an adequate basis for developmental psychology.[18] In that light, it is not surprising that Darwin, of all people, should have been well equipped for a fresh look at his firstborn. In the field of biology, Darwin's ideas were a thorough expression of interactionism: the development of a new species is neither an unfolding expression of properties already implanted in the organism nor a direct reflection of the impact of the environment upon it: all development is a unique product of the interaction of organism and milieu.

The same point of view provides the best guide for a fresh look at each growing child. The a *priorist* looks mainly inward at the mind of the philosopher to discover the hypothetical adult already there; the empiricist looks "objectively" at the environment that will relentlessly shape the child. Only the interactionist is prepared to look *at* the child, to see him as a new person developing in *his* concrete circumstances.

There was another obstacle to the serious study of the child. In the story of Genesis, the first man and woman make their appearances as fully formed and functioning adults. Whether on the level of species or of individual evolution, the scientist is prepared to undertake developmental inquiry only when he divests himself of creationist mythology. This Darwin had done shortly before undertaking his first and in a real sense only investigation of human psychology, his brief study of the mind of an infant. How fitting it was for him to begin with a baby.

All through the M and N notebooks there are intimations of the

---

18 This theme pervades Piaget's work, but see especially *Biologie et Connaissance* (Paris: Gallimard, 1967).

importance of babies. During the period just before his own marriage, Darwin paid attention to his friends' and relatives' children, asked the parents questions, and watched the babies himself. None of this was very methodical, but a few lines of questioning thought emerged. Are early childhood memories retained throughout life, or are the specific events forgotten so that only habitual patterns of behavior endure? (Compare *M* 7 and *N* 62) As we have seen, this question had a definite relation to his speculations on the inheritance of acquired characteristics.

Chimpanzee disappointed and sulky. Drawn from life by Mr. Wood. Illustration from *The Expression of the Emotions in Man and Animals.*

In his many comments on the development of emotion, even in these early notes, Darwin attended mainly to the *expression* of various emotions in babies. The main line of his thought is that much emotional expression is unlearned and instinctual, and that an evolutionary link can be found uniting human and animal emotions. But he pays some attention to the development of emotion through the child's recognition of emotion in others. (See, for example, *M* 51, *M* 58, *N* 7) He was interested in the way in which the individual expression of emotion affects the relationships between individuals, and he was sensitive to the mutual interplay of feeling between parent and child. (See *M* 101, *N* 37)

Consistent with Darwin's primary reliance on objective observation, there are relatively few comments on the subjective character of emotions. He does discuss the nature of happiness as a flow of pleasurable ideas. (*M* 118, *M* 124) And in one passage, written three weeks before his marriage, he muses fleetingly on the subjective character of love. Typically, even here he opens the question through the avenue of outward expression before going on to say something about the inner substance:

> What passes in a man's mind, when he says he loves a person—do not the features pass before him marked, with the habitual expression of those emotions, which make us love him, or her.—it is blind feeling, something like sexual feelings—love being an emotion, does it regard (is it influenced by) other emotions? [*N* 59, January 6, 1839]

Approaching the topic of emotion through the study of expression has a somewhat indirect quality, like most of Darwin's psychological efforts. It must be remembered that even a thoroughgoing and systematic knowledge of the outward expression of emotions—facial expressions, blushes and erections, postures and movements—will never tell us how an emotion *feels*. For this, one must somehow consult the inner person or remain in ignorance. The whole subject of emotional expression gains its chief interest from our recognition, whether tacit or explicit, of the connection between outer expression and inner experience.

Darwin does not seem to have been denying this link or minimizing the importance of inner experience. There are in these notebooks many passages of a highly subjective nature. But he does seem to have worked on the assumption that one profitable path to follow in constructing a science of psychology is from the outside in—that is, moving from the objective to the subjective.

Instinct and Intelligence

Underlying Darwin's evolutionary line of thought lay a particular psychological approach to the nature of instinct. For adaptive behavioral change to precede and influence structural change, it is necessary that previously inherited structures do not completely determine behavior. In other words, instinctive behavior must be somewhat variable and intelligently guided in ways that depend on the immediate circumstances of life.

It was an essential part of his thinking that small variations in function might precede small evolutionary changes in structure. In the phase before he had worked out the theory of natural selection, he believed simply that the fortuitous requirements of a particular situation would evoke an adaptive variation in behavior, which might then become habitual and finally perhaps instinctual; this evolution of a durable new behavior would be coupled with appropriate structural changes to record and preserve it. After he had worked out the idea of natural selection, the idea that functional change can precede and influence structural change took on new force. Those functional changes which were supported by ensuing structural changes would be not only consolidated and preserved, but often enhanced, if natural selection happened to move the course of evolution in the same direction as the initiating functional change.

Darwin's view of instinct was at odds with the main thrust of Natural Theology. As applied to the subject of instinct, the argument from Design held that a designing Providence had created a structure that would invariably, like clockwork, carry out His purposes. The organization of the nervous system for each species could be compared to one setting of a cylinder in a portable organ or music box, the placement of the pegs on the cylinder determining the order in which different notes would be struck—i.e. the predetermined behavior of each species. Kirby, in borrowing this analogy from a French zoologist, Virey, knew without doubt Whose "invisible hand" had designed the instrument, set the cylinder for each of His creatures, and turned the organ too.[19]

For Darwin, on the other hand, it would have been awkward to admit predetermined complex behaviors not flexibly adapted to a changing environment; he would then have had to introduce some entirely new mechanism to account for the evolution of higher forms of intelligence. Far simpler theoretically for him to accept the operation of rudimentary forms of reasoning and problem-solving behavior as integral parts of instinctive acts. Then the course of evolution could run smoothly, producing a continuously changing balance among different sorts of psychological functions, one evolving out of the other.

Thus, for the Natural Theologian, reason was something "super-added" to instinct. Darwin resisted the sharp distinction between instinct and reason. For him, an element of intelligent adaptation was an integral aspect of the lowest instinct, even in the behavior of worms and plants: "A little dose . . . of judgment or reason, often comes into play, even in animals very low in the scale of nature." (*Origin*, 208)

---

19 Rev. William Kirby, *On the Power, Wisdom and Goodness of God as Manifested in the Creation of Animals and in Their History, Habits and Instincts* (London, 1836), Vol. 2, pp. 243–244. This was the seventh Bridgewater Treatise. Kirby was an eminent entomologist of his day.

Natural Theology in the eighteenth and early nineteenth centuries flourished in an age when the behavior of deterministic machines, such as clocks and music boxes and Babbage's calculating engine (see above, p. 208), provided the only comprehensible physical analogies of complex behavior. For the Natural Theologian the seeming music-box perfection and precision of complex instincts was a source of wonder and pleasure, and a testament to the existence of the designing hand of the greatest Mechanic of all. Darwin's answer to Natural Theology, in his chapter on instinct in the *Origin,* showed how such instincts might evolve without the guidance of any such designing hand.

In spite of Darwin's "little dose" of reason, his extended discussion of instinct did not unmistakably lay the ground for an examination of more flexible mental powers or faculties. It would certainly have been possible to accept the argument of the *Origin* on the evolution of instincts and then to draw the line, leaving higher mental faculties displayed in man as the special handiwork of God.

In the *Origin* the only chapter dealing with the evolution of behavior is the one entitled "Instinct," and the discussion is organized around three examples of instinct as Darwin understood it—cuckoos laying their eggs in other birds' nests, a species of ant making slaves of another species, and hive bees making cells. These examples are described in some detail, to make the point that very complex patterns of behavior can be transmitted through heredity, that these patterns are adaptive for the organisms in question, and that these specific instinctual patterns vary in such a way as to make it possible to account for their evolution through natural selection.

But if one looks for psychological faculties in Darwin's writing, they begin to appear. In the essay of 1844 the chapter on instinct contains a four-page discussion of the distinction between faculty and instinct, somewhat more detailed and clearer, but much the same as in the pages of the N notebook.[20]

The distinction between faculty and instinct is not made in the long chapter on instinct that Darwin prepared in 1857 for "Natural Selection," the long volume on evolution, the writing of which was interrupted by Wallace's letter and the consequent necessity to hammer out the *Origin* in 1859. Nor does he make the distinction in any of the six editions of the *Origin.*

But if we turn to the *Descent of Man* with an eye newly educated by the pages of the N notebook, we find an abundance of faculty psychology. The key chapter headings are Chapter 3 and Chapter 4, "Comparison of the Mental Powers of Man and Lower Animals," and

---

[20] Charles Darwin, *Foundations, op. cit.*

Chapter 5, "On the Development of the Intellectual and Moral Faculties During Primeval and Civilised Times."

Why did this important theoretical distinction suffer such vicissitudes in Darwin's writings? Most likely, the consideration of the gradual improvement of mental powers or faculties is more compatible with a discussion of the psychological evolution of humanity than is the rather mechanistic notion of the congealing of specific habits into hereditary instincts.[21]

In the M and N notebooks, Darwin's first references to faculties are all very brief. Only after his reading of Algernon Wells' lecture on instinct did he write more extensively on the subject.

The line between faculty and instinct is not sharp. Both are conceived of as hereditary. At some points, Darwin discusses faculties as though they are part of instincts. At other moments, faculties seem to be independent mental powers that can be put to work in the service of behavior, whether that behavior is organized in an instinctive pattern or not. If flexible powers are utilized in instinctive patterns of behavior, it follows that the instinctive pattern itself will be expressed in flexible rather than rigid ways. This conclusion conforms with Darwin's general treatment of instinct, and with modern findings as well.[22] There is nothing in Darwin's general style of thought that would require him to choose between these two conceptions. His theory of branching evolution can easily embrace a plurality of mechanisms.

In the eighteenth and nineteenth centuries there were many attempts to find a psychological line between man and animals that would be at once theologically safe and scientifically justifiable. Everyone had to grant the marvelously adaptive and seemingly intelligent character of infra-human behavior. One could attribute such processes to mechanisms designed by God, and label them "instincts." This approach, both mechanistic and theistic, removed God from the

---

21 In the nineteenth century, faculty psychology was viewed in some quarters as a theologically acceptable alternative to the mechanistic associationism of David Hartley. The associationists and, later, the early behaviorists did their best to eliminate both "faculty" and "instinct" from the list of scientifically acceptable concepts; they wished to show that all psychological functions could be reduced to simple reflexes modified by associations acquired during the life of the individual. The leading faculty psychologist of the eighteenth century, the Scotsman Thomas Reid, listed some 30 faculties. J. P. Guilford, with modern American organization and technology at his disposal, has found 120 in the intellectual domain alone. See David Hartley, *Observations on Man, His Frame, His Duty, and His Expectations* (London: Leake and Frederick, 1749) ; Thomas Reid, *op. cit.;* and J. P. Guilford, *The Nature of Human Intelligence* (New York: McGraw-Hill, 1967) .

22 See Colin Beer's article "Instinct" in the *International Encyclopedia of the Social Sciences* (Macmillan and Free Press, 1968) , for a clarifying discussion of the bewildering variations in the concept of instinct.

immediate arena of life processes. It left open the decision as to the source of those adaptive variations in behavior that could not be understood as the functioning of an unvarying machine.

On this point there was some dispute among Natural Theologians, since it was not clear whether lessening God's immediate control over events should be interpreted as lessening His power or heightening His glory. To give only one example of this way of thought, since the occurrence of seemingly intelligent animal behavior was indisputable, one zoologist argued as follows: flexible and intelligent adaptation implies consciousness; animals are certainly not conscious; therefore, intelligent behavior in animals demonstrates the intervention of another consciousness—i.e., God's.[23]

While there were some differences of opinion among Natural Theologians, the key issues on which they agreed were not only the reasonableness or adaptiveness of animal behavior, but the absence in animals of conscious reasoning and self-conscious awareness of the activities of the mind, both in intellectual and in moral matters.

In contrast, Darwin was interested in showing the evolutionary continuity between man and other animals in two ways. On the one hand, he believed, non-human animals show some rudiments of consciousness. On the other, humans act in ways not fully guided by conscious, rational thought. Having forsworn the attempt to write a full-blown psychology, Darwin was not as explicit as we might have liked him to be on these matters. But his protégé, George Romanes, to whom Darwin turned over all his notes on psychological processes, was very clear: consciousness evolved gradually, making its first rudimentary appearance in the coelenterates (e.g., jellyfish, coral).[24]

On the matter of unconscious processes, Darwin alluded repeatedly to several cases: unconscious selection, unconscious classification, and the transformation into habitual, unconscious routines of behaviors initially performed on a conscious, rational basis. These kinds of unconscious processes fall short of Freudian theory, in which the Unconscious becomes a domain for the play of taboo ideas, proscribed and inaccessible to conscious thought. Of this psychoanalytic Unconscious there are only a few glimmerings in Darwin's M and N

---

23 John Oliver French, "An Inquiry Respecting the True Nature of Instinct and of the Mental Distinction Between Brute Animals and Man," *The Zoological Journal*, Vol. 1, 1824, pp. 1–32. French concluded, "That intellectual and scientific qualities do not become objective in the minds of brutes . . . and therefore that so much of intellectual or scientific design as appears conspicuous in their actions, must be the effect of intellectual and scientific powers or energies, acting upon them in a region of their minds above the sphere of their proper consciousness" (p. 32).

24 George J. Romanes, *op. cit.* As we have seen, Darwin might well have placed the "dawn of consciousness" even earlier.

notebooks, and nothing at all in his published writings. In Freud's thought, conflict led to repression. But the main thrust of Darwin's writing about the subject was that inner conflict could be induced by the comparison of present impulses with the memory of past impulses and actions; and that such conflict expands the possibility of choice, enhances consciousness and self-consciousness, and furthermore that it has thus led to the evolution of self-awareness and moral conduct.[25]

In the *Origin,* Darwin could not discuss these matters at all, since he had decided to avoid all consideration of higher mental processes. In the *Descent of Man,* the questions of consciousness and conscience are subtly but briefly considered. Darwin's aim there was not to develop a definite and systematic science of psychology, but only to show how psychological problems might be attacked in a manner harmonious with evolutionary theory.

In the *Origin,* then, Darwin gave a one-sided presentation of his own psychological views. To avoid the issue of man's evolution, he had to say as little as possible about mind, but he could hardly evade the whole subject of adaptive behavior. His compromise was to deal at length with instinctual behavior and not at all with higher mental processes. This distortion was corrected only when he published *The Descent of Man,* twelve years later.

There can be little doubt that this tactic of publishing such a truncated psychology in 1859 was born of his wish to reduce the intensity of the forthcoming conflict with his adversaries. In a twentieth-century context, it is easy to see Darwin's restraint as a kind of intellectual cowardice. Two things should be said in mitigation. In 1859 he had not in fact done the work of marshaling evidence and argument necessary for the writing of *The Descent of Man* and its sequel, *The Expression of Emotion in Man and Animals.* But there is a more significant fact. In the perspective of history, the chapter on instinct in the *Origin* appears as a compromise and a delay. But viewed in its contemporary setting, it can be read as a blunt and direct attack on the existence of God as supported by the argument from Design.

To see the force of Darwin's attack, one has only to compare his treatment of instinct with the chapter by his old favorite of adolescent days, the arch-Natural Theologian, William Paley. Writing of the instinctive maternal behavior of a sitting bird, Paley concluded, ". . . I never see a bird in that situation, but I recognize an invisible hand, detaining the contented prisoner from her fields and groves . . . ,"[26] the hand of God.

---

25 See *Descent of Man,* especially Chapter 4, which is devoted to the "moral sense."
26 Paley's works have gone through many editions. I quote from *The Works of William Paley, D.D., with a Life* by Alexander Chalmers (5 vols., London, 1819), Vol. 4, *Natural Theology,* p. 249, the chapter entitled "Instincts."

Earlier in the same work Paley devoted an entire chapter to the structure of the eye as evidence of the designing intelligence of God, suggesting that "the examination of the eye was a cure for atheism."[27]

Darwin, for all his caution, would have no part of this cure. His chapter on instinct concluded, ". . . to my imagination it is far more satisfactory to look at such instincts as the young cuckoo ejecting its foster-brothers,—ants making slaves,—the larvae of ichneumonidae feeding within the live bodies of caterpillars,—not as specially endowed or created instincts, but as small consequences of one general law, leading to the advancement of all organic beings, namely, multiply, vary, let the strongest live and the weakest die." (*Origin,* 243–244)

Darwin had studied animal behavior largely to elucidate the origins of human mental processes and was completely unabashed in his search for primordial signs of higher mental processes in lower animals and in his use of a vocabulary based both on human introspection and on behavior description. Within a few years, however, the British psychologist Lloyd Morgan announced his dictum, "In no case may we interpret an action as the outcome of the exercise of a higher psychical faculty, if it can be interpreted as the outcome of the exercise of one which stands lower in the psychological scale." Rather than searching for the beginnings of human mentality in other animals, "Morgan's canon," as it became known, led comparative psychologists to do their best to reduce such beginnings to terms that were, as far as possible, non-intellectual, non-introspective, and non-human.[28]

This reductionist trend reached its acme much later in the radical behaviorism of J. B. Watson, who did his best to expunge all references to inner experience from scientific psychology. In one form or another today, notably in the writings of B. F. Skinner, behaviorism has been enormously influential. In so far as behaviorism has been successful, Darwin's achievement has been completely distorted. Rather than considering mental processes as part of natural science, the behaviorists have lost sight of Darwin's evolutionary aim and eliminated mind from psychology.

In a sense, the twentieth-century behaviorists and the nineteenth-century Natural Theologians share an important premise: mind is super-natural. From this premise the behaviorists draw one conclusion: mind is an unscientific concept and all subjectivity must be eliminated from psychology. The Natural Theologians took a different tack—the attempt to incorporate mind and all other living phenomena in natural science by subjugating science to theology. It would

---

27 *Ibid.,* p. 26.
28 C. Lloyd Morgan, *Introduction to Comparative Psychology* (1894), Chapter 3.

have troubled Darwin to know that his "opening to the left" would in a few decades lead some scientists toward excising and even exorcising man's mind from the domain of legitimate scientific inquiry.

Darwin on Himself

Introspection into his own mental processes played a large part in Darwin's early work on psychological problems. For him, self-examination was strictly a method; his manifest aim was not self-discovery but an understanding of the operation and evolution of mind in general. Sometimes his introspections are written in the first person, sometimes he writes of a generalized person but in such a way that it is obvious he is drawing on his private experience. The style of the M and N notebooks is definitely not that of a private diary or confessional autobiography. Nevertheless, in this impersonal setting Darwin set down many notes that tell us something about himself.

As a man whose work it is to think, Darwin finds he has chosen a difficult vocation. Flights of imagery and disconnected thoughts come easily enough to him, but connected thinking—involving a series of complex decisions and the maintenance of several parallel streams of thought—is hard, exhausting work. He believes the difficulty stems from the complexity and novelty of each effort, rather than from the raptness of his attention, for he is quite able to lose himself in music or private daydreams in which all his attention is focused on one thing without experiencing the fatigue of reasoning or inventive thought.

Yet the spontaneity and flow of his notebooks and letters give a strong impression of someone who finds it easy and enjoyable to think, hard to refrain from intellectual work or play. His various remarks on the "hardness of thought" (see, for example, *M* 34) can scarcely mean that he always found it hard. They probably mean that Darwin thought persistently, whether it was coming easily or not, and that he often pushed himself beyond the onset of fatigue.

In the *Descent of Man* Darwin wrote of the combination of intellectual faculties forming "the higher mental powers": curiosity, imitation, attention, memory, reasoning. and imagination. (*Descent*, Chapter 3). The list of topics Darwin covered reads almost like an inventory of subjects chronically neglected by twentieth-century psychologists until the upsurge of cognitive psychology beginning in the 1950s. Of imagination he wrote, "By this faculty he [man] unites former images and ideas, independently of the will, and thus creates brilliant and novel results." (*Descent*, 74) The passage goes on to argue that the higher animals "possess some power of imagination." In the M and N notebooks, when he compares himself with his sisters and in other passages, he seems to be saying that he has a highly developed imagination, good powers of attention, and enough of the other faculties to form a useful repertoire.

The impression one forms of Darwin's intellect from what he says of himself in these notebooks is not strikingly different from his modest description of himself in his *Autobiography,* written nearly forty years later. There is one difference. In the *Autobiography,* in the section "An Estimation of My Mental Powers," he says little of his imagery, while the notebooks are full of powerful images as well as descriptions of himself as a person with strong visual imagery. There are, however, passages in the *Autobiography* in which he does describe his imagery. For example, in telling of his passion for entomology, especially collecting beetles, during his Cambridge years, he writes of "the indelible impression many of the beetles which I caught at Cambridge have left on my mind. I can remember the exact appearance of certain posts, old trees and banks where I made a good capture." (*Autobiography* 63) Also, in answering Francis Galton's "Questions on the Faculty of Visualising," Darwin gives an account of himself as someone with fairly strong visual imagery. (*LL* 3, 238–39)

The images of the notebooks are not merely arid records of objective facts useful in inductive reasoning. On the contrary, Darwin's images are full of feeling and show beyond question that when he observed nature he did so with the full range of human emotions.

I have already discussed some of Darwin's fears. This subject was introduced early in the present book in order to explain his tortuous detours and delays in publishing his ideas. But fear would hardly form the basis for the positive feeling toward nature necessary to do good science of any kind, least of all for a synthesis embracing the whole natural order. Everywhere in these notebooks we come upon more positive emotions: love of beauty, sense of reverence, sympathy, curiosity, and love of truth. Not only these vaunted "human feelings" but Darwin's enjoyment of sensual impressions—sights, smells, tastes, rhythms, and sexual passion—are found in these pages. Darwin was a thinking-feeling animal, and the thinking part was in good contact with the feeling part.

Darwin's eventual published approach to the subject of emotions focused on expression rather than on emotion as such; indeed, we can see this approach taking shape in the M and N notebooks. It is therefore of great interest that Darwin, before deciding on this tactic of cataloguing the "objective" observable aspects of emotion, had gone through a period of self-examination in which he recorded and reflected upon his own subjective world, his private emotional life. Nearly 100 years after Darwin wrote these notes, Watson, the founder of American behaviorism, criticized William James for departing from the Darwinian model of "thoroughly objective and behavioristic" descriptions of emotional reactions. Watson objected to James' reliance on introspection without realizing how much James' precursor, Darwin, had done the same.[29]

Darwin recorded three dreams in these notebooks, all within a two-month period. As I have already discussed, dreams are ambiguous, and various interpretations of one dream may be simultaneously plausible. While we cannot know what these dreams really meant for Darwin, trying to set down what they might have meant is a way of expressing the feelings Darwin conveys to one reader of these notebooks. For brevity, I am omitting various other interpretations that have come to mind. I give here only one for each dream, in a way that brings them together as a group, which seems reasonable, considering their closeness in time.

"*Going home.*" In August 1838 Darwin was genuinely baffled. He had been for some time struggling with a group of problems whose solution eluded him. Several times in the preceding months he had discussed the "hardness of thought." On September 7, one week after this dream, he wrote that, considering what his predecessors had done, "I pretend to no originality of idea. . . ." (C 69) The dream of packing a trunk for Shrewsbury, his birthplace and family home, seems like a womb wish of going home for help. But it is not a dream of disorganized retreat. In the dream Darwin is still in command, giving orders to his servant.

"*Death and immortality.*" I have already discussed Darwin's dream of execution and restoration to life. When Darwin had this dream, he was only one week away from his reading of Malthus and his insight about the role of natural selection in evolution. As I have shown, this insight was not really very sudden. Darwin may well have felt that he was getting close to an important moment of truth. But finding the solution carried with it the responsibility of publication, the certainty of exposure, and the threat of harsh criticism.

"*Still fragmented.*" Darwin's incisive insight about natural selection on September 28, 1838, did not at once transform his thinking. Many puzzles remained, and it would require much hard work to mine the vein opened by the insight, and to satisfy himself of its explanatory power. On October 30, when he recorded the dream of reading the French book and understanding every word but not the sense of the whole, it was as though he had read the book of nature and understood it piecemeal but had not quite seen how his own

---

[29] See J. B. Watson, *Behaviorism* (University of Chicago Press, 1961). First published 1924.

insight could serve as the unifying thread with which to weave a great new synthesis.

While the main import of Darwin's numerous remarks on unconscious processes was the harmony of unconscious mental work with conscious goals, he does seem to have had some feeling for the existence of unconscious conflict and repression. In the M and N notebooks, each of the three dreams was immediately followed by fleeting remarks with an obvious bearing on this subject. After the dream of Going Home, he wrote, "One's Reflective Consciousness is curious problem, one does not care for the pains of ones infancy—one cannot bring it to one self.—nor of a bad dream. . . ." (*M* 115) After the dream of Death and Immortality he wrote, "What is the Philosophy of Shame & Blushing?" (*M* 144) After the Still Fragmented dream he wrote, "It does not hurt the conscience of a Boy to swear, though reason may tell him not, but it does hurt his conscience, if he has been cowardly. . . ." (*N* 34)

Freud and Ernest Jones picked up Darwin's sensitivity to these issues. They both cited a remark of Darwin's about the tendency to forget unpleasant events such as facts or ideas opposed to one's cherished theories. Darwin handled this problem by immediately writing a memorandum about any such point.[30]

I do not mean to suggest that Darwin anticipated Freud's ideas about unconscious processes in an explicit or even a conscious way, but only that he was willing to examine his own thoughts and emotions in a spirit of accepting non-rational components of human experience.

As reflected in the "Still Fragmented" dream of October 30th, Darwin had good reason to feel that he had not yet achieved a satisfying synthesis resolving all of the main problems that faced him. True, he now had the key idea of evolution through natural selection. But he had not worked out an acceptable answer to the genetical problems—heredity and variation—which had figured so prominently in his motives for beginning the M and N notebooks. True, he had increased his confidence in his ability to defend the proposition of psychological continuity between man and other animals. But he had not advanced very far toward developing a convincing scientific psychology harmonious with his own image of man.

Just how far he was from such a goal is reflected in the fate of his psychological ideas as they were incorporated into the body of late nineteenth- and early twentieth-century thought. Consistently, Darwin had striven to approach the subject of continuity both by showing the beginnings of human intelligence and morality in infra-human animals *and* by showing the traces of our animal origins in the non-

---

30 Sigmund Freud, 1901, *op. cit.*

rational components of human psychology. But he did not construct a psychology sturdy enough to protect the unity of this thought from three important deformations.

Behaviorism, psychoanalysis, and social Darwinism all drew upon his work. But all three were movements which placed overwhelming emphasis on the animal origins of man as against the "far more perfect creature" Darwin thought he saw in the making. (*Autobiography*, 92)

Darwin's argument for the evolutionary continuity of human and animal mentality was steadily transformed into the anti-mentalism of behavioristic psychology. A leading behaviorist has acknowledged that this required three steps: Darwin ascribed mental powers to animals, Lloyd Morgan continued the development of comparative psychology by advocating the elimination of mind as a legitimate concept in the study of animal behavior, and J. B. Watson endeavored to "re-establish Darwin's desired continuity without hypothesizing mind anywhere."[31] I believe Darwin would have been happier with the Gestalt psychologists' treatment of animal intelligence, which preserved the idea of continuity by developing objective methods for studying insightful problem-solving behavior in infra-human species.[32]

The social Darwinists, of course, have had their day. They used Darwin's idea of the struggle for existence to support their view of the pitiless struggle of man against man as a defensible social arrangement among human beings. Ironically, Darwin never entertained such an idea. As I have shown, his conception of the struggle for existence was one of struggle to meet all the conditions of life. It would be entirely in harmony with his thinking to insist that the struggle for survival of the human species must be, in the years to come, a struggle to develop social forms that enhance cooperation and rational, long-term planning for collective ends rather than short-sighted, individualistic efforts for private gain. In the *Origin,* in his chapter on instinct, Darwin devoted by far the most space to his discussion of the hive-making behavior of bees. While he did not mean to suggest that the behavior of social insects was consciously cooperative, he was quite explicit that the struggle for survival pertains to the swarm as a whole, not to a contest of bee against bee. (*Origin,* 235)

In the *Descent of Man* Darwin developed an extended argument for the view that conscious, intelligent behavior "for the good of the community" was a natural product of evolution (*Descent,* 124) . In the heyday of competitive capitalism, Darwin's ideas were seized upon and

---

31 B. F. Skinner, *The Behaviour of Organisms: An Experimental Analysis* (London: Appleton-Century, 1938), p. 4.
32 Köhler, *op. cit.*

distorted to justify "rugged individualism" and the exploitation of man by man.[33] But today the pressure of circumstances has led many people to re-think the meaning of survival and to search out ways of working for it in a spirit of collaboration rather than mutual destruction.

Psychoanalysis began as a movement stressing the non-rational, instinctual roots of human thought and conduct. Unlike the behaviorists, Freud was not opposed to "mentalism." He knew that in organic evolution, primitive forms tend to be replaced by the later products of evolution. But he thought that mental evolution had followed a somewhat different course: "As a rule the intermediate links have died out and are known to us only through reconstruction. In the realm of the mind, on the other hand, what is primitive is so commonly preserved alongside of the transformed version which has arisen from it that it is unnecessary to give instances as evidence."[34] Psychoanalysts for a long time emphasized the predominance of the primitive over the more evolved forms of mental life. But, in the tradition of both Darwin and Freud, they have always been deeply interested in the interplay of the rational and the non-rational. In recent years there has been a change in the balance of these ideas. There is now a strong tendency within psychoanalysis to give a somewhat hopeful answer to a question Freud once posed: "The fateful question for the human species seems to me to be whether and to what extent their cultural development will succeed in mastering the disturbance of their communal life by the human instinct of aggression and self-destruction."[35]

In the main, the three movements I have been discussing all suggest a dark outlook for humanity. Man's hopes rest on a rational and cooperative use of our highest intellectual and moral abilities, on our capacity to become not only human but humane. Fortunately for Darwin's inner tranquility, he lived before the possibility of man's rapid self-extermination had become a household question. The balance he struck among these complex considerations was romantically optimistic and, I hope, true. In the closing passage of the *Descent of Man* he was no longer delaying the expression of his ideas or softening them by phrases pandering to religious sentiments:

> We must, however, acknowledge, as it seems to me, that man
> with all his noble qualities, with sympathy which feels for the most
> debased, with benevolence which extends not only to other men but

---

33 See Richard Hofstadter, *Social Darwinism in American Thought*, rev. ed. (Boston: The Beacon Press, 1955).

34 Sigmund Freud, *Civilization and Its Discontents*, translated and edited by James Strachey (London: Institute of Psycho-Analysis, 1930).

35 *Ibid.*

to the humblest living creature, with his god-like intellect which has penetrated into the movements and constitution of the solar system —with all these exalted powers—Man still bears in his bodily frame the indelible stamp of his lowly origin. [*Descent*, 619]

By his use of the word "god-like," Darwin was finally rendering unto man that which is man's.

CHAPTER 12

Creative Thought:
The Work of Purposeful Beings

Origin of man now proved.—Metaphysics must
flourish.—He who understands baboon would do
more toward metaphysics than Locke.

Charles Darwin, M notebook,
p. 84, August 16, 1838

Men make their own history, but they do not make it
just as they please; they do not make it under circumstances chosen by themselves, but under circumstances
directly encountered, given and transmitted from the
past.

Karl Marx, *The Eighteenth Brumaire of Louis
Bonaparte* (New York: International Publishers,
1963), p. 15

Darwin spoke of man's "god-like intellect." But is man really god-like?
Has he an image of himself? Can he create a being in his own image?
Can he deliberately create anything?

The last question may seem the most peculiar, since the answer,
"yes," is so obvious. Man has invented so much, changed the face of
the earth, painted, written, sung, and dreamed. Yes. But in what sense
has any of this been *deliberate?*

Darwin had his moments when he saw the force of these questions: "I verily believe free will & chance are synonymous.—Shake ten
thousand grains of sand together & one will be uppermost,—so in
thoughts, one will rise according to law." (*M* 31, written between July
15 and July 22, 1838) But he did not draw despairing conclusions from
his personal blend of determinism and probabilism. He recognized a
connection between the evolution of intelligence and the evolution of
morality. He took an optimistic view of man's future, and he believed
that understanding his theory of evolution would make man more
moral rather than less: "Two classes of moralists: one says our rule of
life is what *will* produce the greatest happiness.—The other says we

have a moral sense.—But my view unites both & shows them to be almost identical & what *has* produced the greatest good or rather what was necessary for good at all *is* the instinctive moral sense."[1]

In the same passage Darwin comments on the importance of civilization and education in bringing the accumulated experience of man to bear on changing man's "moral sense."

Despite Darwin's own positive feelings, one modern view of life has emerged, owing much to Darwin, in which man suffers a double indignity. His future is both determined and unpredictable. He can neither do nor know anything important about his own destiny. This cannot even be called "man's fate," for in the classical view there were at least gods and perhaps poets who knew what fate held in store.

Modern determinism sees the world as operating according to natural law rather than divine fiat. But deterministic laws and fate are equally inexorable. Neither leaves any room for human invention and choice to change the future of the individual or of the species.

One version of the human plight was expressed by Camus. Sisyphus is condemned for all time to rolling a stone up a hill and watching it roll down again. He thinks about the meaninglessness of such a life, contemplates suicide, and decides against it, the decision itself being part of his fate. While life is boring and repetitious without end, at least Sisyphus knows what is in store for him and the task before him is merely meaningless—rolling a stone is no better or worse than any form of common labor. Although Camus does not dwell on the point, Sisyphus can also have some feeling of individual identity—his task is a special punishment set for a deed he himself has committed.[2]

A view of human life has arisen in which the individual is subject both to deterministic and probabilistic laws in such a way as to make the idea of free and purposeful creativity meaningless. To the extent that life is governed by deterministic laws, the argument runs, there is no way of affecting the future because it has all been determined by circumstances beyond personal control. Meanwhile, wherever probabilistic laws prevail, there is no way of intelligently influencing the future because things are chancy and unpredictable.[3]

It may help to give this view a name. Because it combines determinism and chance in a thoroughly materialistic way, and proceeds on this basis to deny any significance or reality to mental processes, we may label it *hypermaterialism*. It should be clearly dis-

---

[1] "Old and Useless Notes," #30, written October 2, 1838.

[2] Albert Camus, *The Myth of Sisyphus* (London: Hamish Hamilton, 1955).

[3] For an excellent discussion of the relation between determinism and probabilism, see David Hawkins, *The Language of Nature: An Essay in the Philosophy of Science* (New York: Doubleday, 1967).

M Notebook, p. 84. *Courtesy of Cambridge University Library.*

tinguished from other varieties of materialism. This hypermaterialist position is advocated by Skinner, who seems to use Darwin as a point of departure but writes, "We can follow the path taken by physics and biology by turning directly to the relation between behavior and the environment and neglecting supposed mediating states of mind."[4]

To take account of the seeming occurrence of intelligent, purposeful creativity, the hypermaterialist picture must be modified in describing the creative person. But an image of the creative individual which stems from such an alienated image of Everyman inevitably carries some of the same stigmata.

The idea of a purposefully creative individual seems to conjure up the old argument from Design. Fear of teleology has influenced various ways of dealing with the appearance of deliberate innovation. There have been two basic approaches, both of which have had as their theoretical function the elimination of the striving, purposeful person who successfully carries out his creative aims. One approach externalizes and depersonalizes the creative process, attributing responsibility for it entirely to the *Zeitgeist* or spirit of the age, objective circumstances, or even chance contingencies. In this view, the individual's thought and action are nothing but direct reflections of

---

4 B. F. Skinner, *Beyond Freedom and Dignity* (London: Jonathan Cape, 1972). I do not deny that there are both deterministic and probabilistic laws. Of course there are. But the reductionist tendency to see deterministic laws operating in small, atomistic events has been coupled, in the hypermaterialist view, with a tendency to deny the existence of self-regulating mechanisms, i.e., to see the larger patterns of nature as completely chancy. In my view, the opposite approach is more plausible. At the local levels, indeterminacy is prominent; in the larger patterns, local irregularities are smoothed out by natural self-regulating mechanisms. In human activities, purpose is one such self-regulatory process, keeping thought and action on a steady course in the face of all sorts of chancy vicissitudes. For a fuller development of a similar idea see Paul A. Weiss, "The Living System: Determinism Stratified," in *Beyond Reductionism: New Perspectives in the Life Sciences,* edited by Arthur Koestler and J. R. Smythies (Boston: Beacon Press, 1971).

factors in the controlling environment: the person is a vehicle and not an agent.

The other approach drives the creative process entirely inward, desocializing it, and minimizing the role of conscious, disciplined effort. The creative thinker is a "sleepwalker" who stumbles onto his best ideas in dreams or other unguarded moments. Underlying this approach is the premise that conscious thought is not free, that it runs in "predestinate grooves" dictated by the prevailing ideas of the day, and only unconscious mental activity is free enough of these constraints to permit creative work. Not all thoughts are free, only dreams.

This overemphasis on unconscious, non-rational mental work gains some support from accounts of creative processes in which dreams and other involuntary activities have played a striking role.[5] These accounts are numerous and they deserve attention, but their meaning is not simple. Rather than looking at such incidents as documenting the paramount role of unconscious processes, we can see the latter as part of the activities of a person governed by a ruling passion.

The usual view of unconscious processes is that they express the way in which a person is divided against himself. But a person is not always so divided. When he bends all his efforts toward some great goal, the same problems which occupy his rational, waking thoughts will shape his imagery and pervade his dreams.

In such cases the occurrence of useful dream work is a symptom not of inner conflict but of unitary commitment of the whole person. Anyone who has ever had such an experience will remember the moment of welcoming, the waking joy of discovering what one has thought. Of course, for such products to become useful, they must be seized upon and reworked by the creative person, thoroughly awake and aware of what he is doing.

Such a conception of the creative thinker, as relatively well-functioning and integrated, harmonizes better with the fact of his successful creativity than does a view of him as divided and stumbling. If creative thought were a matter of sudden and sporadic acts or of happenstance, well-organized steady functioning would not be so important. But I believe it is a slower growth process in which the person must persevere against obstacles and use all the resources at his command. When we say that great insights come only to the prepared

---

[5] Especially when the idea of the Unconscious was young, some scientists were delighted to discover that some of their work was play. One of the best accounts of such an incident is by the mathematician Henri Poincaré: *Science and Method* (London: Nelson, 1914; first French publication, 1908). Many of these incidents have been described by Koestler, *op. cit.*

Charles Darwin in 1882. "As for myself, I believe that I have acted rightly in
steadily following and devoting my life to Science. I feel no remorse from having committted any great sin, but have often regretted that I have not done
more direct good to my fellow creatures." (*LL* 3, 359; written in 1879) *Courtesy of Cambridge University Library.*

mind, we do not mean that the mind is prepared merely by steeping it in pre-digested knowledge. The way is made ready by active search and inquiry. The welcoming mind belongs to one who has prepared it by his own efforts, as a field in which new ideas can flower.

If the production of new ideas depended mainly on unconscious processes, or if the recombination of ideas into new patterns depended mainly on chance, there would be little room left for such purposeful growth. The concepts of freedom and purpose are inseparable. If freedom means anything, it means the opportunity to do something of one's own choosing. What would freedom be for an aimless atom?

At this point in the discussion it is always tempting to open a path for purposeful creativity by introducing a new kind of person, someone who can transcend determinism and chance. Perhaps, although Everyman is impotent, there are a few great men of enlarged consciousness and superior resolve who can be deliberately creative. Enter the Hero!

We should not carelessly dismiss the concept of greatness, but it is important to be clear on this point. The mere assertion that there are some individuals of extraordinary ability who transcend the hypermaterialist image of the world is a denial of the problems and not a solution. Substituting the group for the individual will not work either. Faced with the suggestion that the individual is impotent, it seems reasonable to propose that the powers of the group may be equal to a task that defeats the individual. Again, we should not dismiss the human group, for it is essential to the creative process even when the individual seems to work alone. But without an escape from the hypermaterialist trap, the group can be just as much a prisoner of determinism and chance as the individual. Perhaps more so, for, at least in modern Western society, people often work at cross-purposes: while an individual may have his own clear-cut goals, society's product may seem more rather than less aimless.

To understand the relation between purpose, freedom, and creativity, we need to examine further the role of chance in creative work. For purposes of this discussion a thought process can be sub-divided into these two parts: the production of new ideas and the reorganization of ideas (both old and new) into new patterns. In saying this, of course, I am using *ideas* to refer to elements or sub-units of which larger patterns are composed.

We know very little as yet of the process by which a new idea is produced. Let us suppose that each new variant is not an isolated idea but a change in the properties of some larger mental structure of which it is a part. Let us suppose, furthermore, that those parts of a system of ideas that are free to vary at any given moment are variable only within certain limits. This would be analogous to what we might say of any other part of a living system—that it is variable in its functioning, but within limits that depend on its place in the system as a whole.

There are many things we do not know. How are individual ideas produced? Are new ideas common or rare? Are they recurrent or unique? In spite of all this ignorance, there are a few definite things we can say.

A new idea can be recurrently new in one brain in the special sense that the first time it occurred it was not incorporated in a stable structure and therefore on a later occasion it *feels* new; or in the sense that its recurrence marks the transformation of some larger system, which did not occur the first time. The recurrence of the same novelty in the realm of ideas would be analogous to the repeated occurrence of the same mutation in the field of genetics. The immediate cause of the mutation may be some unknown, random event; its precise recurrence suggests to the geneticist that the mutation itself is one of a finite number of states that can be assumed by a given complex molecular structure.

The belief that a useful theory of creativity absolutely requires us to understand the source of variant or new ideas is akin to Darwin's feeling, against which he struggled, that his theory of evolution must include an explanation of the cause of heritable variation. Of course, we would like to know the answers to these questions, but we can do useful work by taking the occurrence of variants as given, and then studying the process of search, selection, and reorganization in which a new argument is constructed.

If the occurrence of each new idea is a unique event, we can hardly apply the laws of chance to such events, since these laws deal only with statistical aggregates of many events that can all be treated as members of the same population. But even if new ideas are unique events, we still want some conception of the role of chance in the growth of thought. There is a way.

We need an approach that would do justice to our image of the creative person as well organized, purposeful, aware of the manifold possibilities that exist in the world, and therefore free to choose among them. We need an approach that respects the kinship of mental processes with other living systems: variation and novelty are not chaotic or unrelated to the organism's past, but express the degrees of freedom characteristic of a particular organization as it stands at one moment in its history.

Every living organization has internal structure, so that the functioning of each of its separate parts influences the others and all function together as a more or less harmonious whole. This is what we mean by an organism. Each such living entity is dependent on its environment and yet independent of it, for each organism has stored within it the means of continuing to sustain itself and to preserve its organization under a range of circumstances. This stable organization is what we mean by the identity or integrity of an organism. The living world is therefore made up of such partially independent systems, each functioning according to its own internal laws of organization. From time to time, each organism comes into contact with and interacts with another system whose past history and present functioning are independent of its own.

This is the crucial fact. When the paths of previously independent systems intersect, the result is something new, not predictable from our knowledge of the special laws governing each system in isolation.

We need only add that the very occurrence of any particular intersection is unpredictable from those special laws. It follows that the sum of these interactions is, like Darwin's irregularly branching tree of nature, a collection of occasions, each a lawful event, but their totality unpredictable from the knowledge of their parts. This is the way to conceive of the operation of chance in the panorama of unique events we know as wild nature.

Any time we want to search for some lawful relationships, we can submerge the differences among things unique, find some similarities and class like with like. Then the laws of such aggregates can be found. But if we want to conceive of living nature as a whole, we must also remember that it is made up of partially independent entities, each with a life of its own, interacting from time to time in irregular and unpredictable ways.

What can be said of the relation among organisms can also be said of the relation of organs within an organism. We would not need the concept of a distinct *organ* if the organism were composed of perfectly interdependent parts, like the gears of a clock. Each organ follows its own laws, and while these must of course contribute to the harmonious result we call life, the laws of one organ are not the laws of another.

To treat all organs and all organisms as obeying the same laws is a constrictive denial of the chancy interaction of independent systems. At the same stroke, it is the denial of freedom. This was one of William Blake's meanings in his early revolt against the heavy determinism of eighteenth-century scientific thought when he wrote, "One Law for the Lion and Ox is Oppression."[6]

But freedom does not arise from mere individuality. If the lion and ox must each obey its own completely deterministic law, neither has freedom. Freedom, or the possibility of choice, arises from the existence in each of us and in the world around us of multiple

---

6 William Blake, *The Marriage of Heaven and Hell.*

potentialities. Each of us is a storehouse of possibilities. The interactions among individuals are marked by the fact that each person, no
matter how lawful his internal functioning may be, is an independent
system. This gives rise to the unpredictable character of his encounters
with others.

Something similar can be said of the internal creative life of each
person. We have already seen how Darwin's work was divided into a
number of separate enterprises, each with a life of its own. This type
of organization has several constructive functions. It permits the
thinker to change his ideas in one domain without scrapping everything he believes. In this way he can go on working purposefully on a
broad range of subjects without the disruptive effects that would ensue
if every new idea and even every doubt immediately required a
reorganization of the whole system of thought.

At the same time, the organization of thought in partially independent systems developing unevenly and each following somewhat
different laws provides the setting for the chancy interactions that give
each creative process its unique flavor. For example, as we have seen,
in the summer of 1838 Darwin was studying biological variation, and
he was searching for a mechanism of selection. Neither process alone
would generate a workable theory of evolution. As it happened, on
September 23 he wrote in his notebook: "Saw in Loddiges garden 1279
varieties of rosses!!! proof of capability of variation." (*D* 118) On
September 28 he recorded his reading of Malthus and his insight about
superfecundity and natural selection: ". . . until the one sentence of
Malthus no one clearly perceived the great check among men." (*D*
135) Other sequences might have produced the same happy coupling
of ideas; by "chance" this is the one that occurred.

There is a danger in this formulation. It seems to reintroduce the
whole notion of chance recombination and sudden insight as the main
feature of creative work. This is especially true because the particular
example I have given uses only two elements, variation and selection,
and therefore smacks of Koestler's combinatorial theory of "bi-sociation," in which it is always just *two* ideas that come together in a new
juxtaposition.[7] But some thinkers can keep more than two things in
mind. In discussing the structure of Darwin's argument I have shown
how many threads had to be woven together to make a coherent
theory. Darwin's interest in variation and selection were not isolated
events but growth products evolving from a changing argument governed by his ruling passion, the deliberate search for a theory of
evolution.

---

[7] Koestler, *op. cit.* Actually, selection as Darwin used it was a complex idea derived
from superfecundity and conservation of population number, so the "twoness" of
this bi-sociation is debatable.

The partially independent systems whose interactions produce the unique creative event are by no means limited to the internal thought processes of one person. He is engaged with others, and he is in touch with the world around him. Darwin went to the zoo to see what he could see, and he noticed something he could incorporate in his thinking about variation: "George the lion is extraordinarily cowardly.— the other one nothing will frighten—hence variation in character in different animals of same species." (N 98) Evidently, if he were not thinking about variation he might have noticed something else. But it is also true that he would not have been thinking about variation in this way if the world were not full of such individual differences, or if he had not wandered enough to see many of them with his own eyes.

The evolution of enduring purposes partially de-couples the individual from his environment. But he is not entirely free, only free to choose among possible things: attainable goals and feasible paths to reach them. This was the meaning of the old idea that "freedom is the recognition of necessity." In a chancy world it needs some revision. If you have effectively organized your experience of the world and the record of your own actions in it, you can take better cognizance of the choices open to you. You are better able to choose one of the paths that increase the likelihood of reaching your goal. You can avoid wasting time looking for regularities that do not exist. The more you are aware of the actual probabilistic structure of your environment, the more able you are to search for a really favorable opportunity, rather than plunging through the first open door. For the creative person, *carpe diem* has a special meaning: since he is trying to do something that has never been done before, he must look for the rare opportunity and then seize it. To recognize what is rare, one must have the kind of knowledge of the world that is gained only by moving about in it.

But since we are talking about the freedom to do something, simply knowing the world is never enough. One must construct an image of the world and a plan of action. As we study Darwin's thinking, we see him revising both his theories and his plans. His notebooks are mainly devoted to recording his ideas and useful information, but frequently enough he writes down clear-cut statements of intent: "If I be asked by what power the creator has added thought to so many animals of different types, I will confess my profound ignorance.—but seeing such passions acquired & hereditary & such definite thoughts, I will never allow that because there is a chasm between man . . . and animals that man has different origin." (C 222–223)

On the winding path from intention to achievement all sorts of propitious occasions arise: those for valuable observations, timely recollections, fortunate personal contacts, disturbing confrontations, and seminal encounters with ideas. In a way, the individual manufactures them through his own activities, and they emerge from a very dense network of personal experience. Only hindsight tells us that some of these experiences are more important than others. Some are publicly observable and recordable, but for the most part they are extremely fleeting and private.

Darwin's notebooks are an intermediate case. Although they are written partly in a private, telegraphic style, they can be read by others and are in that sense a public record. Some passages are clearly intended for inclusion in published works.

There is certainly a private level of experience of which only traces appear in Darwin's notebooks: notions that seem too absurd to be written down, transient thoughts still too fleeting or awkward for written expression, taboo ideas that can be expressed only when muted or transformed. And there is another sort of thinking that leaves very little trace, although it is not rejected or suppressed: the personal imagery one uses to carry a thought along, the personal knowledge one gains of a situation only by actually being in it—seeing, hearing, feeling, tasting, smelling it. Doing, enjoying, remembering, imagining it. This is the fine-structure of experience, well nigh invisible except to the person himself.

For some purposes it does not matter that there is a level of experience that is largely idiosyncratic, private, and non-communicable. Since there are always many possible paths between any two points, it does not matter exactly how one gets from place to place. The same visible structure or ecologically significant act can emerge via many different routes. The fine-structure of experience is therefore not closely disciplined by the requirements of interaction with the environment.

This partial de-coupling of the fine-structure of experience from the environment does not mean that the fine-structure is unimportant. The particular ordering of a group of bricks in a brick wall does not matter, but the bricklayer may not leave one out. The particular path to a goal may not matter, but the path must be continuous. The fine-structure is the sensible continuity of experience.

To an outsider, an act that could be readily replaced by another act may seem superfluous. Darwin invented or reshaped much of the material he used. Logically, some of this work could have been avoided, since there was such a wealth of pertinent data available. But to argue that any real man could have done without the concrete work of marshaling the evidence is to argue that such personal knowledge is not necessary. The evidence runs the other way.

Admittedly, we do not have a theory of thinking that can explain exactly why the acquisition of knowledge must be so private and personal, even when the desired end product is the public knowledge of science. For the moment, all we can say is that this highly individualized and private level of experience seems to be ubiquitous. Knowing what we do about living systems in general, the best guess is that a process which appears so regularly and universally must have some function other than to torment behaviorists.

I once watched a very small boy deepening his "personal knowledge" of the system of numbers. He already knew something about counting, in the limited sense that he could rattle off the numbers from one to ten, and he had a shaky grasp of the operation "plus one"—e.g., if you add one item to a collection of six items, you will have seven. Now he was investigating the operation "minus one." His method was very direct. He dumped all the cookies from a jar onto a table, counted them, then announced to himself, "Ten. I wonder how many there will be if I take one away." He pushed one aside, put the remainder back in the jar, dumped them out again, then announced to himself, "Nine. Now I'll see how many are left if I take one away." And so on. Only when he got down to about four cookies was he willing to hazard a guess—or, better, make a hypothesis, $4 - 3 = 2$.

This story is a good illustration of the enormous density of personal experience that is packed into the simplest ideas. The growth of knowledge is an orderly process. Experience is not a chaotic series of encounters with the environment, but a sensible structuring and restructuring of ideas. The personal knowledge packed into an abstract idea is put there by the growing person himself, through his own activities, assimilating what he can into existing structures and thereby strengthening them, occasionally noticing anomalies that require the revision of these structures to accommodate experiences that would otherwise not find a stable place.

What I have said up to now means only that there is a possible role for the individual in history—or, more properly, many possible roles. Which one will he choose to play?

In good part the answer depends on his own progress and invention as he proceeds.

Darwin felt the need for a theory of genetics, to account for variation and heredity. One can hardly say that this was a thoroughly unrealistic goal or an impossible task. Mendel solved the main problems in the same epoch, with technical resources not very different from Darwin's. At least, Darwin would have been delighted to achieve what Mendel had done by 1863. From a purely experimental point of view, Darwin did come very close to some of Mendel's results. It was at the conceptual level that he missed something.

Failing, at some turning point he realized that he did not absolutely have to solve certain problems in order to carry out his life's task. He turned aside from the problems of genetics long enough to write the *Origin*. Why Darwin was not able to do what Mendel did, I cannot say. In one sense, he did not try hard enough. For him, the problems of variation and heredity were always subordinate to the problem of evolution. If he had not seen a way of treating variation and heredity as unexplained premises, he might never have thought out the theory of evolution through natural selection. But he could never have so treated them if he did not view his overarching task as being the construction of an evolutionary theory.

Mendel, too, saw the relation between genetics and evolution. When he began his experimental work, he saw himself as repairing a major gap in Lamarck's theory of evolution; a few years later, when the *Origin* appeared, Mendel accepted Darwin's views and continued his work on genetics.[8] No theory of evolution is complete without an explanation of heredity and variation, but such explanations do not constitute a theory of evolution. Both Darwin and Mendel saw that the two sorts of issues, genetics and evolution, were in some measure separable. They made different decisions about the use of their personal resources. This is crucial in understanding the role of the creative individual in the history of thought. Among the inviting and forbidding array of unknowns at the frontiers of his own knowledge, he must choose his life's work.

When we speak of the integrity of the individual, we mean precisely this. He does not reorganize his ideas upon every encounter with the world. Rather, he does his best to incorporate the flow of experience into the existing structure of his own knowledge in accordance with his own purposes.

Viewed in this way, an often neglected feature of scientific theories comes to light. A theory is not only a way of organizing existing knowledge, and of generating specific predictions that can be tested empirically. These aspects of theory have often been discussed. But a theory is also a way of handling the personal flow of information. In the work of science, there is not always a tight coupling between theoretical and empirical work. Various systems for the accumulation of data have lives of their own, somewhat separate from any particular theoretical enterprise.

Information organized under one aegis may be detachable from it and usable in another context. In the case of a creative scientist like Darwin, who was constructing a wide new synthesis, one of the important tests of the value of his theory would be its ability to affect the flow of information. Darwin, throughout his life, put his ideas to this

---

8 See Hugo Iltis, *Life of Mendel* (London: Allen and Unwin, 1932); and W. Bateson, *Mendel's Principles of Heredity* (Cambridge: University Press, 1909).

kind of test: he immersed himself in a field of empirical enquiry, not simply to test a particular prediction or solve a specific problem, but to see how well his theory would deal with *whatever* he might find: the complexities of fossil and living barnacles, leaf-cutting bees, orchids, sea-soaked seeds, babies' emotional expressions, variations in pigeons.

During the years 1837–39 Darwin behaved in the same way. One source of the very personal knowledge he was then reworking is well known—the experiences of the *Beagle* voyage. These were probably the most theoretically intense years of Darwin's life. Nevertheless, we see him hungrily searching out new experiences even during those years of thought. The *Origin* is not only a great re-synthesis of existing knowledge, it is permeated with Darwin's own discoveries.

The flow of experience, therefore, like life itself, must be continuous. The ordinary struggle to incorporate experience into existing schemas of thought, again like the struggle for life, is also continuous. But innovation must be either a slower process or a more sporadic one. The theory of creativity as a few creative acts or sudden insights is one way of dealing with the problem of integrity: the person and his way of thought remain the same most of the time, until he has a great transforming insight. The theory of creativity as a growth process is a different way of preserving the integrity of the individual. From moment to moment, changes are small. Even when great changes occur, certain invariant schemas remain intact, so that the person and his way of thought are recognizably the same before and after the transformation.

The view of knowledge as a growing structure is not new. In the history of science it has been well expressed by Thomas Kuhn and in the psychology of cognitive development by Jean Piaget. In scientific work each such structure or *paradigm* embraces an accepted theoretical position, an array of agreed-upon facts, and a set of accepted methods for working within the framework of the paradigm. By definition, the paradigm is a social phenomenon, a way of thought shared by a group of scientific workers. As the work proceeds, difficulties typically accumulate—observations that do not fit expectations, previously unnoticed theoretical weaknesses that come to light. Eventually, the increasing weight of these difficulties produces a sense of crisis, and a phase of revolutionary scientific activity erupts, leading to the emergence of a new structure of ideas.

This is an attractive view. It deals with the organized character of thought, and it makes room for growth and change without treating complex ideas either as direct and inevitable copies of structures existing in nature, or as chance concatenations. In spite of these attractions, this view lacks certain human dimensions. The notion of paradigm does not deal with the psychology of creative individual thought, but with the history of thought in scientific groups—in particular, groups sharing a given paradigm.

When we turn to the individual, new points emerge. His work is not carried on within the framework of a single paradigm. It is organized in a number of enterprises, forming an ensemble that expresses his unique purposes. Some of these enterprises may be shared or at least readily shareable with some of his contemporaries, others not. But the uniqueness of the single enterprise is not, in any case, the important point. The individual is always the unique host of a living network of enterprises. Consequently, any single enterprise has a different meaning for him than it has for others with whom he may share it. Darwin the pigeon fancier was not like the other pigeon fanciers with whom he consorted. For him, the selective breeding of pigeons was part of a grand plan to come as close as possible to an experimental attack on the evolutionary process. Darwin the student of variation and heredity was not like Mendel, also a student of these problems of genetics. For Darwin, these could be subordinated to the problems of evolutionary theory—with the result that he did not have to solve and did not solve the problems of genetics. For Mendel, a different group of problems were uppermost; he could not treat heredity as an unexplained premise, and so he worked under a different set of imperatives. Darwin the evolutionist was not like Wallace, his co-discoverer of the theory of natural selection. Darwin felt the need of a theory that would account for the evolution of man's mind, while Wallace sought to avoid such a materialist explanation of mind.

Each person makes a different set of decisions about the use of his personal resources, thereby both setting the scene for the fortunate accidents of thought that occur and choosing among them when they do. Thus, Darwin could notice behavioral variations in pigeons and use them in a theory of the evolution of mind because he was at once the pigeon fancier, the evolutionist, and the materialist.

The fact that he was all these things at once meant that a unique and productive intersection of many enterprises could occur in his thinking. At the same time, the existence of this ensemble was not an accident but the deliberately cultivated fruit of Darwin's work. He organized his life in order to construct a new point of view, one that would deal with adaptation in a changing-world without any recourse to supernatural forces.

In his explorations of the world, the individual finds out what needs doing. In his attempts to do some of it, he finds out what he can do and what he cannot. He also comes to see what he need not do. From the intersection of these possibilities there emerges a new imperative, his sense of what he must do. How "It needs" and "I can" give birth to "I must" remains enigmatic.

Appendix
The Many Voyages of the *Beagle*

How many voyages of the *Beagle* were there? There were two on the high seas that concern us. But every real voyage gives rise to many voyages of the mind. Captain FitzRoy's account is of interest to us because it provides a basis for comparison with Darwin's *Journal of Researches*. And in Darwin's mind, the *Beagle* plied the seas, circumnavigating the globe, incessantly, each time leading him to new discoveries.

Darwin did not publish his theory of evolution until 1858, twenty years after he had puzzled it out. How much of this revolutionary way of thought crept into his writing in the intervening years? That is the question to which this essay is addressed. Darwin wrote a lot. Keeping a perfect secret is hard to do. It takes decision and unremitting self-discipline.

How well did Darwin keep his secret? Is it fair to speak of a "secret"? It might be better to ask How did Darwin manage the exchange of ideas and information between himself and others? What questions did he ask? What answers did he give? The subject has two parts, the answers and the questions. Darwin was certainly slow and restrained in revealing his answer to the "question of questions"—the origin of species. But he was quite open in expressing the plethora of puzzles and the wider sense of wonder that gave rise to his whole approach to the question. The *Journal* does not give the answer Darwin had worked out, but it does frame the questions in a manner that prepared the way for his conclusions.

This duality is reflected by an odd omission in Darwin's quotation of a few lines from Shelley in the second edition of his *Journal*. Darwin was recalling his reaction to a geological formation in Patagonia, one suggesting the almost unimaginable expanse of geological time. He wrote,

> There is not a tree, and, excepting the guanaco, which stood on the hill-top a watchful sentinel over its herd, scarcely an animal or

a bird. All was stillness and desolation. Yet in passing over these scenes, without one bright object near, an ill-defined but strong sense of pleasure is vividly excited. One asked how many ages the plain had thus lasted, and how many more it was doomed thus to continue.

> None can reply—all seems eternal now.
> The wilderness has a mysterious tongue
> Which teaches awful doubt.
> (*Journal*, 1845, p. 168)

The three lines of poetry are from Shelley's "Mont Blanc." The odd thing is that Darwin stopped his quotation in the middle of the line. Shelley goes on to present an alternative response to the awesome mysteries of nature:

> None can reply—all seems eternal now.
> The wilderness has a mysterious tongue
> Which teaches awful doubt, or faith so mild,
> So solemn, so serene, that man may be,
> But for such faith, with nature reconciled.

In my view, even during the voyage and certainly by 1845, when he made this poetic insertion, Darwin went easily beyond "awful doubt." He spent most of his life "with nature reconciled" under the green and pleasant banner of a solemn, serene faith in the power of human reason and steady scientific effort to penetrate the mysteries and to make sense of the world.

Darwin's account of the voyage of the *Beagle* has been described as an "important travel book."[1] It first appeared as one of three volumes published as the *Narrative of the Surveying Voyages of His Majesty's Ships Adventure and Beagle, between the Years 1826 and 1836, Describing Their Examination of the Southern Shores of South America, and the Beagle's Circumnavigation of the Globe*. Volume 1, mainly written by Robert FitzRoy, is an account of an earlier expedition by the *Adventure* and the *Beagle*, 1826–30. The captain of the *Adventure* was Commander Phillip Parker King, senior officer of the expedition. At the outset, the *Beagle* was commanded by Captain Pringle Stokes. After twenty-one months at sea, Captain Stokes, suffering a profound depression, shot and killed himself.

Robert FitzRoy was then appointed commander of the *Beagle*, a post he held for the remainder of this voyage and during the later

---

[1] R. B. Freeman, *The Works of Charles Darwin, an Annotated Bibliographical Handlist.* (London: Dawsons of Pall Mall, 1965), p. 13.

one, the *Beagle's* circumnavigation of the globe, 1831–36. FitzRoy wrote lengthy accounts of both voyages, and these, with Darwin's, comprise the three-volume set. Darwin's volume was also printed separately under the title, *Journal of Researches into the Geology and Natural History of the Various Countries Visited by H.M.S. Beagle, under the Command of Captain FitzRoy, R. N. from 1832 to 1836*. But in my copy of the very first printing of the three volumes, Darwin's had a half-title on a separate page: "Volume III, Journal and Remarks, 1832–1836, by Charles Darwin, Esq., M.A., Sec. Geol. Soc." It is these little noticed "remarks" that will be our main concern in the following pages. By examining them, I hope to show that Darwin's *Journal* was far more than a travel book.

Everyone knows that interspersed with adventure stories, evocations of tropical scenery, and accounts of primitive customs, there are many marvellous passages describing the geology and the fauna and flora of the places visited. What is not so well known is that the "remarks" in the *Journal* give a very rich picture of Darwin's thinking, his theoretical point of view at the time he was writing. The steps in which the *Journal* was written are many and somewhat complex. In this essay, I deal only with what Darwin published in 1839 and in 1845. The 1839 version was mainly written in 1837, just as Darwin was becoming a convinced evolutionist. Its publication was delayed in order to permit its appearance at the same time as the volumes being prepared by FitzRoy, who was not so speedy a writer as Darwin.

Between 1837–38 Darwin worked out the theory of evolution through natural selection. On September 28, 1838, when he wrote down his first clear statement of the principle of evolution through natural selection, the first edition of the journal of the voyage had already been set in type. In other words, the first published version of the *Journal* was written while Darwin was trying out various preliminary formulations of possible theories of evolution. On October 27 he wrote the preface and certain addenda to the *Journal,* but he was not ready to use this occasion to reveal the new direction of his thinking.

Over the following years, he thought much about evolution. In 1839 and in 1842 he wrote brief preliminary sketches of the theory. On July 5, 1844, he finished a 230-page "Sketch of Species Theory," as he called it, setting forth his views much as they eventually appeared in the *Origin of Species*. Nine months later, on April 25, 1845, he began work on the second edition of the *Journal*, keeping at it steadily for exactly four months.

In many ways, the 1845 edition reflects the changes in Darwin's thinking. But it takes careful reading to see this, as Darwin's theoretical remarks are fragmented and interspersed with the stories of travel and adventure.[2] An advertisement for the 1845 edition quoted a review: "The author is a first-rate landscape painter." Darwin's "painting" is indeed fine, but here our task is to cut it away so that we can see something of his theory as he expressed it in the two versions of the *Journal*.[3]

Possibly the most important result of the very first expedition was FitzRoy's resolve to carry a trained naturalist on any subsequent voyage. Thinking of the unknown mineral resources of Tierra del Fuego, he wrote, "I could not avoid often thinking of the talent and experience required for such scientific researches, of which we were wholly destitute; and inwardly resolving, that if ever I left England again on a similar expedition, I would endeavour to carry out a person qualified to examine the land." (*Narrative*, Vol. 1, p. 385) Darwin became the "person qualified."[4]

The method I have used to compare the two editions of the *Journal* was laborious but simple. I sat with both editions in front of me, searching for any changes in the text, turning the pages of both books as I went. The changes are many and sometimes subtle. What I will do now is take the reader with me through these books. I have organized the material primarily on thematic lines. Although this does destroy the temporal and geographical sequence of the voyage, it makes it easier to bring out the theoretical significance of

[2] Nora Barlow, Darwin's granddaughter, noticed a number of the changes between the two editions of the *Journal* and mentioned them in the notes of her edition of the *Beagle Diary*. But in her introductory remarks she says only, "Much was added, and as the whole had to be somewhat shorter, much had to be altogether cut out or condensed. This abridgment she found particularly troublesome." (*Beagle Diary*, p. xxix) Gertrude Hemmelfarb and Gavin de Beer each noted some of the significant passages, but relied on the first edition. See Himmelfarb, *Darwin and the Darwinian Revolution* (New York: Doubleday, 1959) and de Beer, *Charles Darwin* (New York: Doubleday, 1964). Camille Limoges gives in three lines a succinct but dismissive summary of some of the changes: "In 1845, for the second edition, he augments the account of details that he believes only explicable from an evolutionary perspective, but without expressing the latter" (*La Sélection Naturelle: étude sur la première constitution d'un concept, 1837–1859* [Paris: Presses Universitaires de France, 1970], p. 31, my translation). In spite of their great intrinsic interest, the documents of the voyage have been curiously little studied.

[3] For a description of the growth of Darwin's geological ideas during the voyage, see Howard E. Gruber and Valmai Gruber, "The Eye of Reason: Darwin's Development during the *Beagle* Voyage," *Isis* 53, 1962, 186–200.

[4] Another qualified man, Robert MacCormick, appears in FitzRoy's list of seventy-four persons on board the *Beagle* when Darwin sailed with him. As the ship's surgeon, MacCormick would have been acting in an established tradition of the Royal Navy had he doubled as naturalist. But he left the ship in 1832, probably because he did not get along with FitzRoy and the other officers. In any case, it is clear from FitzRoy's account that he regarded Darwin as the ship's naturalist, describing him as "Mr. Charles Darwin, grandson of Dr. Darwin the poet . . . a young man of promising ability, extremely fond of geology, and indeed all branches of natural history." (*Narrative*, Vol. 2, pp. 18–19) See also Jacob W. Gruber, "Who was the *Beagle's* naturalist?" *The British Journal for the History of Science*, Vol. 4, 1968–69, 266–282.

the work and the changes in Darwin's published position from one version to the other.

Not only those ideas which changed between the two editions are of interest to us. There are certain themes that reflect constants of Darwin's thought that are essential to his work as an evolutionist. In every case, I indicate which of the two versions of the *Journal* I am citing and whether or not there has been (in my opinion) a significant change.

This way of tracking Darwin's expression of his ideas in 1837 and 1845 is not intended to show their embryonic development during the *Beagle* voyage: that would require a special and exhaustive study of his scientific notebooks during the voyage, a task that no one has yet carried through.

In most cases it will be self-evident that the theme under discussion has a bearing on Darwin's evolutionary ideas. But the same set of themes can be woven in different patterns, composing different theories. In *Darwin on Man,* I have tried to show how one man did this at several points in a period of intense theoretical work. The meaning of any theme changes somewhat, depending on the theoretical design into which it is threaded. In understanding the pattern as a whole, then, part (but only part) of our task is to identify these themes.[5]

The *Journal* is, obviously, not an explicitly theoretical work. Still, Darwin introduced many important themes and made them visible enough to any reader who happened to be on a similar track. Although neither version can be read as a full and coherent account of the theory he held while writing or rewriting the *Journal,* each is an expression of a belief system, and the differences between them reflect changes in the theoretical situation over a period of eight or nine years.

Carrying out a reorganization like this entails a series of interpretive acts, which depend on the point of view of the investigator. For instance, in 1834, observing the mules used in the mines of Chile, Darwin wrote, "The mule always strikes me as a most surprising animal: that a Hybrid should possess far more reason, memory, obstinacy, powers of digestion & muscular endurance, than either of its parents.—One fancies art has here outmastered Nature." (*Beagle Diary*, p.247) Almost the same passage appears in both editions of the *Journal*. If there were other such instances, inclusion of hybridization as a theme would be appropriate, especially since Darwin wrote about it in the *Origin* and in the

---

[5] For an interesting discussion of "thematic analysis," see Gerald Holton, *Thematic Origins of Scientific Thought: Kepler to Einstein* (Cambridge: Harvard University Press, 1973).

drafts leading up to that work. Darwin's early interest in hybridization is interesting, as it may ultimately have led him to study the works of breeders and thence to see the analogy between artificial and natural selection. But hybridization is hardly a theme of the *Journal*. Moreover, the passage about the mule was not included under the theme of evolution per se precisely because it appears in the *Diary* at a time when we have good reason to think that Darwin was not yet thinking of himself as an evolutionist. At most, we might say that this was the sort of material that Darwin *later* tried to assimilate to an evolutionary schema.

As will become evident, some of Darwin's important theoretical expressions were made as brief passing remarks. Others became extended essays, the longest of which was the seventeen-page discussion of the formation of coral reefs. On two subjects, the causes of extinction and varying species of the Galapagos archipelago, I have quoted the *Journal* quite extensively, in order to convey the character of the essays.

The theoretical ideas in these journals fall into three types: (a) constants, ideas that occur in both versions of the *Journal*; (b) deletions and corrections, ideas that Darwin came to view as incorrect or doubtful, and that he removed or reduced in emphasis from 1839 to 1845; and (c) insertions, ideas that Darwin went to the trouble of adding in the later version. To these must be added a fourth type, (d) omissions, beliefs that Darwin held but excluded from the *Journal*. It only makes sense to speak of theoretical omissions if the *Journal* is thoroughly impregnated with Darwin's theory. To show how that condition is fulfilled, we turn now to an examination of twelve themes.

1. Relation between food supply and population. This relationship figured prominently in Malthus's *Essay on the Principles of Population*, on which Darwin drew. Darwin explores this theme in a number of ways. Two points emerge: he does not think the relationship is very simple, and he was interested in it very early.

In January 1832 he explored the country around Porto Praya in St. Jago, the main island of the Cape Verde archipelago. "A single green leaf can scarcely be discovered over wide tracts of the lava plains; yet flocks of goats, together with a few cows, contrive to exist."[6] Rainfall is sporadic; after heavy torrential rains "a light vegetation springs out of every crevice." It withers, and hay forms naturally, upon which the animals live. (1839, p. 2)[7]

During the spring of 1832 he stayed around Rio de Janeiro for

---

[6] This observation occurs in the *Beagle Diary*, entry for January 23, 1832, in about the same form.

[7] Citations from both editions of the *Journal* are identified by year and page number.

some months. Ordinarily, he remarks, in different parts of the world similar relationships exist between species, but this must occur naturally. He cites a recurrent relationship between certain fungi and certain beetles—a relationship found in England as well as in Brazil. "We here see in two distant countries a similar relation between plants and insects of the same families, though the species of both are different." Then he adds the important qualification: "When man is the agent in introducing into a country a new species, this relation is often broken; as one instance of this I may mention that the leaves of the cabbages and lettuces, which in England afford food to such a multitude of slugs and caterpillars, in the gardens near Rio are untouched." (1839, p. 37) The presence of an appropriate food supply does not in itself guarantee the presence of another organism that will feed upon it.

In 1832 and 1833 Darwin spent some time in Argentina in the vicinity of Bahia Blanca, south of Buenos Aires. He made some important discoveries of the fossils of very large mammals (see below). The general aridity of the country and sparseness of vegetation led him to consider the relation between the size of animals of a given fauna and the density of vegetation necessary for their support. He inserted a six-page essay on this subject in the *Journal*, synthesizing his own findings with those of others, and observations of existing ecosystems with his growing knowledge of those long past.

> That large animals require a luxuriant vegetation, has been a general assumption, which has passed from one work to another. I do not hesitate, however, to say that it is completely false; and that it has vitiated the reasoning of geologists, on some points of great interest in the ancient history of the world. The prejudice has probably been derived from India, and the Indian islands, where troops of elephants, noble forests, and impenetrable jungles, are associated together in every account. If, on the other hand, we refer to any works of travels through the southern parts of Africa, we shall find allusions in almost every page either to the desert character of the country, or to the numbers of large animals inhabiting it. When the *Beagle* was at Cape Town, I rode a few leagues into the country, which at least was sufficient to render that which I had read more fully intelligible. (1839, pp. 98–99)

He expands on this theme in three pages summarizing information about Africa given to him by Dr. Andrew Smith, whom he met while in Cape Town in 1836, toward the end of the voyage. Smith had recently come back from an important expedition. The two naturalists "took some long geological rambles" together, which gave them the opportunity for wide-ranging talks. (*Beagle Diary*, p. 409) Darwin concludes this passage about Africa with an observation of his own about camels and then goes on to make a new point about the same subject, incorporating observations of another fellow explorer.

It should have been remembered that the camel, an animal of no mean bulk, has always been considered as the emblem of the desert.

The belief that where large quadrupeds exist, the vegetation must necessarily be luxuriant, is the more remarkable, because the converse is far from true. Mr. Burchell observed to me that when entering Brazil, nothing struck him more forcibly than the splendour of the South American vegetation, contrasted with that of South Africa, together with the absence of all large quadrupeds. . . . After the above facts, we are compelled to conclude . . . that among the mammalia there exists no close relation between the *bulk* of the species, and the *quantity* of the vegetation, in the countries they inhabit. . . .

. . . We must grant, as far as *quantity alone* of vegetation is concerned, that the great quadrupeds of the later tertiary epochs might, in most parts of Northern Europe and Asia, have lived on the spots where their remains are now found. I do not here speak of the *kind* of vegetation necessary for their support; because, as there is evidence of physical changes, and as the animals have become extinct, so may we suppose that the species of plants have likewise been changed. (1839, pp. 101–103)

The theme reappears throughout the *Journal*. Darwin wonders about the food supply of whales and seals, and petrels and albatross found in the southern Atlantic. Thinking about the food chain, he wrote:

In deep water, far from the land, the number of living creatures is extremely small. . . . Between latitudes 56° and 57° south of Cape Horn the net was put astern several times; it never, however, brought up any thing besides a few of two extremely minute species of Entomostraca. Yet whales and seals, petrels and albatross, are exceedingly abundant throughout this part of the ocean. It has always been a source of mystery to me, on what the latter, which live far from the shore, can subsist. I presume the albatross, like the condor, is able to fast long; and that one good feast on the carcass of a putrid whale lasts for a long siege of hunger. It does not lessen the difficulty to say, they feed on fish; for on what can the fish feed? It often occurred to me, when observing how the waters of the central and intertropical parts of the Atlantic, swarmed with Pteropoda. Crustacea, and Radiata, and with their devourers the flying-fish, and again with *their* devourers the bonitos and albicores, that the lowest of these pelagic animals perhaps possess the power of decomposing carbonic acid gas, like the members of the vegetable kingdom. (1839, p. 190)

In 1845 he amended his speculation to take new discoveries into account. But he saw that filling in one link in the chain did not completely solve the mystery: "I presume that the numerous lower pelagic animals feed on the Infusoria, which are now known, from the researches of Ehrenberg, to abound in the open ocean; but on what, in the clear blue water, do these Infusoria subsist?" (1845, p.167)

The question comes up in a rather more personal form in Patagonia in 1834: "A good-sized fly (Tabanus) was extremely numerous, and tormented us by its painful bite. The common horsefly, which is so troublesome in the shady lanes of England, belongs to this genus. We here have the puzzle, that so frequently occurs in the case of musquitoes on the blood of what animals do these insects commonly feed? The guanaco is nearly the only warmblooded quadruped, and they are present in numbers quite inconsiderable, compared to the multitude of flies." (1839, p. 200)

2. Struggle. The idea of struggle for existence, of course, embraces the previous theme of relation between food supply and population. When Darwin later wrote of the struggle for existence, he referred, as he put it, in "a large and metaphorical sense" to all the forces favoring the existence and reproduction of a given organism, as against all those opposed.[8] Looking at his life work as a whole, we can see that the idea of struggle had an even more general and pervasive character. People struggle against each other. The land struggles with the sea. Life and Death contend.

In this section, I consider those instances in the *Journal* where the idea of struggle is quite explicit. In a sense, the capture of one animal by another belongs in the preceding section. But we would miss something about Darwin's feelings toward nature if we simply grouped together his descriptions of goats foraging for hay and of spiders brilliantly ensnaring their struggling victims. Darwin was a fine entomologist, and there are a number of such descriptions in which he, with equal brilliance, captures such insect struggles in print.

Halfway between the Cape Verde Islands and the northeastern coast of Brazil there is a desolate uninhabited island, St. Paul's Rocks. The *Beagle* hove to and spent a day in the vicinity. While Darwin spent some time ashore geologizing, boats were lowered and some of the seamen fished. In his diary he merely wrote, "They caught a great number of fine large fish and would have succeeded much better had not the sharks broken so many of their hooks and lines." (*Beagle Diary*, p. 36, February 16, 1832) In the

---

[8] For a discussion of the different meanings of "struggle," see Edward Manier, *The Young Darwin and His Cultural Circle*, (Dordrecht and Boston: D. Reidel, 1978).

Journal this became "The sharks and the seamen in the boats maintained a constant struggle which should secure the greater share of the prey. . . ." (1839, p. 10)

Two weeks later the *Beagle* put in to Bahia in Brazil. Darwin describes a kind of blowfish, a Diodon antennatus, its habits and its ingenious defense mechanisms. "It could give a severe bite, and could eject water from its mouth to some distance. . . . By the inflation of its body, the papillae, with which the skin is covered, become erect and pointed." (1839, p. 14) In the 1845 edition of the *Journal,* he adds the following: "I have heard from Dr. Allan of Forres, that he has frequently found a Diodon, floating alive and distended, in the stomach of the shark; and that on several occasions he has known it eat its way, not only through the coats of the stomach, but through the sides of the monster, which has thus been killed. Who would ever have imagined that a little soft fish could have destroyed the great and savage shark?" (1845, p. 35)

The *Journal* is studded with examples of the idea that every organism has its natural enemies that check its increase. Riding overland from Bahia Blanca to Buenos Aires, he recollects, "The plains abound with three kinds of partridge, two of which are as large as hen pheasants. Their destroyer, a small and pretty fox, was also singularly numerous." (1839, p. 131) He also saw much of the effects of human warfare, especially wars of extermination waged by Europeans against Indians in South America and aborigines in Australia and New Zealand.

3. Extinction: Monads or Malthus? Darwin's preoccupation with geology led him to make many important discoveries of fossils, and thus to think about the process of extinction. In the 1839 edition of the *Journal,* there is a three-page essay on the causes of extinction. The way it is cast reflects Darwin's 1837 monadic theory of evolution, which uses the idea of a species life span to account for the "death" of species. In the 1845 version, this passage is somewhat longer, and a profound change has been introduced. Gone is the idea of the species life span. In its stead is a passage astonishingly similar to the moment of Malthusian insight entered in the third transmutation notebook, on September 28, 1838. Using Malthusian theory as a point of departure, Darwin expands on the many and often unknown factors that control the numbers of any species. The two versions have in common the insistence on searching for natural causes that operate continuously, producing slow and gradual transformations in nature—the theme of uniformitarianism or "anticatastrophism." One version expresses his thinking as it stood in July of 1837, the other, the epoch-making intellectual transformation that his ideas underwent in the next fifteen months.

I reproduce here the whole passage of the later version. This is not the first time it has been reprinted. The observant botanist John Lindley reprinted it all in his *Gardener's Chronicle* on August 16, 1845, just after it appeared.[9]

It is impossible to reflect on the changed state of the American continent without the deepest astonishment. Formerly it must have swarmed with great monsters: now we find mere pigmies, compared with the antecedent, allied races. If Buffon had known of the gigantic-sloth and armadillo-like animals, and of the lost Pachydermata, he might have said with a greater semblance of truth that the creative force in America had lost its power, rather than that it had never possessed great vigour. The greater number, if not all, of these extinct quadrupeds lived at a late period, and were the contemporaries of most of the existing seashells. Since they lived, no very great change in the form of the land can have taken place. What, then, has exterminated so many species and whole genera? The mind at first is irresistibly hurried into the belief of some great catastrophe; but thus to destroy animals, both large and small, in Southern Patagonia, in Brazil, on the Cordillera of Peru, in North America up to Behring's Straits, we must shake the entire framework of the globe. An examination, moreover, of the geology of La Plata and Patagonia, leads to the belief that all the features of the land result from slow and gradual changes. It appears from the character of the fossils in Europe, Asia, Australia, and in North and South America, that those conditions which favour the life of the *larger* quadrupeds were lately co-extensive with the world: what those conditions were, no one has yet even conjectured. It could hardly have been a change of temperature, which at about the same time destroyed the inhabitants of tropical, temperate, and arctic latitudes on both sides of the globe. . . . Did man, after his first inroad into South America, destroy, as has been suggested, the unwieldy Megatherium and the other Edentata? We must at least look to some other cause for the destruction of the little tucutuco at Bahia Blanca, and of the many fossil mice and other small quadrupeds in Brazil. No one will imagine that a drought, even far severer than those which cause such losses in the provinces of La Plata, could destroy every individual of every species from Southern Patagonia to Behring's Straits. What shall we say of the extinction of the horse? Did those plains fail of pasture, which have since been overrun by thousands and hundreds of thousands of the descendants of the stock introduced by the Spaniards? Have the subsequently introduced species consumed the food of the great antecedent races? Can we believe that the Capybara has taken the food of the Toxodon, the Guanaco of the Macrauchenia, the existing small Edentata of their numerous gigantic prototypes? Cer-

---

[9] See *Darwin on Man,* p. 24 n.

tainly, no fact in the long history of the world is so startling as the wide and repeated exterminations of its inhabitants.

Nevertheless, if we consider the subject under another point of view, it will appear less perplexing. We do not steadily bear in mind, how profoundly ignorant we are of the conditions of existence of every animal; nor do we always remember, that some check is constantly preventing the too rapid increase of every organized being left in a state of nature. The supply of food, on an average, remains constant; yet the tendency is every animal to increase by propagation is geometrical; and its surprising effects have nowhere been more astonishingly shown, than in the case of the European animals run wild during the last few centuries in America. Every animal in a state of nature regularly breeds; yet in a species long established, any *great* increase in numbers is obviously impossible, and must be checked by some means. We are, nevertheless, seldom able with certainty to tell in any given species, at what period of life, or at what period of the year, or whether only at long intervals, the check falls; or, again, what is the precise nature of the check. Hence probably it is, that we feel so little surprise at one, of two species closely allied in habits, being rare and the other abundant in the same district; or, again, that one should be abundant in one district, and another, filling the same place in the economy of nature, should be abundant in an neighbouring district, differing very little in its conditions. . . .

In the cases where we can trace the extinction of a species through man, either wholly or in one limited district, we know that it becomes rarer and rarer, and is then lost: it would be difficult to point out any just distinction between a species destroyed by man or by the increase of its natural enemies. . . . If then, as appears probable, species first become rare and then extinct—if the too rapid increase of every species, even the most favoured, is steadily checked, as we must admit, though how and when it is hard to say—and if we see, without the smallest surprise, though unable to assign the precise reason, one species abundant and another closely-allied species rare in the same district—why should we feel such great astonishment at the rarity being carried a step further to extinction? An action going on, on every side of us, and yet barely appreciable, might surely be carried a little further, without exciting our observation. Who would feel any great surprise at hearing that the Megalonyx was formerly rare compared with the Megatherium, or that one of the fossil monkeys was few in number compared with one of the now living monkeys? and yet in this comparative rarity, we should have the plainest evidence of less favourable conditions for their existence. To admit that species generally become rare before they become extinct—to feel no surprise at the comparative rarity of one species with another, and yet to call in some extraordinary agent and to marvel greatly when a species ceases to exist, appears to me much the same as to admit that sickness in the individual is the prelude to death—to feel no surprise at sickness—but when the sick man dies, to wonder, and to believe that he died through violence. (1845, pp. 177–80)

As I have described in *Darwin on Man,* the monadic theory of evolution appeared only fleetingly in Darwin's first notebook on evolution. It is of the highest interest, therefore, to see that one of its cornerstones, the species life-span idea, made its way into the 1839 *Journal,* only to be removed from the 1845 version. In the 1839 *Journal,* the passage on extinction concludes with the metaphoric comparison of the extinction of a species with the *aging* of an individual. In the 1845 version, this metaphor is replaced by the comparison of extinction with *sickness* leading to death, i.e., inability to contend with antagonistic forces.

The 1839 version is strange to modern eyes.

These cases of extinction forcibly recall the idea (I do not wish to draw any close analogy) of certain fruit-trees, which, it has been asserted, though grafted on young stems, planted in varied situations, and fertilized by the richest manures, yet at one period, have all withered away and perished. A fixed and determined length of life has in such cases been given to thousands and thousands of buds (or individual germs), although produced in long succession. Among the greater number of animals, each individual appears nearly independent of its kind; yet all of one kind may be bound together by common laws, as well as a certain number of individual buds in the tree, or polypi in the Zoophyte.

I will add one other remark. We see that whole series of animals, which have been created with peculiar kinds of organization, are confined to certain areas; and we can hardly suppose these structures are only adaptations to peculiarities of climate or country; for otherwise, animals belonging to a distinct type, and introduced by man, would not succeed so admirably, even to the extermination of the aborigines. On such grounds it does not seem a necessary conclusion, that the extinction of species, more than their creation, should exclusively depend on the nature (altered by physical changes) of their country. All that at present can be said with certainty, is that, as with the individual, so with the species, the hour of life has run its course, and is spent. (1839, p. 212)

4. *The superfecundity of nature.* We have seen how Darwin argues that forces limiting population—and therefore sometimes contributing to the extinction of a species—are a necessary part of the "polity" of nature. This presupposes that nature is fecund, even "superfecund," and would in some sense produce too much, were it not for these limiting factors. But too much *what?* There are at least three major senses in which organic nature may be productive. First, the total *biomass* produced may vary. (This would be the

product of the number of individuals—regardless of species—times their average weight.) Second, the number of *individuals* in a given species, or overall, may vary. And third, the number of *species* may vary.

Darwin enjoyed the fecundity of nature and was aware of each of these meanings. In his first efforts to construct a theory of evolution, the number of species was treated as approximately constant and the existence of a species as the main unit of analysis. In his more mature theory, matters were more complex. On the one hand, selection operates on individuals. On the other hand, Darwin later went to much trouble to prove that divergence, that is, the formation of many and distinct species, was a necessary part of the evolutionary process. Thus nature is potentially prodigal both in the number of individuals and in the number of species, and a coherent order of nature entails limits on each.

These themes of fecundity are present in both editions of the *Journal*. In the 1845 version, changes are made that draw certain issues more sharply. He describes the amount and variety of life to be found in a salina, or salt lake, in Patagonia—protozoa, algae, worms, flamingos. "How surprising it is that any creatures should be able to exist in a fluid, saturated with brine, and that they should be crawling among crystals of sulphate of soda and lime." (1839, p. 77) In a footnote in the 1839 version, he adds, "Well may we affirm, that every part of the world is habitable: Whether lakes of brine, or those subterranean ones hidden beneath volcanic mountains—warm mineral springs; the wide expanse and depths of the ocean; the upper regions of the atmosphere; and even the surface of perpetual snow;—all support organic beings." (1839, p. 77) From the contents and tone, as well as from its position in a footnote, we may guess that this remark was added in 1838, when the *Journal* was going to press. By 1845, the addition was integrated into the text itself.

In the waters of the Falkland Islands, he found a seaslug that produced an enormous number of eggs, but not as many mature individuals. He went to some trouble over this point. The following excerpt appears as a footnote in both editions:

> I was surprised to find on counting the eggs of a large white Doris (this sea-slug was three and half inches long) how extraordinarily numerous they were. From two to five eggs (each three-thousandths of an inch in diameter) were contained in a spherical little case. These were arranged two deep in transverse rows forming a ribbon. The ribbon adhered by its edge to the rock in an oval spire. One, which I found, measured nearly twenty inches in length and half in breadth. By counting how many balls were contained in a tenth of an inch in the row, and how many rows in an

equal length of the ribbon, on the most moderate computation there were six hundred thousand eggs. Yet this Doris was certainly not very common: although I was often searching under the stones I saw only seven individuals. (1839, p. 258n)

However, in the 1845 version, a crucial sentence is added. *"No fallacy is more common with naturalists* [than] *that the numbers of an individual species depend on its powers of propagation."* (1845, p. 203, Darwin's italics)

Describing Tierra del Fuego, he writes of the remarkable amounts of seaweed to be found in its cold, uninviting waters. Of course, a large amount of seaweed must be distinguished from a rapid rate of growth. In the 1845 version, he added a note from Wilson's *Voyage round Scotland* on the extreme rapidity with which a bed of seaweed can restore itself.

In the years following the voyage, Darwin read the work of the German naturalist Professor Christian Ehrenberg on living and fossil microorganisms. These organisms often produce striking examples of the fecundity of nature. Large masses of organic beings are composed of these productions, and important geological formations are composed of their fossil remains. In July 1836, the *Beagle* visited the island of Ascension. Some geological observations made then were not mentioned in the 1839 *Journal;* perhaps Darwin could not make sense of them. In the intervening years, he took advantage of Ehrenberg's competence in this area and inserted the following passage in the 1845 version:

A hill, formed of the older series of volcanic rocks, and which has been incorrectly considered as the crater of a volcano, is remarkable from its broad, slightly hollowed, and circular summit having been filled up with many successive layers of ashes and fine scoriae. These saucer-shaped layers crop out on the margin, forming perfect rings of many different colours, giving to the summit a most fantastic appearance; one of these rings is white and broad, and resembles a course round which horses have been exercised; hence the hill has been called the Devil's Riding School. I brought away specimens of one of the tufaceous layers of a pinkish colour; and it is a most extraordinary fact, that Professor Ehrenberg finds it almost wholly composed of matter which has been organized: he detects in it some siliceous-shielded, fresh-water infusoria, and no less than twenty-five different kinds of the siliceous tissue of plants, chiefly of grasses. From the absence of all carbonaceous matter, Professor Ehrenberg believes that these organic bodies have passed through the volcanic fire, and have been erupted in the state in which we now see them. ... Where on the face of the earth can we find a spot, on which close investigation will not discover signs of that endless cycle of change, to which this earth has been is, and will be subjected? (1845, pp. 465–466)

There is more here, evidently, than the observation of profusion in number and kind of microorganisms. It is an example of cooperative work: Ehrenberg examined Darwin's specimens, and Darwin reported the results at a meeting of the London Geological Society on June 4, 1845.[10] There is also Darwin's sense that the earth has been the scene of this abundance everywhere and for aeons of geological time.

This was a theme that stayed with Darwin over the years. In 1860, he replied to a long critical letter from the botanist W. H. Harvey, who had many objections to the *Origin of Species.* Among the points taken up was the rapidity with which life could spread over the globe from some first origin. Darwin wrote, "I dissent quite from what you say of the myriads of years it would take to people the world with such imagined protozoon. In how very short a time Ehrenberg calculated that a single infusorium might make a cube of rock: A single cube on geometrical progression would make the solid globe in (I suppose) under a century." (*ML,* Vol. 1, p. 164)

5. *The Tangled Bank.* In the celebrated closing paragraphs of the *Origin of Species,* Darwin evokes the great image of a "tangled bank," one great ecological chain standing for all of nature. From the superfecundity of each species and the complex relations among them all, flow the principles of struggle, selection, and evolution. Life teems with interactions. "The relation of organism to organism [is] the most important of all relations," wrote Darwin in the table of contents of the *Origin.* This theme appears throughout the *Journal,* in both versions. It is one of the constants of Darwin's thought.

In 1834, back in Tierra del Fuego (the *Beagle* had been there two years before) Darwin wrote at length of *Fucus giganteus,* a large and abundant seaweed:

> The number of living creatures of all Orders, whose existence intimately depends on the kelp, is wonderful. A great volume might be written, describing the inhabitants of one of these beds of sea-weed. Almost all the leaves, excepting those that float on the surface, are so thickly encrusted with corallines as to be of a white colour. We find exquisitely delicate structures, some inhabited by simple hydra-like polypi, others by more organized kinds, and beautiful compound Ascidiae. On the leaves, also, various patelliform shells, Trochi, uncovered molluscs, and some bivalves are attached. Innumerable crustacea frequent every part of the plant. On shaking the great entangled roots, a pile of small fish, shells, cuttle-fish, crabs of all orders, sea-eggs, star-fish, beautiful Holuthuriae, Planariae, and crawling nereidous animals of a mul-

---

[10] See Paul H. Barrett, ed., *The Collected Papers of Charles Darwin,* Vol. 1, pp. 199–203.

titude of forms, all fall out together. Often as I recurred to a
branch of the kelp, I never failed to discover animals of new and
curious structures. . . . I can only compare these great aquatic
forests of the southern hemisphere, with the terrestrial ones in the
intertropical regions. Yet if in any country a forest was destroyed,
I do not believe nearly so many species of animals would perish as
would here, from the destruction of the kelp. Amidst the leaves of
this plant numerous species of fish live, which nowhere else could
find food or shelter; with their destruction the many cormorants
and other fishing birds, the otters, seals, and porpoises, would
soon perish also; and lastly, the Fuegian savage, the miserable lord
of this miserable land, would redouble his cannibal feast, decrease
in numbers, and perhaps cease to exist. (1845, p. 237)

Perhaps no passage better captures Darwin's awe at the variety,
fecundity, and interconnectedness of nature than an entry in the
Beagle Diary written in Brazil, early in the voyage.

But these beauties are as nothing compared to the Vegetation; I
believe from what I have seen Humboldt's glorious descriptions
are & will for ever be unparalleled: but even he with his dark blue
skies & the rare union of poetry with science which he so strongly
displays when writing on tropical scenery, with all this falls far
short of the truth. The delight one experiences in such times be-
wilders the mind; if the eye attempts to follow the flight of a
gaudy butter-fly, it is arrested by some strange tree or fruit; if
watching an insect one forgets it in the stranger flower it is crawling over; if turning to admire the splendour of the scenery, the
individual character of the foreground fixes the attention. The
mind is a chaos of delight, out of which a world of future & more
quiet pleasure will arise. I am at present fit only to read Humboldt; he like another sun illumines everything I behold. (*Beagle
Diary*, p. 39)

6. *Selection.* I do not think there is any explicit, even if veiled,
expression of the unitary idea of evolution-through-natural-
selection in the *Journal*. As we have seen, there is much on the
theme of wholesale extermination of species, especially as a function of changes in food supply. But this is not quite the same idea
as a bias acting *within* a species, promoting the survival of some variants and not others, thus making for a change within the species.
However, although this theme of bias does not occur in a directly
evolutionary context, there are at least two suggestions that Darwin
was thinking along that line. They occur in both editions and seem
to be spontaneous uses of this "thought-form." From the way they
are put, the points seem to have occurred to Darwin during the
voyage. It is my guess that he had this thought-form available to
him quite early, even though he did not apply it to the species
question until much later. And clearly, although he expressed him-

self rather fully on many subjects when writing the *Journal,* this was one area in which he held almost everything back.

Darwin gave many descriptions of warfare between Europeans and Indians in South America. In 1834 he was in Chile and heard of a very successful leader of one roving band of Indians. "Pincheira was a capital horseman, and he made all around him equally good, for he invariably shot any one who hesitated to follow him." (1845, p. 259)

Maybe Darwin had selectivity on his mind at the time he was preparing this section of his *Journal,* for immediately following the Pincheira entry, there occurs one of the few other examples I could find of this theme. It is neither a biological nor a social example, but a description of the refining of gold ore.

> When the ore is brought to the mill, it is ground into an impalpable powder; the process of washing removes all the lighter particles, and amalgamation finally secures the gold dust. . . . It is beautiful to see how the exact adaptation of the current of water to the specific gravity of the gold, so easily separates the powdered matrix from the metal. The mud which passes from the mills is collected into pools, where it subsides, and every now and then is cleared out, and thrown into a common heap. A great deal of chemical action then commences, salts of various kinds effloresce on the surface, and the mass becomes hard. After having been left for a year or two, and then rewashed, it yields gold; and this process may be repeated even six or seven times. . . . This is an exact counterpart of what takes places in nature. Mountains suffer degradation and wear away, and with them the metallic veins which they contain. The hardest rock is worn into impalpable mud, the ordinary metals oxidate, and both are removed; but gold, platina, and a few others are nearly indestructible, and from their weight, sinking to the bottom, are left behind. After whole mountains have passed through this grinding-mill, and have been washed by the hand of nature, the residue becomes metalliferous, and man finds it worth his while to complete the task of separation. (1845, p. 261)

It is worth noting Darwin's perceptive analogy between humanity's way of refining gold and nature's way of making metallic veins. Years later, the analogy between artificial and natural selection was to become one cornerstone of his theory of evolution.

7. Variation and Divergence. Staying close to home, one comes to make a set of distinctions and classifications appropriate to the limited range of one's experience. Traveling more widely, extending that range, one encounters many cases that do not fit the system that was formerly constructed. Darwin had to leave his home-grown system behind him, suffer the consequent confusion, and build a new system.

Darwin reminisced about his own experiences during the voyage:

> When a young naturalist commences the study of a group of organisms quite unknown to him, he is at first much perplexed to determine what differences to consider as specific, and what as varieties; for he knows nothing of the amount and kind of variation to which the group is subject; and this shows, at least, how very generally there is some variation. . . . His general tendency will be to make many species, for he will become impressed, . . . with the amount of difference in the forms which he is continually studying. . . . As he extends the range of his observations, he will meet with more cases of difficulty; for he will encounter a greater number of closely-allied forms. . . . When, moreover, he comes to study allied forms brought from countries not now continuous, in which case he can hardly hope to find the intermediate links between his doubtful forms, . . . his difficulties will rise to a climax."
> (*Origin*, pp. 50–51)

Here Darwin is struggling with a point that stems from the psychology of perception. Traveling widely, one sees large differences and these submerge the young naturalist's perception of smaller ones. Staying close to home does not guarantee the outcome, but a restricted range may invite awareness of the finer nuances.[11]

Distinguishing within-species variation from between-species differences is not easy. But in the long run, the difficulty may be productive in encouraging an evolutionary way of thought. Darwin continues: "These differences blend into each other in an insensible series; and a series impresses the mind with the idea of an actual passage." (*Origin*, p. 51)

The versions of the *Journal* do not dwell on these issues. Darwin was clearly entranced with variety in nature. For both perceptual and conceptual reasons, he focused this attention on interspecific variation. This subject leads almost directly to the issue of evolutionary branching, and in several places the *Journal*, is openly

---

[11] Heinz Werner experimented with "micromelodies"—musical compositions made with a compressed scale using intervals about one-sixth of the half-tone of a conventional scale. The listener gradually becomes accustomed to this miniature musical world, and from an initially blurred and wavering sound, patterns of rhythm and melody appear (Werner, *Comparative Psychology of Mental Development,* [Chicago: Follett, 1948]).

Now imagine the contrary case, someone attuned to these finer nuances being exposed to the wider scale of our ordinary music. I believe it would seem at first a disorganized, wildly swinging cacophony of sound.

suggestive of a process by which one species becomes, or gives rise to, several others.[12]

From his travels in central Chile, Darwin describes two related species of field birds, locally known as "el Turco" (the Turk) and "Tapacolo" (cover-your-posterior), each with its own strange habits. He dissected them, examined their anatomy and the undigested contents of their crops, as well as their visible habits. From all this he concluded, "This bird seems in a certain degree to connect the thrushes with the gallinaceous order." (1845, p. 265) In a footnote, he remarks that a previous writer, "Molina, though describing in detail all the birds and animals of Chile, never once mentions this genus, the species of which are so common, and so remarkable in their habits. Was he at a loss how to classify them, and did he consequently think that silence was the more prudent course? It is one more instance of the frequency of omissions by authors, on those very subjects where it might have been least expected." (1845, p. 265n.) Apart from explaining Molina's motives, which are unknown to us, it would seem that Darwin wanted to use the omission to raise a question in the reader's mind, a question about a mystery to which he held the key.

But taxonomic links in themselves are only suggestive of evolutionary "passages." The case is strengthened if these connections can be related to facts of distribution in geographical space and geological time. Darwin describes two species of ostrich, clearly related to each other, one found in the north and the other in the south of Patagonia. In the 1845 version of the *Journal*, he is pleased to say that the ornithologist Gould has named one of these *Rhea darwinii* for its discoverer.

Continuing his descriptions of the birds of South America, he summarizes his observations of several species of snipe-like birds, concluding, "This small family of birds is one of these which, from its varied relations to other families, although at present offering only difficulties to the systematic naturalist, ultimately may assist in revealing the grand scheme, common to the present and past ages, on which organized beings have been created." (1845, p. 107)

In his transmutation notebook written at about the same time, he went further. Writing about the interrelationships among species differences, geographical space, and geological change, he says, "I look at two Ostriches as strong argument of possiblity of such change; as we see them in space, so might they in time." (*B* 17)

These ornithological passages remain about the same in both

---

[12] Later on, probably in 1858, Darwin finally had to solve the difficult theoretical problem of explaining the *necessity* for continuing divergence in the system of nature, which does not follow from the empirical fact of branching.

editions of the *Journal,* although Darwin was probably aware of possible evolutionary relationships during the voyage. But his most striking and justly famous account of the finches of the Galapagos Archipelago was much changed between the two versions (see below, pp. 287, 299).

He described a wonderful deposit of fossils of nine extinct quadrupeds he found near Bahia Blanca, on the pampas of Argentina. Darwin concludes with the Toxodon, a large, hoofed mammal a little like a modern rhinoceros, but as his account shows, not really fitting into any scheme that ignores its place in evolutionary time:

> Lastly, the Toxodon, perhaps one of the strangest animals every discovered: in size it equalled an elephant or megatherium, but the structure of its teeth, as Mr. Owen states, proves indisputably that it was intimately related to the Gnawers, the order which, at the present day, includes most of the smallest quadrupeds: in many details it is allied to the Pachydermata: judging from the position of its eyes, ears, and nostrils, it was probably aquatic, like the Dugong and Manatee, to which it is also allied. (1845, p. 95)

Descriptively, the two versions of the *Journal* are quite similar on this subject. In the 1839 version, Darwin included a summary of anatomist Richard Owen's analysis of the *Beagle* fossils as reported in a paper at the London Geological Society, April 19, 1837. But the 1845 version adds one sentence, virtually giving a word picture of a segment of Darwin's branching model of evolution: "How wonderfully are the different Orders, at the present time so well separated, blended together in different points of the structure of the Toxodon." (1845, p. 95) Here is the diagram he might well have drawn (Dugong and Manatee are large aquatic herbivores):

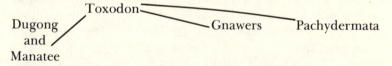

Darwin believed that the first emergence of stabilized variants in several species of mammals that had been imported to the Falkland Islands (off the southeastern coast of Argentina) less than a century before his visit took place in a much shorter time scale. The language of the 1845 version is especially redolent with what we know he had already written more fully in his private notebooks: "It is a curious fact, that the horses have never left the eastern end of the island, although there is no natural boundary to prevent them from roaming. . . . Considering that the island does not appear fully stocked, and that there are no beasts of prey, I was particularly curious to know what has checked their originally rapid increase." (1845, p. 194) (I defer Darwin's answer to this question until the section on rudimentary organs and maladaptive variations.)

In the 1845 version, Darwin adds an important item of information, provided after the voyage by Captain Sulivan, which ends with a remark noteworthy because he makes a prediction about the future course of species change:

> The cattle, instead of having degenerated like the horses, seem as before remarked, to have increased in size, and they are much more numerous than the horses. Captain Sulivan informs me that they vary much less in the general form of their bodies and in the shape of their horns than English cattle. In colour they differ much; and it is a remarkable circumstance, that in different parts of this one small island, different colours predominate. Round Mount Usborne, at a height of from 1,000 to 1,500 feet above the sea, about half of some of the herds are mouse or lead-coloured, a tint which is not common in other parts of the island. Near Port Pleasant dark brown prevails, whereas south of Choiseul Sound (which almost divides the island into two parts), white beasts with black heads and feet are the most common: in all parts black, and some spotted animals may be observed. . . . Captain Sulivan thinks that the herds do not mingle; and it is a singular fact, that the mouse-coloured cattle, though living on the high land, calve about a month earlier in the season than the other coloured beasts on the lower land. It is interesting thus to find the once domesticated cattle breaking into three colours, of which some one colour would in all probability ultimately prevail over the others, if the herds were left undisturbed for the next several centuries. (1845, pp. 194–195)

Darwin quickly became alert to the evolutionary import of the isolation on newly formed islands of species formerly joined to continental populations (see *Darwin on Man*, p. 138). In his theory of coral reef formation, the steady subsidence of the ocean floor and consequent separation of previously joined regions play an important role. Summarizing this theory in the 1839 edition of the *Journal*, he writes,

> If the theory should hereafter be so far established, as to allow us to pronounce that certain districts fall within areas either of elevation or subsidence, it will directly bear upon that most mysterious question,—whether the series of organized beings peculiar to some isolated points, are the last remnants of a former population, or the first creatures of a new one springing into existence. (1839, p. 569)

Note the cryptic tone of the passage and the conjunction *or*. A species is either disappearing or appearing. This dichotomous formulation conceals rather more than it reveals of his evolutionary thought. In the 1845 version, this whole passage is deleted, and the whole tone of the 1845 treatment of species conveys a much clearer idea of continuous transformation.

8. *"The law of the succession of types."* Darwin speaks often of cases in which, in the same geographical region, one species becomes extinct and another, closely allied, replaces it in the scheme of nature. Similarly, he speaks of a species in one region being replaced in the ecology of a neighboring region by another, closely allied species. Now these are not outright statements that natural evolutionary change accounts for the facts, since it is possible that a supernatural creator simply chose to emplace organisms in this way. But we know that when Darwin was writing of these changes, he had evolution in mind.

In Patagonia, he marvels at the similarity of extinct and living forms found in the same region. He announces the "law of the succession of types" in the 1839 *Journal.* In the 1845 version, this relationship is still a matter of great interest, but not simply as a "law" relating distinct classes of facts. Rather, it illuminates the "appearance" of new species.

> In one spot . . . earthy matter filled up a hollow, or gully, worn quite through the gravel, and in this mass a group of large bones was embedded. . . . Then immediately occurred the difficulty, how could any large quadruped have subsisted on these wretched deserts in lat. 49° 15'? I had no idea at the time, to what kind of animal these remains belonged. The puzzle, however, was soon solved when Mr. Owen examined them; for he considers that they formed part of an animal allied to the guanaco or llama, but fully as large as the true camel. As all the existing members of the family of Camelidae are inhabitants of the most sterile countries, so may we suppose was this extinct kind. The structure of the cervical vertebrae, the transverse processes not being perforated for the vertebral artery, indicates its affinity: some other parts, however, of its structure, probably are anomalous.
>
> The most important result of this discovery, is the confirmation of the law that existing animals have a close relation in form with extinct species. As the guanaco is the characteristic quadruped of Patagonia, and the vicuna of the snow-clad summits of the Cordillera, so in bygone days, this gigantic species of the same family must have been conspicuous on the southern plains. We see this same relation of type between the existing and fossil Ctenomys, between the capybara (but less plainly, as shown by Mr. Owen) and the gigantic Toxodon; and lastly, between the living and extinct Edentata. At the present day, in South America, there exist probably nineteen species of this order, distributed into several genera; while throughout the rest of the world there are but

five. If, then, there is a relation between the living and the dead, we should expect that the Edentata would be numerous in the fossil state. I need only reply by enumerating the megatherium, and the three or four other great species, discovered at Bahia Blanca; the remains of some of which are also abundant over the whole immense territory of La Plata. I have already pointed out the singular relation between the armadilloes and their great prototypes, even in a point apparently of so little importance as their external covering. . . .

The law of the succession of types, although subject to some remarkable exceptions, must possess the highest interest to every philosophical naturalist, and was first clearly observed in regard to Australia, where fossil remains of a large and extinct species of Kangaroo and other marsupial animals were discovered buried in a cave. (1839, pp. 208–210)

In the 1845 version, he added a more succinct summary of the facts and included some new ones. He concludes the section with a sentence going as far as he then wished, or dared, to reveal himself, promising that "this wonderful relationship in the same continent between the dead and the living" would someday "throw more light" on the appearance of new species. And well he might promise, since he already held the necessary lamp ready.

The relationship, though distant, between the Macrauchenia and the Guanaco, between the Toxodon and the Capybara,—the closer relationship between the many extinct Edentata and the living sloth, ant-eaters, and armadillos, now so eminently characteristic of South American zoology,—and the still closer relationship between the fossil and living species of Ctenomys and Hydrochaerus, are most interesting facts. This relationship is shown wonderfully—as wonderfully as between the fossil and extinct Marsupial animals of Australia—by the great collection lately brought to Europe from the caves of Brazil by MM. Lund and Clausen. In this collection there are extinct species of all the thirty-two genera, excepting four, of the terrestrial quadrupeds now inhabiting the provinces in which the caves occur; and the extinct species are much more numerous than those now living: there are fossil ant-eaters, armadillos, tapirs, peccaries, guanacos, opossums, and numerous South American gnawers and monkeys, and other animals. This wonderful relationship in the same continent between the dead and the living, will, I do not doubt, hereafter throw more light on the appearance of organic beings on our earth, and their disappearance from it, than any other class of facts. (1845, p. 177)

Fourteen years later, in the *Origin*, he wrote a sentence remarkably similar both in wording and intent. It was 1859. He was revealing his general theory of evolution but still refraining from any treatment of the evolution of the human species. In his concluding remarks on the significance of the theory he wrote: "In the distant future I see open fields for far more important researches. Psychology will be based on a new foundation, that of the necessary acquirement of each mental power and capacity by gradation. Light will be thrown on the origin of man and his history." (*Origin*, p. 488)

9. Biogeography. H.M.S. *Beagle* was a vessel of the Royal Navy engaged upon an imperial mission—to learn more about the far corners of the world, the better to expand and control the domain of empire. Many of Darwin's writings describe the functioning of the colonial system directly or exploit it metaphorically for theoretical purposes.

In the *Essay* of 1844, in the section on geographical distribution, he wrote of the way in which, since organisms are not necessarily "perfectly adapted" to their milieux, a newcomer (invader, migrant, colonist—the term varies) may win out in competition over the indigenous species. "We know the European mouse is driving before it that of New Zealand, like the Norway rat has driven before it the old English species in England." (*Essay*, p. 153) It was not a bad summary of the imperial history of England, first colonized by Scandinavians, then colonizing the four quarters of the earth.

In the *Origin,* the subject of geographical distribution grew into two chapters, over one-eighth the total length.[13] About the same length is devoted to the geological record, so the evidence for evolution from the relations among species over space and time comprises about one-quarter of the book. During cycles of elevation and subsidence of the earth, the ocean level falls and rises, making islands where there was continuous terrain and mountains where there were islands. Again Darwin wrote in human terms: "The various beings thus left stranded may be compared with savage races of man, driven up and surviving in the mountain-fastnesses of almost every land, which serve as record, full of interest to us, of the former inhabitants of the surrounding lowlands." (*Origin*, p. 382)

The subject of geographical distribution is complex. Interest in it had been growing rapidly for about a century. There are three great classes of facts to be explained. First, similar habitats do not necessarily have similar organisms living in them. Thus, organisms do not seem to be made directly for their habitats. Second,

---

[13] See Gareth Nelson, "From Candolle to Croizat: Comments on the History of Biogeography," *Journal of the History of Biology*, Vol. 11, 1978, pp. 269–305, for an interesting account of different theoretical models of biogeographical relationships, beginning with Buffon's seminal work in 1761.

neighboring or interconnected regions do have similar organisms. Island inhabitants resemble those of nearby continents; nearby islands have similar species, and so forth. But the concept of distance must be modified to take into account the presence of all sorts of geographical barriers to the establishment of a single interbreeding population. Finally, neighboring regions often have similar, but not identical, species. Each variant form tends to be adapted to the special conditions of its local habitat or station.

As Darwin came to see, these facts can all be explained by a biogeographical theory with three main elements. (1) Each species arises only once—there are no "multiple creations." (2) There is a continual process of migration and dispersal of every organism from any point of origin, limited, of course, by various geographical barriers. The evolution of means of dispersal and extension of range is one of the adaptive functions of living creatures. (3) In the new habitats in which organisms are thus forever finding themselves, further adaptive modification occurs. Depending on the total set of circumstances, this process of dispersal and modification repeats itself as new species are formed.

The influence of Charles Lyell is evident throughout Darwin's treatment of this subject: "Geology is the science which investigates the successive changes that have taken place in the organic and inorganic kingdoms of nature." These are the opening words of Lyell's *Principles of Geology*, which Darwin studied all during the voyage. But it would be a mistake to ascribe everything in this field to Lyell. Biogeography was widely discussed, and Darwin drew on many sources, the richest of all being his own experiences during his five-year circumnavigation of the earth.

In the published journal of the voyage, there are many indication of Darwin's biogeographical thinking, and some of his use of it within the evolutionary approach he was elaborating. The facts of geographical distribution were a major stimulus for thinking about evolution. They are an important part of the evidence that cries out for an evolutionary explanation. The 1839 version gives a great deal of this evidence; the 1845 version of the *Journal* is far more suggestive of the relation of these facts to evolutionary thought.

The history of the earth and the facts of geographical distribution were inseparable. "Daily it is forced home on the mind of the geologist, that nothing, not even the wind that blows, is so unstable as the level of the crust of this earth." (1845, pp. 309–310) Darwin discusses Indian ruins found in an extremely arid part of the Cordillera, too arid for human habitation. This suggests to him a change in climate caused by a gradual elevation of the land, but this must have happened very slowly.

I have convincing proofs that this part of the continent of

South America has been elevated near the coast at least from 400 to 500, and in some parts from 1,000 to 1,300 feet, since the epoch of existing shells; and further inland the rise possibly may have been greater. As the peculiarly arid character of the climate is evidently a consequence of the height of the Cordillera, we may feel almost sure that before the later elevation, the atmosphere could not have been so completely drained of its moisture as it now is: and as the rise has been gradual, so would have been the change in climate. On this notion of a change of climate since the buildings were inhabited, the ruins must be of extreme antiquity. But I do not think their preservation under the Chilian climate any great difficulty. We must also admit on this notion (and this perhaps is a greater difficulty), that man has inhabited South America for an immensely long period, inasmuch as any change of climate effected by the elevation of the land must have been extremely gradual. At Valparaiso, within the last two hundred and twenty years, the rise has been somewhat less than nineteen feet: at Lima a sea-beach has certainly been upheaved from eight to ninety feet, within the Indo-human period: but such small elevations could have had little power in deflecting the moisture-bringing atmospheric currents. Dr. Lund, however, found human skeletons in the caves of Brazil, the appearance of which induced him to believe that the Indian race has existed during a vast lapse of time in South America. (1845, pp. 342–343)

Darwin does not specify how many years he has in mind. But if the human species had a single origin and then slowly dispersed over the earth, there must have been many hundreds of centuries between its first appearance somewhere far away and the lifetimes of those men and women who made the buildings and whose skeletons caught Darwin's imagination. Even during the voyage he thought of our species as part of nature: the phrase "man and . . . all other animals" appears in the *Beagle Diary* (entry for December 29, 1834). Although he might not have used such a revealing phrase in the published *Journal,* his use of human historical evidences in a biogeographical argument was revealing enough.

If one great region, formerly united, becomes separated through geological change into two regions between which migration is impeded, and if great periods of time are allowed, all of the species in each region may evolve in such a way that two distinct "provinces" will emerge. Fossil remains will be the same in the two provinces, but living organisms will be different. This would be a case of evolutionary divergence on a grand scale. More than once, Darwin described the formation of such provinces.

If we divide America, not by the Isthmus of Panama, but by the southern part of Mexico in lat 20°, where the great table-land presents an obstacle to the migration of species, by affecting the climate, and by forming, with the exception of some valleys and of a fringe of low land on the coast, a broad barrier; we shall then have the two zoological provinces of North and South America strongly contrasted with each other. Some few species alone have passed the barrier, and may be considered as wanderers from the south, such as the puma, opossum, kinkajou, and peccari. South America is characterized by possessing many peculiar gnawers, a family of monkeys, the llama, peccari, tapir, opossums, and, especially, several genera of Edentata, the order which includes the sloths, ant-eaters, and armadilloes. North America, on the other hand, is characterized (putting on one side a few wandering species) by numerous peculiar gnawers, and by four genera (the ox, sheep, goat, and antelope) of hollow-horned ruminants, of which great division South America is not known to possess a single species. Formerly, but within the period when most of the now existing shells were living, North America possessed, besides hollow-horned ruminants, the elephant, mastodon, horse, and three genera of Edentata, namely, the Megatherium, Megalonyx, and Mylodon. Within nearly this same period (as proved by the shells at Bahia Blanca) South America possessed, as we have just seen, a mastodon, horse, hollow-horned ruminant, and the same three genera (as well as several others) of the Edentata. Hence it is evident that North and South America, in having within a late geological period these several genera in common, were much more closely related in the character of their terrestrial inhabitants than they now are. The more I reflect on this case, the more interesting it appears: I know of no other instance where we can almost mark the period and manner of the splitting up of one great region into two well-characterized zoological provinces. (1845, pp. 138–139)

With our hindsight, the biogeographical and evolutionary significance of the species found in the Galapagos archipelago almost leaps to the eye. But as Darwin himself put it, not to the eye of the body "but rather after reflection, the eye of reason." (*Beagle Diary*, p. 400, written April 12, 1836, after visiting Keeling Island) This process of reflection takes some time and hard work. It leads to searching out new information, asking new questions, and finding people who can answer them. Darwin used the time between the two versions for this work, and the natural history of the Galapagos was almost completely rewritten.

The natural history of these islands is eminently curious, and well deserves attention. Most of the organic productions are aboriginal creations, found nowhere else; there is even a difference between the inhabitants of the different islands; yet all show a marked relationship with those of America, though separated from that continent by an open space of ocean, between 500 and 600 miles in width. The archipelago is a little world within itself, or rather a satellite attached to America, whence it has derived a few stray colonists, and has received the general character of its indigenous productions. Considering the small size of these islands, we feel the more astonished at the number of their aboriginal beings, and at their confined range. Seeing every height crowned with its crater, and the boundaries of most of the lava-streams still distinct, we are led to believe that within a period, geologically recent, the unbroken ocean was here spread out. Hence, both in space and time, we seem to be brought somewhat near to that great fact—that mystery of mysteries—the first appearance of new being on this earth. (1845, pp. 360–361)

The remaining land-birds form a most singular group of finches, related to each other in the structure of their beaks, short tails, form of body, and plumage: there are thirteen species, which Mr. Gould has divided into four sub-groups. All these species are peculiar to this archipelago; and so is the whole group, with the exception of one species of the subgroup Cactornis, lately brought from Bow Island, in the Low Archipelago. Of Cactornis, the two species may be often seen climbing about the flowers of the great cactus-trees; but all the other species of this group of finches, mingled together in flocks, feed on the dry and sterile ground of the lower districts. The males of all, or certainly of the greater number, are jet black; and the females (with perhaps one or two exceptions) are brown. The most curious fact is the perfect gradation in the size of the beaks in the different species of Geospiza, from one as large as that of a hawfinch to that of a chaffinch, and . . . even to that of a warbler. . . . Seeing this gradation and diversity of structure in one small, intimately related group of birds, one might really fancy that from an original paucity of birds in this archipelago, one species had been taken and modified for different ends. (1845, pp. 362–363)

The tortoises which live on those islands where there is no water, or in the lower and arid parts of the others, feed chiefly on the succulent cactus. Those which frequent the higher and damp regions, eat the leaves of various trees, a kind of berry (called guayavita) which is acid and austere, and likewise a pale green filamentous lichen (Usnera plicata), that hangs in tresses from the boughs of the trees. (1845, p. 365)

I have not as yet noticed by far the most remarkable feature in the natural history of this archipelago; it is, that the different islands to a considerable extent are inhabited by a different set of beings. My attention was first called to this fact by the Vice-Governor, Mr. Lawson, declaring that the tortoises differed from the different islands, and that he could with certainty tell from which island any one was brought. I did not for some time pay sufficient attention to this statement, and I had already partially mingled together the collections from two of the islands. I never

dreamed that islands, about fifty or sixty miles apart, and most of
them in sight of each other, formed of precisely the same rocks,
placed under a quite similar climate, rising to a nearly equal
height, would have been differently tenanted; but we shall soon
see that this is the case. . . .

The inhabitants, as I have said, state that they can distinguish
the tortoises from the different islands; and that they differ not
only in size, but in other characters. Captain Porter has described
those from Charles and from the nearest island to it, namely,
Hood Island, as having their shells in front thick and turned up
like a Spanish saddle, whilst the tortoises from James Island are
rounder, blacker, and have a better taste when cooked. . . . The
specimens that I brought from three islands were young ones; and
probably owing to this cause, neither Mr. Gray nor myself could
find in them any specific differences. I have remarked that the
marine Amblyrhynchus was larger at Albemarle Island than
elsewhere; and M. Bibron informs me that he has seen two distinct aquatic species of this genus; so that the different islands
probably have their representative species or races of the
Amblyrhynchus, as well as of the tortoise. My attention was first
thoroughly aroused, by comparing together the numerous specimens, shot by myself and several other parties on board, of the
mocking-thrushes, when, to my astonishment, I discovered that all
those from Charles Island belonged to one species (Mimus trifasciatus); all from Albemarle Island to M. parvulus; and all from
James and Chatham Islands (between which two other islands are
situated, as connecting links) belonged to M. melanotis. These two
latter species are closely allied, and would by some ornithologists
be considered as only well-marked races or varieties; but the
Mimus trifasciatus is very distinct. Unfortunately most of the
specimens of the finch tribe were mingled together; but I have
strong reasons to suspect that some of the species of the subgroup Geospiza are confined to separate islands. If the different
islands have their representatives of Geospiza, it may help to
explain the singularly large number of the species of this subgroup in this one small archipelago, and as a probable consequence of their numers, the perfectly graduated series in the size
of their beaks. (1845, pp. 375–376)

The only light which I can throw on this remarkable difference in the inhabitants of the different islands, is, that very
strong currents of the sea running in a westerly and W.N.W. direction must separate, as far as transportal by the sea is concerned, the southern islands from the northern ones; and between
these northern islands a strong N.W. current was observed, which
must effectually separate James and Albemarle Islands. As the archipelago is free to a most remarkable degree from gales of wind,
neither the birds, insects, nor lighter seeds, would be blown from
island to island. And lastly, the profound depth of the ocean be-

tween the islands, and their apparently recent (in a geological sense) volcanic origin, render it highly unlikely that they were ever united: and this, probably, is a far more important consideration than any other, with respect to the geographical distribution of their inhabitants. Reviewing the facts here given, one is astonished at the amount of creative force, if such an expression may be used, displayed on these small, barren, and rocky islands; and still more so at its diverse yet analogous action on points so near each other. I have said that the Galapagos Archipelago might be called a satellite attached to America, but it should rather be called a group of satellites, physically similar, organically distinct, yet intimately related to each other, and all related in a marked, though much less degree, to the great American continent. (1845, p. 379)

The phrase "creative force" is ambiguous here. It might conceivably mean "activity of the Creator" or it might mean "factors stimulating evolutionary change." Darwin's cryptic handling of this issue does not make it easy to tell just where he is at any given point in the development of his ideas. But the changes in what he wrote do suggest the direction of movement of his thought. In the 1839 edition, he wrote: "If the theory should hereafter be so far established, as to allow us to pronounce that certain districts fall within areas either of elevation or subsidence, it will directly bear upon that most mysterious question,—whether the series of organized beings peculiar to some isolated points, are the last remnants of a former population, or the first creatures of a new one springing into existence." (1839, p. 569)

This sharp dichotomy between the extinction of the old and the evolution of the new reflected Lyell's idea of multiple creations and successive repopulations of the earth. The dichotomy was not so easy to maintain in Darwin's later thinking, and the passage was dropped from the 1845 version.

10. Strange Contrivances, Maladaptations, and Rudimentary Organs. Darwin looked with both acuity and relish at the many beautiful adaptations of structure and habit by which organisms carry out the task of living. As I have pointed out in *Darwin on Man,* he drew on the work of the natural theologians who dwelt on the perfection of adaptive mechanisms as a sign of the handiwork of God, the Divine Artificer. But Darwin's theory required that adaptation be somewhat less than perfect. Adaptation is a process; organisms adapt to meet changing conditions; an adaptation which seems perfect under one set of circumstances will not be so when they change, as circumstances inevitably do.

Thus we find in the *Journal* evidence both of Darwin's delight in the seeming perfection of nature and his keen discernment of the flaws in that system. Of course, the fossil record and the massive facts of extinction were, for Darwin, evidence of imperfection, or better, of the limitations of particular adaptations. But in this section we deal with imperfections on a smaller scale.

In northern Argentina, Darwin saw a fine thing, a spider "aeronaut," as he called it, with a pretty way of getting about in the world:

> One day, at St. Fé, I had a better opportunity of observing some similar facts. A spider which was about three-tenths of an inch in length, and which in its general appearance resembled a Citigrade . . . while standing on the summit of a post, darted forth four or five threads from its spinners. These, glittering in the sunshine, might be compared to diverging rays of light; they were not, however, straight, but in undulations like films of silk blown by the wind. They were more than a yard in length, and diverged in an ascending direction from the orifices. The spider then suddenly let go its hold of the post, and was quickly born out of sight. (1845, p. 160–161)

But all is not always so well. In the Falkland Islands, Darwin learned, the horses were headed toward extinction, apparently from a species-suicidal habit. He reflected on possible explanations in a passage added to the 1845 version of the *Journal*.

> That in a limited island some check would sooner or later supervene, is inevitable; but why has the increase of the horse been checked sooner than that of the cattle? Captain Sulivan has taken much pains for me in this inquiry. The Gauchos employed here attribute it chiefly to the stallions constantly roaming from place to place, and compelling the mares to accompany them, whether or not the young foals are able to follow. One Gaucho told Captain Sulivan that he had watched a stallion for a whole hour, violently kicking and biting a mare till he forced her to leave her foal to its fate. (1845, p. 194)

In Uruguay, in Maldonado, Darwin saw the Tucutuco, "a curious small animal . . . a Gnawer with the habits of a mole."

> The man who caught them asserted that very many are invariably found blind. A specimen which I preserved in spirits was in this state; Mr. Reid considers it to be the effect of inflammation in the nictitating membrane. When the animal was alive I placed my finger within half an inch of its head, and not the slightest notice was taken: it made its way, however, about the room nearly as well as the others. Considering the strictly subterranean habits of the tucutuco, the blindness, though so common, cannot be a very serious evil; yet it appears strange that any animal should possess an organ frequently subject to be injured. Lamarck would have been delighted with this fact, had he known it, when speculating*
> *Philosophie Zoologique*, tom. 1., p. 242 [Darwin's note, H. G.].

(probably with more truth than usual with him) on the gradually-*acquired* blindness of the Aspalax, a Gnawer living under ground, and of the Proteus, a reptile living in dark caverns filled with water; in both of which animals the eye is in an almost rudimentary state, and is covered by a tendinous membrane and skin. In the common mole the eye is extraordinarily small but perfect, though many anatomists doubt whether it is connected with the true optic nerve; its vision must certainly be imperfect, though probably useful to the animal when it leaves its burrow. In the tucutuco, which I believe never comes to the surface of the ground, the eye is rather larger, but often rendered blind and useless, though without apparently causing any inconvenience to the animal: no doubt Lamarck would have said that the tucutuco is now passing into the state of the Aspalax and Proteus. (1845, p. 52)

The two versions of the *Journal* are alike in their descriptions of the Tucutuco. But in 1845, Darwin inserted his remarks on "acquired blindness." Although he seems to pass the responsibility for these remarks to Lamarck, Darwin cannot quite refrain from endorsing the views he attributes to his precursor.

In contrast to the highly evolved mammalian eye, too specialized to be readapted for another purpose, when birds' wings lose their function of flight, other functions evolve. This intrigued Darwin, and in the way he puts his summary of the facts, we see that for him adaptations of this sort are only one evolutionary step away from rudimentary organs. "Thus we find in South America three birds which use their wings for other purposes besides flight; the penguin as fins, the steamer as paddles, and the ostrich as sails: and the Apteryx of New Zealand, as well as its gigantic extinct prototype the Dinornis, possess only rudimentary representatives of wings." (1845, p. 202)

A key point, sometimes misunderstood, in Darwin's theory of evolution, is that only some (indeed, very few) new variants are positively adaptive. Only those few survive to breed and increase their own kind. Whether or not they do depends on the particular circumstances of their lives.

Darwin gave a clear example of these relationships in his account of an unusual breed of oxen found in Banda Oriental, in Uruguay. The passage, so close to a frank statement of his beliefs, did not appear in the earlier edition but was added in the 1845 version of the *Journal*.

On two occasions I met with in this province some oxen of a very curious breed, called nāta or niata. . . . Their forehead is very short and broad, with the nasal end turned up, and the upper lip much drawn back; their lower jaws project beyond the upper, and have a corresponding upward curve; hence their teeth are always exposed. Their nostrils are seated high up and are very open; their eyes project outwards. When walking they carry their heads low, on a short neck; and their hinder legs are rather longer compared with the front legs than is usual. Their bare teeth, their short heads, and upturned nostrils gave them the most ludicrous self-confident air of defiance imaginable.

Since my return, I have procured a skeleton head, through the kindness of my friend Captain Sulivan, R.N., which is now deposited in the College of Surgeons. Don F. Muniz, of Luxan, has kindly collected for me all the information which he could respecting this breed. From his account it seems that about eighty or ninety years ago they were rare, and kept as curiosities at Buenos Ayres. The breed is universally believed to have originated amongst the Indians southward of the Plata; and that it was with them the commonest kind. Even to this day, those reared in the provinces near the Plata show their less civilized origin, in being fiercer than common cattle, and in the cow easily deserting her first calf, if visited too often or molested. . . . The breed is very *true;* and a niata bull and cow invariably produce niata calves. A niata bull with a common cow, or the reverse cross, produces offspring having an intermediate character, but with the niata characters strongly displayed: according to Señor Muniz, there is the clearest evidence, contrary to the common belief of agriculturists in analogous cases, that the niata cow when crossed with a common bull transmits her peculiarities more strongly than the niata bull when crossed with a common cow. When the pasture is tolerably long, the niata cattle feed with the tongue and palate as well as common cattle; but during the great droughts, when so many animals perish, the niata breed is under a great disadvantage, and would be exterminated if not attended to; for the common cattle, like horses, are able just to keep alive, by browsing with their lips on twigs of trees and reeds; this the niatas cannot so well do, as their lips do not join, and hence they are found to perish before the common cattle. This strikes me as a good illustration of how little we are able to judge from the ordinary habits of life, on what circumstances, occuring only at long intervals, the rarity or extinction of a species may be determined. (1845, pp. 152–153)

11. On human imperfection and perfectibility. Throughout his long life, Darwin was aware of the imperfections of his own species. As time wore on, he wove this awareness into his theory. If, on the one hand, man had been created perfect and then fallen from grace— rapidly in some theologies, slowly in others—this would not accord with the theory of evolution through natural selection. If, on the other hand, human beings were, like other animals, variable in their intellectual and social characteristics, they might slowly construct their systems of knowledge and their codes of ethics. He concluded the pertinent section of the *Descent of Man,*

To believe that man was aboriginally civilised and then suffered utter degradation in so many regions, is to take a pitiably low view of human nature. It is apparently a truer and more cheerful view that progress has been much more general than retrogression; that man has risen, though by slow and interrupted steps, from a lowly condition to the highest standard as yet attained by him in knowledge, morals and religion. (*Descent*, p. 145)

Although Darwin's ideas on the evolution of intelligence and social conduct do bear some resemblance to modern sociobiology, it should be pointed out that the theoretical aims of these modern descendants of Darwin have diverged far from his. These sociobiologists are interested in demonstrating the *fixity* of human conduct; Darwin was interested in its *evolution*, including a superior state still to come, far in the future. Darwin was interested in including the human past in biological evolution as part of a more general insistence on scientific materialism. He had more than a glimmering of a second and powerful process of cultural evolution, which narrowly selectionist sociobiologists often lack.

The imperfections of war, slavery, and other forms of inhumanity seemed as "natural" to Darwin as any other imperfections in the order of nature. Nevertheless, as I have stressed in *Darwin on Man*, Darwin came from a family tradition opposed to slavery, and he exhibited the same feeling on his first encounters with that institution. But he did not say much about it in the 1839 version of the *Journal*, perhaps because it was still too close to being an official document. In 1845 he added a long and bitter attack on slavery.

On the 19th of August we finally left the shores of Brazil. I thank God, I shall never again visit a slave country. To this day, if I hear a distant scream, it recalls with painful vividness my feelings, when passing a house near Pernambuco, I heard the most pitiable moans, and could not but suspect that some poor slave was being tortured, yet knew that I was as powerless as a child even to remonstrate. . . . Near Rio de Janeiro I lived opposite to an old lady, who kept screws to crush the fingers of her female slaves. I have stayed in a house where a young household mulatto, daily and hourly, was reviled, beaten, and persecuted enough to break the spirit of the lowest animal. I have seen a little boy, six or seven years old, struck thrice with a horse-whip (before I could interfere) on his naked head, for having handed me a glass of water not quite clean; I saw his father tremble at a mere glance from his master's eye. These latter cruelties were witnessed by me in a Spanish colony, in which it has always been said, that slaves are better treated then by the Portuguese, English, or other European nations. I have seen at Rio Janeiro a powerful negro afraid to ward off a blow directed, as he thought, at his face. I was present when a kind-hearted man was on the point of separating for

ever the men, women, and little children of a large number of
families who had long lived together. . . .

It is argued that self-interest will prevent excessive cruelty; as
if self-interest protected our domestic animals, which are far less
likely than degraded slaves, to stir up the rage of their savage
masters. It is an argument long since protested against with noble
feeling, and strikingly exemplified, by the ever illustrious Humboldt. It is often attempted to palliate slavery by comparing the
state of slaves with our poorer countrymen: if the misery of our
poor be caused not by the laws of nature, but by our institutions,
great is our sin; but how this bears on slavery, I cannot see; as well
might the use of the thumb-screw be defended in one land, by
showing that men in another land suffered from some dreadful
disease. Those who look tenderly at the slaveowner, and with a
cold heart at the slave, never seem to put themselves into the position of the latter;—what a cheerless prospect, with not even a
hope of change! Picture to yourself the chance, ever hanging over
you, of your wife and your little children—those objects which nature urges even the slave to call his own—being torn from you
and sold like beasts to the first bidder! And these deeds are done
and palliated by men, who profess to love their neighbours as
themselves, who believe in God, and pray that His will be done on
earth! It makes one's blood boil, yet heart tremble, to think that
we Englishmen and our American descendants, with their boastful
cry of liberty, have been and are so guilty; but it is a consolation to
reflect, that we at least have made a greater sacrifice, than ever
made by any nation, to expiate our sin.

The passage contains an evident allusion to a violent argument
with Captain FitzRoy about the treatment of slaves, which almost
led to Darwin's being put off the *Beagle* early in the voyage. Captain RitzRoy believed that slavery was a "tolerable evil."[14] Darwin
did not.

12. The transformation of creation. As I have discussed in *Darwin
on Man,* throughout his notebooks and his later writings, Darwin
used "creationist" language from time to time, always in an ambiguous way. The same is true in both versions of the *Journal.* He
speaks more than once of a species having been "created" in or for
a certain habitat. He might have meant "created by God," but, on
balance, I believe that he meant only "appeared in and adapted to"
the place in question. Such a formula is neutral with respect to the
manner of origin.

There is one passage which evolved in a striking way from the

---

[14] Early in the voyage (April 15th, 1832), Darwin described at some length the
cruelty of a slaveowning Irishman he met in Brazil. Obviously alluding to the ship-
board argument with FitzRoy, he concluded, "Against such facts how weak are the
arguments of those who maintain that slavery is a tolerable evil" (*Beagle Diary,* p. 55).

Beagle Diary to the 1839 *Journal* to the 1845 *Journal*. It is worth examination, for it is the most explicitly creationist passage in these works. In 1836 in Australia, he reflected on the complex array of similarities and differences found in the biogeographical patterning of the earth. In different quarters of the earth there are different but related species, with similar habits.

In the *Beagle Diary* in 1836—prompted by his observations of the larva of an ant lion, which traps prey by digging holes and by throwing sand over its victims that have fallen into these pitfalls— Darwin wrote a kind of abbreviated dialogue among three discussants: A Disbeliever, to whom the differences among species suggest distinct and unrelated appearances of different species; an implicit Believer (Darwin himself?), to whom the similarities among nature's contrivances in different places suggest that "one hand has surely worked throughout the universe"; and a Geologist (Darwin's capitalization!), who proposes the hypothesis of multiple creations.

> A little time before this I had been lying on a sunny bank & was reflecting on the strange character of the animals of this country as compared to the rest of the World. An unbeliever in everything beyond his own reason might exclaim, "Surely two distinct Creators must have been at work; their object, however, has been the same & certainly the end in each case is complete". Whilst thus thinking, I observed the conical pitfall of a Lion-Ant:—a fly fell in & immediately disappeared; then came a large but unwary Ant. His struggles to escape being very violent, the little jets of sand described by Kirby (Vol. 1. p. 425) were promptly directed against him.—His fate, however, was better than that of the fly's. Without doubt the predaecious Larva belongs to the same genus but to a different species from the Europaean kind.—Now what would the Disbeliever say to this? Would any two workmen ever hit on so beautiful, so simple, & yet so artificial a contrivance? It cannot be thought so. The one hand has surely worked throughout the universe. A Geologist perhaps would suggest that the periods of Creation have been distinct & remote the one from the other; that the Creator rested in his labor. (*Beagle Diary*, p. 383)

In the 1839 version of the *Journal*, the direct reference to the "Creator" is gone, and only the "one Hand" remains—which might well mean only one natural law operating uniformly everywhere. In the 1845 version, the "Hand" too is gone, and all that remains is a footnote describing the behavior of the insect.[15] On noticing this tranformation, I was reminded of Einstein's collaborator, Leopold

---

[15] See *Darwin on Man*, pp. 132–133, for further discussion of the passage from the *Beagle Diary*. Darwin's granddaughter Nora Barlow has also pointed out this transformation in the three versions in her notes on the *Beagle Diary*, which she edited for publication.

Infeld. In his biography, Infeld describes the gradual fading of his image of God; first there was truly a white-bearded partriarch in the sky and finally, after a passage of years, only the clouds.

Conclusion. To understand Darwin's behavior in revising the *Journal,* we need to consider the sequence of his publications in relation to the sequence of his private writings. These components can be represented schematically as follows:

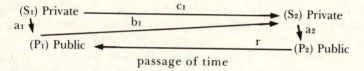

$$(S_1) \text{ Private} \xrightarrow{\quad c_1 \quad} (S_2) \text{ Private}$$

passage of time

In general, any thinker or writer must first work out ideas and then decide whether or not to publish them (arrow a_1). Publication itself has consequences that affect the ongoing thought processes (arrow b_1). Apart from these effects, the person goes on working and thinking (arrow c_1). At some point, a new decision to publish occurs, and the cycle begins again (arrow a_2). I have added the time-reversed arrow r (for 'reflection') to indicate that the thinker-writer may well be aware of and take into account the relation between present and past publications. Writing is not only an expressive act, it is a reworking of self-consciousness.

Consider these cases:

Withholding. The thinker-writer has developed an idea but decides not to publish it ($P_1 < S_1$).

Substitution. The thinker-writer changes one idea for another. Generally, this will be a correction, but there are other possibilities (P_2 replaces P_1).

Insertion. The thinker-writer adds ideas that were not previously published. This may be because his or her knowledge and thinking has gone forward in a new way, or it may represent a decision to publish ideas that were previously withheld ($P_2 > P_1$).

In Darwin's case, this abstract schema can be given particular form as follows:

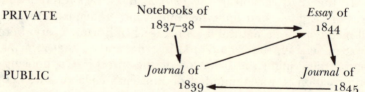

PRIVATE   Notebooks of   *Essay* of
                  1837–38   1844

PUBLIC   *Journal* of   *Journal* of
                  1839   1845

Admittedly, Darwin wrote most of the 1839 *Journal* before he began the notebooks. But the delay in publication caused by Fitz-Roy's slower pace in preparing his account of the voyage gave Darwin the chance to revise. And he did so, at least until October

27, 1838 (i.e., one month after the insight occasioned by his reading of Malthus), when he wrote the preface and twenty pages of addenda.

It is clear that both in 1839 and in 1845, Darwin withheld important ideas. In 1839, he avoided evolutionism and withheld any direct statement of the theory he then held. In 1845, he threw out a few hints of his evolutionism but withheld any suggestion of the theory of evolution through natural selection, which was by then at least seven-years and three drafts old.

Darwin also eliminated one idea that had become, for him, an error. He believed in 1837 that the species life-span idea was a tenable explanation of extinction, and that is could be accommodated within his earlier theories of evolution. But by 1845, it was neither tenable nor necessary. Extinction could be explained as an outcome of the complex struggle for existence, and so it appeared in the 1845 *Journal.*

The four months of hard work he put into the revision of the *Journal* were not for the purpose of concealment. On the contrary, the revision was an effort to express as much of his thinking—by then quite mature—as he felt he could manage, given all the constraints operating upon him: familial questions, professional and religious pressures, and unsolved scientific problems. He had, of course, worked out much more than he was prepared to publish. The momentum due to his 1844 completion of the *Essay* must have generated enormous internal pressures toward publication of his ideas. "It is like confessing a murder," Darwin wrote to his friend Hooker in 1844, about his belief in the mutability of species. The thorough revision of the *Journal* was his solution to the conflict.

Understanding this truncated, half-concealed form of expression raises interesting questions about the relation between Darwin and Alfred Russel Wallace. Their supposedly independent invention of the theory of evolution through natural selection has long stood as one of the most striking cases of this kind. I believe it might be better to see Darwin and Wallace as carrying out a half-knowing dialogue across decades, productive for both of them.

On April 11, 1846, Wallace wrote to his friend and future collaborator in exploration, H.W. Bates, "I was much pleased to find that you so well appreciated Lyell. I first read Darwin's 'Journal' three or four years ago, and have lately re-read it. As the Journal of a scientific traveller, it is second only to Humboldt's 'Personal Narrative'—as a work of general interest, perhaps superior to it."[16]

In his *Journal,* as we have seen, Darwin wrote about "the law of

---

[16] A. R. Wallace, *My Life, A Record of Events and Opinions,* Vol. 1, (London: Chapman and Hall, 1905), p. 256.

the succession of types." In 1855, Wallace published a paper on the same theme, stating that "every species has come into existence coincident both in space and time with a pre-existing closely allied species."[17] Darwin read this paper, and a correspondence sprang up, which the two men continued for twenty-seven years. In 1858, Wallace sent Darwin a sketch of the theory of evolution through natural selection, not knowing that by that time Darwin had travelled much further down the same road. Sketches of the theory by both men were read at the famous meeting of the Linnaean Society in 1858. Darwin was forced to abandon writing his "big book"—by then about two-thirds finished—and instead wrote the *Origin of Species*. The dialogue between the two men may be said to have continued even after Darwin's death, for in 1905 when Wallace published his autobiography, he included a six-page discussion of the theoretical differences between the two of them, concluding, "It will thus appear that none of my differences of opinion from Darwin imply any real divergence as to the overwhelming importance of the great principle of natural selection, while in several directions I believe that I have extended and strengthened it."[18]

It is nearly twenty-five years since I first looked at these journals with the intention of comparing them. I had set myself the task of making such a comparison in order to find out what it was like to work as a historian of science. I hoped, after a brief foray, to get on with the project of exploiting the findings of historians of science in a study of the psychology of thinking. The facts took me by surprise. In particular, the changes Darwin had introduced in 1845 seemed to point like a flashing arrow to the way in which he had managed his great secret—by telling much of it in print, in this fragmented way, holding back only a few crucial points. It seemed to me that a person untrained in historical research, like me, ought not to have made this little discovery about Darwin. By 1956, it should have been well known.

I drew three conclusions from this initial work. First, it appeared that psychologists had paid very little attention to the process of keeping secrets, although this is an important aspect of human conduct. Second, historians of science had not really studied the Darwin materials at the level of detail that would be useful to a cognitive psychologist. If I wanted to write broadly about the psychology of creative thinking and base my conclusions on detailed case studies, I would have to do them myself. Little did I know how difficult it would be to get past my first case. Finally, as to Darwin's

---

[17] A. R. Wallace, "On the Law which Has Regulated the Introduction of New Species," *Annals and Magazine of Natural History,* 2nd series, 1855, Vol. 16.
[18] Wallace, *My Life,* Vol. 2, p. 22. Throughout these volumes, there are many other reprises of the discussions between the two.

conduct, I still believed most of what I had read about his character: he was dull, neurotic, and unhappily subject to the tyranny of his domineering father. This picture now seems to me to be unfounded and probably absurd. I did not then understand much about his thinking. It seemed to me that "planting" fragments of his theory in an apparently surreptitious way must have been motivated by a desire to establish his claim to priority, like an explorer who cannot actually colonize a territory but instead only "plants the flag."

Staking a claim in this way seemed a little ignoble of Darwin but not really important to me. I left the *Beagle*-comparison project behind and went on to my chosen work, to reconstruct his thought processes from his notebooks—a complex effort in which a few others have since joined. Now, having at last written this appendix, I see things somewhat differently, Darwin wrote as he thought and thought as he wrote. The *Journal,* because of its wide-ranging and free-flowing narrative format, was an excellent medium for self-expression. It reflects and expresses Darwin's belief system and way of thought. As these changed, the *Journal* changed. "Planting fragments" was the wrong image.

I now see Darwin as simply expressing himself quite spontaneously and editing out or withholding certain crucial things he was not ready to bring forth. To be sure, he did hold something back, something terribly important, the theory of evolution through natural selection. That theory sprang not simply from his rich encounter with nature. It grew from his way of thinking about nature. Now we can see that the *Journal* is suffused with this way of thought.

A final note. In January 1981 I had the good fortune to read an important new article soon to appear in the *Journal of the History of Biology,* "Darwin and His Finches: The Evolution of a Legend," by Frank J. Sulloway. This ingenious study shows in minute detail how and why Darwin "mingled together" (Darwin's phrase) specimens from different islands in the Galapagos archipelago, thereby beclouding their evolutionary significance. Contrary to the legend that has since sprung up, seeing the Galapagos finches did not lead Darwin to the theory of evolution. While Darwin was in the early stages of his evolutionary theorizing, his distinguished collaborator, the ornithologist John Gould, was sorting out the *Beagle* specimens as best he could, which was well enough to be quite helpful to Darwin. Only a hint of the evolutionary significance of the Galapagos materials appears in the 1839 version of the *Journal,* because the evidence was not well understood at the time Darwin was writing (mainly in 1837). By 1845, as I have discussed above, this material was far more fully elaborated. The 1845 version of the *Journal* includes a now celebrated illustration showing "the perfect gradation in the size of the beaks in the different species" of Darwin's finches.

Acknowledgments

This book has been long in the making, and I have needed help from many quarters, always generously given. For access to various scattered Darwin manuscripts and related documents I am grateful to many libraries and their staffs, among them the American Philosophical Society, the Athenaeum, the British Museum, the John Crerar Library, the Detroit Public Library, the Library of Congress, the New York Public Library, the Royal Botanic Gardens at Kew, the Shrewsbury Public Library, and Shrewsbury School. University libraries in which I have worked with manuscripts and rare books include the University of Colorado, Cornell University, Edinburgh University, the University of Geneva, Harvard University, Keele University, the University of Michigan, Michigan State University, Oxford University, Rutgers University, and Yale University.

Most of my work has, of course, been done in the Cambridge University Library with its magnificent collection of Darwin materials. Without the assistance of Peter Gautrey this book would have been impossible. I am especially indebted to Dr. Sydney Smith of Cambridge University for sharing unstintingly his matchless knowledge of the Darwin manuscripts and for the many ways in which he has given me hospitality and practical help.

I also remember pleasant and fruitful days at Down House, Darwin's old home, both wandering about the grounds and sitting in his study using the books that are still kept there. I thank Mr. S.

Robinson, custodian of Down House, and Dr. Hedley Atkins of the Royal College of Surgeons for permission to work there.

Lady Nora Barlow has been helpful to me in many ways, in giving me a better feeling for Darwin family traditions, in making important material available to me, and in discussions of Darwin's thought. Dr. June Goodfield, Dr. Stephen Toulmin, and Dr. Robert M. Young all encouraged me to pay close attention to the question of materialism in Darwin's early development. Among the many other individuals with whom I have had valuable discussions of the Darwin materials, or who have helped me in searching for them, I would like to mention J. D. Bernal, Henry Bredeck, Edward Carlin, Gilbert Cohen, Ralph Colp, Gavin de Beer, James J. Doele, Harold Fruchtbaum, Emanuel Hackel, Guy Hamilton, Julian Huxley, Mladen Kabalin, Chester Lawson, James Lawson, Ralph Lewis, Clinton Lockert, Edward Manier, James K. Merritt, Everett Mendelsohn, M. J. Rowlands, Natalia Rubailova, Martin Rudwick, Ronald A. Sinclair, Robert Stauffer, Bruce Stewart, George Stocking, Hew Strachan, Arthur Thomas, and Walter A. Weiss. Valmai Gruber has been at numerous points a true collatorator in my work.

I am indebted to various institutions for leaves of absence and other forms of help: the University of Colorado, the New School for Social Research, and the Institute for Cognitive Studies at Rutgers University, where I have enjoyed the irreplaceable stimulation of my colleagues. Many students have been helpful in various ways, especially Charles Bebber, Virginia Bernier, Joan Colsey, Donald Hovey, and William Walsh. For financial aid in this work I am indebted to the American Philosophical Society, the Fund for the Advancement of Education, and the National Institute of Mental Health. Many periods, long and short, in which to reflect upon creative thinking as a growth process were spent in Geneva at the Centre d'Epistémologie Génétique, due to the hospitality of my late friend Jean Piaget.

Colleagues who have read and criticized all or large parts of the book include Solomon E. Asch, Colin Beer, Thomas K. Bever, John Ceraso, Dorothy Dinnerstein, Phillip Liss, Charles St. Clair, John Schmerler, Jacques Vonèche, and Robert M. Young. I am grateful for their comments but do not hold them responsible for my shortcomings.

Discussions with many people helped me to formulate the ideas in the appendix to the second edition. I especially thank Jeanne Bamberger, Jerome Bruner, Andrea DiSessa, Stephen Jay Gould, Thomas Kuhn, Philip Morrison, and Phyllis Morrison, as well as Benson Snyder, who opened a valuable forum to me at the Division for Study and Research in Education at M.I.T.

ILLUSTRATIONS

Frontispiece: Charles Darwin in 1840. Reproduction of a preliminary sketch for the George Richmond watercolor of 1840. Courtesy of Nora Barlow.

Page 11: Fuegian. Drawn by Conrad Martens, artist on board H.M.S. *Beagle.* From *Narrative of the surveying voyages of HMS Adventure and Beagle.*

Page 22: M Notebook, p. 57. Courtesy of Cambridge University Library.

Page 25: Emma Darwin in 1839. From the portrait painted by George Richmond. Courtesy of American Museum of Natural History.

Page 40: C Notebook, p. 123. Courtesy of Cambridge University Library.

Page 42: A cartoon ridiculing Darwin. From the *Hornet* of March 22, 1871. Courtesy of Cornell University Library.

Page 50: M Notebook, p. 123. Courtesy of Cambridge University Library.

Page 53: Anti-war petition signed by Darwin. Courtesy Cambridge University Library.

Page 66: Wedgwood anti-slavery medallion. Modeled in black jasper on white jasper background by William Hackwood for Josiah Wedgwood. First produced in 1786. Courtesy Josiah Wedgwood and Sons Ltd.

Page 74: Darwin as seen by a fellow student. Pen-and-ink drawing, reproduced here in original size. Artist unidentified but possibly William Darwin Fox, Darwin's second cousin. Courtesy of Cambridge University Library.

Page 96: Charles Darwin in 1854. Photograph by Maull and Fox. Courtesy of Nora Barlow.

Page 127: Darwin's changing world view.

Page 135: Archipelagoes and the Branching Model.

Page 142: Tree diagram. From the B Notebook, page 26. Courtesy of Cambridge University Library.

Page 143: Tree diagram. From the B Notebook, page 36. Courtesy of Cambridge University Library.

Page 160: Galapagos finches. From *Voyage,* 1845, p. 379.

Page 171 (*top*) : D Notebook, p. 134. Courtesy of Cambridge University Library.

Page 171 (bottom): D Notebook, p. 135. Courtesy of Cambridge University Library.

Page 178: Jemmy Button in 1833 and 1834. Drawn by Captain Robert FitzRoy. From *Narrative of the surveying voyages of HMS Adventure and Beagle.*

Page 182: Anti-slavery medal, 1838. By Patrick Reason. From *The Massachusetts Review,* Vol. XIII, 1972. Courtesy of Emma and Sidney Kaplan.

Page 197: Taxonomic tree. Drawn by Darwin on April 21, 1868. Courtesy of Cambridge University Library.

Page 216: N Notebook, p. 5. Courtesy of Cambridge University Library.

Page 228: Chimpanzee disappointed and sulky. Drawn from life by Mr. Wood. Illustration from *The Expression of the Emotions in Man and Animals.*

Page 245: M Notebook, p. 84. Courtesy of Cambridge University Library.

Page 247: Charles Darwin in 1882. Photograph by Leonard Darwin. Courtesy of Cambridge University Library.

Index